HV6722.C2 T46 2009
Betting their lives :
33663005147307
EGN

DATE DUE

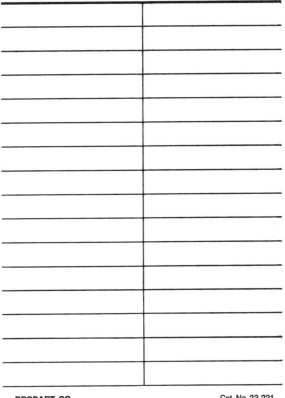

BETTING
THEIR LIVES

The Close Relations
of Problem Gamblers

Lorne Tepperman

OXFORD
UNIVERSITY PRESS

OXFORD
UNIVERSITY PRESS

8 Sampson Mews, Suite 204, Don Mills, Ontario M3C 0H5
www.oupcanada.com

Oxford University Press is a department of the University of Oxford.
It furthers the University's objective of excellence in research, scholarship,
and education by publishing worldwide in

Oxford New York
Auckland Cape Town Dar es Salaam Hong Kong Karachi
Kuala Lumpur Madrid Melbourne Mexico City Nairobi
New Delhi Shanghai Taipei Toronto

With offices in
Argentina Austria Brazil Chile Czech Republic France Greece
Guatemala Hungary Italy Japan Poland Portugal Singapore
South Korea Switzerland Thailand Turkey Ukraine Vietnam

Oxford is a trade mark of Oxford University Press
in the UK and in certain other countries

Published in Canada
by Oxford University Press

Library and Archives Canada Cataloguing in Publication

Tepperman, Lorne, 1943–
Betting their lives : the close relations of problem gamblers /
written by Lorne Tepperman.

Includes bibliographical references and index.

ISBN 978-0-19-543059-2

1. Compulsive gamblers—Canada. 2. Compulsive gamblers—Family
relationships—Canada. 3. Compulsive gambling—Canada. I. Title.

HV6722.C3T46 2008   363.4'20971   C2008-903961-0

Cover image: Andy Hwang/iStockphoto

2 3 4 5 – 15 14 13 12

This book is printed on permanent (acid-free) paper ∞.
Printed and bound in the United States.

Contents

Acknowledgments

This book is based on the findings of two studies funded by the Ontario Problem Gambling Research Centre (OPGRC), studies completed in 2003 and 2005, respectively. I want to first thank OPGRC and its director, Rob Simpson, for having faith in these projects. I hope this book justifies that faith.

Many people contributed to the completion of this book, and I will thank them in (roughly) chronological order. Gambling and addictions expert Dr. David Korn collaborated on both studies reported in this book. He offered wise advice that helped in designing the study, creating the questionnaire, recruiting the people we studied, and collecting the data. Jennifer Reynolds, as project manager for the 2005 study, was closely involved with collecting the data and drafting the project report. David and Jennifer were key figures in the success of the 2005 research project, on which this book is mainly based. Marion Lynn played a similar role in managing the 2003 project.

Sandra Colavecchia, who recently received her doctorate in sociology at the University of Toronto, made up questions that focused on the financial organization of gamblers' households, analyzed couples' responses, and contributed to the final 2005 report. A special thank-you goes to our 2005 interviewers: Tara Hahmann, Maja Jovanovic, and Tamar Meyer. Their patient, careful, and sensitive interviewing was important for the success of the study, and I am grateful for their work in transcribing the interviews. Also, I am indebted to doctoral student Tara Hahmann for analyzing and reporting on some of the qualitative data and drafting reviews of the therapeutic literature. In both studies, Agata Falkowski-Ham entered the quantitative data, programmed data analyses, and provided interpretations of the quantitative data, making it easier to see the linkages between our qualitative (open-ended) and quantitative (closed-ended) material. Linn Clark contributed critical intelligence and editorial skill that improved the research reports that preceded this book.

Several undergraduate research assistants at the University of Toronto drafted preliminary reports on our findings, especially important in the two years when this monograph was being prepared. I am indebted to undergraduates Dana

Gore, Matt Kopas, David Li, Mike McPhail, Miranda Ng, Crystal Tse, and Jennie Wong, who helped by analyzing and reporting on the transcribed interview materials. Undergraduates Rebecca Daniels, Joanna Guerriere, and Lianne Percival, and Master's student Elizabeth Martin contributed valuably to the literature review on families and gambling. Undergraduate Angela Kalyta was important in critiquing, reorganizing, and improving the manuscript in creative ways—and especially in mining the rich interview materials for insightful quotes. Master's student Sasha Stark supervised the work of our many assistants and reorganized and revised many sections of the manuscript. In the end, she also shortened many of the chapters. Undergraduates Alex Tepperman and Sarah Fox helped revise and clarify this manuscript in its final version. Toronto sociologist Horace Henriques read and reviewed an early draft of the manuscript. Thank you, Horace. As well, Rob Simpson of OPGRC commented usefully on drafts of the manuscript. My wife, Sandra Wain, offered very useful suggestions about ways to improve the edited version of the manuscript. And editor Nancy Mucklow did a wonderful job of pulling everything together in the final, clean, and coherent book you are holding in your hands. Finally, thanks go to Sasha Stark, Sandra Duong, Edward Thompson, and OUP editor Leslie Saffrey for a close reading of the page proofs.

I am indebted to our respondents in both studies and hope that our research makes a difference to their lives. The people who agreed to speak to us had confidence in this project and in the importance of our research, and we are thankful for that. Their contribution to research on problem gambling will help educate both health professionals and other families affected by this issue.

As we get older, we discover who we are and how we came to be that way. With that lesson in mind, I dedicate this book to four people who played a deep, hidden role in fashioning this study. My father taught me to love books. My Aunt Toby showed me the importance of a social conscience. My teacher George Homans showed me how to use a sociological imagination. And my colleague Eric Single reminded me what a sociological understanding of addictions might look like. I am deeply indebted to these four important people.

Lorne Tepperman
Toronto, May 2008

DREAMING THE NUMBERS

I remember that my father would go to sleep in the afternoons so that he could dream. We were not allowed to wake him up . . . My mother would say, "Don't wake him up because he has to dream the number that is going to come out." He would dream of numbers. He would dream of something, and then there were sayings that if you dream with a dead man talking, play 47; if you dream with a dead man that doesn't talk, play 48, and so on.

Estrella, age 42

I.

Problem Gambling

Chapter 1

Introduction

This is a book about gambling and its effects. However, it is not a book about why people gamble. Almost everyone gambles at some time or another—if not with bets at a racetrack or casino or online, then with lottery tickets, real estate transactions, or risky stock purchases. As we will see in this study, people gamble for various reasons and in various ways. Mainly, they gamble to make money without investing much effort.

Why gamble? Because, given the choice, most people would rather acquire money quickly and easily. They dream of winning a lot of money, just by luck. Most people would love to win a large pot of money and be without financial constraints on where and how they live. Gambling dangles that promise before our eyes.

So there is little need to explain gambling. Nor is there any effort here to explain systematically why some people—roughly 5 percent of those who gamble—graduate from a leisure pastime to what we shall call "problem gambling." Current explanations of problem gambling (some of which are discussed in this chapter) tend to be weak and unpersuasive. Statistically, each has little explanatory power. Therapeutically, each contributes little to the prevention or cure of problem gambling, and more research is needed. All we can say with certainty is that currently, many variables—social, cultural, psychological, and possibly biological—contribute to a general understanding of problem gambling.

The people who graduate from gambling to problem gambling are betting their lives—their incomes, jobs, marriages, friendships, and even health—on winning a lot of money, just by luck. Today, the dominant explanations of problem gambling are psychological or psychiatric in nature. By contrast, this book places its focus on social and cultural factors. In the end, research may generate a grand synthesis—a theory that incorporates all the factors that affect problem gambling, along with the complex ways in which they interact.

This book is mainly about the *effects* of problem gambling on both the gamblers themselves and their families. Following in the sociological tradition, this book asks the following questions: first, how do problem gamblers and their families *interpret*—make sense of—gambling and the gambling life? Second, how does the fascination with gambling affect gamblers' marriages, work, schooling, and other social relations? Third, how does problem gambling result in gamblers being labelled and stigmatized? Fourth, does labelling and stigmatization confirm and strengthen the person's identity as a gambler? Fifth, what role can spouses play in helping gamblers change or regulate their gambling? Sixth and finally, how can therapists help problem gamblers and their spouses control or end their problem gambling?

In answering these questions, we examine areas both inside and outside the gambling literature. This is an exploratory study, which means it asks more questions than it answers. It achieves its goal if it points to fruitful new directions for inquiry. During this investigation, we discuss (among other things) existing research on families stressed by illness; the reasons people keep and disclose secrets; ethnocultural variations in gambling beliefs and practices; factors that ease the exit from old roles and entry into new ones; and theories about the reasons people develop gambling problems.

Above all, we hear the voices of the people interviewed in the course of our studies: problem gamblers and their spouses. We hear about problem gambling—its pleasures and pains—in their own words. Better than any theories or second-hand descriptions, this direct report of experiences with the gambling life and its effects on marriage submerges the reader in the troubled sea of problem gamblers. The book ends with a theory about the ways we might re-organize treatment for problem gamblers, to take advantage of what this study has found out.

This book is mainly a work of *grounded theory,* research that grows out of the words of our respondents, so we need to begin by discussing who we interviewed.

Interviewees

In the spring of 2005, we advertised the study in Toronto newspapers to attract subjects. We also posted similar notices around the University of Toronto campus to recruit younger gamblers. The advertisement read as shown at the top of the following page.

Two months later, after only a modest response from the partners of gamblers, we posted another set of advertisements specifically aimed at recruiting additional partners, as shown in the second box on the next page.

Initially, we did not know how many responses to expect. We had hoped for 120 respondents altogether (we ended up with 90). Nor did we have a clear idea who would respond, though we expected a mix of people: some occasional

RESEARCH PARTICIPANTS NEEDED

- Do you like to gamble? Are you a partner of someone who gambles?
- Are you currently in a committed relationship?
- Looking for people who gamble, partners of gamblers, and couples affected by gambling.
- Privacy and Confidentiality is guaranteed
- Partners are interviewed separately
- Each interview will last 1 ½ hours.
- $25 gift certificate will be given for each interview

For information about the study contact (416) XXX-XXXX

RESEARCH PARTICIPANTS NEEDED

- Are you a partner of someone who likes to gamble?
- Are you currently in a committed relationship?
- Looking for people who are partners of gamblers and couples affected by gambling.
- Privacy and Confidentiality is guaranteed
- Each interview will last ½ hours.
- $25 gift certificate will be given for each interview

For information about the study contact (416) XXX-XXXX

gamblers, some frequent gamblers, and some problem gamblers. In the same vein, we expected a mix of spouses: some who were enthusiastic about gambling, others who were tolerant or indifferent, and others still who were negative and troubled.

Despite movies and advertisements that tend to picture gamblers as glamorous, high-spirited, and dynamic, we expected to see a mix of ordinary people. I had already watched people buy lottery tickets at corner convenience stores.

I had already visited casinos in Ontario, Brisbane (Australia), and Durban (South Africa). I had even twice visited Las Vegas for conferences of gambling researchers, and over the course of these experiences I had viewed the kinds of people who gamble with some regularity. Here are my impressions.

The first obvious fact is that most gamblers look just like you and me—except for that frisson of electrons that sometimes circles them like a halo. I have seen how people behave in a busy casino, where (it seems) energy fields waft from them, like perspiration or dew. The room itself assaults its occupants with mechanized noise, flashing neon lights, the dense smell of cigarette smoke, and the nervous intensity of gamblers interacting rapidly and silently with dealers and machines. No doubt about it: the casino atmosphere of organized gambling is agitated—often, gamblers themselves look electrified.

Yet it is not only Las Vegas that has this agitating effect on gamblers. I have watched people buy lottery or scratch-and-win tickets at the corner convenience store. They, too, more than regular customers coming in for milk or bread (say), show an edge of anticipation in their interactions with the "dealer." Often, they joke or chitchat nervously as they purchase their tickets. Often they are animated and conversational, well beyond the norm in a convenience store. Their mood changes after losing. Typically, they leave without speaking, their goals on this day thwarted. They may very well come back the next day and do it over again.

So, in our sample, I expected to see people a lot like the people I already knew: a varied group, with diverse strengths and weaknesses, vices and virtues—that is, ordinary people. But we encountered a different selection. Many who came in for interviews had suffered a succession of setbacks because of gambling. Often, their lives had become one-dimensional, largely eaten up by gambling. Their lives were much less glamorous than gambling advertisements suggested. In fact, many were leading lives that were stressful, unhappy, and unhealthy.

Our interviewees came not to boast about their successes and delights but to muse about their failures and worries. Many seemed to want a change without having the strength or resources to bring change about. All wanted to testify about how gambling had changed their lives, though they seldom knew where to start or how to continue with their account. Often they lacked eloquence, though it was clear they felt deeply about the things they said. For the most part, they were earnest and troubled.

I was especially eager to learn about the marital relationships of these people. Yet we heard no romantic stories of sudden wealth and delightful vacations for two. Instead we heard about seemingly endless conflicts over money, unpaid bills, lies told and discovered, shabby misjudgments that humiliated the family, lost or depleted savings, and dashed hopes. We heard family stories defined by regret, estrangement, and loneliness.

In the end, we saw a sizeable gap between what the mass media tell us about gambling—and what the public has consequently come to believe about gambling—and the reality of gambling for these people. The illusion is glamorous but the reality, we heard, is often shabby and harsh. That, for me, emerged as the "problem" of problem gambling. A formidable range of promotions, advertisements, and inducements seduce ordinary people into activities that, taken to extremes, disappoint many and too often spell disaster for a large minority. Some appear unable to free themselves from the pull of gambling before forfeiting their careers, marriages, or health. Very often, the victims blame themselves. They are told they are not "responsible gamblers."

Yet through the mass media, the gambling industry, and the government, society continues to encourage and praise people who embark on the same path. In this way, we raise one generation after another to think that gambling is glamorous and worthwhile. Little wonder that some spend—indeed, overspend—their time and money trying to win at games of chance.

The "Gambling Problem"

The practice of gambling can best be viewed as falling along a continuum that ranges from nongamblers at one end, through recreational gamblers in the middle, and problem gamblers at the other extreme (Currie *et al.*, 2006; Hardoon, Gupta, and Derevensky, 2004). Over time, a fraction migrates from the non-gambler "population" to recreational gambling, and others migrate to the problem gambler "population." In time, we may come to understand precisely how and why such migration occurs. Until we do, designing effective preventive strategies remains a difficult challenge.

How widespread is the so-called "gambling problem," and why should we care? A 2005 Ontario population survey using the Canadian Problem Gambling Index (CPGI)—this will be discussed in more detail later—reported that "the large majority of participants" (90.7 percent) had not experienced gambling-related problems in the past year, with 36.6 percent classified as non-gamblers and 54.1 percent as non-problem gamblers. Of the total sample, 5.8 percent were classified as at risk of gambling problems, and 2.6 percent were classified as having moderate problems. Less than 1 percent (0.8 percent) were classified as having severe gambling problems. (Wiebe, Mun, and Kaufman, 2006:14). These estimates are probably the most relevant to our current study, since it examines a sample of Ontario gamblers.

While estimates vary between populations and over time, they all suggest that roughly 1 Canadian adult gambler in 20 has a current or prospective gambling problem. This means that in a population of roughly 32 million Canadians, of whom 75 percent are over age 20, roughly 1.2 million Canadians have a gambling problem or are at serious risk of a gambling problem.

The CPGI is a survey questionnaire developed to measure problem gambling. The index includes a range of questions to help pinpoint the extent of a given individual's compulsion to gamble.

Most problem gamblers end up disturbing the lives of other people—partners, parents, children, employees, or friends, for example. That means a substantial number of Canadians are affected by problem gambling. In this book, we try to attach a human meaning to these statistics by looking closely at the effects of problem gambling on a sample of Torontonians. This study was conducted in Toronto, but it could just as well have been in Vancouver, Montreal, Halifax, Edmonton, or any other part of North America. The effects are the same, whatever the jurisdiction or community size. Though our sample is small, it provides a ground-level, everyday sense of the problem. As sociologist C. Wright Mills urged, our data show the "biographic" or personal side of a growing public issue—in this instance, the personal side of a gambling problem.

Here's an interesting statistic from the United States. Likely, the figures are similar for Canada, though comparable statistics are not currently available. According to CareerBuilder.com's latest survey, 41 percent of all working Americans often or always live from paycheque to paycheque. CNN reports that "Scrambling to make ends meet is an exercise all too familiar in many homes. One-third of workers report they don't have enough income to live comfortably. To achieve this, more than half said they would need to earn more than $500 per paycheque. Thirty-seven percent of workers said they have one income for their households, while 16 percent say they work more than one job just to make ends meet" (CNN 2007). It doesn't take much imagination to realize that people who live from paycheque to paycheque (or welfare cheque to welfare cheque) and are chronically short of money would be in big trouble even from small, regular gambling losses. Many of the people we interviewed for our study of problem gambling fall into this category.

This problem needs more study if we are to understand it fully. Moreover, problem gambling is likely going to get worse before it gets better, and it has

Problem Gambling Behaviour
- Bet more than you could afford
  - How often have you bet more than you could really afford to lose?
- Increased wagers
  - How often have you needed to gamble with larger amounts of money to get the same feeling of excitement?
- Returned to win back losses
  - How often have you gone back another day to try to win back the money you lost?
- Borrowed money or sold anything to gamble
  - How often have you borrowed money or sold anything to get money to gamble?

Adverse Consequences
- Felt gambling problem
  - How often have you felt that you might have a problem with gambling?
- Suffered criticism
  - How often have people criticized your betting or told you that you had a gambling problem?
- Feelings of guilt
  - How often have you felt guilty about the way you gamble or what happens when you gamble?
- Financial problems
  - How often has your gambling caused any financial problems for you or your household?
- Negative health effects
  - How often has your gambling caused you any health problems, including stress or anxiety?

the potential to get much worse if we fail to address it effectively. Research evidence consistently shows that as gambling *opportunities* increase—at casinos, racetracks, bars, corner stores, or on the Internet—so do gambling problems. Non-problematic gambling is the pool from which problem gambling emerges. So, to prevent problem gambling—that is, to reduce the risks of onset—we must address the larger environment in which gambling is structured and marketed by an aggressive global gambling industry.

Gambling has become a major global industry in the last 20 years, and it continues to grow rapidly. No longer—as in the days of American columnist Damon Runyon (1884–1946)—is gambling restricted to colourful characters and exotic locales. Gambling is advertised everywhere as fun and entertaining. What's more, national, provincial or state, and local governments are helping to promote gambling to raise their own revenues. Governments reason that people are going to gamble anyway, so it makes sense for them to regulate it and take a percentage of the revenue.

As with alcohol and drugs, gambling has historically also been a major source of revenue for organized crime. Accordingly, in the second half of the twentieth century, many governments moved to legalize and regulate gambling and take a share of the profits. From here, it was a small step to promote gambling and increase those profits, which are seen as "non-tax" revenues or even "voluntary taxation." Some of this money is directly reinvested in "public goods" such as charitable foundations (and in fact, some of the money raised this way is even spent to do research on problem gambling).

The gambling industry has done its best to highlight the positive economic and social effects of gambling, as in this newspaper story recently reported in the *Toronto Star*:

April 8, 2008
THE CANADIAN PRESS
Canada's largest and most financially significant entertainment industry is gambling, accounting for 267,000 full-time jobs and contributing $15.3 billion a year to the economy, according to the Canadian Gaming Association.

The industry group's report released Tuesday and based on 2006 data says 57 percent of gambling revenue—$8.7 billion—supported government services and charities.

The other $6.6 billion "was spent to sustain operations, paid out as salaries, and used to purchase goods and services."

The gaming association's research, described as the most comprehensive study ever conducted on the economic impact of gaming in Canada, found 135,000 people are directly employed in the industry, and indirect gambling-related employment such as food and entertainment services swells the total to 267,000 full-time jobs. For 2006, this translated into $11.6 billion in labour income, the association says.

"Gaming has grown significantly over the past decade to become an essential pillar of the entertainment industry in Canada," stated association president Bill Rutsey.

"It is now demonstrably clear how the majority of spending in the industry goes directly back to Canadians in the form of paycheques, construction in communities, and revenues for the programs and services and charities that we value."

At the same time, the gambling industry has promoted an image of gambling that is fun, exciting, and often dashingly naughty. That international gambling centre, Las Vegas, has championed the idea that "What happens in Vegas, stays in Vegas." This slogan suggests that any secret mischief can be "left behind"—nobody will find out, for example, if you went to bed late, ate too much, drank too much, smoked too much, had an affair, and so on. Gambling, by definition, is a game of chance and, the slogan suggests, life should (occasionally) be a game of chance too. It suggests that people—in gambling and in life—might do well to sometimes take exciting chances and try to beat the odds.

Thanks to aggressive advertising and marketing, gambling has become an overwhelmingly popular pastime for many North Americans (Ladouceur, 1996; Shaffer, Hall, and Vander Bilt, 1999; Canadian Partnership for Responsible Gambling, 2007). Yet, this expansion of interest in and access to gambling has led to a corresponding increase in concern about the health issues associated with gambling (Currie *et al.*, 2006).

Gambling has become a public health issue, in the sense that it has social causes and harms the health of many people. Gambling is more than the expression of a personal taste, individual psychopathology, or genetic inclination. It is a behaviour that is learned socially through observation, experimentation, and emulation in social surroundings or through the modelling and examples set by social role models. Often, as we see later, people first learn the essentials of gambling in families during childhood.

Family life is a significant source of learning and encouragement for many gamblers and one key risk factor for subsequent problem gambling. In turn, families themselves—including cultures—supply beliefs about gambling and also reward or punish would-be gamblers. For example, cultures may encourage gambling by portraying it as an activity that tests daring, skill, courage, luckiness, or intelligence; they may also discourage it by viewing it as foolish or wasteful. Mass culture also affects gambling. Currently, mass media advertising supplements these cultural messages with positive images of gambling. So, to understand a person's gambling—and even his or her problems with gambling—we have to understand both the family and sociocultural messages the person brings to a gambling event. Failure to consider these contributions makes therapy and behaviour change significantly more difficult.

Just as gambling has social causes, it also has social (and health) consequences for families and communities. As we will see, gamblers can lose in many ways when they play the odds at games of chance. Many who took part in our study suffered disastrous financial losses at the track, the poker table, the bingo hall, or the slot machine—and they lost much more than money. Imagine children growing up in a household where mom or dad periodically loses the month's grocery money. Imagine a husband or wife who suddenly finds the savings account has been emptied out, the house has been mortgaged, and creditors are phoning at all hours to demand payment.

It is hard for most people to imagine the precariousness of life with a problem gambler. It is hard to imagine living with someone who is financially out of control—who every day risks everything you have worked years to earn, buy, and save. Yet many spouses feel powerless as their partner steals family money or pawns family possessions to gamble. Some families have to sell their homes and move to rented quarters because a parent has created more debt than they can carry. Some families live as "afterthoughts"—second priorities after gambling. Occasionally, spouses get fed up and leave to protect themselves and their children.

In our study, many gamblers and their families had faced these situations. Their stories, their own words, show that excessive gambling can cut a wide swath of destruction through families, careers, relationships, and future prospects. For these reasons, problem gambling becomes deeply important to the community, as does the fact that it is growing. As a society, we neglect these problems at our peril. Nor should we suppose the people most directly affected solve the problems on their own. Often the people most at risk are least able to protect themselves.

As a central theme in this book, we consider the possibility that families— which often promote and reward gambling behaviour—can also play an important part in regulating gambling and mediating the harm. To limit the scope of this study, we focus on the role of spouses[1]: how they are affected by problem gambling and how they deal with it. Ultimately, our goal is to develop a sociological approach to problem gambling that makes a contribution by helping people—including therapists, gamblers, and the families of gamblers—understand and change family responses, so that they better reduce harm associated with gambling.

This book is limited in its ambitions. First, family regulation is the only harm-reduction strategy we consider in this book. Of course, other harm-reduction strategies are helpful too, such as regulating the gambling industry and its advertising, improving public health education about the dangers of gambling, and limiting the spread of gambling (such as lotteries) in schools, hospitals, churches, and governments. All these are harm-reduction strategies, in that they assume people will continue to gamble. They all put forward ways to prepare for and moderate the dangers of excessive gambling—for treating the currently addicted and also preparing for the next generation. Problem gambling is no longer limited to adults; it affects young people as well (Poulin, 2000) and influences the likelihood of gambling problems in the future (Currie *et al.*, 2006).

Second, this book takes a mainly *sociological* approach to problem gambling. Much of the social science research on gambling takes a more *psychological* approach: that is, it focuses on the thoughts, emotions, and behaviours of problem gambling, without considering the social context. For example, some researchers view problem gambling as the product of cognitive distortions—such as errors in thinking—about the likelihood of winning and the merits of chasing losses. Thus, cognitive-behavioural counselling encourages gamblers to think and act differently, whatever their personal inclinations. But this psychological model of behaviour change places the onus for "responsible gambling" on the particular gambler. Many policy-makers, industry representatives, and the public seem to share this viewpoint, and it is reflected in everything from government gaming policies to treatment and prevention programs.

Notably missing is the sociological perspective. Sociology goes beyond an analysis of just the individual to include the social context that surrounds the gambler. Its underlying logic is that even in instances when the act of gambling is solitary (as with online gambling or video lottery terminals (VLTs)), the results echo throughout the gambler's social network. And since people's gambling

---

1   The term *spouse* will be used to refer to both legally married spouses and common-law partners.

influences the lives of those around them, the reverse is also possible: that people around the gambler exert influence on the gambler's attitudes and habits. This book explores the informal control of gamblers' attitudes and habits by partners significant to them.

Our findings show that spouses who are more deeply *embedded* in the social world of their gambling partners have more awareness of and influence over their partner's gambling than spouses who are not embedded in the same social world. Embeddedness in a common social network increases the likelihood that partners disclose gambling (and related) problems to one another and share thoughts about these problems. Embedded spouses are more likely to be aware of changes in the gambling problem (for example, the occurrence of a heavy financial loss, lost job, or increased preoccupation). Most important, such spouses are more able to influence and control the gambling of the other and are more able to promote treatment compliance. These findings lead us to conclude that problem gambling may be more effectively controlled by increasing the embeddedness of couples in common social networks.

Spouses who are kept in the dark—and many spouses are—are less able to gauge the extent of their partner's gambling and the severity of related problems. Partly for this reason, they are correspondingly less able to influence their partner's behaviour or promote treatment compliance.

In short, our study offers a descriptive account of how spouses influence problem gambling—new knowledge that has the strong potential to influence prevention and treatment programs. We hope it helps others to develop treatment programs that involve gamblers' spouses, new counselling techniques for couples, and public education on how to talk to partners about their gambling.

The purpose of this book, then, is to explore the lives of people who gamble dangerously and to ask how gambling affects their lives—especially, their everyday lives of work and marriage. It is also intended to explore how harmful gambling can interact with marriage. We wanted to know the ways in which, and with what degree of success, most adults try to regulate their partner's gambling. Finally, our study reveals how embeddedness affects a gambler's readiness for treatment.

The Research Method

Because we did not use a systematic random sample, the findings of this study are only exploratory and suggestive. In total, 90 adults from the Greater Toronto

Area volunteered to take part in this exploratory study. Of these, 59 declared themselves as having (or potentially having) a gambling problem. Another 31 declared themselves as spouses of people who have (or potentially have) a gambling problem. The 90 people included ten couples who agreed to answer extra questions that specifically focused on financial issues.

As noted earlier, we recruited the sample by advertising in newspapers, local gambling education websites, and the meeting places of Gamblers Anonymous and Gam-Anon. We used a survey questionnaire (containing roughly 90 closed-ended questions) and an interview (containing roughly 30 open-ended questions). Couples willing to engage in the separate interview were asked an additional 20 open-ended questions. We cross-referenced the findings of this study with those from our earlier exploratory study of 360 respondents, titled *At Home with Gambling* (Tepperman *et al.*, 2003). The primary focus of that study was the role of family and ethnocultural influences on people's gambling. That sample was drawn from the Greater Toronto Area as well. Both studies revealed a great deal about the nature and extent of problem gambling.

In the current study, all participants were initially assessed using the Canadian Problem Gambling Index (CPGI) to determine their gambling status. The average CPGI score was 15 (out of a possible 27), and most respondents fell into the "problem-gambling" category, which is marked by a minimum score of 8. Only 7 of 59 gamblers in our study scored between 1 and 8 points on the CPGI, though they too are considered at increased risk of a gambling problem. (A score of zero indicates "no risk" of problems.)

In addition, we collected information about the range of marital problems associated with problem gambling. Most intimate relationships in this study showed great strain and turmoil; many of the gamblers and spouses we studied were considering separation or divorce. Ironically, the spouses were often unaware of the emotional turmoil that gamblers were experiencing and the extent of their gambling-related difficulties. Neither the gamblers themselves nor their spouses felt confident that spouses could influence or moderate gambling problems.

Our results show that problem gambling lessens the quality of marital relations and increases the distance between husbands and wives. So, as the CPGI score increases, the respondents' similarity with his or her partner decreases, as does the time spent together. Marital harmony diminishes. The partners often lead separate lives, with little knowledge of the people in their partner's life.

Many respondents know only a few of their partner's best friends and co-workers by first name, and vice versa.

We saw that relationships could get better or they could get worse—it depended largely on the severity of the gambling problem and on the degree of embeddedness. As embeddedness increased, relationship quality improved. For example, respondents with high scores on the embeddedness scale (see Chapter 9) usually knew their partner's innermost hopes and fears and had a closer relationship with them. Gambling tended to undermine this embeddedness. The problem gamblers were more likely than the moderate gamblers to have unstable, weak, or conflictual relationships with their partners and were less likely to be embedded in the same social world.

Gamblers in weak relationships were also less willing to change their gambling practices. Moreover, the spouses of problem gamblers had less ability to influence their partners to undertake change. Only embedded gamblers—those who spent more time with and had closer relations with their partners—were usually willing to consider and undertake change.

The practical implication is that gamblers and their partners would benefit from strengthening their relationship while they work on the gambling problem. Admittedly, we do not know the direction of this association. It may be equally true that a reduction in gambling strengthens the relationship.

Organization of this Book

In the first part of this book, the opening chapter discusses "the gambling problem" in a general sense. Subsequent chapters review the existing literature on gambling as a family activity with family origins and family-related outcomes. In particular, we consider the ways problem gambling affects marital relations. The third chapter in this part outlines the research methods we used in this study.

The second part of the book focuses on the gambling practices and beliefs described by the respondents in the study. It includes descriptions of gambling, their lives with gambling, their marriages, and a range of other related topics. Using direct quotes from our respondents, we examine five main themes within our findings. First, many of the gamblers we studied were suffering a downward spiral of social, economic, and family impacts. Second, though most spouses recognized problems in their intimate relationships, they were often unaware of the full nature and extent of these problems and their connection to gambling. Third, the lack of spouses' awareness both reflected and supported weak couple embeddedness—a tendency of gamblers and their spouses to live in largely separate social worlds. Fourth, this weak embeddedness, in turn, allowed potentially harmful gambling practices to continue and marital relations to deteriorate further. Fifth, and most especially, the weak embeddedness and poor marital relations undermined the spouse's ability to influence the gambler to undertake treatment or change.

The final part of the book summarizes these conclusions and considers limitations of the study. Then it turns to solutions, discussing ways that spouses and therapists can help problem gamblers control their harmful behaviour, and offering recommendations for policy, practice, and research aimed at solving these problems. In particular, we consider ways in which therapists who work with problem gamblers and their spouses might make use of our findings. We end with a sociological theory of problem gambling that holds implications for future research and for changes of focus in therapy for problem gamblers.

Last Words

Our interviewees showed remarkable courage and generosity in agreeing to be interviewed in this study. They hoped to gain insight into their problems and receive a measure of help (although we assured them we would not provide treatment or advice). Many wanted a chance to "testify" about the problems they were experiencing—to put their views on the record and to be "heard," as people need to do when they have suffered a lot. All were looking for answers in their own histories to the central question: Why is this happening to me?

Our respondents were often hampered by powerful urges they could not understand, bitter conflicts at home that coloured their view of themselves and gambling, and lack of access to the tools they needed to examine their lives. They had notions and observations about gambling and its effects, but lacked cohesive theories. They had tactics for coping but no way to evaluate them. They knew their own experiences but often could not see them in a wider context. They could see their personal troubles but usually could not see the public issues behind these troubles. They lack what C. Wright Mills calls a *sociological imagination*—the ability to link personal troubles and public issues.

Finally, though many of our respondents were intelligent and insightful people, they often had trouble talking about their experiences. For most, these were emotion-laden memories. For some, difficulties were compounded by the fact that English was their second language. So, when we read their words, we must keep in mind that they were groping for the right words. In this book, I have endeavoured to clarify the speakers' intent without putting words in their mouths. In this respect, my job has been to act as a translator as well as theorist and analyst. I have tried to do this with care and respect.

To psychologists, problem gamblers are people with a psychopathology built upon cognitive distortion and dysfunctional motivations—people in need of treatment and support. To sociologists, like myself, problem gamblers are citizens of a particular class, time, and place. They are ordinary people grappling with everyday issues of financial insecurity, consumerism, and socially created beliefs about glamour, social standing, and wealth. I hope their voices in this book add new levels of context and shed a new, though less glamorous, light on aspects of gambling as a pastime, a problem, and an industry.

Chapter 2
Groups, Families, and Gambling: A Sociological Approach

This chapter lays a theoretical groundwork for the study that follows. But to understand the need for this elaborate groundwork—for what may sometimes seem like an unnecessary digression for no more than academic motives—the reader needs to know a little about the development of this project. This study has a long history and it grows out of things I found—and didn't find—over a period of eight years.

In spring of the year 2000, partly by chance, I first met physician, gambling researcher, and addictions counsellor Dr. David Korn. In a casual conversation, David got me interested in problem gambling; that conversation has never ended. Wanting to extend my research on families in a new direction, I realized that problem gambling would provide interesting new challenges. With this in mind, I worked with David to develop a project proposal on the family's role in ethnic gambling. We received funding for our research from the Ontario Problem Gambling Research Centre (OPGRC), and carried out the study in 2001–2002. I report some findings of that study in the pages that follow, where I refer to it as the *At Home With Gambling* study (Tepperman *et al.*, 2003).

The Missing Links

In preparing for that study and carrying it out, I discovered two very remarkable facts about the field of gambling research. First, problem gambling has never been studied from a sociological perspective. By the time I began my first gambling research, I had been studying sociology for nearly 40 years and studying families specifically for about 15 or 20 years. Imagine my surprise, then, when I found *nothing* that was recognizably sociological in the field of published gambling research. Second, very little had been published about families either. Most of the available research was concerned with the characteristics of individual gamblers, as if they somehow existed in a social and familial vacuum—or perhaps on a desert island, totally alone, with no company but a roulette wheel or a slot machine.

It seemed outrageous. People and their behaviour are not understandable outside a social context. But David confirmed that family influences on gambling had not been studied or written about to any noticeable degree.

This finding puzzled me, and I began to wonder whether gambling was an area—unlike other areas of life—that simply did not lend itself to sociological study. I knew only one sociologist who had done any work on gambling: Dr. Eric Single, whom I had seen from time to time at the University of Toronto. Eric invited me to his home for a chat. He further confirmed my impression that little recognizably sociological work had been done on gambling, but he convinced me that it could be done. Partly he did so through anecdotes that helped me imagine what directions such research might take: for example, the study of group influences around a gambling table. Partly, he did so by analogy: for example, by referring to work he had done on the regulation of drinking and drunkenness in licensed establishments.

I left Eric's house convinced that I could work in this area and that there was much to be done. I completed the ethnic gambling study with David in 2003. What we found out in that study strengthened my belief that families do influence gambling practices, from childhood onward. I believe we cannot possibly understand adult gambling without understanding what adult gamblers learned (and saw and heard) as children, as young adults, and thereafter. Work remains to be done, to study the learning and encouragement of gambling practices in schools, workplaces, and various leisure settings. And of course, much work remains to be done on the effects of the mass media and advertising on gambling.

The Influence of Culture

Our 2003 study was, admittedly, an exploratory study, since it was based on a small, non-random sample of respondents from six different ethnic ancestral groups in the Greater Toronto Area. In hopes of strengthening my findings about ethnic differences, in 2004, I sought and received funding from OPGRC for another study. In this study, I re-analyzed data from Dr. Jamie Wiebe's first survey of a random sample of Ontarians (Wiebe, Single, and Falkowski-Ham, 2001). Jamie collaborated on my new study, as did Agata Falkowski-Ham, who had earlier collaborated on my *At Home* study and earlier had collaborated with Jamie on the Ontario survey.

To estimate ethnic variations, we painstakingly re-coded an ethnic ancestral variable in that sample. To estimate neighbourhood influences on gambling, we linked Jamie's survey to the most recent available (1996) public use Census data for Greater Toronto, using postal codes. The results were messy to analyze, but they largely confirmed that ethnic influences were as we had found them in the *At Home* study, even when we took into account the statistical influences of other variables (such as neighbourhood poverty and unemployment rates, for example).

This study showed that gambling in Canada varies from one ethnic group to another. Consider, for example, the English, the Chinese, and the Aboriginals. Chinese and Aboriginal people, both in Canada and elsewhere, tend to gamble a lot more than average and are more likely than average to show signs of gambling problems. By contrast, both in Canada and in their home country, people of English background (despite a long history of gambling by both working-class and aristocratic people) gamble less than average Ontarians and are less likely than average to show signs of gambling problems.

To understand these ethnic variations better, I re-analyzed data from the Ontario Prevalence Survey. There too I found that members of different Ontario ethnic groups score differently (on average) on CPGI. Again, Chinese-Canadian and Aboriginal people scored significantly higher than average, with more gambling problems; and English-ancestry people scored significantly lower than average, with fewer gambling problems. Through the use of public use sample data from the Census of Canada, I found that living in certain neighbourhoods (called "enumeration areas" in the Census) predicts higher problem gambling scores than living in other neighbourhoods. In short, both neighbourhood context and personal background affect gambling, though personal background is the stronger influence of the two. However, the same patterns emerge. In particular, people from neighbourhoods with a higher-than-average Aboriginal residency tend to have higher-than-average CPGI scores, independent of the personal ancestry of the individual respondent.

Finally, sophisticated and powerful tools of multivariate data analysis confirmed that ethnic ancestry does indeed influence gambling patterns, both positively and negatively. Thus, the 2003 study supported the findings of earlier exploratory research. It showed the central importance of social variables in explaining problem gambling, and this strengthened my resolve to press on.

The Influence of Families

During this period, I also wrote a textbook on social problems and another on deviance. The deviance textbook, particularly, renewed my interest in bringing a sociological focus to gambling research. It reminded me about the importance of *informal social control* in social life—the many ways people routinely keep their friends, family members, and workmates from doing foolish, thoughtless, or even dangerous things. It occurred to me that families might try to control problem gambling in this way.

I sought a small grant from OPGRC and carried out a systematic review of the published literature on informal control or regulation. I found almost nothing about informal control related to gambling, and only a little research on the informal control of other risky behaviours, such as excess drinking, smoking, dangerous driving, and unprotected sex. Again, this strengthened my belief that there was sociological work to do in this area. I reasoned that if informal control of gambling existed, we would likely find it first in the relationship between a gambler and his or her spouse. So, I wrote a research proposal to study this, OPGRC funded the proposal, and together with David Korn and Jennifer Reynolds, we carried out the 2005 study on which this book is mainly based.

As subsequent chapters describe, spouses do try (with varying degrees of success) to regulate the gambling of their partners who gamble to excess. This book is about the ways they try to do this and reasons why many fail most of the time.

We can distinguish patterns in the family problems that arise from problem gambling and patterns in the efforts spouses make to control this gambling. Further, these patterns remind us of patterns sociologists see in other families facing other kinds of problems. There is a continuity—a similarity or connection—that allows me to think we will be able to bring to bear existing sociological theories about groups and families on the study of problem gambling: we will not have to invent a new sociological approach just for problem gambling.

The remainder of this chapter reviews the sociological research upon which this book is based. If you are a problem gambler or the spouse of a problem gambler, you may prefer to jump ahead to the sections on results and practical advice. However, theories are very practical and useful tools to help us examine our own lives.

For researchers and therapists, the following sections will provide familiar sociological insights about groups, especially processes of informal control in groups, and show how they relate to gamblers. Since families are groups, we discuss the specific role that families and spouses play in providing informal control in a variety of health-related matters, especially addictions.

A Sociological Approach to "Becoming"

Sociologists have different methods for studying how people take on social identities, but one of the most useful is the *symbolic interactionist* (SI) approach. SI is a way of viewing society as a product of continuous face-to-face interaction in different settings. SI focuses on the processes by which people build society through these interactions: how people interpret and respond to the actions of others, and how social structures result from these processes.

Two questions of special interest to symbolic interactionists are:

- How do people become the kind of people they are? That is, how does the *self* (and self-control) develop?
- How do people reach new understandings about a situation, and how do they learn the proper behaviour for that situation?

All sociologists view learning as a social process; but symbolic interactionists are most concerned with understanding how people come to take on the norms, values, attitudes, beliefs, and behaviour patterns of the people around them. A related but more general question is, how do people come to be *themselves*? By *self*, we mean a person's experience and awareness of having a personal identity that is separate from that of other people. Sociologists believe that people develop this sense of self in the same way that they internalize their culture. How, for example, does someone become a "gambler," sociologically speaking? And how does one become a "problem gambler"? What experiences create and consolidate the identity we label "gambler" or "problem gambler"?

Social theorists differ in their accounts of the emergence of the self, but they agree on one thing: social interaction is central to its development. American sociologist Charles Cooley (1902) was the first to emphasize the importance of the self in the process of socialization. He stressed the role of the social environment in the development of a self-concept. According to Cooley, people form concepts of themselves as they see how other people react to them. The so-called *labelling theory* of deviance comes directly out of this principle.

A more complete approach to socialization can be found in the work of the American social theorist George Herbert Mead (1934). Mead suggested that children go through several phases as they learn to internalize social expectations. For symbolic interactionists, social life is like a game, and we learn to play the game—to take coordinated roles and anticipate the role-play of others— when we are children.

Learning to be a "gambler" and taking on a "gambler's identity" is very obviously the result of playing games with other people (or with machines). The gambler identity is established through interaction in this situation where there are clear winners and losers, rewards and punishments.

Symbolic Interactionism, Communication, and the Lure of Deviance

Symbolic interactionists want to understand how people acquire new meanings and relationships as they interact with other people in a cultural context. These meanings are social because people create them, share them, learn them, and often pass them down from one generation to the next. A related important concept is a person's *definition of the situation*. People act meaningfully in relation to their own definition of reality, not someone else's.

According to symbolic interactionists, relationships require continuous communication—negotiation, talk, bargaining, and compromise. Negotiation requires social skills, and we all learn social skills through interaction from our childhood upwards. Communication is often easiest if we can lead people to see a situation our way. Thus, controlling and structuring communication is critical for the success of a relationship, because it sets the agenda for negotiation and interpretation. We will see the importance of communication in our discussions of the marital relationships of gamblers later in this chapter. There, at the collision of identities—gambler versus spouse—we see people struggling to identify their concerns, goals, and motives.

In studying deviance and social problems, followers of the SI perspective analyze the ways that society defines certain behaviours and conditions as *deviant acts* and regards some people as *deviant people*. Consistent with the basic premise of labelling theory, Herbert Blumer (1971) proposed that labelling of social problems happens in two stages. The first stage is *social recognition*, the point at which a given condition or behaviour—for example, drug use—is first identified as a potential social concern. Then *social legitimating* takes place: society formally recognizes the social problem as a serious threat to social stability. But symbolic interactionists are less interested in explaining *primary deviance*—that is, the reason why people break society's rules. They are more interested in the way society responds to the rule-breaking. From their standpoint, it is the social response that "creates" deviance and deviant communities.

Nearly a century ago, Georg Simmel (1950 [1902]) offered important insights into the social construction of deviance and deviant communities.

Simmel explained that society includes two *worlds*. The first world is the openly acknowledged world of socially acceptable activities—school and work, family life, sports, etc. The second world is the (slightly) hidden deviant activities—sexual affairs, drug addictions, treacherous plots, violent acts, prostitution. This second world is ignored by most people most of the time but is in full view to people with the skill and desire to see them. Simmel showed how these second worlds—or deviant communities—are based on yet build away from the first "real" world of our everyday sense experience.

Simmel also helped explain the social role of strangers. Strangers occupy an interesting role in every group, community, or society. Strangers are outsiders who, for some purposes, are allowed inside a group. When strangers interact with that group, for self-protection, they control information flow by hiding some information about themselves (also known as *impression management*). Because of their partial exclusion, strangers are free to do things that are forbidden to the group's insiders. In that way, they are able to display and exemplify alternative ways of living. As we see in this book, a large part of the lives of problem gamblers is spent at the margins of conventional society: between intimates and strangers, secrecy and openness. In effect, many gamblers live in both the first and second worlds of their society.

Howard Becker (1963), a symbolic interactionist trained in the Chicago School, emphasized that deviance should not be explained in terms of psychology or personality. Everyone is capable of deviance, and everyone practices deviance from time to time (just as everyone is a stranger in one setting or another). For Becker, the important issue is how a person discovers deviant behaviour, learns to participate in it, and adjusts to the label of deviant—in effect, how deviant communities form and how people create deviant identities.

In one classic work, Becker analyzed the ways that people progress into (and out of) the recreational use of marijuana. He emphasized that deviance is rarely practised solo; it is almost always a social accomplishment. So, for example, people need others to help them recognize and enjoy the chemical effects of marijuana. Without this social context, they are unlikely to enjoy and repeat the experience. Moreover, smoking marijuana often becomes a social activity in its own right, as enjoyable for its sociability as for its chemical effects.

The most important symbolic interactionist tool for understanding deviance is *labelling theory*. Sociologists regard Edwin Lemert as a pioneer in the development of this approach for his work on *societal reaction theory*, first published in his 1951 work, *Social Pathology: A Systemic Approach to the Theory of Sociopathic Behavior*. His work examined *secondary deviance*—rule-breaking acts that follow from a deviant label. His theory holds that contrary to what we might expect, people labelled as deviant are *more* likely to engage in deviant behaviour, because that fits in with their new self-image (and with their new, more restricted social opportunities).

Labelling starts with a perception of difference. Some people attract attention through their deviant behaviour. The application of a label, whether formally or informally, may result in a changed self-image or social exclusion. As a result, labelling is the starting place for understanding deviant life paths, identities, and communities.

Labelling theory turns attention away from the person doing the deviant activity and toward the people doing the labelling. What social forces or institutional goals increase the rate of labelling of deviants? What factors influence the social construction of crimes? That is, what makes certain acts deviant or criminal at some times, but not at others? Why is gambling, which used to be criminal or (at best) unrespectable, now legal and widely considered fashionable? The answers to such questions cannot be found in the reasons why people break rules or commit crimes. In other words, these questions require *sociological* answers, not *psychological* answers.

These questions also lead us to study marginal, fringe, and deviant communities. Any large society contains a dominant culture and various subcultures that flourish within the dominant framework. Deviant communities are the social mechanisms that promote and maintain deviant subcultures. They also give their members social support for remaining deviant and create alternative social worlds. In addition, they develop deviant subcultures—their ideological reason for existing. The two—deviant communities and deviant subcultures—are analytically distinct; but in practice, there is no deviant subculture without a deviant community, and vice versa.

Sociologists' interest in deviant subcultures is closely related to an influential theory of crime and deviance first named in the early twentieth century as *differential association theory*. In 1924, the theory's author, Edwin H. Sutherland, published *Criminology*, which became a standard textbook; and by 1947, four editions of the book had been published. An eminent researcher, his books *The Professional Thief* (1937) and *White Collar Crime* (1949) introduced new ideas in the field of criminology.

Sutherland was not the first criminologist to argue that deviant and criminal behaviours have cultural, rather than individual (psychological or biological), roots. People imitate what they see other people doing. In communities where crime is common, accepted, and even highly organized—such as the Neapolitan *camorra* about which Gabriel Tarde[2] wrote in the late nineteenth century—otherwise normal people are likely to engage in crime too.

Symbolic interactionism also provides an insight into the ways that social issues (or *social problems*) arise. Social problems are socially created, or *constructed*. The *social construction approach*—growing out of symbolic interactionism—examines how problem situations come to be defined as social problems. No problem, no matter how big, can gain widespread attention and concern without social construction. Even the most catastrophic social acts—such as genocidal mass murder—need a social explanation (Alexander, 2002). All interpretations and understandings of moral responsibility (blame) have a social history. They are never self-evident or without an ideological background; they may include claims and counter-claims, and sometimes differing visions of right and wrong. To say this is only to affirm that everything people say and do has a social-historical background. From the smallest issue in a single community to the biggest issue on the world stage, social problems are rooted in a particular time and place, with a particular social meaning that someone has constructed.

Symbolic interactionists have always been interested in outsiders, minorities, deviants, and rebels, and their communities and subcultures. Young people, for example, have always interested sociologists, whether organized in gangs, cliques, classrooms, or mass audiences. Immigrant communities and subcultures are equally interesting. Even people with unusual features, such as autism or deafness, interest sociologists, because they are more likely than others to develop deviant identities and lead somewhat deviant or unusual lives. Symbolic interactionists argue that labelling and social reaction prolong the deviant behaviour, creating a career out of an attribute.

People work out life strategies for dealing with their peculiarities and disabilities. Socialization and labelling shape people's identities and stabilize their

---

2 Tarde was an early theorist of crime, which he regarded as deviant activity based on imitation and learning. A more recent example of popular deviant activity was the black market in the formerly communist Eastern Europe, where a majority of people practised bribery and corruption as a matter of course. Today, Mafia-like gangster groups operate even more openly there than in the past. These examples show that corruption and criminality develop their own subcultural value systems wherever conditions are ripe for them.

activities. Social constraints and opportunities, socialization, and even biology may all influence the contingencies involved in activity throughout the life course (Ulmer and Spencer, 1999). This holds true whether the behaviour is conforming or deviant, criminal or law-abiding, desirable or disgusting, socially useful or socially parasitic.

In summary, symbolic interactionists emphasize the importance of interaction, negotiation, symbolic meanings, stigmatization, and the effects of labelling on a person's sense of self; and all are factors that can determine deviant and conforming behaviours. Underlying all this is the human need to make sense of life, self, and society. We will find these ideas useful in understanding problem gamblers and their families throughout this book.

How Groups and Families Protect Themselves

People do not merely think and interpret other people's actions, as symbolic interactionism seems to imply. They also take action to further their own interests and protect the *groups* to which they belong. Sociological theories about groups—associated with research on small groups and social systems, especially by the sociologist George Homans—can provide us with deeper insight into group influences, especially into the ways groups protect themselves against deviant activities and deviant identities. Since families and couples are small groups, our research falls into this category.

As a way into this problem, our study focused on that single most important relationship people are likely to have: the relationship with an intimate partner, husband, or wife. Our thinking was that if anyone in the gambler's group could informally influence the gambling of problem gamblers at all, their intimate partners—or spouses—could do it. We reasoned that spouses are in a far better position than parents, children, friends, workmates, acquaintances, and even bosses to exercise some control over problem gambling. They should have more information about their spouse and his or her gambling.

The informal ways people control one another are many, but they mainly comprise two processes: rewarding wanted behaviour and withholding rewards for unwanted behaviour. Rewards between spouses include respect, love, sex, friendship, emotional support, and sometimes money. One thing that makes couples—indeed all groups—unique is their shared history of good and bad experiences, including the history of rewards and punishments they have given one another. This may sound bloodless and abstract, but that is only because it applies as readily to work groups, cliques, teams, clubs, bands, and gangs as it does to marriages and families. At ground level, among real people in real situations, it is exciting—and it works!

The discussion that follows uses the terms *rule-breaking* and *norm violation* interchangeably. Both connote the violation of social—especially, family—expectations about obedience: unwritten and often unspoken rules about family behaviour. So, for example, most families assume—without saying so—that their members protect the family's financial security and avoid risking family property, savings, or personal earnings. When a problem gambler endangers the family by betting and losing the family car or house, a child's educational savings, or even a large chunk of his or her own wages, that gambler is breaking the family rules—in effect, violating the family norms. In such instances, the family often responds by applying sanctions. That is, it attempts to regulate, control, or punish the offending behaviour.

Our discussion here begins with a brief examination of *informal social control*, which can be defined as conformity to (or compliance with) social norms and the expectations members of a group have about one another's behaviour. The theory of social control is based on classic work by George Homans in *The Human Group* (1950). Homans draws data from the findings of five earlier studies of small groups and makes several key propositions about social control.

First, he notes that *no social rule or custom sustains itself—people have to sustain it*. Our obedience to or compliance with rules occurs because of the responses of others. We know how social control works because we can see what happens when a person violates a rule or norm. Typically, members of the group withdraw their rewards, including even their friendship and trust. They become less willing to do favours for the rule-breaker. Members likely feel and express less sentimental attachment to the rule-breaker. Even a high-ranking rule-breaker may lose his or her standing as a group leader. Basically, social control comes from the existing structure of mutual dependence in a group. If a member violates the rules of the group, he or she undermines that mutual dependence and threatens the group. In turn, the group threatens the violator with a loss of the privileges associated with membership in the group.

Thus, *norm violation*, or rule-breaking, and social control exist in the context of particular people within particular groups. Group histories and personal histories define the boundaries of acceptable and unacceptable behaviour. So problem gambling has to be evaluated differently in families where gambling—even frequent gambling—has long been a part of the repertoire of family behaviour, compared to families where gambling has been rare or nonexistent. In nongambling families, the norm violation of overspending because of a gambling problem is noticed far sooner than in gambling families, where gambling-related troubles are almost expected. In turn, this means members of gambling families may be far less vigilant and responsive to gambling problems.

Homans further notes that *social control is not a separate element within a social organization*. When confronted by norm violation, families do not suddenly "go into action" as social controllers, using techniques specially devised for this purpose. Rather, they are always engaged in social control over transgressions against the family rules. The same processes that regulate normal, everyday family transactions—especially exchange and reciprocity—limit the likelihood a person will break the family rules.

Thus, families are likely to use the same repertoire of informal controls to deal with problem gambling that they use to deal with other rule infractions. Families may need to be taught new ways to informally control problem gambling if their existing methods aren't working. Though familiar forms of control can be successful with everyday problems, they may not work well with a gambling problem.

Additionally, some families are more attentive to norm violations than others. Some families are measurably more cohesive than others, expecting and receiving a higher degree of member commitment and conformity as a matter of course. There are many sociological theories to account for such interfamily variations, none of them specifically addressing problem gambling. What we should note at this point is that some families are more experienced than others at dealing with significant norm violations associated with problem gambling.

According to social control theory, each member of a group has a lot to lose by breaking the group's rules. So, for example, a husband who loses the rent money gambling on poker stands to lose the love and friendship of his wife. Some spouses even withhold sex when they are angry about such rule infractions. A father who loses his daughter's college fund stands to lose his daughter's respect. Likewise, a son who borrows money from his parents or friends to pay gambling debts stands to lose their affection and future co-operation.

Though some rule-violators seem unaware of the price in family conflict they might pay for their behaviour, many others are aware of it and continue to gamble anyway. In a sense, what we mean by a gambling "problem" or gambling "addiction" is precisely that the gambler seems unable to avoid predictable punishment and pain by giving up gambling. What is far more common is that problem gamblers usually imagine they will not be found out.

Homans' third observation is that *a norm violation activates the system of relations so as to reduce future norm violations.* Family responses to a norm violation are often strong enough to deter further norm violations. However, families may fail to deliver strong enough responses if they lack valid information about the extent of the violation, if they have wide latitude of acceptance, or if they are unable to muster an effective response. Some families are too frightened, reserved, conflicted, polite, or unexpressive to respond forcefully.

Homans adds that *punishment does not necessarily produce control.* A healthy, well-functioning group or family responds forcefully and quickly to rule-breaking, usually by withholding the rewards and support that family members typically rely on. This is usually what we mean by a "normal" or "well-functioning" family. A family that does not or cannot enforce its own rules is dysfunctional. It will usually show other symptoms of family dysfunction—other evidence of continuing conflict and an inability to make and follow plans.

Variations in Family Responsiveness

A stable, balanced, healthy, or well-functioning family is one in which rule-breaking normally leads to system-wide *activation*, whether through punishment or a withdrawal of rewards. This activation consciously and almost ritually reasserts the dominance of the group over its members, affirms the boundaries of acceptable behaviour and strengthens the bonds between the remaining (that is, conforming) family members.

Of course, in doing these things, families rarely act with self-conscious unity. Usually, members of the family act with different thoughts, beliefs, and ideas. Different family members may be faster or slower to condemn a rule-breaker, for example. They also differ in their willingness and ability to hold back rewards the rule-breaker desires. These differences between members introduce new, secondary tensions and conflicts into the family, but they do not indicate that the family is dysfunctional. A *dysfunctional* family is one that for various reasons can rarely or never behave in a concerted way. It can rarely or never enforce group norms, seek group goals, amass group resources, or protect group members.

Health Consequences

On the one hand, then, families are healthy, self-protecting groups that maintain themselves by controlling norm violations. Rule-breakers such as problem gamblers are ostracized or expelled from the group as a result. Thus, problem gamblers can find themselves quite alone. For a time, they may ignore their effective loss of membership in the family, especially if they are preoccupied with the excitement and pleasure of gambling.

Yet on the other hand, people are social by nature—and that includes problem gamblers. Most want to live with other people and form long-term bonds with them. Both men and women (but especially men, as we discuss later) do better as members of families than on their own. Ostracization and loneliness often lead to physical and mental health issues. So, an added cost of rule-breaking and punishment by the family is the increased risk of physical and mental decline. Likely, some of the physical decline, emotional instability, and comorbidity associated with problem gambling is because of this loss of social control and the decline of social order in the family.

Homans also described a connection between anxiety and ritual. The research literature on gambling (and addiction literature more generally) tends to assume that anxiety is a personality trait or a state induced by stressful external events. From this perspective, addictive behaviour—especially, problem gambling—is a way of quelling anxiety by focusing attention on the "here and now." Problem gamblers celebrate the feeling of being "in the moment." Indeed, many develop elaborate rituals in preparation for play or follow ritualistic patterns while playing.

Researchers often quickly infer from this that gamblers adopt ritualized gambling because of anxiety. Yet a gambler's anxiety is often compounded by the stress of family sanctions and expulsion. As families punish and exclude their members who break the rules against excess gambling, the gamblers become more anxious, ritualistic, and driven to gambling. Thus, without co-operation from the family, including a reduction of family-related stress and anxiety, this vicious circle cannot be stopped. As Homans also points out, a person can be healthy and free only when he or she willingly conforms to the group's rules. Thus, for healing to occur, the group must choose, freely and wisely, to re-admit the problem gambler into the group on probation.

Self-Protection

Because healing depends on family acceptance and reduced stress, families may need to continue providing emotional support to problem gamblers, even though their first self-protective instinct may be to expel and/or punish them. For many gamblers, a spouse's love, understanding, and care help reduce anxiety and the attendant need for gambling. Yet a spouse's first instinct is often self-protective: to pay off the gambling debts, hide the gambling behaviour, and lie for the gambler, while emotionally punishing the gambler with anger and guilt.

This relationship stress contributes to further gambling and alienates the partners from each other even more. They find it hard to deal with the guilt, anger, and resentment of other family members. Gamblers need to face the consequences of their actions, to help them define the gambling as problematic; yet they need emotional support to do so. Similarly, spouses need to assess their reactions: carrying a guilty sense of responsibility for their spouse's actions is emotionally destructive.

For all these reasons, we may conclude that treatment strategies have to involve partners. The problem gamblers need to learn new, healthy behaviours, and so do their partners. Often, their partners become just as sick and distressed as the problem gamblers.

Some rule-breakers preemptively solve the problem of detection and/or expulsion by building an alternative world—new friends and acquaintances, even new lovers and "family members." These new groups are likely willing to accept the gambler's behaviour such as it is. But this "new world" is essentially running away from the problem. In the end, the problem gambler has to come to terms with the socially disruptive nature of problem gambling. The literature on social control in small groups gives us a strong reason to believe that families can play a major role in solving gambling problems.

Social Management

Spouses also use a variety of social tools to control their gambling partners. In a work titled *The Process of Social Organization* (1978), sociologist Marvin Olsen elaborates on Homans' ideas on social control. He highlights the systemic character of families, and the ways that families are like larger organizations in the way that they train and control their members. His theoretical principles about social control have been gleaned from numerous sociological studies of groups and organizations.

Olsen notes that *groups use social control to maintain their boundaries, regulate member activities, perform key functions, and maintain order.* Every family is a social organization in this sense. Key features of a family include a role structure (parent, child, student), a division of labour (chores, income), often a power structure (head of household, decision-making processes), the accumulation and use of collective resources (furniture, bank accounts), and an organizational culture and normative structure (holidays, daily rituals).

Then Olsen goes beyond Homans' idea of the priority of rewards and punishments by asserting that *groups accomplish social control primarily through two processes: social sanctions (rewards and punishments) and social management (shaping the context in order to modify the actions). Social management* refers to creating opportunities and constraints that influence or modify the actions of family members. Some spouses don't use social management to change a partner's gambling behaviour. Some actually promote gambling, while others merely ignore it. But some spouses use their relationship with the gambler to promote or *manage* their change through social means.

For example, spouses can use the *embeddedness* of their relationship—the degree to which they and their partner share one social world—to manage problem gambling in one of two ways. First, a high degree of embeddedness means that the problem gambler's activities are probably highly visible and constantly under surveillance by the spouse. This visibility can have the effect of controlling or limiting rule-breaking behaviour. Second, a high degree of embeddedness also means that the spouse is steering the gambler's time, money, and energy into couple-based activities, effectively reducing gambling opportunities. If handled properly, a spouse can use this kind of social management to change the gambler's behaviour.

Channels for More Effective Control

Olsen also states that *groups use bureaucratization to organize their functions and help them reach their goals.* Certainly, the typical family does not "bureaucratize." However, like bureaucracies, families sometimes have pressing goals. For example, when a family member develops a gambling problem, the family needs to find ways to reorganize itself to survive. How can a family find the most effective, efficient response? Because families are small groups, they must find this response without the range of resources typically available to a larger, richer corporate organization. Often, families can be amazingly productive, given their (usually limited) resources.

Olsen notes that *social control means establishing procedures to help the group survive.* Olsen lists examples of these procedures:

- training or socialization of members
- sharing of common goals
- establishment of a division of labour
- development of a consistent set of norms and rules
- co-ordination of organizational activities

- creation of procedures for resolving conflicts
- transmission of procedures for changing the organization.

This list, though incomplete, hints at the wide range of activities a family must undertake to survive as a group.

The control of family members is incidental to achieving these goals. Ideally, if you are part of the family, you take part in these types of activities and share the rewards. These are the contexts within which family systems manage, control, and channel personal choices. In practice, some family members are usually more heavily engaged than others in meeting these system goals and enforcing social control. Often, it falls to the gambler's spouse—as the only other adult in the household—to fill all these roles.

Decision Making and Power in Families

Olsen maintains that *social control includes procedures for communicating, problem solving, and coping in periods of uncertainty*. Certainly, larger organizations often have specialized internal units dedicated to solving problems, reducing conflicts, and coping with organizational strain. In families, people often have to seek help from external units. When problem gambling develops, people already burdened by many problems must deal with the added problems on top of their usual agenda. Outside units—for example, addictions therapists, doctors, and social workers—may offer needed advice and help. But for various reasons, some families may be unable to locate or unwilling to use such services. One role of therapy, then, is to persuade people that they need outside expert help.

Olsen adds that *social control includes decision-making procedures and structures for collective decisions*. Often, a gambling problem compromises the decision-making capacity of a family. One of the adult members of the family has effectively disappeared or is refusing to co-operate in solving the problem he or she has caused. For the same reason, a family may be unable to enforce decisions made without the participation or co-operation of a key adult member.

Effective enforcement may need the collaboration of the errant spouse's parents, older children, siblings, friends, or employer. Achieving this kind of collaboration is likely harder for a family than for a corporate organization, in which intra-unit collaboration is common. Sometimes the effort to exert control results in *parentification*—a process in which children (even young children) are obliged to parent their parents. Parentification is rarely healthy or helpful for the children and the family.

Finally, Olsen observes that *centralization of power and control is common in all groups, but it can be avoided if power and control are distributed among the members.* This issue of power relations continues to be a central concern in feminist research on families. For example, in families where the male adult is the sole breadwinner, decision-making power can be centralized in male hands. Since the 1960s, women have been able to redress gender imbalances of power and control. But many families, owing in part to gendered differences in earning power and ethnocultural traditions, continue to run as paternal dictatorships. This has particular significance when the male family ruler becomes a problem gambler, since it means the family has little capacity to control the problem. Control over the family's material resources rests largely in the gambler's hands. However, control over trust, affection, and ready compliance may rest in the hands of other family members.

Families as Health Promoters

The Health Effects of Marriage

Research in both health studies and family sociology has shown that, on average, marriage is good for people. By far, the most comprehensive and sociologically authoritative discussion of the positive role of marriage in people's lives is *The Case for Marriage: Why Married People Are Happier, Healthier, and Better Off Financially*, by Linda Waite and Maggie Gallagher (2000). This thorough review of the literature shows that more than any other social arrangement, marriage has the power to significantly improve people's lives.

Despite claims that there is a "his marriage" and a "her marriage," marriage benefits women as well as men. Having a good relationship with one's partner affects the mental health of a wife, just as it does the mental health of a husband (Spotts *et al.*, 2005). Yet the research shows that protective effects of marriage are stronger for men than for women (Kiecolt-Glaser and Newton, 2001). Unmarried women have 50 percent higher mortality risks than married women, whereas unmarried men have 250 percent higher mortality risks than married men (Ross, Mirowsky, and Goldstein, 1990). In addition, research shows that women are far more likely than men to oversee the health of their loved ones. For example, women are more likely than men to try to manage the health of their spouse, thereby improving the lives of married men (Umberson, 1992). In contrast, men are more likely to take their marital support responsibilities lightly. In addition, men receive social support from marriage much more than women. Women's support networks are usually larger and better tended than men's and often include close friends and relatives as confidantes. By contrast, men are much more likely to rely only on their spouse as their sole source of support (Phillipson, 1997). For these reasons, marital disruption is more harmful for men than for women (House *et al.*, 1988).

Married people are, on average, healthier than unmarried people. But the quality of a marital relationship also affects health. People in troubled marriages are generally in poorer health than people in happy marriages (Burman and Margolin, 1992). People in unhappy, stressful marriages run an even higher health risk than divorced people (Williams 2003).

Marriage provides people with their most meaningful social ties, and the lack of meaningful social ties constitutes a major health risk for death and disease. The *positive* effects of social support on health are as large as the *negative* effects of risks such as smoking, high blood pressure, obesity, and physical inactivity (House, Landis, and Umberson, 1988). The structured and organized lifestyle we normally associate with marriage, which includes ongoing supervision by one's spouse, is important in promoting healthy behaviours and discouraging harmful acts (Hawkins and Booth, 2005).

Thus, through close supervision and care, marriage promotes mental and physical health. But a health problem such as drug or alcohol abuse or a social problem such as problem gambling is likely to have effects on both the gambler and his or her spouse, reducing marital quality. The spouses of problem gamblers have to deal with issues that bring new strains to marital relationships. Heineman (1987) notes, for example, that spouses often have to handle threatening phone calls from creditors, repay loans which they co-signed, and wrestle with economic burdens placed on the family. Spouses and partners of problem gamblers also find that they can have little trust in the gambler.

Family Reasons for Problem Gambling

Problem gambling can significantly harm a marriage and thereby harm the health of people in the marriage. At the same time, marital distress can irritate gambling problems (Boyd and Bolen, 1979; Wildman, 1989). This reciprocity leads us to ask which comes first: a bad marriage or a gambling problem? Do gambling problems occur in certain types of families more than in others? Do some people select partners who are already gamblers, have gambling-susceptible personalities (for example, they are born risk-takers), or are likely to react to conflicts by escaping into gambling? If some people unwittingly but consistently select gambler partners, then gambling problems will be especially resistant to family or spousal intervention because they are built into the fabric of the spousal relationship.

More importantly, how important are "innate" personal factors compared with other gambling-related causes? So far, the gambling literature has little to say in answer to this question. Yet gambling researchers have identified at least three possible reasons why people develop gambling problems: a susceptibility to gambling due to a distorted view of the odds of winning (Turner *et al.*, 2002; Blaszczynski, 2002); an emotional vulnerability to gambling (Getty *et al.*, 2000; Blaszczynski, 2002); and a chemical, genetic, neuropsychological, or physiological vulnerability.

As mentioned above, problem gambling has many similarities to other addictions, notably drug and alcohol addictions. The National Research Council (1999) documents similarities that include arousal and euphoria (comparable to the high experienced from drug use), tolerance development (needing to gamble for longer periods of time or increase wager amounts in order to be satisfied), and the experience of withdrawal (when prevented from gambling). Focusing on these similarities, many studies take a biological approach to understand the progression through stages of gambling. This approach comes from a disease model that assumes biological or genetic causes of addiction—neurobiological and genetic factors that predispose certain people to addiction (Peele, 2002).

In addition, many studies have found that problem gambling runs in families. Studies have found that youth who gamble excessively are more likely than average to have learned to gamble with family members (Gupta and Derevensky, 1997). Often, problem gambling imitates, or grows out of, parental gambling (Browne and Brown, 1994). We see support for these findings in our own study, below.

These studies leave us wondering whether the relationship between parent gambling and child gambling is genetically-based or socially-based. For example, a series of twin studies found more similarities in gambling behaviour among 42 sets of identical twins, who share all their genes, than among 50 sets of fraternal twins, who share only half their genes (Winters and Rich, 1998). This effect was significant only for male twins playing high-stake games. Results for female twins and lower-stake games were statistically much less significant. These results are similar to those found in a study on alcoholism, where the genetic risk was much higher for men than women (McGue, Pickens, and Svikis 1992).

In contrast, other researchers have adopted a social psychological model of addiction that focuses on social causality, psychological forces, and the behavioural associations of addiction (Peele, 2002). These researchers view addiction as a compulsive pursuit characterized by preoccupation, disorganization, and desperation. Despite continuous losses, gamblers believe that gambling will solve their problems, and they continue along this path until they have lost everything.

Though rare, some literature on gambling symptoms talks about the influence that families can have on the gambler's career as an "addict." While many problem gamblers follow a downward spiral until they hit rock bottom, not all gamblers do. Some 40 to 60 percent of people who develop a gambling problem show a clinical remission without professional help (McCown and Howatt, 2007). Gamblers who follow this path are said to have *matured out*.

Researchers find a similar pattern of spontaneous remission in studies of other chronic mental disorders, including depression, anxiety, and bipolar disorder. Spontaneous remission occurs at roughly the same rate in gambling as in other addictions. However, the conditions under which a matured-out gambler returns to gambling again are poorly understood. As with drug and alcohol addictions, people who spontaneously stop their problem gambling follow a varied course, and some relapse. What is less clear is how families produce or support such a result.

Spouses and Addiction Treatment Success

Often, problem gamblers and their spouses report high levels of marital discord and related troubles. For this reason, many therapists have started including family members in therapy for problem gamblers (Darvas, 1981; Ciarrocchi and Reinert, 1993).

One reason to include family members in therapy is the research suggesting that spouses of problem gamblers often take longer to recover than the gambler him- or herself. Family members—especially spouses—may need therapy or clinical support long after the gambler has stopped gambling. Factors delaying the recovery of spouses include the financial devastation they continue to live with and their perceived lack of control over family life. In essence, spouses feel that they continue to be at the mercy of the gambler and his or her wish to gamble (Ciarrocchi and Reinert, 1993).

Research is only beginning to study the treatment of couples affected by problem gambling. No one so far has studied the influence of a couple's embeddedness (the degree to which couples occupy each others' social worlds) or lack of embeddedness on a partner's willingness to seek treatment for a gambling problem. Within the subfield of alcohol and drug addiction research, several studies have examined the role of the spouses and social support in relation to treatment strategies. Yet none of these specifically considers couple embeddedness. In drug treatment programs, relationship dynamics—power, control, dependence, insecurity, and decision making—all influence treatment engagement, but these differ by gender and partner drug use (Riehman *et al.*, 2000). Drug addiction literature reveals that social support influences the effectiveness of treatment for drug addiction in four associated ways:

- **Presence of support**: Support reflects social integration, which in turn predicts a lowered risk of relapse (Tracy *et al.*, 2005) and better functioning post-treatment.
- **Relationship stability and treatment outcomes**: Stability in a relationship (remaining in the relationship, as opposed to separating or divorcing) is associated with better substance-use outcomes (Rowe and Liddle, 2003)
- **Quality of support**: Good-quality marital relationships and marital happiness are associated with higher rates of abstinence and a lower rates of using drugs post-treatment (Tracy *et al.*, 2005). Conversely, poor marriage quality is associated with weak outcomes. (O'Farrell and Hooley, 1998).
- **Substance use by social network members**: The presence of a spouse who does not use addictive substances predicts a higher likelihood of abstinence one year post-treatment (Powers, 1993; Powers and Anglin, 1996).

Substance abuse and addictions can be regarded as family diseases or conditions. Lavee and Altus (2001) found that for problem gambling in particular, the majority (76 percent) of relapses result from social pressure, interpersonal conflict, or problems coping with intrapersonal negative emotional states. Successful treatment for any type of addiction calls for family involvement whenever possible. Behavioural Couples Therapy (BCT)—therapy to change the behaviours of one member of the couple by providing therapy to both members of the couple—strengthens marital relationships by improving couple communication, and it also significantly improves treatment outcomes (O'Farrell and Fals-Steward, 2005; McCrady et al., 1986; O'Farrell, 1993, 1996, 2003; O'Farrell and Hooley 1998; Kelly et al., 2002). BCT for addictions focuses in part on supporting abstinence and in part on building the marital relationship through communication, shared activities, and positive feelings (O'Farrell et al., 2003). Researchers report that couples who take part in this treatment have better treatment outcomes than patients who receive standard, individualized treatment.

In addition, both substance abuse and problem gambling undermine marital, family, and child functioning in several ways (Collins, Leonard, and Searles, 1990; Jacob, 1992; Rotunda, Scherer, and Imm, 1995; West and Prinz, 1987). At the same time, the conduct of family members also influences the person at risk of addiction. Part of the problem we encounter in trying to understand the role of families in regulating addiction comes from this mutual or reciprocal causation: addiction increases the risk of family problems, and family problems increases the risk of addiction.

Influences of Families on Problem Gamblers

Although there has been little research into the informal regulation of problem gamblers by their spouses, sociologists have long studied general forms of informal control of behaviour. For example, in his book *Behavior in Public Places* (1963), sociologist Erving Goffman developed a vocabulary for classifying and discussing situational behaviour controls and the mechanisms by which people enforce and avoid them. In addition, anthropological studies have found cultural variations in informal social control, such as gossip and shaming (see, for example, Baumer et al., 2002).

Some researchers have studied the informal control of deviant and health-risk behaviours, including sexual risk behaviours (Ahlberg, Jylkäs, and Krantz, 2001), cigarette and substance abuse (Carter and Kahnweiler, 2000; Gittelsohn et al., 2001; Kennedy et al., 1997; Kumar et al., 2002; and Room, Bondy, and Ferris, 1996) and criminal behaviour (Carr, 1998; Grasmick and Bursik, 1990). These studies describe how groups enforce norms over undesirable behaviour.

Thus, therapists have the foundational concepts to begin researching family-based therapies for compulsive gambling. They can start with the hypothesis that families can promote changes in gambling behaviour by using informal social control, chiefly rewards for change and punishments (specifically emotional and relationship strain) for a failure to change.

Some studies already support this hypothesis. Hodgins *et al.* (2002) found that the top reasons gamblers cited for quitting are financial concerns, emotional factors, and concerns about family and children. Family members can influence a gambler's access to money, which affects whether the gambler stops or continues gambling. As well, family members have other means of pressuring the gambler to quit or consider quitting. An earlier study (Hodgins *et al.*, 1999) found that while all gamblers in the study noted that their gambling had begun to interfere with their lives, only one third of the participants who stopped gambling without professional treatment noted "hitting rock bottom" as a reason for quitting.

More than anything, family members can help the gambler identify the problem. People closest to a gambler are best able to see the warning signs of a problem and recognize that their loved one is behaving strangely. The problem gambler has to recognize and acknowledge the problem before taking any steps towards recovery.

In particular, the gambler needs to acknowledge that the problems resulting from his or her behaviour outweigh the benefits (DiClemente, 2003). Gamblers often keep family members in the dark about the extent and effects of their gambling problems. Kliska and Aranoff (1997) describe how one compulsive gambler was able to hide his problem from his spouse and family. He owned a successful business, so his family was reluctant to pry into his private activities, for fear of bringing to light disreputable information. Researchers also point out that because so many problem gamblers deny that they have a problem, family members often fail to recognize the problem exists (Anderson, 1994).

Influences of Problem Gambling on Marriages

For decades, researchers have recognized that spouses can play an important role in addiction therapy. The more connected an addict is to his or her family, the more likely he or she is to recover. This insight can be generalized to a wide range of illnesses and personal problems: if they know the nature and extent of the problem, spouses can help.

Problem gambling is hard to prevent or cure because of its secrecy. Therefore, by forcing disclosure, spouses should be able to help the gambler admit the extent of the problem. Eliminating secrecy would make the problem more visible and easier to control through informal means. A spouse could contribute to this visibility and control by building a shared social life with the problem gambler.

Cotler (1971) first explored this approach by discussing behavioural changes that could curb problem gambling. The patient in this case study was a 32-year-old male who gambled excessively at cards. He had separated from his wife and was living from paycheque to paycheque. Cotler used several techniques in the patient's therapy. The first assignment he gave the gambler was to replace one night of gambling with some other activity he enjoyed, such as golfing or watching a ballgame. The patient's wife agreed to take part in this therapy, spending time with the gambler in activities unrelated to gambling. In time, the spouse returned, and the gambler was able to work his way back into the family. After sixteen sessions, the gambler was almost free of his problem. Cotler concluded that by increasing the number of nongambling-related social activities, the gambler succeeded in repairing damage to his marriage.

One issue that spousal or couples therapy must address is the damage gambling has done to the relationship and the potential for gambling therapy to repair marriages. Lorenz and Shuttlesworth (1983) examined the difficulties spouses face in living with a problem gambler and the ways they try to resolve these difficulties. The study found "84 percent of those [spouses] responding considered themselves emotionally ill as a result of their experiences" (72). For example, about half of the respondents reported that the gambling spouse lost interest in sex during periods of gambling. Respondents also reported that the gamblers' interactions with the family decreased during periods of gambling. Spouses listed their reasons for staying with the gambler: fear of facing the world alone, love for the gambler, belief the gambling would stop, and a wish to keep the family intact for the sake of the children.

This study suggests that spouses of problem gamblers need significant amounts of professional or social support. Many spouses in this study described their failed efforts to get help from doctors, clergy, and lawyers. None of these professionals were able to help the spouses, and most even failed to refer the spouse to Gam-Anon.

A survey of the (female) spouses of problem gamblers present at Gamblers Anonymous conferences provides similar results. Many of these spouses reported suffering physical and mental problems as result of their husbands' problem gambling (Lorenz and Yaffee, 1988). Many of their problems centred on loneliness and sexuality. Yet after their partner gave up gambling, the proportion reporting sexual satisfaction rose from one-third to two-thirds.

These results show us that problem gamblers are often isolated from their spouses. They spend little time together and often have unsatisfying sexual and emotional lives. Another study—this time, of the (male) gamblers themselves—confirms these findings. Lorenz and Yaffee (1989) compared the results of the survey of partners (discussed above) to a similar survey of the gamblers themselves. Both surveys found that sex became more satisfying for both partners after the gamblers had stopped gambling. Like the wives, the gamblers report they felt isolated during the desperation phase of their gambling problem.

The most interesting finding here is that the marriages of problem gamblers often remain intact, despite serious difficulties. Researchers also note there is a lower incidence of extramarital affairs among problem gamblers and their spouses than in the rest of the population. This finding points to a high level of emotional and sexual commitment, which in turn suggests the potential to revive and improve the marital relations of these gamblers. In addition, a reduction in gambling behaviour will likely help improve marital relations.

Influences of Marriage on Problem Gambling

An even bigger question is, can an improvement in marital relations reduce problem gambling? If so, how?

One strategy is for the spouse to replace the gambler's gambling time with other activities. Jacobs (1987) discusses the need for *community reintegration* because the gambler has been absorbed in solitary activities which have "alienated, weakened, or severed former family ties" (191). Jacobs encourages gamblers to participate in Gamblers Anonymous but adds that they should not spend all their leisure time there either: "[Their] time must be filled with planned alternate and rewarding experiences (preferably shared with people close to them) so they do not slip back into parallel play with former gambling associates and environments" (191).

But obstacles may hinder the gambler's reintegration into family activities. In large part, this is because the spouse harbours doubts and hostile feelings towards the problem gambler. Franklin and Thomas (1989) assert that "the treatment plan of any compulsive gambler is incomplete if it does not address the needs of the family" (142). They conclude that early involvement of family members in treatment is critical, despite the obstacles. The main obstacle is the spouse's resentment and anger. Another potential obstacle is the gambler's attempts to sabotage his or her spouse's participation in treatment.

Research on alcoholism has found that the inclusion of spouses in treatment increases the likelihood that the treatment will succeed. McCrady *et al.* (1991) compared the treatment outcomes of 45 alcoholics and their spouses in three treatment programs: one group had minimal spouse involvement (MSI), another group had alcohol-focused spouse involvement (AFSI), and the third group had alcohol-focused spouse involvement plus behavioural marital therapy (ABMT). Compared to subjects in the other two treatment groups, subjects who received the ABMT treatment "showed more improvement in proportions of abstinent days and abstinent plus light drinking days over the last 9 months of follow-up." Likewise, compared to subjects in the other two treatment groups, they were "less likely to experience marital separations and reported greater improvement in marital satisfaction and subjective well-being" (McCrady *et al.* 1991, 1415). By learning to change their thinking and behaviour, couples were better able to deal with relapses. The researcher concluded: "Marriages do not necessarily improve just because a person receives alcohol treatment. Rather, specific attention to the marital relationship is a necessary element of the treatment" (1422).

Relationship quality is another key feature in successful treatment outcomes. Successful marriages are cohesive and adaptable relationships. Social, cultural, and recreational activities are all important for personal growth. Moos *et al.* (1990) report: "A recreation orientation in the family was associated with less alcohol consumption and depression, a higher likelihood of abstaining, and (as expected) more social activities" (121). In general, "cohesive, well-organized, and socially active families are associated with better treatment outcome" (123). Thus, treatment outcomes improve when compulsive gamblers engage in more social activity with their family and spouse. O'Farrell (1995) confirms that shared recreational and leisure activities can improve a recovering alcoholic's chances of success. The all-consuming nature of alcoholism often results in a decrease in the number of activities the drinker engages in with their family. Reversing this is necessary for the successful reintegration of the alcoholic into his or her family circle.

To revive emotional connections between spouses, spouses can be taught to make use of *core symbols*—symbols endowed with special personal meaning—to increase positive feelings and interactions within the marriage and in this way revive the marriage. Revisiting core symbols that used to be special to the couple can help the addict and spouse to increase positive feelings. But O'Farrell warns that this type of treatment may only be effective if it is implemented after the partners have already begun to feel friendly with each other again.

Other therapists have found that to achieve the degree of embeddedness needed to reform a gambler, the couple must also work on their sexuality and emotional intimacy. Steinberg (1993) stresses the difficulty in reestablishing sexual and emotional intimacy after compulsive gambling treatment. Often, problem gamblers are loners, alienated from others. Many are neither seeking nor capable of sharing intimate emotions with their spouse.

How Families Promote Help-Seeking Behaviours

In 2002, an estimated 18.9 million Canadians gambled; and of those, 1.2 million (5 percent of the adult population) had the potential to become or already had become problem gamblers (Marshall and Wynne, 2003:5). Of the problem gamblers, "56 percent had tried to quit, but could not" (12). Yet little is known about what motivates problem gamblers to finally seek help for their problem.

Helping a partner change ingrained behaviours can be difficult. Substance abuse literature suggests that the effectiveness of a helping partner varies with gender (Riehman *et al.*, 2003). Female drug users are more likely than male drug users to be motivated toward treatment by the influence of their intimate partner (Riehman *et al.*, 2000). Female heroin users, for example, may benefit more than male heroin users from having their partners in treatment with them (Anglin *et al.*, 1987). The drug literature also suggests that men and women differ in their reasons for entering treatment: "Men are more likely to report family pressure and spousal opposition to drug use as reasons for entering treat-ment, while women tend to receive less support from their partners for entering treatment" (Grella and Joshi, 1999: 392).

Yet many spouses complicate the process of change by enabling problem behaviour. *Enabling behaviour* is a learned set of behaviours by significant others that are likely to reinforce negative behaviour, thus increasing the likelihood of such behaviour in the future. Enabling behaviours create environments that reduce the likelihood of a change in problem behaviours. An abstinent spouse, for example, is more likely than a substance-using spouse to motivate an addict towards reduced use or abstinence (Ferrari *et al.*, 2005). But a spouse who drinks or uses drugs—especially if they do so in the company of the addict—is encouraging, if not enabling, addictive behaviour and significantly reducing the chance the addict shakes the habit or meets other harm reduction goals.

Early addiction research tended to blame family members for addiction problems. Early theorists believed the wives of alcoholics had disturbed personalities that influenced their husband's drinking (Downs, 1982; Paolino *et al.*,1978). The literature hinted that these women may have intentionally married alcoholics to shift focus away from their own inadequacies, and that they often intentionally sabotaged their husband's efforts to quit. Many of the wives in these studies had grown up in households where addiction of some sort was present. This led some theorists to conclude that the wives expected or even needed addictive behaviour from their spouse.

Most recently, alcoholism researchers have put forward a *stress and coping theory*, which shifts the focus from individual pathology to the bigger picture of everyday life with an alcoholic. It is based on observations that spouses are continually dealing with difficult and stressful situations. Hurcom *et al.* (2000) praise programs that teach spouses to "reward drinkers for abstinence, set up activities that preclude drinking, reduce 'nagging' behaviours, develop a degree of independence from the drinker, and practice ways of coping with the negative consequences of drinking" (494).

But what is the best course of action for the spouses of problem gamblers? How can they help and support the problem gambler while discouraging the addictive behaviour? Though counter-intuitive from some angles, the answer is simple: avoid enabling behaviour. Velleman *et al.* (1993) write: "Conventional wisdom now indicates that significant others typically engage in different and often changing means of coping with substance abusers and report experiencing significant mental and physical strain as a result ... Clinicians have identified particular coping behaviours displayed by the family members (in most cases the spouse or parents) of alcoholics or other chemically dependent persons that usually include specific types of caretaking and attempts to stabilize situations caused or exacerbated by one member's substance abuse" (258).

Spouses of addicts often repeat certain behaviours when they try to cope with their situation. Pokorny (1972), one of the early writers on the issue of spouses and addiction, concludes from his observations that the wives of problem gamblers play a key role in perpetuating or changing the gambling of their husbands. Boyd and Bolen (1979) also describe what would now be called enabling and codependent behaviours, and they too conclude that the wives of problem gamblers strongly influence their decision to seek treatment.

Shopping Addictions and Sex Addictions

Shopping addiction and sex addiction have interesting similarities to problem gambling. All are compulsive, repetitive behaviours that cause problems for families. Like problem gambling, shopping addiction results in overspending and drains family resources; and sex addiction results in secret activities that compromise family trust. All three may lead the individual to spend a great deal of time outside the family, without the family's understanding or approval.

Moreover, the three addictions appear to be linked. Kausch (2003) studied 113 gamblers admitted to a treatment program. He found that most people who gamble compulsively also suffer or have suffered from another addiction. These include addictions to substances, as well as sex and shopping compulsions. About 30 percent of the 94 cases were individuals who had a problem with compulsive sexual behaviour. Roughly one quarter felt they had a problem with compulsive shopping. Often, there is an overlap among the three compulsive behaviours. This may be a type of comorbidity, or it may just reflect a general increase in gambling in society: since more people gamble, more people with other addictions are likely to become problem gamblers. It seems likely that people who are prone to compulsive behaviour are more susceptible to the risks created by increased gambling opportunities.

Grant and Steinberg (2005) confirmed this pattern in a study into the relationship between problem gambling and sexual addiction. They explored the sexual behaviours of 225 men and women over the age of 21 who met the DSM-IV criteria for pathological gambling. Of them, 44 respondents (17 women and 27 men) showed co-occurring compulsive sexual behaviours. According to Grant and Steinberg, this high rate of correlation makes it important for patients diagnosed as problem gamblers to also be screened for compulsive sexual addiction.

So how do families—especially, spouses—deal with sexual and shopping addictions? The answers could shed light on family interventions into problem gambling.

Though sparse, discussion of spouses in the shopping addiction literature suggests some potential courses of action. The Faber et al. (1987) study of 19 women and 4 men in a self-help group for compulsive shoppers often mentions spouses in conjunction with discussions about secrecy (Faber *et al.*, 1987). Most respondents took pains to hide their behaviour from spouses. They said they were mainly concerned that their spouse would find out. Along similar lines, Mellan (1995) recommends that spouses adopt a sympathetic but detached approach to addicted shoppers. She also advises spouses to be patient with setbacks and avoid seeing them as failures. They should share their own struggles and vulnerabilities with their overspending partners to encourage trust in the relationship.

In contrast, the role of spouses receives a great deal of attention in the literature on sex addiction, because of the strong significance our society places on sexual fidelity in romantic relationships. According to Carnes (1985), the secrecy that comes with sexual addiction can damage many of the sex addict's close relationships: "Addicts progressively go through stages in which they retreat further from the reality of friends, family, and work. Only the individual addict knows the shame of living a double life—the real world and the addict's world" (4). Carnes also says that family members often become entangled in their own web of lies to avoid dealing with the issue head on. This can have harmful effects on the addict's chance of recovery.

Schneider (1989) also discusses secrecy about sexual addiction and its impact on spousal trust. Schneider examined a sample of married couples who identified themselves as sexual addicts or co-addicts. The couples were all receiving treatment of one kind or another: joint counselling, group psychotherapy, peer counselling, or attendance at self-help groups for both individuals and couples. All reported facing the difficulty of re-establishing trust after the sexually compulsive behaviour had been disclosed. How much information to reveal to the spouse about extramarital sexual behaviour is another recurring issue.

The families of sex addicts are often so fully deceived they end up taking part in the lies themselves, in effect, enabling the addictive behaviour. It is important for the families of sex addicts to become aware that by helping their loved one preserve a facade of normalcy, they are also helping the addiction to continue. Sex addicts are often highly isolated in both social and emotional terms, feeling "unknown and unwanted at an important deeper level" (Schneider, 1989:55). Without the help and co-operation of their families, many of these sex addicts would be quite alone.

Therapists should help sex addicts find alternative activities they enjoy, in particular activities they can do as part of a group or with a family member.

It is also important for the sex addict's family to be involved in the treatment. Therapists must recognize that even if the family is sympathetic, marital relationships may be irreparable after the sex addiction is disclosed. Moreover, families need positive ways to cope with relapse to avoid pushing the addict back into isolation.

In a study of cyber-sex addiction, Schneider (2003) surveyed 91 women and 3 men whose spouses were cyber-sex addicts. Respondents reported experiencing many negative emotions because of their partner's sexual behaviour, such as betrayal, loneliness, and abandonment; and many blamed their partner's deception for these negative emotions and feelings. Several respondents were considering divorce and separation, and around one quarter had already separated from their spouse at the time of the questionnaire. Many revealed that their partner's cyber-sex addiction had seriously damaged their sexual relationship in several ways.

Promising Pathways

Recent work by Bonnie Lee and her colleagues, and by David Hodgins and his colleagues, has put into practice many of the ideas and principles in this chapter. Both Lee and Hodgins acknowledge the wisdom of working with both gamblers and their partners to solve the problems associated with problem gambling. In one recent paper, Hodgins *et al.* (2007a) measured the harmful effects of problem gambling on the psychological well-being of *concerned significant others* (CSOs). As gambling symptoms worsen, so do reports of the partner's personal distress. Relationship quality and satisfaction drop as a result.

In a related study, Hodgins *et al.* (2007b) found that even minimal interventions can help these CSOs (including spouses) dramatically. Almost any help provides needy CSOs with solace and insight. CSOs benefit from a variety of interventions, including workbooks, telephone support, and more directed *Community Reinforcement and Family Training* (CRAFT) counselling. Hodgins' studies are discussed more closely in Chapter 13, which focuses on the CRAFT method of couple therapy. Hodgins' study reports that "CSOs require more guidance and follow-up support to achieve [desired] goals using the CRAFT procedures and strategies" (215).

Lee and her team (Lee and Rovers, 2008; Lee, Rovers, and Maclean, 2008) report on the use of another couples-based therapy for problem gamblers called *Congruence Couple Therapy* (CCT). Using a mixed methods approach, Lee and

Rovers (2008) show that CCT has considerable success reducing the symptoms of problem gambling while also improving the gambler's marital relationship. Important relationship problems concerning communication, intimacy, support, and decision-making are improved through CCT, as shown by the qualitative and quantitative data gathered from gamblers, spouses, and therapists. What's more, the CCT method is easily taught and learned, according to evaluation results in Lee, Rovers, and Maclean (2008).

Lee and Rovers' studies are critical because they show the success of couple-based therapy. But there is potential to explore the idea of spousal control more than Lee and Rovers did. There is also a need to study the quality of relationships and its effects on increased control. In addition, the CCT model does not fully deal with the problems of enabling behaviour on the part of spouses. A broader couple- and family-therapy model that included these three factors would improve on CCT.

Both Hodgins and Lee have put family-based therapy options for problem gambling firmly on the therapy agenda. Unlike psychologists who fixate on changing an individual's behaviour and perceptions, Hodgins and Lee recognize that behavioural and perceptual tendencies reside in whole people who live in group contexts. To understand those people, we must study their personalities, histories, and current socio-demographic conditions. What's more, to understand the behaviours and perceptions of people in marital relationships, we also need to study their relationships. Just as behaviours are embedded in personalities and personal histories, behaviours are also embedded in and shaped by close relationships.

Closing Words

The literature on the connection between families and problem gambling, as well as with alcohol and drug abuse, sex addiction, and shopping addiction, is small but growing. More research is needed to explore the role that spouses play in the lives of problem gamblers. The present study aims to contribute to this body of literature.

The chapters that follow describe the effects of problem gambling on gamblers' families, strategies that intimate partners use to discourage gambling, and conflicts that arise when they try to force their gambling spouses to seek treatment. Together, they present a very thorough picture of the life situation these couples face, and the social costs of gambling for ordinary Canadians.

Chapter 3
The Research Project

This chapter discusses the methods used in this exploratory study of problem gamblers and their partners or spouses. An exploratory study like this one, by its nature, is intended to be groundwork for future research and to provide basic information about the problem.

An Exploratory Study

The 2005 study upon which this book is based is first and foremost an exploratory study. Exploratory studies are conducted when little is known about a field of inquiry, and basic groundwork and test instruments are needed to assess the value of future study and propose the next steps. For our research, little is known about the relation between problem gamblers and their partners, so it would have been premature to frame clear theories about the influence partners can have on gamblers. Second, studies into problem gambling are problematic because there is no listed population from which systematically to draw a sample of respondents. Because of the stigma attached to problem gambling, few people are willing to take part in such a study. As a result, the sample used in this study was not random: individuals and couples self-selected to take part. Thus, the results may not represent general attitudes and behaviours in the population.

This research has its flaws, so we make only modest claims and interpret our findings with caution. In any exploratory study, there is no claim or expectation that the findings are final and decisive. Rather, in doing an exploratory study, the researchers recognize they are giving up such claims and expectations. Yet exploratory research has its advantages. It allows us to explore the terrain more richly and closely than is often possible in more systematic studies, where stated hypotheses have to be tested. Exploratory studies often use inductive methods of information collection that let findings, hypotheses, and theories percolate upward from the data. That is what we have done here, and we believe our rich, evocative results justify the effort. The result of an exploratory study in this style is called a *grounded theory*. This book ends with such a theory.

Following Ferris and Wynne (2001), we have defined problem gambling as *gambling that creates negative consequences for the gambler, others in his or her social network, or for the community*. This study measures problem gambling using the nine-item Problem Gambling Severity Index (PGSI) of the Canadian Problem Gambling Index (CPGI).

The diagnostic items in the CPGI are the following:

- chasing losses;
- escalating to maintain excitement;
- borrowing or selling to get gambling money;
- betting more than one can afford;
- feeling guilty;
- being criticized by others;
- harm to health;
- financial difficulties to one's household; and
- feeling one might have a problem with gambling.

The first four items describe gambling itself; the last five describe the *effects* of gambling.

We can summarize the CPGI items in a narrative. Gamblers start on the path toward problem gambling when they chase losses, hoping to make up the money they have lost through a big win. Often, this behaviour rests on the faulty belief that with every loss, the player comes closer to winning. Meanwhile, they start raising their bets to preserve excitement in the same way that alcoholics increase the amount they need to drink to achieve a given intoxication. They then start to do almost anything to get the money for gambling, including selling or pawning valuables and borrowing from friends and institutions. By this stage, gamblers are usually betting far more than they can afford to lose.

Somewhere in this process, gamblers start feeling guilty: they know they are doing something unwise, even dangerous. Family and friends have started criticizing them for excessive gambling and the debt that results from it. Health problems may result from the stress associated with indebtedness, guilt, and criticism. Too little rest, improper eating, and an excessive use of alcohol, coffee, cigarettes and other drugs also harm the health of problem gamblers. Financial difficulties occur, which causes family members to criticize more, which increases guilt and health problems. Finally, problem gamblers face the fact that they have a problem with gambling.

In our research as elsewhere, the scoring for problem gambling in the PGSI falls into four categories:

Non-problem gamblers	(score of 0)
Low-risk gamblers	(scores 1–2)
Moderate-risk gamblers	(scores 3–7)
Problem gamblers	(scores 8–27)

In PGSI, problem gamblers have a score of 8 or higher. But for practical purposes, this study defines problem gambling more broadly to include every adult who is at moderate risk of problems or higher. Though most of the gamblers in this study have scores above 8 on the CPGI, all have scores above 3, so they are all at risk to some degree (for more on definitions of risk, see Wynne and Smith, 2002:18–19). In the Ontario prevalence survey by Wiebe, Single, and Falkowski-Ham (2001), roughly 13 percent of gamblers fall into a "problem gambling" category defined as scores above 3.

The Public Health Approach

Our research adopts the public health approach to gambling developed by Korn and Shaffer (1999). Public health has a tradition of addressing emerging and complex health matters that affect the population and specific subgroups of the population. The value of a public health approach is that it examines broad impacts rather than focusing solely on problem gambling in individuals (Skinner, 1999). It views gambling along a continuum and considers wider health, social, and economic costs and benefits. In addition, it typically gives priority to the needs of vulnerable people and identifies strategies for action (Korn and Shaffer, 1999). It also studies the distribution and determinants of gambling-related problems in the population and organizes measures to prevent, lessen, or manage the effects. Finally, it aims to control the occurrence and spread of gambling-related problems. Within this framework, gambling is defined as "risking something of value on the outcome of an event when the chance of winning is less than certain and determined by chance" (1). Such an approach focuses on populations, not individuals. In this way, it is similar to a sociological approach, in contrast to psychological and psychiatric approaches.

Though our focus widened as our study progressed, our first and central objectives remain the following:

- to describe the extent and character of problem gambling in a non-random sample of Toronto residents;

- to examine the extent and character of marital problems associated with this problem gambling;
- to describe the degree of network embeddedness of these couples—the degree to which they occupy each other's worlds;
- to find out how gambling problems, marital problems, and network embeddedness affect readiness for treatment.

Our most general question is, how do adults try to regulate the behaviour of their partner's gambling? This question spawns some related questions. How does problem gambling affect the marital (or close) relations of problem gamblers? What efforts do the intimate partners of these gamblers make to control this gambling? How successful are these efforts? Finally, what strategies or tactics work best in controlling the gambling of spouses?

As noted earlier, 90 adults from the Greater Toronto Area self-selected to take part in this study, 59 of which self-declared as having or potentially having a gambling problem. Another 31 self-declared as partners of people who have or potentially have a gambling problem. Of those 90 adults, 10 couples[3] agreed to take part in an extra couple's unit of the study. Couples who enrolled in this portion of the study were interviewed separately.

The sample was recruited using advertisements placed in newspapers, local educational gambling websites, and at meeting places of Gamblers Anonymous and Gam-Anon. Interested people were asked to phone the project office telephone, where they were screened for inclusion in the study. Project manager Jennifer Reynolds received the calls and screened respondents for inclusion in the study, using the following script:

Informed Telephone Consent Script

Hi, my name is Jennifer Reynolds, and I'm from the University of Toronto. We're conducting a study on the gambling activities and attitudes of adult Ontarians and we would like to include your views.

---

3   Originally, 11 couples agreed to participate in the couples' component of the study. One respondent had to drop out for personal reasons; however, her spouse still agreed to be interviewed.

Some of the survey questions may be sensitive. The survey will ask you questions about:

- the types of gambling activities you and your partner participate in, and the amount of time and money spent on gambling
- any problems you have experienced from your own or your partner's gambling
- how you and your partner have handled gambling-related problems
- use of alcohol and other drugs
- your background such as level of education, marital status
- your general well-being

The study will provide important information on the nature and impact of gambling among Ontarians.

The survey will take approximately 90 minutes. You can quit the survey at any time or refuse to answer any question. *Confidentiality will be maintained to the extent permitted by law*, and you will not be identified in any report that may arise from this study. Only the researchers on this project will have access to all of the information collected. If the data is shared with other researchers in the future, all identifiers would be removed.

I would like to start off by asking you some questions about gambling to see if you qualify to participate in the study:

Do you currently like to gamble?   YES   NO

If NO, are you a partner of someone who likes to gamble?   YES   NO

Are you currently in a committed relationship?   YES   NO

If YES, do you feel that your gambling may be a problem
for you or your partner?   YES   NO

Do you consent to participate in this study?   YES   NO

To be included in the study, people had to meet the following criteria:

- They had to be living with an intimate partner within the last six months before the study.
- They had to score in the "at-risk" or "problem" range of the PGSI (3 or higher), or have partners who scored in this range.
- They had to admit that gambling might pose a problem for their relationship.

After the screening by telephone, Jennifer then asked those who met the criteria to come in for an interview at the University of Toronto and to invite their partners to take part as well. Some partners agreed to participate and they went through the same process of screening and in-person interviewing as the gamblers. Only a minority of partners participated. All participants were assured of the confidentiality of these responses. All consented to take part in an individual interview or to be part of a couple's interview. Three sensitivity-trained interviewers conducted the interviews. All interviews were tape-recorded for accuracy (when permission was granted) and transcribed for later analysis. To ensure anonymity, pseudonyms replaced real names in all the transcripts. Only pseudonyms were used in the analyses and write-up of findings. Thus, no one reading this book can connect the statements made with the individual respondents who made those statements.

CPGI and DSM-IV Designations

Our respondents were judged to be *problem gamblers*,[4] based on the CPGI. They were not assessed using the Diagnostic Statistical Manual for Mental Disorders (DSM-IV), which would have been the basis for a diagnosis of *pathological gambler*. Yet most of our participants meet the DSM-IV criteria for *pathological gambler*. This is evident in the high scores our participants received on the CPGI, as well as in the behavioural traits our respondents described in their personal interviews.

The CPGI defines problem gambling as "gambling behaviour that creates negative consequences for the gambler, others in his or her social network, or for the community" (Wynne, 2003:2). In contrast, the DSM-IV diagnoses an

---

4 This book mainly discusses *problem gamblers*—a term specified by the use of the Canadian Problem Gambling Index, which we have employed. In the gambling research literature, a wider variety of terms is used, including *pathological gambler* and *addictive gambler*.

individual with pathological gambling if they meet at least five of the following criteria:

- preoccupation—the individual experiences frequent thoughts about gambling;
- tolerance—the individual needs larger or more frequent wagers to achieve the same excitement;
- withdrawal—the individual experiences restlessness or irritability with efforts stop or reduce gambling;
- escape—the individual gambles to improve mood or escape problems;
- chasing—the individual tries to win back gambling losses with more gambling;
- lying—the individual tries to hide the extent of his or her gambling by lying to family, friends, or therapists;
- stealing—the individual steals to seed their gambling addiction;
- loss of control—the individual is unsuccessful at reducing his or her gambling;
- illegal acts—the individual has broken the law to get gambling money or recover gambling losses;
- risked significant relationship—the individual gambles despite risking or losing a relationship, job, or other significant opportunity;
- bailout—the individual turns to family, friends, or another third party for financial help because of gambling (Stinchfield, Govoni, and Frisch, 2001).

This list is similar to the nine-item Problem Gambling Severity Index (PGSI) of the Canadian Problem Gambling Index (CPGI), described above. The DSM-IV definition is more detailed; but the core elements that define a gambling problem are essentially the same in both definitions.[5]

Both the PGSI and DSM-IV measures have undergone extensive scrutiny to ensure strong reliability and high validity. In fact, the final version of the CPGI definitions was altered so the two measures could be systematically compared (Stinchfield *et al.*, 2001; Wynne, 2003). Both reliability and validity measures of

---

5   The term *pathological gambler* implies an extreme case of problem gambling, which is what many of our participants described to us. So, we could apply both the terms *problem gambler* and *pathological gambler* interchangeably; but for consistency, this book uses the term *problem gambler*.

the PGSI were shown to be highly correlated with the DSM-IV. The PGSI also showed good sensitivity, as it is able to identify 83 percent of people diagnosed by the DSM-IV as pathological gamblers. On specificity, the PGSI matched perfectly (100 percent) with the DSM-IV in classifying people with gambling problems. In summary, both the CPGI and DSM-IV yield satisfactory reliability, validity, and classification accuracy, and come to similar or identical conclusions.

Then why use the CPGI definition? There is one important difference between the two definitions. The CPGI (specifically the PGSI) was meant for use as a screening tool to detect people in the general population who are at risk of developing a gambling problem (Wynne, 2003). By contrast, the DSM-IV is a diagnostic tool intended for use to decide whether an individual has a health problem. Typically, a diagnostic assessment is done after an individual has been screened as positive. Thus, the screening definition is more appropriate for this study.

The two procedures also use somewhat different measurement and classification strategies. The CPGI takes a more *dimensional* approach to classification, whereas the DSM-IV uses a *categorical* approach (Ferris and Wynne, 2001). The CPGI assesses gamblers on five dimensions and ranks them according to five subtypes (nongamblers, non-problem gamblers, low-risk gamblers, moderate-risk gamblers, and problem gamblers). In contrast, the DSM-IV categorizes the individual in an either/or manner: either a person is a pathological gambler or is not. Because of its dimensional approach, the CPGI is more useful for classifying people who fall just short of the criteria that would identify pathological gambling according to the DSM-IV.

For our purposes, the CPGI is a better measurement tool because it identifies at-risk individuals early to prevent them from developing a problem. The DSM-IV has been criticized for arbitrary criteria that fail to diagnose people who are one point short of the "pathological" classification. Ferris and Wynne (2001) argue the CPGI goes a step beyond DSM-IV by incorporating social and environmental factors into assessing problem gambling. These factors allow for more sensitive measurement. The CPGI captures some of the under-represented populations in the gambling literature—such as women and ethnic minorities—who are sometimes overlooked by general clinical tools such as those in the DSM-IV.

In conclusion, we believe it is reasonable to relate findings from the literature on pathological gamblers to our findings on problem gamblers, because the two concepts—and their related measures—are similar. Many of the respondents in our study fell at the extreme end of the gambling spectrum and displayed characteristics of pathological gambling.

Data Collection Tools

Our exploratory research study uses both quantitative and qualitative methods. For the main interviews, we used a survey instrument containing roughly 90 closed-ended questions and 30 open-ended questions. Couples willing to join in the separate couple's interview were asked an extra set of open-ended questions (roughly 20 questions). Interviews were expected to last 90 minutes, though some interviews were shorter, and some were much longer, running to several hours.

The questions asked fell into three main categories:

- **Gambling questions:** From both members of a couple, we took a history of the problem gambler's gambling: when it started, how it progressed, and whether (and when) help was sought. Both members of a couple were also asked detailed questions about their own gambling in the past year, their partner's gambling, and efforts the partners made to control their partner's gambling.
- **Relationship questions:** We used the Dyadic Adjustment Scale (Spanier, 1976), a widely known self-report questionnaire, to measure general marital adjustment. We also used the Network Embeddedness Scale (Tepperman *et al.*, 2002; Calzavara *et al.*, 2003) to get a clear picture of the couple's closeness and embeddedness.
- **Background questions:** We asked respondents basic demographic questions: age, sex, marital status, marital history, education, occupation, income, size of community lived in, and ethnic ancestry. These data were used to assess the representativeness of our sample and to allow exploratory inferences about the effects of these variables (especially education and ethnicity) on partner regulatory practices.

The questionnaire was pretested on six people (four gamblers and two partners) who answered advertisements posted around the University of Toronto's St. George campus, as well as one potential interviewer and two collaborators on the project.

Despite extensive efforts, we were unable to recruit 60 spouses of gamblers for the study, as hoped. As a result, our spouse sample is smaller than intended. Like the gambler sample, it cannot claim to be representative, and the sample may be biased. This study would also have benefited from interviewing more gambler-spouse couples. Of the 20 couples, only 10 consented to couple interviews.

The interviews we did were revealing. The respondents were usually candid, open, and willing to share their feelings. Our three interviewers describe the experience of collecting these data. Their reports help us understand just how personally important and revealing are the transcribed interview materials we examine below.

One reports the following experience in her interviewing:

> As a researcher, you create a professional distance between the respondent and yourself, but it was hard not to be taken aback by the [respondents'] tearful stories or happy anecdotes once the interview was over and they made their way out of the office. Some people were desperately in need of someone to talk to about their problems.

She also notes how hard it was for many respondents to find the words they needed to frame their experiences, fears, and emotions:

> It was obvious to me that some participants were struggling to construct a coherent account of their lives with respect to gambling. I found myself having to constantly impose structure on the interview by probing and trying to gain a chronological and context-laden answer.

Another too speaks of the interview process as intensely emotional:

> There were times that the participant's experiences affected me so deeply … thinking about what that specific person had experienced. I can still recall a few interviews that I conducted more than seven months ago that had a significant impact on me, clearly remembering the exact details of the respondent's experience without even referring back to their transcript.

The research offered her a sense that she had helped as well as understood the people she was studying:

> I took pleasure in knowing that several interview participants stated that the interview had been cathartic for them by helping them realize and artic- ulate things about their gambling or their partner's gambling that they had

not thought of or expressed before. Other respondents stated that they felt that through their talking about and actualizing their gambling problem in the interview, they felt that they were taking a first step to cut back or modify their gambling. At the end of a number of these interviews, many participants stated how helpful it was to talk about how their gambling or their partner's gambling was affecting their relationship and how it was easy to talk to someone who was not their partner, friend, or relative. For many participants, the interview provided an opportunity to vent their emotions and frustrations, to sound-out their beliefs and knowledge, to reflect on their or their partner's behaviour, and an opportunity for self-awareness.

A third interviewer describes her experience in similar ways. She found people were eager, even desperate, to tell their stories.

I have had incredible interviews with both gamblers and partners who have opened up to me in ways that I could never have expected. I have had people sincerely thank me at the end of an interview for listening to them . . . that they needed to talk, and felt so much better now that they had told their stories.

She said the research process transformed her own understanding of gambling and especially, problem gambling:

Everywhere I went, I started seeing gambling advertisements, overhearing conversations about poker, catching a glimpse of the celebrity poker tournaments on television, and even though all these things existed before I began interviewing gamblers, they just seemed much more prevalent because I was more knowledgeable about the inner workings of gamblers.

It is impossible to conduct honest research on a topic like problem gambling without making genuine human contact with the people who are telling their important, sad, and even frightening stories. Within the limits of time and money imposed on our study, our interviewers got the real goods for us. Our job below is to interpret that story.

Assessing Our Sample
To find out whether and to what degree our sample represented the general population, we compared the characteristics of our sample with Wiebe *et al.*

CPGI Score

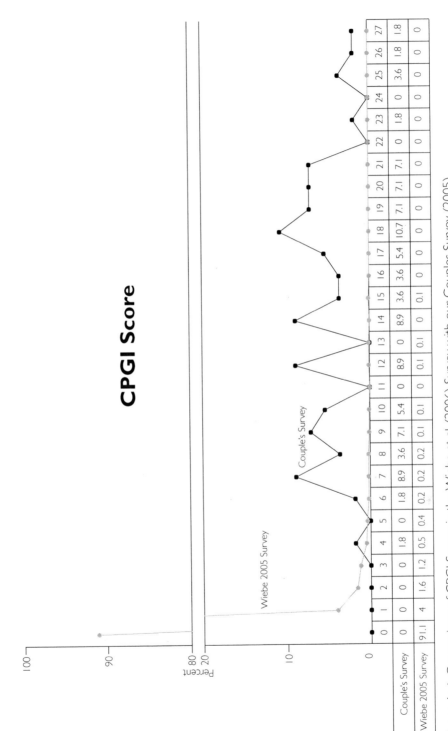

	0	1	2	3	4	5	6	7	8	9	10	11	12	13	14	15	16	17	18	19	20	21	22	23	24	25	26	27
Couple's Survey	0	0	0	0	1.8	0	1.8	8.9	3.6	7.1	5.4	0	8.9	0	8.9	3.6	3.6	5.4	10.7	7.1	7.1	7.1	0	1.8	0	3.6	1.8	1.8
Wiebe 2005 Survey	91.1	4	1.6	1.2	0.5	0.4	0.2	0.2	0.2	0.1	0.1	0	0.1	0.1	0	0.1	0	0	0	0	0	0	0	0	0	0	0	0

Figure 1: A Comparison of CPGI Scores in the Wiebe et al. (2006) Survey with our Couples Survey (2005)

(2006), a study of gambling and gambling problems using a large random sample of Ontarians.

First and most important, our sample comprised mainly people with a moderate or severe gambling problem, while Wiebe's random sample of Ontarians represented a wide range of gamblers and nongamblers. This is evident in the graph in Figure 1, which compares the CPGI scores of our sample with those of the Wiebe study.

Table 1: CPGI Classification from Wiebe et al. (2006)

	Frequency	Percent	Valid Percent	Cumulative Percent
Valid				
Nongamblers (N/A)	1,333	37.0	37.2	37.2
Non-problem gamblers (0)	1,932	53.6	53.9	91.2
At risk (1-2)	198	5.5	5.5	96.7
Moderate problems (3-7)	91	2.5	2.5	99.2
Severe problems (8+)	28	0.8	0.8	100.0
Total	3,582	99.4	99.9	

These data show that our sample, made up entirely of people with moderate or severe gambling problems (CPGI> 3), is highly unrepresentative of the Ontario adult population. But is it representative of the Ontario gambling population that is at risk of a gambling problem?

To answer this question, we compared our sample with respondents from the Wiebe sample who scored 1 or higher on the CPGI scale. We found the following differences:

- Our gamblers were more likely to be male than the at-risk or problem gamblers in Wiebe's study (61 percent compared with 41 percent).
- They were older on average than the gambling population in Wiebe's sample (60 percent in the 25–59 age range compared with 42 percent).
- They were (by design) far more likely to be married and living with a partner (78 percent versus 46 percent), and they were much less likely than gamblers in Wiebe's sample to have never married.
- They were more likely than the gamblers in Wiebe's sample to have completed a post-secondary college degree (27 percent compared with

14 percent) but less likely to have studied in a university (31 percent versus 42 percent).

- They were more likely than Wiebe's sample to be employed part-time; otherwise, there was no difference between samples in present job status. However, the household income of our sample was far lower than that of the gamblers in Wiebe's sample. In our study, 28 percent of households earned less than $20,000, compared with only 10 percent in Wiebe's sample. Another 36 percent earned between $20,000 and $40,000, compared with only 17 percent in Wiebe's sample. At the other extreme, 18 percent of Wiebe's sample report household earnings of $100,000 or more, compared with no cases in our sample.

Thus, our respondents had CPGI scores that were higher on average than those of at-risk, moderate, and severe problem gamblers in the general Ontario population. These comparisons show that, overall, the participants in our study were poorer, less well educated, and more severely harmed by gambling than the average Ontario at-risk or problem gambler.

The *At Home With Gambling* Study (2003)

As noted earlier, we backed up the results of our current study with data from an earlier, unpublished study we did of gamblers in the Toronto area, also funded by the Ontario Problem Gambling Research Centre. The *At Home With Gambling* study (Tepperman *et al.*, 2003) focused on family and cultural influences on gambling.

The total sample of that exploratory study consisted of 360 Toronto-area respondents, 60 from each of six ethnocultural groups: Aboriginal, British Isles, Caribbean, Chinese, Latin American, and Russian. Because no complete counts of these communities exists, and because of the difficulty in gaining access to some of these groups, we had to rely on alternatives to random sampling: namely, convenience, self-selection, snowball methods, and targeted sampling. We interviewed people who live in many different family and household arrangements to find out whether there is a connection between gambling and family or household cohesion, stability, and type.

From each respondent in this 2003 study, we collected information on various topics related to socio-demographic features, ethnocultural identification, gambling beliefs and activities, and family life. Data from that study revealed that all three sets of sociological variables (socio-demographic variables, family variables, and ethnocultural identification) contributed significantly to gambling behaviours. The study found that gambling status is strongly correlated with marital disruption, family discussions of gambling (especially discussions between brothers), and certain ethnocultural backgrounds (especially Aboriginal, Chinese, and Russian).

In addition, problem gamblers in the *At Home* sample had different worries and preoccupations from the adult respondents who gambled without problems or did not gamble at all. Problem gamblers were 10 times more likely than non-problem gamblers to report that they worried about their gambling. They also worried about how they are going to prevent other people (their families, bosses, or co-workers) from finding out about their gambling problem, and how they are going to avoid losing their jobs and their families. Moreover, secondary characteristics that were associated with problem gambling, including self-identified, co-occurring addictive behaviours, such as alcohol, cigarette, and drug use, also worried the gambler respondents.

Problem gamblers also had different personal histories from the other respondents. By their own report, the problem gamblers began gambling at an earlier age than other adult respondents. They were also more likely to remember the outcome and report having won their first game. They were also more likely to have had close friends who gambled and who talked about gambling.

Family life may have played a part in developing these problem-gambling patterns. Respondents who grew up seeing or hearing about gambling by their parents were more likely to have become adult problem gamblers than respondents who did not see or hear about parents' gambling. Among both adult and adolescent gamblers, we found intergenerational transfers of gambling habits. Adult respondents who grew up in a gambler's household were about twice as likely as other respondents to have their own children growing up hearing about their parent's gambling. Also, adult respondents who saw or heard about their grandparents gambling at home when they were growing up are over twice as likely as other respondents to have their own children growing up hearing about their grandparents' gambling. Obi and Raylu (2004) confirm this finding, noting that parents may transfer their beliefs about gambling to their offspring, and these beliefs perpetuate gambling. Further, people who witness their family members gambling may incorporate such activities into their own behaviour (Gupta, 1997).

Other issues reported by problem gamblers in the 2003 *At Home* study were gambling by other family members, financial and non-financial problems in the family, marital breakdown, and fewer than average family activities.

Still, these problem gamblers largely viewed gambling positively. They believed that success in gambling was a test of luck, experience, and intelligence.

Presentation of the Findings

The results of the 2003 *At Home* study are echoed in the 2005 study upon which this book is mainly based. Both studies reveal that partners may be unaware of the extent of the problem gambling and its effects. Gamblers themselves often feel that their partners can have little influence on their gambling or openness to treatment. Although this study did not involve recommending counselling strategies to participants, all were provided with a list of organizations they could contact for help with problem gambling.

The chapters that follow quote the taped and transcribed interviews with gamblers in both the 2003 and 2005 studies, and from the spouses in the 2005 study. The quoted passages are as the participants spoke them, with only superfluous utterances ("um," "like," "sort of" and "you know") removed to ease the reading, and occasional bracketed words inserted to clarify the meaning in context.

The number of quoted passages has been kept to a minimum. We have analyzed and interpreted the numerical data, then translated the results into words for the reader. As often as possible, we have also allowed our respondents to report our findings in their own words.

II.

GAMBLING AND FAMILY PROBLEMS

Chapter 4
Gamblers and Gambling Practices

Gambling in Ontario

Problem gambling—the betting of people's lives on easy money, obtained by luck—exists in a context. It requires us to understand what non-problem gambling is. The most recent statistics on non-problem gambling in Ontario are provided by Wiebe *et al.* in 2005, the same year we collected the data for this book.

Wiebe surveyed a total of 3,604 Ontario adults aged 18 and older in both 2001 and 2005. Nearly two-thirds of the respondents report having gambled in the preceding 12 months. Fewer people reported gambling in the 2005 survey than in 2001, but those who gambled in 2005 gambled more often.

Wiebe's 2005 study found significant increases since 2001 in weekly participation in card or board games, casino table games, Sport Select, and speculative investments. The most common form of gambling in Ontario is the purchase of lottery tickets, with 52.4 percent of surveyed Ontarians having done this in the 12 months, followed by raffle tickets (28.7 percent) and scratch tickets (24.9 percent). The least common forms of gambling are Internet-based (1.7 percent) and sports betting with a bookie (0.4 percent). Rates of participation for some kinds of gambling—raffle tickets (28.7 percent), casino slots (16.5 percent), racetrack slots (6.5 percent), non-Ontario casinos (5.2 percent), and slots and VLTs (3.1 percent)—were higher in 2005 than in 2001. Stocks, options, and commodities trading are the costliest gambling activities in both time and money, with a mean expenditure of 58 hours and $5,450 per month.

According to Wiebe's 2005 study, average gamblers spend 2.2 percent of their personal income on gambling, moderate problem gamblers spend 8 percent, and severe problem gamblers spend 21 percent. While the average gambler reports spending only 1 to 1.5 hours per month on casino or racetrack slots and casino table games, people with severe gambling problems report spending between 3.2 and 4.6 hours per month on these same activities.

Gender is the single most important factor distinguishing gamblers in Ontario, with education, income, and age all playing secondary roles. Of the 3.7

percent of Ontarians reportedly engaging in "games of skill," males were far more likely to engage in this activity than females (6.3 percent versus 1.2 percent). In contrast, female participation was reportedly only 0.6 percent and 0.5 percent for arcade or video games and Internet gambling, respectively, whereas male participation was 2.7 percent and 2.8 percent. Gender was a significant factor in sports gambling (with males seven times more likely than females to bet on sports games), speculative investment gambling (with males roughly five times more likely than females to participate), and card and board games (with males three times more likely than females to participate). Participation in bingo was twice as high for women as for men (6.5 percent versus 3.1 percent). It was also highest for young people: people aged 18–24 years had the highest partici-pation rate (7.6 percent). With respect to education, rates of participation in bingo decreased as education levels increased, with the lowest rates of participa-tion among people with a postgraduate degree (2.3 percent).

Just over half of the total sample (52.4 percent) reported having bought a lottery ticket in the year before the survey. Nearly one-quarter (24.9 percent) reported having bought a scratch ticket in the past year, and 28.9 percent reported buying a raffle ticket. In general, lottery purchases increased with age, then decreased dramatically after the age of 60. In contrast to lottery tickets, scratch ticket purchases decreased with age. Lottery ticket purchases also increased with personal income.

As well, 16.5 percent of the total sample reported having gambled at slot machines in Ontario casinos during the preceding year. People with income exceeding $20,000 per year were more likely than those earning less than $20,000 to gamble with gaming machines.

Demographics accounted for many differences in the choice of gambling vehicle in Wiebe's study. Of all respondents, 6.5 percent reported having gambled in Ontario casinos. Males and young adults were overrepresented (11 percent and 17.8 percent, respectively). Further, people with personal incomes of $100,000 and higher were more likely than average to engage in this form of gambling (12.6 percent). Compared to casino gambling, few high-income people participated in sports-related gambling, whereas people with incomes exceeding $100,000 (7.7 percent) made up the largest group betting on horse races.

In addition, a very small percentage of the sample (1.9 percent) reported having taken part in speculative investment gambling. Investment gambling was more popular with males than with females (3.3 percent versus 0.6 percent). Further, people with higher income levels ($60,000+) were more likely than average to engage in this form of gambling. As well, roughly 8.5 percent of the sample reported gambling with card or board games, with males more likely than females (13 percent versus 4.1 percent) to engage in this activity. Participation in card and board games decreased with age.

In short, almost all Ontarians gamble, and there is no sign that this is declining. All of the features of gambling—the game played, the frequency, and the amount spent—vary by the gender, income, age, and education of the individual.

Types of Respondents

The participants in our study can be classified according to demographics. Only about half of the respondents studied were employed full-time, while 19 percent worked part-time, 10 percent were unemployed, and 10 percent self-classified as "other." The remaining 12 percent were outside the labour force because they were not looking for work. Most gambler-respondents in our sample earned a low income. Over 80 percent of the respondents report household incomes of under $50,000 per year, despite many cases of two-income families. Close to 50 percent of all respondents had household incomes of less than $30,000. Nearly 85 percent of the respondents (spouses included) had an education level of a high school diploma or higher.

The descriptions that follow show that the people we studied were not wealthy, glamorous, or particularly insightful. Most of them were struggling to make ends meet, and their gambling problem was causing serious difficulties for them and their families.

What follows are short descriptions of some of the couples who participated in our study. These descriptions show the variety of demographic and situational variables facing these couples, as well as the gambling preferences of the gamblers.

Stephanie and Peter [6]

Stephanie and Peter are married without children. Stephanie has completed some postsecondary education and has a job, while Peter, who is retired, has some high school education. Stephanie is primarily responsible for handling their finances. Peter's annual retirement income is less than $20,000, while Stephanie makes between $50,000 and $60,000. Peter takes care of his personal expenses himself, as does Stephanie. The couple has both separate bank accounts

---

6   All names have been changed.

and a joint account. Stephanie attributes the separate accounts to differences in their spending styles. Peter claims that all their finances are held jointly.

In the past, Stephanie and Peter participated in sports together as well as coaching together. Currently, Stephanie and Peter spend time doing community-focused activities together rather than "personal, between us" activities. Despite all the talking they do, Stephanie feels they are less able to get their ideas across to each other than in the past. Stephanie believes she is "being suckered" into doing more of the housework. Peter feels their housework is divided fairly.

Stephanie is the problem gambler in their family, mainly playing the slot machines at casinos. Stephanie agrees with Peter that her habit has to be kept within bounds, but disagrees with him on the "specifics of what those boundaries are." Stephanie admits she doesn't tell "the whole truth" when talking about how much money or time she spends gambling. Stephanie says she doesn't discuss gambling with Peter, allegedly because her gambling is not a problem yet. Peter says he doesn't think Stephanie is a problem gambler and he has not tried to change her gambling.

Stephanie knows that while Peter and her parents think gambling is mostly harmless, they also think it is a waste of time and money. Peter believes that Stephanie's father had a gambling problem. For her part, Stephanie considers gambling a relaxing and pleasant way to spend time. Stephanie confesses that she is afraid of developing a gambling problem in the future. She does not want her gambling to "become an entity on its own." Both Peter and Stephanie feel Stephanie's gambling has not harmed their relationship. In fact, Peter views her gambling in a positive light, since they have fun together at the casino. He also thinks that Stephanie uses gambling as an "outlet" for the stress she's under at work.

Peter's "niggling concern"—that Stephanie's gambling *could* become a problem—makes him want to appoint himself as her "protector" and "white knight in shining armour." He tries to ensure that Stephanie avoids certain gambling machines at the casino. Stephanie asserts that if she and Peter "had other activities that [they] could share that were enjoyable and [would] fill the time together," she might do it.

Sophie and Anthony

Sophie and Anthony are married and have adult children, one of whom lives with them. The couple emigrated from Kenya 30 years ago. Sophie has some high school education and is on disability insurance, receiving an annual income between $20,000 and $30,000. Anthony has some postsecondary education and an annual income between $30,000 and $40,000.

Sophie is a problem gambler who enjoys the casino. She believes her family isn't affected by her gambling because she doesn't tell them how much money and time she spends doing it. Sophie lies because she is convinced they would become angry and try to stop her from gambling. Like his wife, Anthony believes that Sophie's gambling has not affected their children, especially now that they are adults. Furthermore, Anthony also feels that his relationship with his wife has not been affected by her gambling—it's not a "big deal," as it is merely her "hobby."

Sophie feels guilty and stressed about her gambling and suffers from migraines each time she returns from the casino. Anthony, on the other hand, claims that he has no problem with his wife's wanting to gamble, figuring that she's bored, is on disability, and needs something to occupy her time. When the topic of gambling comes up, it is usually Sophie who mentions it on her way out to gamble that night. Because he drives and she doesn't, getting to the casino can be problematic for Sophie unless Anthony comes along. Sophie and Anthony share their credit cards and have always used a joint account. Sophie took over the task of paying the bills from her husband five years ago. Anthony denies that they have disagreements about money, believing that after the bills are paid, little money is left to fight about.

Sonia and Paul

Sonia and Paul are of Indian descent. They are married, and both are retired. Paul, who has a high school education, earns between $30,000 and $40,000, while Sonia, who has completed a postsecondary education, earns less than $20,000 per year.

Paul is a problem gambler and says that his gambling is an illness and an addiction, adding that he would like to cut out gambling from his life. He says he learned to gamble from his father when he was a teenager. He may also have a drinking problem and often drinks while gambling. Sonia says that when her son was younger, she avoided bringing up gambling to shield her son from arguments. Their son, who is now married and himself a father, refuses to gamble or drink alcohol because of his father's history of gambling and drinking.

According to Paul, Sonia knew about his gambling before she married him, though his gambling only became a problem in the last five years. Sonia says that he promised her that he wouldn't do it after they got married. She says that Paul did stop gambling but started up again. Because of Paul's gambling, the couple has separated twice. About five years ago, the couple decided to put their assets—their home, specifically—in Sonia's name because of Paul's gambling problem. Paul also has no access to the bank accounts that are in Sonia's name. They currently divide the costs of household expenses.

Paul admits that he takes little care of himself when he is gambling, and this worries Sonia. Among other health problems, Paul is diabetic. When he gambles, he doesn't eat or drink properly or take his medicine. Sonia says gambling has destroyed their marriage. They have also lost friends because of Paul's gambling problem. Paul is less fatalistic, feeling they would have a good relationship if only he didn't gamble. Whenever Sonia begins a conversation with Paul about his gambling, they end up screaming at each other, so Sonia avoids the topic. For his part, Paul feels their problems exist because they just don't think alike and don't have anything in common. Sonia claims Paul has taken no initiative to reduce his gambling, a problem Paul has acknowledged.

Sonia tells us that when she was working, she used to spend money foolishly as a way to equalize their spending, using these purchases as a form of revenge against Paul. Since retiring, she has become much more careful about her spending. So far, Paul's gambling has not endangered the couple's financial security. Paul exercises restraint in the amount that he gambles.

Philip and Marcie

Philip and Marcie have been married for 21 years, and they have one adult daughter, who is disabled. Neither completed high school. Philip, who is retired, earns between $20,000 and $30,000 per year. Marcie works part-time and earns less than $20,000 per year. Before this, she was a stay-at-home mother, unable to work because of her daughter's medical condition.

Marcie is the problem gambler in the family, regularly playing bingo and buying lottery tickets. Philip also gambles, but to a lesser degree, favouring the lottery, scratch tickets, and horse racing. He only goes to the occasional bingo game with his wife to keep her company. Playing bingo was a major shared activity for them when they first met. Marcie likes playing bingo and has been playing since childhood. Marcie also feels she has better chances of winning at bingo than at other gambling games. She says she likes it because of the money to be won and the "rush" that comes from winning. She considers bingo to be an important social activity in her life.

Philip has always assumed responsibility for paying the bills. While Marcie claims they have always held separate bank accounts, Philip says they hold only a joint account. Marcie gives Philip money each month to put towards shared household expenses. Neither has a credit card. Each time Marcie wants to go to play bingo, she asks Philip for money. They negotiate how much she spends. The couple argues about the cost of bingo and the time she spends away from home, and Philip believes Marcie's bingo gambling is out of control. Philip refuses to accompany her when she does go if he thinks that they really can't afford it. Philip says that he was aware of her gambling problem before they married. Philip denies that Marcie's gambling has affected their daughter, since "[she] gets anything she wants." Marcie, on the other hand, thinks she has "a terrible gambling problem," and she spends more money on bingo and less time with her family than she feels she should.

Philip feels there is a fair division of housework, and he enjoys the time they share together. In contrast, Marcie feels that her gambling has strained their relationship, believing that Philip is less affectionate and more often argumentative. She sees them drifting apart as a couple. Spending time with her family or in community involvement helps bring them closer together.

Margaret and Bob

Margaret and Bob live with their two-year-old daughter and ten-year-old son. Margaret and Bob both have some high school education, though they are a low-income family on social assistance. Bob earns less than $20,000 per year, while Margaret is a stay-at-home mother.

Bob is the problem gambler in the family, buying Pro-Line and other lottery tickets almost daily. In the past, Bob used to go to the casino with Margaret every two months. They stopped going to the casino after their youngest child was born because, according to Margaret, Bob was very badly addicted to blackjack, spending the rent and food money. For periods of time, Bob would be at the casino every day or whenever he could get the money to go. Margaret says that Bob stopped going to casinos only when she delivered an ultimatum to him, demanding he choose between gambling or her and their then-unborn child. In the end, Bob chose to control his gambling by placing a limit on how much he would gamble. Margaret says that Bob stuck to his self-imposed limit. He would give her "the bank card and everything to hold on to" every time they visited the casino, until they stopped going entirely.

Margaret also buys lottery tickets and used to gamble at casinos, but she does not define herself as a problem gambler. She became aware of her partner's gambling when he started playing Pro-Line. Margaret regularly confronts her husband about his spending on Pro-Line tickets, and he responds by saying that he can't stop. Margaret says she does not know why Bob gambles. Seeing that he doesn't tell her why he gambles, she suspects that he doesn't know why either. Margaret has tried to change his gambling by getting him to agree to set a limit on the money he spends on the Pro-Line tickets a week. This effort has been ineffective. Moreover, Margaret is unwilling to try doing other things to make Bob change his gambling habit. She doesn't think that making him change is worth it if it means losing him. Margaret feels that a professional could do a better job helping him quit than she could.

Bob's gambling has caused them to split up on a few occasions, according to Bob. When Margaret discusses Bob's gambling with him, it is mainly about the money and time spent gambling. Bob tries to avoid the topic of gambling altogether or walks away from the discussion. When Margaret confronts him about having to stop spending so much on Pro-Line, Bob tries to justify what he spends on gambling by comparing it to what Margaret spends on cigarettes. Bob feels that he is cutting down on his gambling slowly, especially on the scratch tickets, lottery tickets, and Pro-Line.

Margaret keeps detailed budgets for household spending. Bob sometimes feels guilty because he knows he could be using his money for something else besides gambling. In addition, his children sometimes "lay the guilt on [him]." Their son usually tells Margaret when his father has bought Pro-Line tickets, and Margaret says Bob responds by poking fun at his son. Margaret describes it as a comical routine between father and son, but there is a hint of tension, as her child is caught in the middle between his parents.

They recently switched from using separate accounts to using a joint account that Margaret controls. Margaret is also responsible for drawing up a monthly budget. Neither Bob nor Margaret has credit cards. Bob says he prefers to ask Margaret for money because he cannot be trusted with their money. Margaret is now responsible for the finances. Otherwise, both Bob and Margaret are about equally responsible for housework, childcare, and solving problems in their relationship. Margaret feels that Bob's gambling has created a financial strain for them and it makes her feel stressed and worried over money matters.

Lee and Doug

Lee and his same-sex partner, Doug, are both involved in gambling. Both are currently unemployed and their individual income is less than $20,000 yearly.

Lee has a high school diploma while Doug completed some postsecondary education.

Lee likes to use gambling, alcohol, and drug use to deal with stress. Doug plays bingo, Pro-Line, Lotto 6/49, Super 7, PayDay, and scratch tickets weekly. He claims he gambles because he lacks money and wants to try to win some, despite his belief the chances of winning are "not very good." Doug even admits that gambling to win money only "gets [him] deeper and deeper into debt." The couple switched from joint accounts to separate accounts about a year ago, and neither has a credit card. Doug has always been responsible for paying the household bills out of his own account. Lee does the monthly grocery shopping. Other than that, neither he nor Lee organizes their finances or tries to budget.

In the 1990s, Lee won $75,000 on a bingo ticket and, since then, he has bought more bingo tickets than Doug would like. Doug says Lee has not tried to make him stop gambling and that none of the arguments they have are over gambling. Lee says that Doug has tried to get him to save his money rather than spend it gambling. Most of the time, they agree on how much to spend on gambling, though Doug would like to see Lee spend less money on bingo. Doug says that he met Lee at a bingo game, so both knew from the beginning that the other person gambled. Lee says that Doug had no idea that he gambled until he took him to a bingo hall five years into their relationship. Lee says he can control his gambling, knows his limit, and does not "blow all of [his] money on bingo."

Besides gambling, Doug and Lee enjoy going to hockey and baseball games or just taking walks. Doug, who usually organizes these outings, does not think that gambling has affected their relationship "a lot." Doug does try to encourage Lee to spend less on bingo tickets, though his efforts are unsuccessful. Lee shares Doug's sentiment that gambling has little effect on their relationship. Lee and Doug share household tasks more or less equally between them. Doug feels that talking things over is the most helpful strategy for resolving problems and ignoring each other is the worst. Lee also adds that when they argue, there is much screaming and yelling.

Kurt and Marie

Kurt and Marie are married. Both have completed postsecondary education and are employed full-time. Kurt's annual salary is between $100,000 and $120,000, and Marie's is between $40,000 and $50,000. Kurt takes greater responsibility for handling the finances. According to Marie, this is because Kurt is "just better at it." Housework and household bills are split evenly between the two of them. Kurt and Marie have a joint account, as well as having their own separate chequing accounts and credit cards. Kurt works out a budget with Marie so they have a good handle on their expenses.

Communication between Kurt and Marie is open and constant, and they seem committed to keeping it that way. Despite their arguments, Marie asserts: "There's been nothing that we haven't been able to solve through many patient discussions and negotiation and compromise." Marie usually organizes the activities that she shares with Kurt, such as eating out, going to the movies or out with friends, or taking walks together. She likes how they can "relax together and do the same sort of thing" during those activities.

Marie gambles at the slot machines in casinos, as well as gambling on bingo, euchre, scratch tickets, and lottery tickets. Kurt accompanies Marie when she goes to casinos, but he rarely gambles. Kurt would like to see Marie reduce the time and money she spends gambling. Ever since they began dating, he was aware that Marie gambled. When they first got together, Marie revealed to Kurt that she liked to gamble. He asked her to exercise self-control when gambling. She explained to him the "rules" that she had set for herself regarding gambling, including never using the casino bank machines. She also keeps the money that she sets aside for gambling separate from the money she has budgeted for food and other things. Marie enjoys gambling for the excitement. Kurt is concerned about what he sees as her use of gambling to fill a "void" of some sort. Marie usually starts the pair's discussions of gambling. Since she does not drive, Marie usually asks Kurt to drive her to a casino. Kurt sees gambling as a way of "buying $100 worth of entertainment," though Marie does not. They also often disagree about how long she will stay at the casino.

Kurt suspects that Marie may have a gambling problem but has not pushed her to seek treatment. Kurt feels the need to "prevent" the problem of his wife turning into a problem gambler by balancing out their visits to the casino. Marie thinks her gambling never gets out of hand, because each casino trip is planned ahead of time. Marie believes her gambling has little effect on their marriage. Kurt worries that her gambling *could* become a problem, as she has an "addictive personality." Kurt says they talk openly about Marie's gambling and his fears about it. Marie says her gambling has not hindered her ability to contribute to savings and RRSPs. On the other hand, Kurt has experienced financial difficulty in the past because of unemployment and student debt.

Josie and Rob

Josie and Rob are engaged and live together. Both Josie and Rob are finishing school and they both work. Rob's income is less than $20,000 per year. They split the housework between them, and each feels they both do a fair share of it. According to Josie, they "can pretty much do anything together" as a couple, whether it is watching television or playing basketball. Rob points out that they have different hobbies and interests. He believes that finding things that both of them enjoy doing together is difficult.

Rob thinks Josie is "fine" with his gambling online and in poker games. According to Rob, no problems between them have arisen from his gambling. He has never sought treatment for his gambling. Rob does not view what he does as gambling. He feels he is merely "playing a game that [he is] really good at." Josie has not tried to stop Rob from gambling, as she does not view his gambling as an issue in their relationship. She does not fully believe that Rob is a problem gambler, but at the same time she is not sure that he isn't. Rob gambles almost every day. The time he spends gambling varies from ten minutes to eight hours. Neither Rob nor Josie feels there has been any conflict or tension brought on by Rob's gambling. Josie thinks this is in part because Rob's gambling has not affected their finances. When Rob is upset about losing, Josie often tries to console him and then tries to change the subject. Otherwise, Rob becomes fixated on how events might have unfolded differently if he had used other playing strategies.

Rob and Josie both have credit cards and have many different bank accounts, some of which are held jointly. Josie took over paying the bills when they first started living together. Though they both look after their investments, Rob takes the lead. They have plenty of knowledge about finances and investments, having both taken a course in financial investments. Josie tries to budget their money but does not always stick to the budget. Rob, on the other hand, does not try to budget at all.

George and Sue

George and Sue are engaged. According to George, they live separately, but Sue spends a great deal of time at his place. According to Sue, she and George moved in together four months before Sue's participation in the study. The housework and household expenses are shared evenly between the two.

Though George and Sue have both completed postsecondary education, Sue works full-time while George remains a full-time student in law school. Sue's annual income is between $30,000 and $40,000 per year, and George's income is less than $20,000 per year. Both are involved in online gambling. George mentions online gambling and poker and that his friends also gamble online. He says he started playing before Sue did. George says his gambling is under control. It is not a source of conflict in their relationship, and he and Sue do not talk about it. According to George, they handle their finances, savings, expenses, and budgeting separately.

According to George, both he and Sue are active and like to do outdoor activities when they are together. Sue, however, says that online gambling has "consumed" their relationship, as it takes up their quality time. Sue states that their online gambling has become a problem only since they started living together. When discussing gambling, she says, they mostly talk about their own experiences, gambling strategies, and reasons they should try to cut down on how much they gamble. Sue says that George is in debt and his finances are tight. He has credit card debt and a line of credit too. Sue tells George to put a "cap" on his gambling if she feels he is spending too much money in one night. The only clear disagreements over money are about what Sue spends on clothing, which George thinks is too much.

Cliff

Cliff is married to his second wife and has adult children from his first marriage. Cliff's wife unexpectedly declined to take part in the study. Cliff is a problem gambler, his gambling problem being one reason why his first marriage ended. Cliff also argues with his current wife about his gambling, especially his betting on horse races. Cliff concedes that his gambling has had a harmful effect on his current relationship. Arguments with his wife revolve around their different gambling habits and attitudes towards gambling, and the time he spends gambling. Furthermore, Cliff purposely hides information about when and how much he wins at gambling.

His partner buys lottery tickets and plays bingo, but Cliff does not think that she has a gambling problem. Over the years, Cliff has sold belongings (his cars, for example) and borrowed money from family or close friends so he could continue gambling. Cliff does not have a bank account or credit cards; he works for cash and pays for everything in cash. He and his current wife keep their finances separate, though they both pitch in to pay for household expenses. They do not budget for the future or have any joint investments.

Zab and Delkash

Zab and Delkash are married with two children, having emigrated together from India. Delkash makes between $80,000 and $90,000 per year, while Zab has an income between $60,000 and $90,000 per year. Zab is the problem gambler and gambles at casinos. The couple uses a joint account; however, Zab says he handles the family finances and bill payments. Delkash says that getting a joint account was a mutual decision, and it was done when they were married. From Delkash's view, getting a joint account made sense because "if there's nothing to hide, then there's no problem with a mutual account. It's better that way because then everything is in the open."

Delkash does not know that Zab has a secret separate account in which he saves money for his gambling, where he puts his overtime pay and work bonuses. Zab also saves money from daily expenses and stows this money away in his separate account. Zab concedes that his gambling has hurt his children. He spends less time with them than he feels he should. Yet Delkash feels that her husband's gambling has not affected their children because "he's always there when they're done school and he only gambles during the night."

Delkash avoids conflict about gambling and does not discuss her husband's gambling in front of their children. According to Zab, Delkash disagrees with him on how long he can stay at the casinos to gamble, and then she usually agrees with him on the "money limits." Zab admits to getting carried away though. Delkash believes Zab likes to gamble due to his greedy desire for more money.

Types of Gambling

The participants can be examined by general categories of the types of gambling they engaged in. Five out of six gamblers in our study said they have played lotteries in the past month. Three in every four (75 percent) of our respondents purchased scratch tickets in the past month, while just over half have played slots at a casino, and 42 percent played casino table games.

Most respondents reported preferring strict games of chance. Only 15 percent of our sample said that they played games of skill in the previous month. Most saw gambling as games involving risk and luck. Less than half the respondents felt that gambling involved skill, experience, or intelligence. When asked how often they currently gamble, 33 percent said that they gambled every day. Nearly 86 percent of the respondents gambled once a week or more, and 95 percent gambled at least once a month.

Becoming a Gambler: Family Influences

None of the respondents in our study gambled with their children, though some said they gamble with spouses and other family members. Yet a majority—nearly 61 percent of our respondents—said that they gambled alone.

Despite this solitary behaviour, a large proportion of the respondents associated gambling with family life. Nearly three out of four respondents said they gambled or played gambling games while they were growing up, and the average age at which respondents started gambling was 17 years. Most of the gamblers in our study were exposed to gambling at a young age, had had family members who gambled (some of whom might be considered problem gamblers), or had a social network that included gamblers.

When asked about children or teenagers gambling in their home, a majority (56 percent) said this doesn't happen. When growing up, a majority did not see or hear about their parents' gambling at home (60 percent) or elsewhere (65 percent). Most gambling knowledge came from teenage friends. Over half of the respondents (59 percent) said that their close friends gambled. This reinforces our view that gambling is a social phenomenon with social roots and consequences. Some respondents claimed that, as children, they went gambling with family members and their siblings would teach them about gambling:

My dad used to play cards quite a bit, and I got interested in it. Then I heard about betting the horses. [I learned] from different people . . . co-workers and friends.

[I started when] I was 12—crap games in the yard and card games in Sunday school. We'd find the spot nearest the fence, so when the cops came, everyone scrammed. Oh God, I was addicted early on.

My uncle . . . taught me to play cards, such games as poker. He was the first man who told me all about the charm of gambling games.

Once, my grandmother took me to the horse races. From there on, I just developed a natural liking for it. We used to play cards with her too . . . This is how I got into poker: her taking me to the races.

I was about 12 when I started playing the cards. I have two brothers . . . They were like, majorly into sports, so I would bet with them.

[I played] War ... for pennies [when] I was a kid. And Blackjack, growing up.

At school we'd play cards, pennies, quarters. Just things like that. In grade school.

Some respondents reported that they have been encouraged to gamble by friends and family even more often than they already do:

When we [my family] go down, the six of us, something we have to do is all get out to a bingo together.

A lot of my friends are gamblers ... If you're a poker player, you get to know other poker players. Or you play the horses and you get to know the horse players, and most of my friends fall into that category, and they're also beer drinkers.

She goes with friends so it's a social thing ... Her friends are also a lot more into gambling and have taught her their ways, to have regular gambling as a part of your life.

The 2003 *At Home With Gambling* study revealed that family influences on gambling often begin in childhood and persist through adulthood. Some families appear to have intergenerational *family gambling cultures*. People who become problem gamblers typically begin gambling at an earlier age than people who are non-problem gamblers. As well, people who saw or heard about their parents gambling at home while growing up are also more likely to have become adult problem gamblers than people who did not see or hear about their parents gambling at home.

In the 2003 study, respondents whose close friends gambled throughout the respondents' teenage years were more likely to develop a gambling problem than were respondents without gambling friends. Some respondents report having learned that gambling was something that family members considered a social activity, something that was fun, exciting, and made a person happy, regardless of whether they won or lost:

My grandma said it was lots of fun ... going out and socializing and playing bingo.

My grandfather was at the racetrack everyday ... He made it seem really exciting. He'd come home sometimes and show us a thousand dollar bill.

Some respondents report that this view influenced their later gambling:

I think that is why I used to go gambling twice a month when I was younger. She [mother] described it as going out with the girls ... They just went out like other people go somewhere with their friends ... [like] going to the movies.

Respondents also reported that what some families found most exciting is the possibility of winning big. They learned what "a big win" would do for their lives:

I heard conversations of my parents and their friends when they'd come to play cards ... Those conversations were full of excitement and dynamics. Besides, we often bought lottery tickets. Every jackpot was followed by excitement and discussions about what could be done with money in case we won.

My father was a gambler ... [He] would openly send us out to get his lottery tickets and his numbers. He would say, "This could be our lucky chance to get the big one" and if he won the money, we would get a lot of things—our education would be paid for, our car, computer, what have you.

Other respondents learned from their families that gambling is not something good people do, or that gambling is associated with bad outcomes. This view was sometimes associated with religious belief or ethical principles of how good and responsible people behave:

Gambling was evil, that's what we were brought up to believe ... I don't know, maybe that's why we flipped, got intrigued ... I had to see how "evil" it was.

They said, "Don't gamble, stay away from gambling, live a clean life. Keep yourself clean and don't get involved."

My grandmother told me that my grandfather was an addicted gambler. They once lived on easy street. Later they became poor because my grandfather lost out in gambling, almost all their property, including precious antiques and several hectares of farmland.

When I was younger, I was taught at home and in school that gambling was bad and could leave "your family broken."

Something most memorable that influenced all my life as a gambler were the long talks with my father. Probably his personal experience persuaded him to teach me since a young age not to ever get seriously interested in gambling. And, probably, those childhood memories stayed with me for all my life.

Many respondents told us their children were learning about gambling by witnessing their own or another family member's gambling, or by talking with them about gambling:

They've seen us gamble—mostly playing cards. They might have heard me say, "I'm going over to Tim's tonight to play cards so wish me luck."

They [the children] said, "Get out, Mom. Go have a good time." They've heard [gambling] is like an entertainment, socializing, getting out, something to do.

Sometimes, children became directly involved in a family member's gambling:

My youngest son [age three], I used to let him break open tickets.

One night when I came home, I thought they were sleeping. I won a thousand dollars. I was so excited . . . but the girls were still awake. And my son goes, "Where did you get that money?" So [my husband] goes, "Oh, she won at bingo." That's when I think they finally connected bingo to money.

Some parents were concerned that their children were learning "bad habits" from themselves and other family members, so they were taking steps to teach their children about gambling:

My daughter's only 14, and she likes to get scratchies, and I told her it's illegal. Also she plays TV bingo, and I tell her she shouldn't get involved in this too much because I have the bad habit . . . [but] she still likes to play it so I let her. It's my fault. I let her.

I told [my daughter] "You see how daddy plays, and he's spending so much money when it would be possible to buy things for that money. See, it's a hundred dollars. For those hundred dollars, you wanted that Barney cassette—we could buy this many Barney cassettes—and he lost it. He just threw it in the garbage." . . . I translated it into material things, so that she could understand what that was.

Her father often buys 6/49 lottery tickets. I told my kid this actually was not very good. He just spent a little money to buy a kind of hope and to mentally adjust himself . . . an activity of speculation. There was little chance to win. It's just to console himself . . . just to hold a sweet dream for the week. [I said,] "If you won 10 million dollars, how would you spend the money?" It's a pleasant thing to think about . . . I told her it's only for fun and not to put your hope completely on that. I don't want her to indulge in speculation.

This chapter examined a cross-section of gambling families in Ontario, highlighting differences in gender, age, and income. It also introduced some of the couples in our study. Not too surprisingly, gamblers often learn as children to associate gambling with hope, excitement, and happiness. Yet this doesn't explain why some grew up to develop a gambling problem. To do that, we need to examine what gamblers believe about gambling.

Chapter 5
Gambling Beliefs of Respondents

Why do some people bet their lives on easy money, on dreams and luck? The sociological approach to gambling focuses on the ways that social life constrains and changes ordinary people. It asks why ordinary, everyday people sometimes do odd, reckless, and even dangerous things. Psychologists or psychiatrists might look for signs and explanations of psychopathology or distorted reasoning. But sociologists look for outside (social) conditions that lead the individual to behave this way—unusual or even destructive conditions that might lead well-adjusted people to act oddly. In a crazy world, it is normal and reasonable to act in what others might think are crazy ways.

The sociological approach focuses on the ways that people's actions and beliefs are shaped by their social experiences—through interaction, socialization, advertising, and encouragement and discouragement by others. People's perceptions and beliefs are shaped by other people. Like other living creatures, humans respond to rewards and punishments. We repeat rewarded activities, avoid punished activities, and (eventually) forget non-rewarded activities. Unlike other animals, people respond to situations and rewards *not* as these situations objectively exist, but as the people perceived them. Yet a person's perception of reality is "real," for it has real consequences.

Therefore, to understand problem gambling, we have to understand what people learned to think and believe about gambling: their knowledge, attitudes, practices, interpretations, and cultural experiences.

Beliefs in the 2003 *At Home With Gambling* Study

The 2003 *At Home* study paid special attention to people's beliefs about gambling, as well as the ways beliefs reflect what people had learned in childhood. These beliefs often varied according to the ethnocultural origin of the respondent, so we have organized the findings by ethnocultural group. We recognize that these snapshots merely sketch the range of variation. Moreover, we understand that there are many other important social influences on gambling behaviour, including age, region, religion, education, socio-economic status, and so on. We merely want to illustrate a level of analysis that lies outside psychological and psychiatric interpretations of gambling—that is, the social context the gambler lives in.

We asked respondents four questions:

(1)   What makes gambling different in your own ethnocultural group?
(2)   How is gambling different for women and men?
(3)   Why do people gamble in your ethnocultural group?
(4)   What would persuade people to quit gambling?

What follows are the most common themes that emerged. This section gives a sense of the enormous variety among and within six ethnocultural groups.

The Aboriginal Respondents (47 Adults)

Most Aboriginal respondents reported knowing someone—often a family member—with a gambling problem. Almost half said that gambling led to financial or other problems in their families. Among Aboriginal adults, 34 percent also reported worrying about an alcohol addiction, 57 percent reported concern over a cigarette addiction, and 13 percent reported concern over a drug addiction. These respondents noted that many members of their group gamble:

> A lot of Aboriginal people gamble a lot. You can ask anybody, just about any Aboriginal person.

Several moderate gamblers among the adult Aboriginal respondents said that there was a historical and cultural context to Aboriginal gambling:

> [Traditionally, there were the] stick games, like when they had celebrations in the northwest, they would have pow-wows, they would have a log, and a lot of these people would sit around and each one would have a stick, it is like the log was a drum. They played a song on it, and with the other hand they would pass a baton around, like behind, and they would bet on where it would stop, when the song was over. There are lots of games, like the moccasin games, you know the old shell game. They would take three moccasins and put something under it and shake it around and people would bet on it.

Gambling is a part of [our culture]. It is a part of our mid-winter ceremonies ... The Peace Bowl Game [is] a game that we play at the end of our mid-winter ceremonies ... a gambling game. You are supposed to bring something that is very near and dear to your heart, be it moccasins, rattles, dress clothes, anything. The teams are divided up into clans ... The prizes get handed out to the winning team ... They say that if you lose something you will get it back in the Spirit world ... They usually start at about 1:00 or 2:00 and keep going until 4:00 or 5:00 [a.m.]. And if there is no winner, then we start the next morning, and we can go for the whole day.

Others reported that Europeans introduced gambling:

I think that for First Nations people, cigarettes, pop, alcohol, gambling, all of those things are very addictive behaviours. For First Nations people, if you look at history, First Nations people never really had ... these kinds of behaviours. Nothing against Europeans, but when Europeans came, [gambling] seems to be something that was in their backgrounds for many, many years. So it was something they introduced.

Others yet traced current problems to the new presence of casinos on reserves:

Until the casinos went up, I hadn't heard anything [about gambling].

Many respondents expressed mixed feelings about the casinos:

Now with the casinos, we have a lot of things we didn't have before. We have cocaine dealers now. We had one of the workers, when the [coffee shop] was opened, while she was putting out the garbage, she was raped and beaten ... That person got away. They never found him. Of course, a lot of good things have happened too, like we have a water treatment plant, we have a dump, we are all on the same water line—water was a real problem before—and we have a daycare for the school, and the arena for the kids and stuff. But when you weigh both factors, my fear is that one day something is going to happen to one of the kids and I don't think the price is worth it.

Several respondents linked problem gambling to addictions such as alcoholism and linked both of these addictions to feelings of alienation and a desire to escape:

There are addictions that go together, and it is almost as though all of those things are an escape from the deeper problems these people experience.

Other respondents cited the centrality of poverty in their lives, and the belief that gambling is the only possible way to get out of it:

The majority of Aboriginals are living in poverty. They have this hope of getting out of that ... having money for once, so gambling probably does appeal to them.

Some respondents believed that Aboriginal people can quit gambling only by drawing on their own heritage, by understanding the power of healing circles, and by getting in touch with themselves as a people. They also recognized the powerful incentive posed by on-reserve casinos and believed that despite the financial benefits, there should be no more casinos placed on reserves.

Aboriginal respondents were divided on the question of gender differences in gambling. Some believed that gender differences appear in the types of gambling women and men are likely to prefer. These reflections tended to include some social or structural commentary:

More women would play bingo than go to the casino, because bingo is more accessible than the casino. If someone doesn't have the transportation, they can hitch a ride with someone else to the local bingo hall. It would be harder to go to the casino. I think men are more comfortable going to a lot of places by themselves. Women might feel more comfortable going with a friend.

Some respondents thought that the women in their ethnocultural group are more attached to gambling than men, though men were described as gambling more aggressively and as being more willing to accept high stakes.

The British Isles Respondents (59 Adults)
Among British Isles respondents, 28 percent believed that they themselves or one of their family members had a gambling problem. Of the 60 respondents, 26 percent worried about their own gambling. Roughly 23 percent said that gambling led to problems within the family environment, especially worries about finances. Twelve percent of adults worried about an alcohol addiction, 29 percent about a cigarette addiction, and 7 percent about a drug addiction.

The British Isles respondents were culturally and socially varied. They were mainly Christian and drew links between Christianity and gambling, arguing that Christians tended to oppose gambling:

> In that kind of Christian—in the sense of Catholic, Protestant, Anglican— background, [gambling] was a behaviour that was not condoned. Particularly, it would have been frowned upon and looked at as a weakness, a sin, and all those kinds of things.

Other respondents saw their group's gambling within the context of a history of aristocratic and social gambling in Britain.

> When you get to the track, you get the women with their beautiful hats. The racetrack in that situation is more of a social [event]. Men take their wives with them. The Queen [went] with the Queen Mother ... This is part of a social thing.

The British Isles respondents cited a range of motivations for gambling, including excitement, stress relief, poverty, and addiction:

> It's a thrill ... I do it for the excitement, really.

> I know doctors that gamble. They're addicts, and they are gamblers, but they don't drink, and they say it's stress-related—it's a stress release for them.

> Poverty has a lot to do with it, you know. It's the chance that you might get some money and be able to change your life.

The respondents had varying views about what it would take to quit gambling:

> If they had trouble at home, I think they would stop [gambling]. That is the biggest factor, or can be a great factor.

> It's like any addiction. You've got to find your own personal boundary ... Maybe a little bit of help might be useful to shorten my recovery to the stage that I am going to decide to quit. Once I've decided that, maybe some kind of counselling can help me to get there. But [first] I have to help myself.

Two-thirds of the British Isles respondents thought that there were gender differences in gambling within their culture:

> I noticed that women seem to go to the casinos and the bingos, but they don't seem to go to the horse races. Not in the same ratio. If you go to a bingo, I would say 90 percent of them are women. If you go to the horse races, there are 90 percent men there up, until they got the casinos and horses combined.

Many linked these perceived gender differences to traditional and distinctive gender roles:

> I've known a lot of women who like to gamble. But women have been the ones to try to maintain the peace in life, in their relationships, in their families, etc. And that's such a heavy responsibility. So they've squashed that down a bit, whereas men are just allowed to do it.

> In terms of my generation, gambling was worse for men because they had the money, and they probably gambled the rent. Women didn't used to work so they could only gamble the egg money.

Some respondents thought these traditions were changing and believed that women are now gambling in part because of an increased access to gambling locales:

> Men like to gamble more than women do. And I think it's always been like that. [But] it might be changing now because of the fact that we have casinos: we have these accessible places to go where we never had that before. When I used to play poker, nobody ever invited the wives or their girlfriends to go and play poker at somebody's house. Now we have casinos all over the place. So environmentally and socially, you have these places for women to go and enjoy themselves that you didn't have before.

The Caribbean Respondents (43 Adults)

Among the Caribbean respondents, gambling was an activity shared among friends, largely as a form of entertainment. Roughly 18 percent of the respondents identified either themselves or someone else in their family as having a gambling problem. Among those reporting gambling concerns, 22 percent said that gambling has led to family, monetary, or other problems. Only 2 percent reported worrying about an alcohol addiction, 21 percent about a cigarette addiction, and 5 percent about a drug addiction.

Some respondents noted that gambling games have a long history in this community, serving as a way of getting people together to enjoy a social evening:

> Where other cultures might play cards, for the Caribbean community, the big-guy thing to do is to play dominoes and bet on dominoes, or some other game, like Ludi.

> In my culture, it's maybe more acceptable for men to gamble. It's a social thing, so that when they get together and have a few beers, they play dominoes.

Just under two-thirds of the adults believed that there are no gender differences in gambling. Those who thought there were differences invariably said that men gamble more than women:

> When I was growing up, women would be home taking care of the children. They weren't the ones that worked and had their own money. The men would have the money, so they are the ones that would gamble.

> My uncle would go ballistic if he found out my aunt gambled. Male domination, that's the way it is.

> Women are supposed to have more financial sense … They know more about family finances, what is needed, so they can't afford to take money and spend it uselessly.

When asked why people in their culture gamble and what would persuade them to quit, many Caribbean respondents cited issues relating to race and class:

> Everyone is striving to make it rich, and within our community the struggle could be harder because of racism, classism. So maybe in our community, because of those types of oppression, [gambling] is an addiction that comes out of those oppressions … I can just speak about my mom: her whole

motivation is to win the big million and then all her financial problems would just go away.

[Caribbean people] don't believe in what society says; they go by what they feel and what they've grown up with. And a lot of them are stubborn, so a lot of them will have to fall on their face in order to stop, or see someone else fall on their face and stop.

The Chinese Respondents (49 Adults)

For the Chinese respondents, gambling is a well-established, traditional social activity. Only three Chinese gamblers in our sample reported gambling alone, since gambling usually occurs with one's spouse or with other family members. Though some respondents mentioned playing card games (*pai gow* and *fan tan*) and horse racing, mah-jong is by far the most popular traditional Chinese betting game our respondents play:

It's thrilling. Men and women, old and young, they all like to play this game, despite their educational background. Playing mah-jong is acceptable to all. In China, these people include senior officials, intellectuals, housewives, aged ladies, and those without jobs. It seems people from all walks of life can accept this form of gambling.

One respondent noted that people usually play mah-jong at home and among friends. Traditional Chinese practices of gambling with friends or relatives are nothing like the "individualized" and "public" gambling in the West:

Chinese people normally play mah-jong and poker with friends, and each time they need four people to play along. In the Western world, however, people gamble on their own. They play slot machines themselves, or they play with dealers. I think the Western ways of gambling are more reasonable. Chinese people gamble against their friends, and this harms the friendship among these people when some of them win but others have to "say Uncle." Such a situation doesn't happen among Western people because they don't gamble against their friends.

The Chinese respondents cited many reasons for gambling: the changes in leisure activity after immigration to Canada, the long history of gambling in Chinese culture, and gambling patterns passed down in the family:

Gambling in China has a long history. This is partly because there are not enough ways of entertainment. Also gambling has become trendy as a kind of recreation activity. Gambling behaviour also passes down from one generation to another. Many families have a gambling history.

For some, gambling is a status symbol that marks financial success. Some also said they see gambling as a way to make money or to show it off. Many respondents believed showing up in a casino is a symbol of distinction because "many rich people go to casino [to] eat, drink, and play." One of our interviewers who belonged to this ethnocultural group added that some people with a Chinese background gamble because they feel that life is otherwise dull and boring. In addition, a language barrier may keep some from communicating effectively with non-Chinese people; thus, casino gambling is one way for them to overcome the communication problems they face.

Few of the Chinese respondents reported worrying about their own gambling. Only 4 percent of the adults reported worrying about an alcohol addiction or a cigarette addiction, and none worried about a drug addiction. About a third denied there are any gender differences in gambling. However, a few respondents did describe gendered behaviour patterns. Those who believed there are gender differences most often framed their views in terms of levels of risk-taking or daring:

Men generally like taking risks, so they are more likely to [be] involved in gambling.

They are both very daring when they gamble. I saw a woman in the casino. She placed a bet of $8,000. She lost it. She put another bet of $8,000. Even those working in the casino were stunned. When a gambler sits at the gambling table, he or she does not even remember his or her father's name.

The theme of women being the caretakers in the family emerged as a caution against women gambling to excess or risking too much money when gambling:

When women gamble, they don't care about their families.

There are differences between men and women in gambling. Women are usually more careful and tend not to bet a big amount of money; and they are considerate and care for their kids. They won't forget to look after their children when they gamble. I noticed some women who were playing mah-jong. They ended it quickly when they knew their children were coming back. Men are different. They tend to put big amounts of money. They are likely to take a risk and forget their children.

The Chinese respondents placed a strong and usually positive value on daring and risk-taking. But though gambling and daring are valued in this culture, family duty is valued much more highly. When asked what would lead people to quit gambling, some said the threat of family destruction could have that effect:

> The best way of helping people to quit gambling is to let them know the consequences of gambling, which often lead to a broken family. It is a disaster for the family and also for family members.

Latin American Respondents (47 Adults)
Of the Latin American respondents, 53 percent stated that they had grown up with a close friend who gambled. Only 12 percent reported that they themselves or someone in the family currently has a gambling problem. Just under one-third of the adults believe gambling has led to family problems. Only three respondents worried about financial difficulties because of gambling. Of the adults surveyed, only 6 percent reported worrying about an alcohol addiction, 23 percent about a cigarette addiction, and one respondent about a drug addiction.

Though gambling is illegal in Cuba, betting games are played there anyway. Several respondents mentioned a lottery called *bolita*, a game that involves participants listening for numbers reported on foreign radio stations. Casinos are popular in Ecuador, while lotteries are popular in Colombia. Most of the Latin American respondents reported poverty as a factor in the way they view gambling:

> Gambling is a way of life for many Colombians, because everyone is so poor. If you want to make money quick ... the boys learn to gamble at twelve, sometimes nine. And there's cockfights, dogfights, even fights with the bulls ... and cards on Friday, and spin-the-wheel, pool, and soccer. In a way, there's more gambling in Colombia than here in Canada.

In contrast to the gambling that occurs in poorer Latin American countries, one respondent noted, gambling is associated with social status in Argentina:

> Going to the races shows you're wealthy; and sometimes the casino too, although now it is more for the masses.

Most respondents believed there were gender differences in gambling. For many, views of gambling aligned with traditional conceptions of gender roles:

> Normally in our culture, the tendency is for the men to gamble in the casinos and outside the home. The women play in the home and play for entertainment and fun, not to win money or experience the feeling of suspense. They play more "innocent" games like the lottery, and normally they play in the home.

One female respondent believed that gambling is an extension of male power over women:

> Women don't gamble because their husbands don't allow them. Besides, women are more responsible with the money; we stick to our budget. Women are not like men; eight guys go to gamble because they become bolder when they are all together. When they're home, they are machos, but when they're coming home, they cross themselves because they are on their own to face their wives.

Many of the respondents' answers reflect views of gender that are specific to Latin America:

> The gambling in Ecuador is mostly for men, for the boys. It's a macho thing. [Women don't gamble] unless they're prostitutes in the red light district and the old French ghetto area. So women are not expected to gamble. They think if a woman wants to gamble, she wants to take away the role of the macho, wants to be daring. It's not a symbol of good character, not a lady-like thing to do. Just prostitutes in the brothel houses [gamble].

Many respondents stressed the relationship between gambling, drinking, and men:

There's a lot of sexism among Latin Americans. When men play cards, women are talking on one side, while they're gambling and drinking on the other side.

Some forms of gambling that are especially popular in Latin America are specifically linked to machismo:

Cockfighting is a very male thing; no ladies come. Dice, poker, cards are male oriented.

Only a few respondents claimed there are exceptions to these deeply entrenched gender roles. Respondents said that the few women who gamble in public tend to belong to richer classes:

There are a lot of women at the casinos over there, but of course, only rich women. Regular housewives don't go to the casinos, and they also don't go to horse races, which are more for men. But there are a lot of women at the casinos.

Several respondents from Cuba and Argentina noted the intersection of superstition and gambling:

In Argentina . . . if one dreams something, it is equivalent to a number, so for example 48 is dead man talking, 15 is a pretty girl, 22 is ducks. And when one dreams [numbers], one can check this index that has been printed and can be obtained at variety stores and public spaces where there could be gambling.

When asked why Latin American people gamble and what would persuade them to quit, respondents focused on the desire for easy money. These respondents associated the possibility of winning easy money with the general openness and generosity of Canadian society:

As a Spanish person, when you come from a Third World country, you always see Canada and the United States as a city of gold, and you always want to reach that limit. You want to be categorized as First World and have your own house. I believe that's everyone's dream. They don't want to live anymore in poverty; they want to advance. And some people take those steps in gambling, believing that in a one-shot kind of a deal, they'll do it.

According to these respondents, the only way Latin American people are likely to stop gambling is if they run out of money or face the threat of losing their family:

> When they stop gambling, it is perhaps because they have gambled away all they had in the piggy bank and haven't won anything.

> Probably to lose the person dearest to them would make them abandon gambling.

The Russian Respondents (52 Adults)

The Russian respondents came with high educational and occupational expectations—and with a love of gambling. For Russian immigrants, gambling is mainly about skill, strategy, and brainpower. Most Russian respondents in this sample reported that they usually gamble with friends, and only 23 percent claimed to gamble alone. Of all the adult respondents, 20 percent stated that either they or someone in their family has a gambling problem. When naming specific concerns about their own gambling, 20 percent worried about finances, none reported worrying about an alcohol addiction, and only one respondent worried about a drug addiction, though one-third worry about a cigarette addiction.

One of the specific features of gambling for many in this group was a fear of exposing their gambling, due to having grown up in a country where it was illegal:

> Attitudes to gambling in our ethnocultural group differ from attitudes to gambling in other groups, because all of us used to live in a closed society. We tried to hide any involvement in gambling. Here it is open.

The respondents mentioned many games that are part of the gambling pattern of their culture, including lotteries, dice, chess, cards, dominoes, and billiards. The only gambling that stands out as uniquely Russian is a rarely mentioned actively—Russian roulette:

In Russia, there is a very cruel kind of gambling, like Russian roulette. It is of Russian nature, I mean a game for life or death. Such an extreme is common for Russians, and gambling leads to suicides and tragic consequences.

While most Russians gamble, some feel neutral about gambling while others talk about it negatively, speaking of the damage that it does to families. In the Russian group, nearly half of the adult respondents did not believe there were any differences between men and women in gambling:

Gambling cannot be differentiated according to sex. Gambling thrills both equally, men and women.

Some claimed that, in general, women prefer "less complicated" games, while men prefer games that are more complex. Of those who perceived gender differences, the majority believed that men are more likely to take risks and lose control:

A woman is a less excitable person because she can stop playing in time. As for men, they are more excitable. It's much more difficult for them to stop gambling if they start winning.

I think men are more venturesome. Maybe they lose their heads more often than women. Young women who don't have families don't think about complications with gambling.

When asked why Russian people gamble and what would persuade them to quit, the respondents' answers varied. They mentioned their immigrant status, a need to make money, and family and cultural histories of gambling.

People gamble because they probably were taught so by their parents or by their social environment. It is also a part of their culture. And what is to stop them? They have to be persuaded that once you cross a certain limit, this can become a bad habit, which can lead to various problems and, even worse, catastrophes.

One respondent claimed that for some Russians, gambling is an important part of their self-expression:

> It is generally in the Russian character—maybe it is a national feature—this trust in luck, in this hit-or-miss, in your chance to get lucky. That's why the Russians are gambling.

> Gambling contains a certain stimulus that encourages a person to live. A gambling game is one of the elements of self-expression.

Few of these respondents seemed to believe that it is possible or important for Russians to stop gambling. They saw it as a central part of their national character and of their lives as immigrants in a new country.

> First of all, they want to distract [themselves] from everyday problems. Then, everyone hopes to improve his or her financial state. Besides, many people in the Russian community don't speak English well, and consequently they don't have many places for visiting. They can't go to theatres or movies, as they won't understand a thing there. And not everybody has friends to communicate with. That's why people choose this way of entertainment and spending spare time . . . I don't think it is possible to convince them to quit gambling.

> As for convincing a person to stop gambling, I don't think anything could convince a person to stop doing what he likes, even if it does harm to him. If it doesn't do harm, why should he stop doing it?

Findings from the Current Study

The more recent 2005 study also explored gamblers' beliefs and opinions. These answers yielded some interesting information on how gamblers define and justify their own gambling. Other research has shown that problem gamblers reason differently than other people (Toplak *et al.*, 2007). Irrational beliefs are often associated with problem gambling (Moore and Ohtsuka, 1999), and faulty ways of thinking lead gamblers to behave against their best interests. Many of our interviewees believed that they can beat the odds and win. Realistically, it is difficult to make money from gambling over the long term. Some respondents recognized their illogical reasoning contributes to their addictive behaviour:

> There's always the fantasy that you might win . . . I have lotto advance and I play the same numbers; I'm just hoping through persistence that I will win.

Right now, I don't have anything so I try to see if I can win money; but it actually doesn't work.

One interviewee provided a clear insight into what many of these gamblers are thinking:

You always hope to win. You may go through a bunch of losses. And every loss, you think maybe the next time, maybe the next time, maybe the next time. I'm sure everyone who gambles says the same thing . . . you always hope that the next time is going to do it. [But] it doesn't happen, or if it does, it's not a humongous huge win where you can say, "I got all my money back that I've ever gambled, so I'm happy."

The 50/50 Theory

Some gamblers followed superstitious practices in hopes of improving their chances of winning.

My gambling is mostly bingo. Filipino people are lucky. They tend to win a lot . . . I have been sitting in the same chair for five years—pretty well since they put that smoking room back there.

These superstitions are similar to the very common logical fallacy, the *50/50 Theory*. Almost half of the respondents shared the faulty belief that they have a 50/50 chance of winning whenever they gamble:

With all of them you have the same chances of winning—50/50.

I think it works out to about 40/60 or 50/50. Last time I relapsed, two weeks ago, I walked in with $300 dollars and immediately I was up . . . within an hour I was up $600 dollars. And then I kept winning and winning and then, for the next couple of hours I lost everything. So, I would say, it is about 50/50.

Gamblers seem to have a skewed perception of their chances. One interviewee thought that for him, the odds of winning are 50 percent, but for a "typical" gambler, the odds are much lower:

For me it is about 50/50, but for overall gambling, I honestly believe that it is about a 30 percent chance.

However, many gamblers said they (correctly) believe the odds of winning depend on the game they are playing:

It depends on the game that you play. I play poker, so the odds are pretty good, but it depends on who you're playing. Poker is a game of skill and luck, so it totally depends on who you're playing. As far as what your chances are of winning, if I were to guess, out of 10 times that I'm playing I might win half of those times. Blackjack and poker, both of those there is skill involved, so if you're good at it, then your odds at winning are pretty high.

Most respondents admitted believing that both chance and skill have something to do with the odds of winning. Several respondents admit that even though their chance of winning is low, they still hope to win big someday:

Chances of winning? Very low. You always hope to win. You may go through a bunch of losses. And [with] every loss, you think maybe the next time, maybe the next time.

You'll win every once in a while. Or you come close. I know there is very little chance of winning big. If you win big, you're going to continue on, so you'll lose it anyway.

Several respondents credited winning to non-game-related factors, such as a superstition (for example, always sitting in the same seat) or a supposed ability to assess the "feeling" of a game or gambling opportunity. One problem gambler explained how she had never been "lucky," which explained her consistent gambling losses:

I was born under a black star, because I've never been lucky. When we were young, my brothers and sisters would go to bingo. My parents would take us. From church, we used to go there. It was for small amounts . . . and everyone would win except me.

Some believed that a person's wish to win would affect whether a person does win. One interviewee claimed: "It also depends on how much you want to win." Other respondents said they had developed certain strategies or habits to increase their chances of winning:

> My system is I put in 20 dollars . . . The minute I see it going up, if it goes anywhere near $200 and up, I push out. I get all my coins out, put my coins to the side . . . put a 20 dollar or 10 dollar back in, [and] that way I have my winnings. That's a smart way to play.

Gamblers in this study often repeated the views that they can influence the outcome of a game of chance through various strategies or habits. With this sense of control and predictability, they feel likely to benefit from their gambling.

Why They Gamble

We asked the gamblers in our study what they liked about gambling and what their most memorable gambling experience was. Many gamblers seek a feeling of excitement or rush of adrenalin as their reason for gambling:

> To feel the thrill. You feel good when you win. The feeling when you're winning is indescribable. Your heart races, you're excited, you feel on top of the world.

> It is just a rush that you get when you win . . . The feeling you get of winning is worth taking the risk of losing. So, that is why I like to gamble. It is that risk—[it's] that sort of excitement you get when you don't know what is going to happen.

For some respondents, gambling is mainly an opportunity to go out with friends, meet new people, and have fun:

> I enjoy it. It is just fun. I guess that it is also a social thing. My partner and I gamble with his friends once a week and it brings everyone together.

Many respondents also described physical changes because of gambling:

> I am nervous that I might win or lose. I get butterflies.

> [Your] palms are sweaty and . . . [you] see the cards coming up and you know, like . . . you [motions as if he is trembling]. It's just a rush. The

rush of . . . I am going to get this card and I am going to win this pot. Nuts.

Because gambling results in these heightened emotional experiences, some admitted to using gambling as a way to overcome stress or depression:

> It relieves a lot of stress. It's relaxing, it takes all your worries away . . . at that time. It's fun. You think you are going to get ahead, you hope you are going to come out ahead of what you put in . . . Afterwards, it just adds to the problem.

Emotional or psychological changes can range from extremely positive feelings (happiness and excitement) to extremely negative feelings (frustration and anxiety). The mood swings mean gamblers can experience great pleasure and joy at one moment, then depression the next. This rise and fall in stress level increases the gambler's need to gamble more, as most of these people use gambling to deal with stress, and creates a never-ending cycle.

One problem gambler explained that gambling causes a constant state of moodiness and instability, leading him to career between positive and negative moods:

> Your moods change . . . you might get in a good mood, you might be in a bad mood. It changes so fast that you don't even see it changing . . . One minute you're in a great, great mood then all of a sudden, bang! You don't even notice it; you're in a bad mood all of a sudden.

A few respondents said that they become introverted when they gamble:

> I'll usually keep to myself . . . If I played stupid, I'd be mad at myself if I felt that I should have won; but [if I] lost because I played dumb, then I'll be mad at myself because of that. But I don't lash out.

While some respondents claimed that gambling is a social activity, others sought an opposite experience when they gamble:

> I find gambling extremely anti-social . . . very, very antisocial . . . because you usually do it alone. You don't talk to anybody. You are hooked up with

this machine, and my thing is slots and roulette. You are sitting with other people who are playing, but you are not talking to them, and there is not a lot of conversation going on. It is escapism.

Sometimes, ordinarily passive people become aggressive risk-takers when they gamble. Interviewees often reported having great difficulty controlling their gambling:

There's an excitement that I will win and I can have more money, so I can buy more things. [You feel] more excitement, like when you play slot machines and look like you are going to win but you didn't notice that you lost all your money.

It's like a rush I get though my body. It's like something is moving all through you. I found it was overpowering last year because I got five numbers on the 649. Last year, I got a thousand dollars, and in two weeks, it was all gone.

[I feel] more excited, more confident. I feel that I own that space there.

Some respondents stated that they gamble for the thrill they get from gambling. For them, gambling serves as a substitute for something missing from their day-to-day lives. Others gamble because it is an escape that takes one of two forms: a mental escape and a physical escape. The mental escape allows them to get away from their lives, to get their mind off their problems by immersing themselves in the gambling:

It gets you out of yourself, so you don't have to focus on yourself.

The minute I go there, I feel so free. I feel that there is nobody to ask me anything. I am the master of that whole place. At home, I have to be on my toes, like I cannot tell anybody that I have a migraine. I cannot tell anybody that I am in pain. I have to rush to make food, so that when they come there is food. The minute that I go [gambling] . . . the first machine I sit in, I start. I play so fast—like a blind person—that I lose. I don't even stop to think. Maybe when people get drugs and they are high, maybe that is what I feel— like I am on top of the world now. Nobody can say anything to me.

For those who use gambling as a literal escape, it gives them an opportunity to physically leave their house and family behind:

> I put on my tunes. I don't drive, so [the Casino Rama shuttle bus] gives me a place to go to. I used to go to a cottage. [But] my parents don't own a cottage anymore, and I don't talk to them anymore. [The bus] gives me the travel I like too.

> I go to Casino Rama, and it's like getting out of Toronto for a couple of hours. There's no one to bug you, you can leave your family at home and it's like a vacation. You just spend your money until you want to go home … You're always home, 24/7, and the kids are crying, screaming, want this, want that, and you want to relax. [Going gambling is] like going to Acapulco.

One respondent felt the incentives casinos offer, including cheap shuttle buses and food vouchers, further motivate many people to use gambling as an escape:

> The sightseeing tours are all arranged, with a tour bus that takes us to the casinos. I'd like to spend more time together [with my partner] not gambling related. But I'm aware of all the incentives out there. For example, you have to play for five hours to get the incentives. [But] if you stay for five hours, you only have to pay two dollars for the bus ride and you get a ten dollar coupon towards playing and a five dollar food voucher.

While escape was an important factor for many interviewees, others claimed to gamble just to win money, a finding consistent with the work of Meichenbaum and Turk (1993). The obsession with winning money leads these respondents to gamble more and more, creating unnecessary stress that harms their health. Ultimately, winning means different things to different people, including the hope of recovering past losses, the hope of making a profit or achieving financial stability, and the dream of "winning big":

> I'm not working. For me, [gambling] brings a different kind of financial stability that being on disability can't do.

> I guess [it's] an easy way to make money.

If I am winning something big, like if I win the $1,000 jackpot, what it does to me . . . how good it makes me feel that I spent $40, and I'm coming home with a thousand.

It's pretty exciting when you read in the newspaper about people winning $4 million. My eyes light up for them, but I wish it was me.

Some respondents said that they gamble because they remember having fun doing so and may have won money at some time. When respondents recalled their most memorable gambling experiences, most first cited a positive gambling experience. Prompted to recall a negative gambling experience as well, fewer could do so. Positive gambling stories were usually longer and more embellished than negative stories and were told with little prompting from the interviewer:

I found a $20 bill on the street. I went to the horses and I won $2,000 dollars with that $20. That sticks in my mind as a very memorable experience. It was March 6, 1990—we're talking 15 years [ago]. I just found it on the street and it just accumulated up to $2,000.

Of the positive experiences, respondents most often cited a first-time experience as their most memorable gambling experience. First-time experiences included gambling for the first time, winning big for the first time, playing a particular game for the first time, or just being in a casino for the first time.

Gambling Behaviour of Spouses

Spouses of gamblers were also asked about their own gambling and beliefs on gambling. Both gamblers and spouses said that gambling involves both luck and risk; but the spouses were less likely to describe gambling as requiring skill or intelligence. Furthermore, nearly half the gamblers said that gambling involves intelligence, but just under one-third of the spouses believed the same. Gamblers also differ in life patterns from their spouse. For instance, while 71 percent of gamblers said they gambled while growing up, only half of the spouses said the same. For the spouses of gamblers, gambling is a social event linked to friends and family, while problem gamblers claimed the gambling itself is what matters, not whom one gambles with.

Nearly half of the spouses said that their spouse gambled at least once a week, while another 39 percent said that they gambled daily. As far as the spouses knew, the gamblers gambled alone or with co-workers. Asked why their partner liked to gamble, spouses ventured the same answers as the gamblers themselves: motivations, energy or rush, the desire to escape, and the chance of winning. From their perspective, the energy or adrenaline rush their partner got when gambling was a significant reason why gambling had become a problem:

> It gives them an incredible high, and it's almost a cocaine type of high. It's very different and unique in gambler's brains.

> It's the acceleration and the rush . . . he's pumped. Oh my gosh, I have never seen that much passion in anything else.

Some spouses believed the energy or adrenaline rush was an extension of the emotional excitement and the stimulation a place of gambling offers:

> She likes the noise and excitement about it. She likes all the bells and whistles, the ringing noises and bright lights.

Spouses also understood that gambling was an escape from daily stresses and pressures—a mental and physical escape:

> It's a stress reliever, to get away from everyday life. When she's in the zone, she's not thinking about anything or anyone else.

According to spouses, the chance of "winning big" is a common motivation for gamblers, which makes them come back for more:

> He dreams of being rich. He has very grandiose thinking.

> She wants to strike it rich . . . easy street, you know what I mean?

Spouses sometimes expressed concern that gambling was fuelled by the gambling spouse's urge to possess more than they had and to be able to afford everything they wanted.

> He thinks he can get ahead [by gambling]. That's his way of getting the things in life that he wants.

> Greed—greed for getting more money.

Last Words

Several themes have emerged in this chapter: gambling gives people an opportunity to win money, to get out of the house, to be among other people, and to
experience the excitement of a gambling locale. These combined experiences
give gamblers a rush, a sense of purpose, a feeling of control, and a focus that
is otherwise missing in their lives. The continued need to gamble is a response
often learned in the childhood home, from relatives or friends, or from the mass
media. It is also sometimes a result of social and financial deprivation, combined
with a carefully engineered encouragement toward mass consumption and
gambling.

The availability of casinos, lotteries, and Internet betting and the fierce
advertising by gambling websites ensure that people with a limited income and
limited opportunities, under stress and with low self-esteem, take their chance
at the brass ring. What they ignore is that this socially programmed escapism is
habit-forming. In time, gamblers can't live without it. The result is a downward
spiral—a series of events that consumes their lives, marriages, and family life.

The next chapter discusses the downward spiral of gambling, a common
sequence of often undesirable events that follows from excessive gambling. We
see that beliefs and opinions about gambling lead to actions that in time can
create large, out-of-control personal problems.

Chapter 6
The Downward Spiral of Gambling

Lives based on dreams and fantasies of easy money often run aground. Reality is too unforgiving. This chapter focuses on the downward portion in the classic problem gambling career, as illustrated by the people we studied. Later chapters talk about efforts that some gamblers make to stop the downward spiral and the radical life changes some make to aspire upward—back to normality and stability.

We use the word *career* here purposely, since the word refers to a patterned sequence of life events that is, to varying degrees, both socially structured and open to personal choice. By implication, we reject the notion—often hidden in the idea of *addiction*—that the life changes described in this chapter are inevitable and symptomatic of the health problem itself: that is, life changes like these are not unavoidable outcomes of the medical condition diagnosed as *addiction*.

So, for example, this book does not argue that a problem gambler can never improve until he or she has "hit rock bottom." Nor does it argue that all personal change—whether upward or downward—must proceed through a set of universal, predictable stages, as Prochaska and his collaborators (1986a, 1986b, 1994) have argued. We use the word *career* because it is morally neutral. Unlike the term *addiction*, it implies neither blamelessness (on medical grounds) nor blaming (on moral grounds).

Choosing the word *career* also prevents risky assumptions about causation. Some of the things that happen to problem gamblers during their downward spiral are common to all problem gamblers. For example, sudden shortages of money are characteristic of problem gambling. In this sense, these types of events and situations are likely *results* of the gambling problem itself.

Other events and situations vary from one gambler to another and reflect other factors: for example, cross-addictions to drugs or alcohol; a relative lack of social, cultural, or financial capital; a particularly good or bad marriage; or mental or physical impairments that predate the gambling problem. For some people, a gambling problem begins the downward spiral; in other cases, gambling is merely the new form of a long-existing problem (for example, depression, substance abuse, or a compulsive personality disorder). Indeed, some might argue from our evidence that, for many gamblers, problem gambling is merely a form of self-medication. Like alcohol, drugs—and (some might say also) like compulsive sex, shopping, stock market speculation, religiosity, curio collecting, and so on—problem gambling is a way of finding meaning, hope, and excitement in a world that many experience as empty, bleak, and boring.

Why many people in our society may feel driven to seek meaning, hope, and excitement through problem gambling (or in the other ways mentioned above)— in other words, to self-medicate with gambling—is the subject for another book. Our goal here is to observe that there are predictable social patterns associated with a downward spiral, and this chapter discusses these patterns through a sociological lens. The most important thing to note about a downward spiral is that it is a process of progressive status loss, destabilization, and disconnection.

A Theoretical Approach to the Downward Spiral

When problem gamblers are spiralling downward, they largely stop conforming to the roles they had previously played and stop participating in the groups to which they had previously belonged. That is, they progressively disengage from the rules and groups to which they had previously attached themselves, entering a condition the famous French sociologist Durkheim called *anomie*. This disengagement, which they do in the interests of gambling more often or more freely, can have disastrous consequences. People fare poorly without rules and groups.

Chapter 2 presented an interesting observation by sociologist George Homans: that a person can be healthy and free only when he or she willingly adopts conformity to his or her group's rules. Ideally, group members feel free, and yet they use this freedom to conform to the group's rules.

This finding is echoed in the sociological research on juvenile delinquency: most delinquents funnel back into conformity with general society as they become adults. Why do young people—so many of whom commit delinquent acts while young—stop committing delinquent acts when they are older? The most widely accepted answer among sociologists is based on *social control theory*— that young people cease delinquency when they have a stake in conformity. That is, while most youth could become delinquent, most refuse because they stand to lose too much by doing so. But those who have a low social standing and a poor quality of life have little to lose; when they join delinquent social groups and gangs, they stand to gain status, belonging, and excitement.

Thus, even so-called deviant behaviour is behaviour that typically conforms to some group's rules.

For problem gamblers, there are similar options for group identity. Let's begin with a simple typology. Imagine two dimensions to this typology. First, gamblers may or may not feel they have a stake in belonging to the "normal," nongambling community, which (typically) includes their spouse, family, friends, and workmates. Second, gamblers may or may not feel they have a stake in belonging to a gambling community, with its particular subculture, activities, and memberships. Thus, we can imagine four logical possibilities for groups to which the gambler might conform (See Table 2).

Table 2: Four Possible Options for Group Conformity

		Perceived Stake in the Gambling Community	
		Yes	No
Perceived Stake in	Yes	Double life	Normal life
the Nongambling	No	Gambling life	Downward spiral
Community			(free fall)

During the downward spiral, none of the people we studied is leading a normal life, characterized by an unambiguous and thorough commitment to nongambling activities and groups. At the same time, we find that none is fully leading a gambling life, characterized by an unambiguous and thorough commitment to gambling. Some interviewees reported having led a *gambling life*, or something close to this, at times in their lives. Some expressed feelings of frustration and alienation from all aspects of their lives. They felt they were not secured to either a normal life or gambling life, a condition of *anomie*. The *downward spiral* is a state of moral confusion, which could also be called *free fall*. Individuals in a downward spiral are emotionally volatile and lack a secure social identity, or self-image, in either area.

Finally, some respondents—perhaps most of the gamblers we studied— reported leading a *double life*. They were trying to preserve a stake in both gambling and normal life. For those gamblers, secrecy was key. They strove to keep the family in the dark about their gambling activities, especially about gambling losses. This chapter presents evidence of the conflict, confusion, and ambivalence many gamblers feel about gambling and normal family life. Note that the stresses felt by the gamblers in our study expressed themselves in the language of extreme emotions: anger, self-loathing, grandiosity, and so on. These extreme emotions are not necessarily symptoms of psychiatric pathology or psychological disorientation; they may be normal adjustments to an abnormal social condition.

The double life resembles the *marginal men* described by Everett Stonequist and Robert Park in the 1930s. The *marginal man* (or *person*) is someone who straddles two cultures in society. The marginal person may be rejected by or feel alienated from one or both of the communities to which he or she aspires to belong. As Park wrote in 1937 about immigrants and minority groups: "The marginal man . . . is one whom fate has condemned to live in two societies and in two, not merely different but antagonistic cultures . . . his mind is the crucible in which two different and refractory cultures may be said to melt and, either wholly or in part, fuse" (892).

Included in no community, marginal men are likely to be anomic, troubled, and socially and morally rootless. Some tell lies in hopes of gaining or preserving inclusion in at least one of their communities. Anxiety, secrecy, deception, and a need for self-medication are recurrent themes in their lives, as they are in this book. This speaks to the basic incompatibility between a gambling life and a normal life, and the problem people face when they find themselves attached to both lives or, suddenly, attached to neither.

The Reality of Problem Gambling

Gambling is often portrayed in movies as sexy or glamorous; yet the real life of a problem gambler is usually chaotic and destructive. In time, the appealing aspects of gambling fade away. Gambling has an enormous downside: losing is more common than winning, and gambling debts pile up quickly. The amounts lost by problem gamblers, whose incomes are small and sometimes insecure, can quickly become insurmountable.

Problem gambling is a social, structural problem of society, a result of a combination of mass advertising, consumerism, ethnocultural values, and family traditions. Problem gambling draws much of its popularity from a gambling-supportive and gambling-friendly culture. Though the first losses are financial, problem gamblers eventually suffer other losses—emotional, physical, mental, professional, and social losses; and other people are inevitably hurt by losses as well.

However, even though gambling problems result from public social forces, gamblers suffer privately, often unable or unwilling to prevent or reverse this damage. The stories of problem gamblers are about gradual decline and debasement. They are also stories of worry, deception, financial insecurity, great loss, self-abuse, anxiety, conflict, comorbidity, declining health, and social isolation. Mostly, though, they are stories about a people trapped in the vicious cycle of gambling, forever subject to small ups and large downs.

Our respondents moved forward and backward in their problem gambling career, sometimes skipping certain stages or markers altogether. While most gamblers shared certain common characteristics or circumstances, each problem gambler experienced his or her own downward spiral uniquely.

Findings from the 2003 Study

While relaxation and escape from worries is a common reason for gambling, increased worry is often the result. Gamblers surveyed in our current 2005 study reveal the same worries as the people interviewed in the *At Home with Gambling* (Tepperman *et al.,* 2003) study. Both sets of respondents said they worry about habituation, family members' gambling, losing money, disclosure, losing their job or family, getting in trouble with the law, and comorbidity.

The 2003 study found that adult problem gamblers were 10 times more likely than non-problem respondents to report that they worry about their own gambling. Among adolescent problem gamblers, nearly 4 in 10 reported worrying about their gambling, compared to only 2 percent of non-problem or low-risk adolescent gamblers.

Regardless of frequency, by worrying about the possibility of habituation, many gamblers recognized the damage that gambling can cause. Adult problem gamblers were nearly three times more likely than non-problem gamblers to say that they or members of their family have a gambling problem. Adolescent problem gamblers were twice as likely as non-problem adolescent gamblers to say that they or members of their family have a gambling problem. This finding fits the theory that adolescent gamblers tend to grow up in households where gambling is commonplace, learning the attitudes and behaviours associated with a gambling problem from their parents.

Gamblers also tend to worry about their gambling life. The adult problem gamblers in the 2003 study were about 14 times more likely (28 percent versus 2 percent) to worry about gambling strategies than non-problem gamblers. Among the adolescent respondents, 23 percent worried about strategies, as compared with none of the non-problem or low-risk gamblers. The adult problem gamblers were nearly 20 times more likely (61 percent versus 3 percent) than non-problem gamblers to worry about their finances. Among the adolescent respondents, 23 percent of problem gamblers worried about their finances, compared with only 2 percent of the non-problem or low-risk adolescent gamblers.

Of the adult problem gamblers in the 2003 study, 14 percent worried that their family would find out that they gamble. None of the non-problem adult gamblers worried about this. Of the adult problem gamblers, 8 percent worried about co-workers finding out, while none of the other adult respondents did. Among the adolescent respondents, 8 percent of problem gamblers worried about their family finding out, compared with only 2 percent of non-problem or low-risk adolescent gamblers. As well, 6 percent of the adult problem gamblers worried about losing their job because of gambling, while no other adult respondents did. The adult problem gamblers were also 11 times more likely (11 percent versus 1 percent) than non-problem gamblers to worry about losing their family because of gambling.

In addition, 9 percent of the adult problem gamblers in the 2003 survey worried about getting in trouble with the law over gambling, though none of the other adult respondents shared this worry. Of the adolescent respondents, 15 percent worried about this issue, while none of the non-problem or low-risk adolescent gamblers did. The adult respondents commonly reported that they worried about other addictive behaviours. Whether adult or adolescent, the problem gamblers were more likely than non-problem gamblers to report that they were worried about an addiction to alcohol, cigarettes, or drugs.

Most gamblers also have an incomplete awareness of the depth of their problem. The majority of gamblers from the 2005 study thought that they had a gambling problem, though they believed it existed only some of the time. This statement shows an indecisiveness that allows some gamblers to acknowledge their problem yet continue with their lifestyle unchanged. More than 60 percent of the respondents realized that their problem comes back to "haunt" them. In fact, more than half of respondents (51 percent) believed that their problem is difficult to deal with. Respondents agreed that the problem is a common one, a notion that potentially decreases the respondent's awareness of his or her own problem. A belief in the universality of the problem is an impediment to the process of seeking treatment.

Gamblers are also aware that gambling causes significant problems for both the gamblers and those around them. In the 2005 study, 47 percent of gamblers said they always went back to gambling to win back the money they had just lost; and 45 percent believed that their gambling problem has at times caused financial problems for themselves and the household. Another 38 percent felt that gambling caused them health problems, such as stress. More than 90 percent abused alcohol and, to a lesser degree, marijuana and hashish.

Gamblers in the 2005 study reported damage to their social well-being and a need for social support. Only 32 percent of respondents said they currently gambled with their spouse. One-third of the participants said that they did not have someone in whom they could confide their feelings. This isolation becomes a compounding problem, since relationships can help gamblers deal with their problem. More than one-third of the participants agreed or strongly agreed that they worried about relapse and they were willing to seek help in the event of a relapse. More than one-third also said they were unsure if they could maintain their progress without external help. This is an important worry, since one of the main reasons why gamblers fail to maintain progress is mistaken expectations: a majority of the respondents did not expect relapses to occur and felt they were still struggling with the problem.

The deceptions, self-deceptions, worries, problems, and social isolation compound to create the downward spiral. With an increased involvement in gambling comes an increased neglect of family members and other close (nongambling) associates. As a result, problem gamblers spend much of their time worrying about the effect of their actions on others. This worry creates more suffering among gamblers, and much of their worry leads to secondary problems, such as gambling to recoup previous losses or hiding losses to prevent conflict with a spouse. The worry continues to grow as the stakes get higher, and the gambler goes into the downward spiral. Gamblers often experience great losses that go beyond the financial, creating major problems in gamblers' personal lives as well.

While each downward spiral is unique, all problem gamblers share important common characteristics. These features include

- a preoccupation with winning,
- a heavy investment of time and money in gambling,
- emotional and behavioural changes when gambling,

- financial difficulties due to gambling,
- anxiety and loss of emotional self-control, and
- a variety of personal health defects.

Usually, the gambler keeps his or her suffering private and hidden. Over time, problems associated with gambling intensify, and the symptoms multiply.

The following section discusses this downward spiral as an "ideal type"—the progression that a typical or average gambler takes. An individual gambler may experience some or all of these circumstances. Gamblers may move in different sequences or different rates of change, compared to other gamblers. The discussion is suggestive of the range and significance of these experiences.

The Problem Gambling Continuum

Initiation

Problem gamblers usually start their gambling career as social or recreational gamblers. There is often a particular event—a coincidental series of wins or one large win—which creates a false sense of optimism that puts recreational gamblers on the path to problem gambling. In fact, many problem gamblers in our surveys said that they experienced a big win their first time gambling. When explaining why they gambled, respondents often referred to the joy and excitement they felt during their first win and their search for more wins to relive this experience.

But there is some variety in reasons behind this initiation phase. Many respondents stated that a major attraction of gambling was the social nature of the activity. Others said the hope of solving all of one's problems with a big win was a big motivator. Several respondents claimed that they enjoyed gambling from the outset because of its relaxing qualities. Women especially stated that they were *relief gamblers*, who see gambling as their personal time. Most gamblers did not see financial reasons (for example, being able to pay off debts) as a cause and explained their gambling in terms of fun or relaxation. Thus, from the beginning, each gambler launches into problem gambling for their own mix of reasons and then lives out their personal downward spiral.

The shift from social or recreational gambling to problem gambling often occurs quickly, within weeks or even days of initiation. What begins as harmless excitement rapidly turns into a physiological reaction that is dependent on gambling. Many gamblers become enthralled with the atmosphere of the casino and the rush of winning or even the mere possibility of winning. These psychological and physiological changes often last for hours after gambling and are noticeable even after the gambler has returned home. Spouses described witnessing a clear personality change in their partner, a change they described as unusually happy or even childlike. Gamblers increased the frequency of their gambling in hopes of experiencing the thrill of a win sooner and more often.

The Negative Reactions

The honeymoon effect of the initiation wears off quickly. Because losses are more common than wins, negative reactions become more frequent than positive ones. Since wins and losses are unpredictable, the result is extreme and uncontrollable mood swings:

> When you're up, you're in a good mood and when you are down it's just like boom—depressed, big time. Angry.

> I get grumpy [when gambling]. And sometimes I change my mood. I get angry if someone tells me not to play this.

Many gamblers in the 2005 study described mentally berating themselves:

> If I played stupid, I'd be mad at myself if I felt that I should have won; [if I] lost because I played dumb, then I'll be mad at myself because of that.

> I don't get aggressive—[just] sad and depressed—those types of feelings, knowing that I didn't win and knowing that I'm not going to get my bills paid—just the after effects.

The negative emotions are as visible as the positive ones, and partners reported often being aware of the negative personality changes. While the gamblers just reported getting more intense while gambling, the spouses claimed they turned into different people:

> It causes a constant preoccupation with the gambling and thinking about the gambling. He loses the ability to engage when he's in that zone … He doesn't bet big amounts of money—it's a dollar or two dollars—but it's more the effects of being in a gambling zone, where he's constantly preoccupied

with it, and he's constantly disengaged with his family and the kids, and he's disengaged from positive feelings.

The problem gamblers were often aware of the mood swings they experienced because of gambling:

> It is just a rush that you get when you win. I am a bad loser (laughs). I really hate losing, so when I lose I really get depressed. But the winning, the feeling you get of winning is worth taking a risk of losing. So that is why I like to gamble. It is that risk—that excitement you get that you don't know what is going to happen. The time just keeps flying there.

Gamblers are willing to risk emotional lows and financial losses to feel the excitement of the next big win. This is more than a willingness to take a risk—it is a *need* to gamble.

Increased Neglect

Despite the losses and the negative emotions they experience, gamblers find themselves devoting more of their time and money to it. Gamblers progress faster into the downward spiral when they start chasing losses. As their emotional attachment to the gambling thrill grows, the frequency of gambling naturally grows, too.

Gamblers often begin to neglect various other aspects of their lives. The most often neglected aspect of a gambler's life is his or her family. According to the spouses in our study, long hours—even successive days—spent gambling took away from family time and the chance to share activities together:

> I said, "I'm no longer going to be willing to, especially on the weekends, wait until 10, 11 o'clock to see you." That's when most couples do things. So I said, "I'm not putting up with that anymore." So he changed it to 8 [o'clock]. It was all right for a couple of weeks, but then he would say, "Oh I can't really come tonight because it is special races from the States." You know, some excuse.

The gamblers admitted that they were very engaged in their gambling and that their spouses didn't like it:

> Irene is very, very against [my gambling]. A lot of it has not so much to do with the money, but the hours. You know you can disappear for two or three days, [but] I don't want to come home after eight or nine hours, I want to stay there.

Once a person's gambling causes them to neglect the family, their ties with the family are weakened and strained, making problem gambling a family problem.

Gamblers also often begin to neglect their work. What keeps some gamblers from skipping work to gamble is the fear of losing one's job:

> The only time I really say no [to gambling] is if I'm going to work. There's been times that I've skipped work to go to bingo, but for the most part, I always choose making money over winning money.

Gamblers also neglect other responsibilities, such as education:

> I may spend more time than I want to doing it. The money aspect of it is not a problem because I play low stakes, but as far as timing is concerned, it might start affecting my school work . . . It's taking time away from my studying.

Time spent away from work and school results in missed skills and a decreased likelihood of success in those spheres. As a result, the gambler's occupational opportunities are reduced. He or she becomes more reliant on gambling as a source of income.

Problem gamblers often become so absorbed in their gambling that they may even neglect their personal health:

> My husband is on insulin twice a day, injections. Now his weight has ballooned so much that he has trouble bending down. Being overweight is a no-no when you've got diabetes; you just can't afford it . . . If it's the health part of it, he'll say, "I told you not to worry, if I drop dead that's my problem." I'll say, "What if you end up in a wheelchair? I have to take care of you. What if you get a stroke?" He'll say, "Put me in a home, I have enough money to pay for it."

Some of the respondents were candid about the issue of health effects. But their only concern was the win, which trumped fears regarding personal health:

> The past six or seven months, I have been doing it [gambling] again very frequently. I have no care for family or even food.

Compulsion and Loss of Control

In time, gamblers feel less of the enjoyment that initially drew them to gambling and more anxiety and loss of control. Worry and guilt become more severe as the gambling problem worsens. The problem gamblers in our study described an increasing number of gambling occasions that were mainly negative—occasions characterized by stress, fear, and anxiety:

> Gambling is very, very stressful . . . I [feel] guilty at the gambling table, guilty that I threw out the money foolishly. I could have thrown the same money out on better things. I could have saved a thousand bucks.

> When you are gambling, you've got anxiety. You are always waiting for the heart [attack] and stroke . . . Just a bit of anxiety that is not necessary and you never end up winning.

Some gamblers admitted they were both preoccupied with gambling and helpless to stop it. This inability to quit gave them a feeling of being out of control, and many gamblers wished they could stop:

> [Gambling's] good in small amounts, but when I get in the rush, it takes over, and again . . . it's more than I can handle sometimes. I did try to figure out how to get away from it, but I always get back into it somehow.

> I am always losing, and then I end up with the migraine, because I get stressed and get worried and angry and all that. I take at least six tablets of migraine [medicine] in my bag every time I go to the casino, because I know I will end up taking it—every time I go—and yet I want to go, I can't say no.

For gamblers far along in their habituation, any amount of winning is never enough. The emotions gamblers described reflect a desperate compulsion:

Money didn't mean anything. I just kept playing. I wanted to win. I owed about $400,000 and I wanted to make some money, and $60,000 wasn't enough. It was never enough.

Though gamblers may be aware when they are out of control, they are unable to justify quitting. The physical and emotional need to gamble overrides any attempt to frame the activity as unnecessary or harmful.

When they are not gambling, gamblers may experience unpleasant emotional and physiological reactions some describe as similar to the "strung out" feeling from an addictive drug:

It is out of control. It was really out of control years ago. It was like Jonesing for drugs. Trying to get money [to gamble] was like trying to get a fix.

Severe problem gamblers often reach a point where they have physically uncontrollable and insatiable needs to gamble.

Comorbidity

Problem gamblers in the 2005 study often displayed *comorbidity*—symptoms of another addiction in addition to problem gambling. Research shows that problem gamblers have high rates of substance abuse, and vice versa (Hardoon *et al.*, 2004; Toneatto and Brennan, 2002). Other disorders may blend with the gambling problem in various ways.

Comorbidity refers to the presence of two or more disorders within an individual (Petry, 2005). There are three ways to imagine the causal relationship between problem gambling and other disorders: (1) problem gambling as the direct *cause* of a secondary disorder, (2) problem gambling as the direct *result* of another more primary disorder, or (3) problem gambling as one of a *pair* of disorders with a common cause (Winters and Kushner, 2003).

Substance abuse and mood and anxiety disorders are two major classes of disorders commonly associated with problem gambling. McIntyre *et al.* (2007) finds that people with bipolar I disorder are more likely to show symptoms of problem gambling than both people with major depressive disorder (MDD) and the general population. Similarly, while problem gamblers are at a greater risk than the general population to also be substance abusers, people with a history of substance abuse are disproportionately more likely to develop a gambling problem within their lifetime than non-substance abusers (Pietrzak *et al.*, 2007).

The first causal type of gambling comorbidity is that gambling may predispose vulnerable individuals to other disorders, thereby causing a secondary disorder. Evidence does show that people are more likely to drink alcohol when gambling than during other control activities. Of course, the causal sequence may be more complicated than this: for example, a chain of negative life events may cause a person to develop both a gambling problem and a drinking problem.

The alcohol-gambling comorbidity indicates that excessive alcohol consumption can lead to a greater willingness to gamble. Thus, in the second form of comorbidity, problem gambling can result from particular disorders (such as problem drinking) that predispose vulnerable individuals to problem gambling. For example, many studies have described how alcohol consumption reduces cognitive processes, such as decision-making, risk-related judgments, and attentional focus (Winters and Kushner, 2003), which may lead a person to act rashly.

The third causal type of comorbidity—that problem gambling and comorbid disorders may share common underlying causes—also informs views on problem gambling comorbidity. Specific risk factors that are common to both problem gambling and specific psychiatric disorders may include personality traits such as disinhibition and inadequate stress management. Psychiatric disorders associated with attentional processes and impulse control, such as ADHD and bipolar I disorder, and genetic configurations mediating appetitive urges may play a part (Winters and Kushner, 2003).

In general, research tends to support more than one causal explanation for any condition. For example, Hodgins *et al.* (2005) finds the age of onset for substance abuse is earlier than the age of onset for problem gambling, which supports the theory that other disorders precede and potentially contribute to problem gambling. However, mood disorders are no more likely to either precede or follow problem gambling, which seems to support the theory that problem gambling and mood disorders may share a common cause.

Some research shows that gambling may promote smoking and alcohol use, which is consistent with the findings in our 2003 and 2005 studies. Several respondents claimed to smoke or drink *only* when they gambled. Other gamblers admitted that they smoke or drink *more than usual* while gambling:

[I've been smoking] since I was 17. But I'm a social smoker and I'm not an every-minute smoker. I'm not going to bingo today until midnight, ten o'clock tonight, and I won't smoke until I get to bingo.

Interviewer: Was there a worst [gambling] experience that you can remember?

B: Yeah, just recently. I mean, basically, not even remembering what I did or how I did or where I gambled. It is, basically, alcohol involved in it.

Interviewer: So you drink usually when you gamble?

B: Yeah. Most of the time . . . all of the time. It is a trigger.

For these individuals, gambling causes or aggravates substance abuse.

Some respondents reported experiencing several coexisting addictions involving destructive, illicit substances. One respondent admitted to using cocaine, alcohol, and cigarettes as stimulants to stay awake while gambling for three days straight:

Sometimes you're up, you can't sleep, what the fuck, so you go out and have a cigarette, smoke some dope, and "Fuck this . . . I fucking have to do a little line here or a drink . . . " Some [gamblers] drink like a fish, so I got out of those games, I don't like those guys, they are too intoxicated, too stupid.

As this respondent suggested, problem gamblers who abuse substances may not be at their best when they wager large sums of money on games of chance.

What is particularly disturbing is that gambling establishments often promote the substance abuse disorders of their patrons. Casinos, for example, often offer patrons free alcoholic drinks:

The drinking just makes you stupid. You don't think about what you are doing, so that's a huge influence. You go to the bar, and everything is so perfect and so central in the casino. The bar is right there, and the tables are right there, and they walk around and serve you drinks, so basically it's a bad mix.

While it is already difficult for gamblers to abstain from gambling, encouragements to abandon all caution make it even more difficult to fight against indulging in other substances, too.

Thus, comorbidities contribute to the downward spiral experienced by problem gamblers by worsening personal health and encouraging addictive behaviour.

The Financial Downward Spiral

Each gambler experiences the financial downward spiral in a different way and to a different degree. Furthermore, each gambler uses different means to cope with this aspect of the problem. When the big win doesn't come, problem gamblers often turn to illegal ways of getting money to recover their losses. Ultimately, the gambler's individual actions result in negative outcomes for self and family.

Desperate Acts in the Name of Gambling

Gamblers are habituated to betting, just as substance abusers are addicted to drugs. Since losing is more frequent than winning, problem gamblers consistently need money to continue betting. Once a gambler has exhausted all personal finances, they begin to look for other ways to get the money they need to gamble.

Often, problem gamblers free up money for gambling by making personal sacrifices. Some of these sacrifices include small changes to buying habits and budgeting:

> I save my weekly and monthly expense and add it to my gambling secret account. For example, I'll walk and save my TTC tokens and put that towards my secret account. I'll avoid eating out and I'll bring my own coffee.

Other sacrifices may include reaching out to important people in the gambler's life who might be willing to help them—such as spouses or parents.

When the need for money increases, and easy sources have been exhausted, problem gamblers often search for legal ways to make more money available. Several gamblers take on another job to support their gambling habit. Some gamblers pick up an extra job so they might have money that is solely theirs, allowing them to continue gambling without any supervision.

When another job is unavailable, or large sums of money are needed immediately, some problem gamblers take out a loan. They may seek loans from banks, loan companies, or relatives:

> I spent seven hundred dollars one night and I just blew it all . . . playing slots and blackjack. We just borrowed and borrowed and borrowed from a couple of people . . . [We borrow] probably once a month . . . Usually I do those payday loan things.

Every month, by the time I get my disability cheque, I owe my mother at least a hundred dollars. Right now, I owe my 16-year-old $500, all from bingo because I'm not winning. Needless to say, he's not very happy because he got his first job this summer. I promised I'd give it to him by October 1, and I don't have it. He's on me every day, upset with me, so it's very hard.

Borrowing money can become as habitual as gambling itself, as problem gamblers often come to rely on it. By habitually taking loans, gamblers increase their debt, worsen relations with friends and family, and ruin their credit.

Efforts to find money to gamble often become less legitimate as gamblers become more desperate. Gamblers often lie about needing help so they can secure loans from loved ones:

I keep losing money, so I keep having to borrow from Peter to pay Paul. It is this circle that I get involved in, where you are forever lying to do this, to do that, to cover that. You forget who you are lying to. You know that there is $10,000 owed here, so you've gotta do that, so you go here and do that, but you've forgotten that you've already paid . . . You end up lying and manipulating things.

Spouses reported becoming irate about this situation:

He pressured me for a lot of money . . . Six weeks after that, [though] I don't work now, he borrowed $1,100 and he never paid it back. That's when I should have walked, because he showed his true colours. He lied about what it was for and the whole nine yards.

Gamblers also lie about the reason they need a loan to keep their problem secret and increase their odds of getting the money. They may not want to hurt or lie to their loved ones, but their ultimate concern is being able to gamble. Often, gamblers have to sell their prized possessions to cover the debts they owe:

I sold a car one time, and then my 56 Oldsmobile, but I got that back. I had two other cars I sold. I had a 69 Dodge Super B that I didn't want to sell [but] I sold it through horses and card games . . . and I had a 69 Plymouth Roadrunner and I sold that. I lost on them because they were both a lot of money and both [brought] next to nothing.

When lying no longer works, gamblers sometimes take up illegal activities. For example, if a gambler knows someone with money and doubts that lying will get them the money, they may just steal it:

> A lot of times, the only times I was gambling regularly, I was embezzling money from work to gamble. It got that bad, and I stopped gambling for a while. Then I started, you know. I eventually got fired, because I started trying to pill money from people's credit cards. Gambling also led me to a shoplifting addiction, because I was just too proud to go to food banks and whatever. I got caught twice in one month and sent to jail.

Gamblers also steal in secondary ways. By gambling away all the household's money, a gambler robs his or her family of its money:

> I used to spend the whole paycheque, the rent, the food, the bill money, everything . . . then I lied about it. She caught on when I lost so much in a month . . . like close to $1,800 in a month.

> He wouldn't give the kids her [birthday] cards. We knew that if she gave them a card, she'd give them money. So he would take everything, everything—he would destroy the card and keep the money. And a couple of times we found the card in his glove compartment and I was like, "Oh my God."

By stealing even birthday money from family members, gamblers place their gambling problem before their family and risk wrecking their personal relations.

Once gamblers have exhausted all of their means of getting money, and they have gambled away all of their financial resources, they are forced to declare bankruptcy:

> I went bankrupt a few years ago. I lost my car and I haven't bothered to get another one. I drive hers.

But even having to declare bankruptcy may not be enough to break a problem gambler's betting cycle.

Though this brings gamblers close to the bottom of the downward financial spiral, it may not end the gambling. Some own up to the desperation gambling has caused:

Gambling has forced me to do a lot of things [I] didn't want to do to get money.

It is remarkable, though, how many of these gamblers fail to learn from their mistakes.

Secrecy and Alienation

When gambling persists, even after a gambler has hit financial bottom, problem gamblers put their families at enormous risk. The use of deception to conceal a gambling problem results in alienation for both the gambler and his or her spouse.

Gamblers rarely use the funds they have culled from various sources to pay off debts. They believe that the big win will restore their life to normal and may even improve it:

I'm having trouble finding [a new apartment] I can afford. Being on disability, I only get $1,400 month, and I can't take something dirty. Everywhere I go they are telling me "It's clean, it's clean." So I've been trying to win and I've been getting the last number for a long time now to win $1,000 because I need two months' deposit. I figure I have spent about $600 [gambling] trying to get my deposit for my apartment, because I can't put two months [rent] together.

The first day I lost $1,500, I went home and thought "How did I lose it, and how do I recover it?" I was stressed out. I ate no food and just thought about how to cover this up. I thought about how I should tell my family. I thought about how to sort out this mess. How to recover the money haunted me. I made a plan for the next day. I said that I would play more sensibly. I told myself I would play some games at less risk. I made an outline—a plan to play this game at a certain risk. I stepped into the casino and for the first hour I was well behaved. Then I lost the money and started saying that I would have to make it up.

What problem gamblers fail to recognize is that gambling can't be used to solve problems. More gambling increases debt; it doesn't reduce debt. The anticipated big win is virtually impossible to get; and even if the gambler did win big, he or she would continue gambling until the big win is gone. Gamblers often change strategies in the hope that they can increase their chances of winning. What they fail to accept is that the odds are always stacked against them.

Since severe financial trouble becomes hard to hide, spouses start asking questions and often ask the partner to stop gambling. Many problem gamblers respond by lying about the frequency of their gambling and the funds lost:

> [Though] I never lie, I'm forced to lie because of this gambling. I lie about how much money I've spent, or lost, and how long I've gambled for, etc.

While gamblers may think that they are successful at hiding their activities from their families, their spouses often know or suspect what is going on.

Moreover, spouses who are kept in the dark are prevented from offering the help or encouragement the gambler needs to stop the gambling. Gamblers who manage to deceive their spouses remain free to spiral out of control:

> If nobody is there to care or to want good things for you or try to push you in the right direction, then you are just going to fall harder, right? How bad it got—with him, gambling was feeding and adding to his depression.

This feeling that nobody cares and nothing matters is Durkheim's *anomie*, a lack of regulation and connectivity that can lead to (among other things) suicide. As Durkheim showed, marriages are particularly good at providing the external control that reduces anomie. But by lying about their gambling problem, gamblers are purposely freeing themselves from this external control and exposing themselves to an increased risk of self-destruction. Problem gamblers often feel a high degree of alienation or isolation from the world outside of gambling:

> I have a problem, because if I bring [home] 300 now, it's nothing. I should bring like 500. That's the most I bring. Sometimes I lose my whole paycheque. So, when I saw your ads, I said, "I think I need help." There is a gambling help line . . . but I never . . . talk about [gambling]. It's good to talk about it. Because most of my friends they don't gamble, I'm the only one. So I don't talk about it. They will not understand me.

Gamblers often find themselves alienated, confused, and broke when they hit the bottom of their downward spiral. They have expended all of their financial resources, they have lied to or stolen from all of their friends and relatives, and they feel that they have no one they can reach out to. Yet even with all of these major problems, some gamblers try to deal with their losses by returning to gambling, meaning the self-destructive cycle of gambling has, once again, come full circle.

Conclusion

This chapter illustrates how many of the gamblers we interviewed were caught in a vicious downward spiral of problem gambling. The gamblers themselves were often aware of their problem and, to varying degrees, they worried about its impact on their lives. Because they rarely won, they often found themselves spinning out of control, compelled to increase their betting while failing to fulfill their responsibilities. When faced with the negative results of their gambling, many chose to make personal sacrifices or commit immoral or illegal activities to fund their habit.

The next chapter explores how the downward spiral affects intimate relationships and family life. What may appear at first to be an isolated experience for the problem gambler quickly reveals itself as a downward spiral also experienced by the problem gambler's loved ones.

Chapter 7

Worsening Family Relations

While gamblers are experiencing their downward spiral, their marital relationships suffer in turn. Problem gambling affects both the individual and the family by increasing stresses on the family. The families of problem gamblers have to respond to the stresses caused by financial difficulty or poverty, caregiving, secrecy, and uncertainty. Families of gamblers respond differently, some better than others.

How Stress Affects Families

Family stress is "a state that arises from an actual or perceived imbalance between a 'stressor' (that is, challenge, threat) and capability (that is, resources, coping) in the family's functioning" (Huang, 1991:289). One factor that always influences stress is the nature of the stressor event itself, as measured by its severity, intensity, duration, and timing. Problem gambling poses problems for families for all these reasons: the crises it causes (for example, unpaid bills or secretive activities) may recur often, and the effects (distrust, deception, anger) may be long-lasting.

How family members view and define the stressor controls the way they react to it. In addition, how they evaluate an event may differ from the way an outside researcher evaluates it. Yet a belief in their ability to cope increases the family's actual ability to cope. Sociologists are interested in learning how stress changes the roles and relationships that make up a family. They study the ways stress affects patterns of communication and interaction, marital satisfaction, or parental competence within the family. Sociologists continue to find that economic pressure on a family increases parental unhappiness and marital conflict. It also increases parent–adolescent conflicts (Conger, Ge, and Elder, 1994). In turn, these hostile exchanges increase the risk of adolescent emotional and behavioural problems. Typically, mental health worsens as economic problems such as unemployment and underemployment increase. Essentially, sociologists are interested in how family members cope and adjust to long-term stressors. A family's success in coping with a stressor event depends on the strength or quality of its crisis-meeting resources, such as cohesion and flexibility.

Family Life Transitions

Family life transitions typically refer to events that are predicted and expected in average families: birth, death, marriage, divorce, retirement, the empty-nest, and so on. They all have disruptive, stressful effects, even though they are common and foreseeable. Migration can also be considered a typical family transition: immigrant families typically face acculturative stress, because of the strains of adapting to a new society, and prolonged stress of this kind can harm a family. Chronic stressors confronting families include poverty, inequality, and unemployment. They all increase stress, reduce resilience, and hinder every part of a family's well-being, even including the physical health of its members. Racism is another chronic source of stress for visible minorities, even for those who are economically successful.

It's into this context of regular family stressors that the additional stress of problem gambling is mixed. For some families, the total burden pushes them to the breaking point.

Caregiving as a Source of Family Stress

More than 20 percent of Canadian seniors receive the help of family members because of long-term health problems (Keating *et al.*, 1999:99). Long-term care for the elderly, disabled, or severely ill (including the addicted) can put great strains on a family's functioning. As a result, caregivers often have to change their social activities or their sleep patterns, or give up holiday plans (Keating *et al.*, 1999:69). In some ways, problem gambling has the same effect on a family as an illness.

Often most of the health-care responsibilities and attendant strains fall on one family member—usually the main adult female. Women are almost twice as likely as men to give someone personal care, and as a result, they experience caregiving strain, work interference, income loss, and role strain (Fredriksen, 1996). Overall, women with better social support and better psychosocial health are more satisfied with the care their spouse is receiving (Dawson and Rosenthal, 1996).

Many families learn to cope with these additional burdens by taking advantage of the resources available. Support from family, friends, and community agencies buffers the impact of caregiving, overwork, and family role strain. Overall, caregivers with larger support networks—especially of women and kin—report lower levels of stress. Close relationships with people who are both personal supporters and caregivers lighten the load of caregiving (Wright, 1994).

Certainly, caring for ill family members drains the resources of the family and especially of the main caregiver. But two broad categories of resources—financial/material and emotional/psychological—are key in permitting certain families to withstand these crises. *Financial/material resources* refers to cash on hand, plus the credit available to borrow money as needed. Time and money ease these strains, but neither resource is equally available to all Canadians. *Psychological/ emotional resources* refers to the caregiver's and family's internal abilities to withstand misfortune: coping skills; self-confidence, calmness, and bravery; feelings of trust and affection for other family members; communication skills; and a willingness to risk change for the collective good. Families with a good stock of psychological/emotional resources are the most able to withstand stresses.

Social support other than family is also important for the main caregiver for achieving and keeping good health. Social support includes information that diffuses through social channels. To be useful, social support must give caregivers the right information and encouragement at the right time. Useful information becomes valuable by passing through people in the caregiver's social network— and people whom the listener trusts and respects confirm the information. With reliable information, the caregiver can make decisions with confidence.

These social networks are also important relative to the person who is ill. Illness is partly a biological event and partly a socially performed drama. In return for being allowed to deviate from their everyday activities and neglect their social duties, sick people have to appear ill, consult a doctor, and follow the doctor's advice. It is through interaction in social networks that people recognize or admit to health problems, contact health professionals, and comply with medical advice.

Doctors play a key role in this social network. They are primary advisers who resolve confusion over conflicting information. Interpersonal trust depends on the degree to which patients see their doctors as competent, responsible, and caring. If their doctors are not available, many patients and caregivers look for replacement help from *support groups*. Yet informal social support groups are more valuable than formal support groups: people get far more of the information and encouragement they need from their personal networks than from special-purpose support groups (Ganster and Victor, 1988). In general, social relationships of all types give people a *sense* that they are receiving social support, and this *sensed* social support is important to their well-being (Gottlieb, 1985). Strong social networks get people to address their medical needs and make adequate use of the health-care system (Freidenberg and Hammer, 1998).

Strong social networks make a difference to the care a sick person receives: large, cohesive networks are best for people's health (Tennestedt and McKinlay, 1987), since they typically promote higher levels of social participation. Social participation, in turn, leads to higher levels of well-being and life satisfaction. Because social networks can be useful in promoting good health, some health programs encourage forming new self-sustaining friendship networks. A key part of all case management is rebuilding social support networks damaged by illness or an inability to cope with severe illness (Pescosolido, Wright, and Sullivan, 1995).

Support and Coping: A Systems View

What makes family life regular and predictable, despite change and occasional turmoil? Every family is locked into certain ways of thinking and behaving, and these patterns provide sameness. Thus, change can help or hinder a family, depending on how healthy their patterns are. For example, the way a family responds to the problems associated with problem gambling depends on the family, its organization, and its history. Changes to any of these factors usually affect interactions between family members. If the interactions were strong to begin with, change may weaken them; if they were weak or dysfunctional in some way, change may provide the impetus to improve them.

In general, big changes transform a family from one form to another. Family rituals may disappear as a result. Family rituals—complex, meaningful patterns of interaction—often mark changes in the lives of family members. They are important to families as sources of strength, because they uphold a family's system of shared behaviours and beliefs and communicate its identity. So, the collapse of family ritual is itself a new problem that needs solving, in addition to the change that created it.

As well, sometimes changes that occur for one individual in the family are out of sync with those of other members. Such out-of-phase changes can cause conflict. Some families are better able than others to adapt to such changes over the life cycle. Similarly, every family has a view (or multiple views) about lifestyle issues. If a family has a negative view of gambling or addiction, and one family member reveals a problem in this area, this poses problems the family must confront. But it must confront them in a manner that is consistent with its culture, traditions, and patterns to prevent further damage to itself.

Some families become very good at solving problems. They change themselves in response to changes in their environment and are capable of learning from their mistakes. Families can change by changing their beliefs, changing their roles, building a sense of optimism, and developing social interests (Dinkmeyer and Sherman, 1989). But solving problems is easiest if the parties share the same beliefs and ideas. These similarities in family relationships, which tend to be stable over time, support family cohesion, which in turn reinforces those similarities (Deal, Wampler, and Halverson, 1992). In well-functioning families, problem solving is an educational process of self-discovery. Families learn different ways to resolve conflict and change disabling ways of dealing with one another.

Though all families change and solve problems, some families do so better, easier, and faster than others because their members grew up with the benefit of experience in well-functioning families. These families have stronger traditions of leadership than others, which helps children grow up with a solid picture of leaders taking charge of problems. Strong families contain members who are willing to take responsibility for the family interest and who try to mobilize support for a plan of action.

Moreover, families with stronger traditions of communication are better able to talk about their problems, which helps them solve them. For example, among the families of patients surviving bone marrow transplants and maintenance chemotherapy, well-functioning families—families that can discuss their problems and hash out their differences—are associated with better adjustment in every respect: physical, emotional, and social (Molassiotis, Van den Akker, and Boughton, 1997). Some families solve problems through communication-based methods, such as family therapy, counselling, and family mediation. Family therapy and participation in support groups can balance one another, providing one forum to talk informally with others and reduce feelings of isolation, and providing another forum to talk formally to treat the complex issues of family dynamics (Goldstein, 1990).

In general, functional families share several characteristics that enable them to face challenges such as the intrusion of problem gambling into their lives. These families often have solid coping skills. In addition, they have good systemic properties: a high degree of *cohesion* and a high degree of *flexibility*. This means that family roles and relationships can change when necessary, yet they are strong enough to last when no one needs or wants change. Families with strong systemic properties can even endure the weaknesses and poor coping skills of their individual members. At the same time, too much cohesion or flexibility is undesirable: an excess of cohesion is repressive, stifling individual development and producing family members who are less competent and flexible than they need to be; and an excess of flexibility reveals that there is insufficient normative support in the family.

But some families are unable to cope with large-scale problems. Unable to deal effectively with their problems, some cope through a harmful form of religious denial, such as the belief that a miracle is going to save them (York, 1987). Since miracles are rare, the problems remain. Weak families indulge in this kind of unrealistic thinking, as well as self-blame, distancing, and denial (Judge, 1998). When problem gambling enters one of these families, the weak structures holding them together can collapse.

Literature on the Effects of Gambling on Families

The most noticeable and difficult recurring problem that families of problem gamblers face is financial difficulty. According to the National Council of Welfare (1996), problem gamblers are more likely to borrow money than non-gamblers. In Quebec, a provincial study found that 83 percent of problem gamblers borrow from friends, relatives, and banks to settle their gambling debts. Roughly one-third of the Quebec sample declared bankruptcy with outstanding debts between $75,000 and $150,000 (Ladouceur *et al.*, 1994). The extent of these financial losses is astonishing.

Lorenz and Shuttlesworth (1983) found that financial difficulties are often so great in gambling families that just over half of the spouses surveyed have to borrow money from family and friends to meet the family's basic needs. Most spouses surveyed also said they financially contribute to paying off their partner's debts, with roughly two-thirds having given up their personal savings, and 46 percent giving up personal earnings to do so.

The financial strain causes an emotional strain. Feelings of anger, resentment, isolation, frustration, depression, and confusion, as well as thoughts of suicide are commonly noted among wives of problem gamblers (Lorenz and Yaffee, 1988; Lorenz and Shuttlesworth, 1983). These emotions result from both chronic financial difficulties and a lack of emotional closeness with one's partner. In one study, roughly 37 percent of respondents said their spouse spends too little time with their children (Lorenz and Shuttlesworth, 1983). A lack of quality time with one's children also impacts the gambler's emotional well-being, especially as it relates to one's attachment with one's children.

In addition, in a NORC survey of ten communities in the United States, six communities reported an increase in domestic violence cases since introducing casinos in their area (National Gambling Impact Study Commission, 1999). Further, Lorenz and Shuttlesworth (1983) found that 43 percent of spouses surveyed were exposed to some form of emotional, verbal, or physical abuse. A related study by the National Council of Welfare (1996) found that spouses of gamblers are more violent than the public average.

Given these negative dynamics, the health of the gambler and his or her spouse are frequently compromised. Lorenz and Yaffee (1988, 1986) found various illnesses, such as high blood pressure, backaches, vertigo, and gastrointestinal conditions, are more common than average among gamblers and their partners. In the same vein, Dickerson (1995) found that spouses of problem gamblers experience both stress-related physical symptoms (sleeping problems, for example) and emotional problems (such as depression or suicidal thoughts), both of which mirror the issues of the problem gambler.

A person's gambling can also lead to unhealthy behaviours in his or her spouse. A study of male problem gamblers found that the wives were likely to develop gambling problems too (Lorenz and Shuttlesworth, 1983). Most likely, these wives used gambling as one of many destructive coping mechanisms to deal with problems caused by their husband's gambling. Other unhealthy behaviours, such as excessive spending, alcoholism, drug abuse, and overeating, are also common as a response to a partner's gambling problem (Zion, Tracey, and Abell, 1991).

Furthermore, studies show that children in gambling families are more likely to experience serious problems in adolescence and later in their adult lives (Browne and Browne, 1993; Griffiths, 1989; Ladouceur et al., 1994). They report feelings of anger, anguish, loneliness, guilt, abandonment, and rejection. Firsthand accounts by children portray chronic absences, which lead these children to view the problem-gambling parent as unreliable and untrustworthy, as well as lacking in concern and love (Darbyshire, Oster, and Carrig, 2001). In a qualitative study, Darbyshire, Oster, and Carrig (2001) found that children between the ages of 7 and 18 come to describe the home environment as unpredictable, inconsistent, and tense.

On average, children with parents who gamble score higher than average on anxiety-related and depressive indicators, as well as showing greater feelings of insecurity, inadequacy, and inferiority (Jacobs *et al.*, 1989), especially if their parents have multiple addictions (Lesieur and Rothschild, 1989). Jacobs and his colleagues (1989) reported that children of gamblers use more tobacco, alcohol, and drugs than other children and show a greater preference for stimulants. Many of these adolescents rank the need for relaxation or stimulation as their main goal. This group also appears to be at a greater risk of developing a permanent addictive pattern of behaviour (Jacobs *et al.*, 1989).

Physical abuse exists alongside neglect in studies on parenting by problem gamblers (Lorenz and Shuttlesworth, 1983; NGISC, 1999; Lesieur and Rothschild, 1989; Jacobs *et al.*, 1989). Lesieur and Rothschild (1989) found a notable increase in the prevalence of physical violence between children with gambling parents versus those with nongambling parents. Physical violence is more likely to come from gamblers' wives (37 percent) than from the gamblers (8 percent) themselves (Lorenz, 1981). This is most likely because gamblers spend more time outside gambling than at home, with their families.

But gamblers have many reasons to preserve their marriages, in spite of gambling-related grievances. These reasons may include love for one's spouse, a spouse's support and understanding, or the need to get a spouse's help for their problem. For spouses, reasons may include a fear of facing the world alone, preserving the family for the sake of the children, love for the gambler, a belief the gambling will end, a lack of confidence, shame and embarrassment over leaving, and a lack of finances (Lorenz and Yaffee, 1986, 1988); and some fear retribution from the gambler if the spouse leaves. Since women are more likely to earn less than their male counterparts, and since they have unstable work paths due to childbearing and parenting, they may feel that they have less opportunity to exit the marriage.

Quantitative Data from the 2003 At Home with Gambling *Study*

Much of what is discussed in the literature on gambling and family life is also present in both the *At Home with Gambling* study and the current 2005 study. Several gambling-related marital issues are visible in the quantitative data.

Data from the *At Home* study (Tepperman *et al.*, 2003) show that adult problem gamblers are nearly three times as likely as non-problem gamblers to report that gambling has led to family problems (51 percent versus 19 percent). Also, families of problem gamblers may be less cohesive than others, as 33 percent of the problem gamblers in the survey reported family activities occurring once a week or less. These problem gamblers were also more likely to be separated, in common-law relationships, or divorced than non-problem gamblers, likely the result of the higher rate of family problems experienced by the problem gamblers.

The family problems, lack of shared activities, and high incidence of divorce among the adult and adolescent problem gamblers in the 2003 study is consistent with the findings in the literature. These problems reveal how gambling evolves from a personal problem to a family problem.

Quantitative Data from the 2005 Study

Although the 2005 study was exploratory, we did collect quantitative data from the interviews and questionnaires, using standard scales and indicators. By performing a correlation analysis to discover relationships between the scales used for data collection, we were able to find patterns in the responses.

Correlation of Scales and Measurement Tools

In this study, like most social science studies, we used a series of standard scales, or composite measures of the variables that interested us most. Some scales have both a name and an acronym: as mentioned earlier, we measured problem gambling with the Canadian Problem Gambling Index, or CPGI. We measured marital (or "dyadic") adjustment with the Revised Dyadic Adjustment Scale (RDAS). We also devised a new scale—the Embeddedness Scale—that is described and explained at length in Chapter 9.

First, we found that the Canadian Problem Gambling Index (CPGI) Scale is negatively correlated with the Similarity to Partner Scale ($r= -.395$), Time Spent with Partner Scale ($r= -.395$), and Revised Dyadic Adjustment Scale (RDAS; $r= -.449$). In other words, as the problem gambling score (CPGI) increases (showing a movement toward problem gambling), there is a corresponding decrease in the gambler's perceived similarity with his or her partner and the time a gambler spends with his or her partner. Similarly, as the problem gambling score increases, the marital adjustment score (RDAS) decreases. This confirms that gamblers have less satisfying and stable relationships with their partners as their gambling problem worsens.

In short, problem gamblers are less likely than non-problem gamblers to feel similar to or close to their partner. They are also less satisfied with their marriage and spend less time with their partner and their marriage. It is impossible to tell from these statistics alone the cause of the relationship between gambling and marriage difficulties. That is, we cannot tell if marital difficulties led to problem gambling, or problem gambling led to marital difficulties, or if each repeatedly aggravated the other. Future research using a longitudinal design is needed to determine decisively whether marital problems cause or worsen a gambling problem, or vice versa, or both. At this point, all we can say with some confidence is that problem gambling and bad marriages occur together. However, our interview data strongly suggest that, at the very least, problem gambling worsens the marital relationships.

Another correlation analysis shows that the Embeddedness Scale (which measures the degree to which a couple shares a social world—a new scale used in this study) is positively correlated with marital adjustment on the RDAS (r =.259) and Awareness of Partner's Hopes and Fears (r= .295). In other words, respondents who score high on the Embeddedness Scale are more likely to know their partner's innermost hopes and fears and are more likely to have a good relationship with their partner.

Finally, the marital adjustment scale (RDAS) strongly correlates with all the other relationship scales in our study. In turn, the various new scales used in this study, including the Embeddedness Scale, correlate well with the well-validated marital relationship scale (RDAS). This correlation lends credibility to all the newer relationship measures used in this study.

While the 2003 *At Home* study compared problem gamblers to non-problem gamblers, our 2005 study compared problem gamblers to their partners. The quantitative data in both studies can help us uncover *how* the problem gambling becomes a family problem. Though problem gambling and bad marriages often occur together, only some of the 2005 respondents complained about their marital relationship or felt estranged from their partner. At times, problem gamblers and their partners disagreed on how to characterize the current state of their marriage.

What the Gamblers Said

The gamblers in the 2005 study reported significant marital strife. Asked how often they quarrelled with their partners, 29 percent said they quarrelled all the time, most of the time, or more often than not. Just over half said that their partners annoyed them more often than not or occasionally. Also, 26 percent said they discussed divorce often. Yet, when asked if they regretted marrying (or living with) their spouse, gamblers' responses mainly ranged between never and more often than not, with only 4 percent responding that they regretted marriage all of the time.

However, the gamblers also reported similarities and compatibilities with their spouses. Over 43 percent said that they and their partner always agree or almost always agree when making major decisions. Regarding sex relations, close to 53 percent said that they almost always or always agreed with their partner. They often reported that they have the same views and tastes as their partner in areas such as entertainment, sexuality, politics, home decoration, pastimes, and spirituality. The only item on which they are mostly reported as having different feelings is on how to spend their money. When asked if they ever have a stimulating discussion of ideas with their partner, 35 percent said that they engage in such discussions once or twice a week. When asked how often they calmly discuss something with their partner, 14 percent said never, 24 percent said once or twice a week, and 22 percent said once or twice a month.

What the Spouses Said

The gambler's spouses didn't paint precisely the same picture as the gamblers. Like the gamblers, they offered a mixture of positive and negative comments about their relationships. Certainly, over half of the spouses reported that they agreed or strongly agreed with their partners on issues such as displays of affection, sex relations, and making major decisions. Moreover, almost one in three reported that they never regretted having married the gambler. Like the gamblers, the spouses reported that they were able to discuss matters calmly.

Yet spouses were more open to expressing significant concerns about their relationship. They were as likely as gamblers to admit to conflicts in their relationships; and they were more likely than gamblers to report that they and their partner got on each other's nerves. In fact, 23 percent said that they got on each other's nerves all the time. Over half of the spouses said they regretted marrying or living with the gambling spouse, while one out of three said that they thought about ending their relationship most of the time or more often than not. By contrast, most gamblers responded that they rarely or never considered divorce, separation, or ending the relationship.

In sum, the quantitative results reveal that spouses are less happy with their marriages than are their gambling partners, though neither expressed a consistently high degree of unhappiness. This contradiction suggests that the gamblers may be practising self-deception to bypass the marital problems their gambling is creating. The difference in opinion between the gamblers and the spouses about their relationship may reflect differences in opinions about gambling and its impact.

Qualitative Findings from the 2003 *At Home With Gambling* Study

The respondents interviewed in the 2003 *At Home* study described several negative effects that gambling has on couples and family relations, such as dishonesty, unemployment, disrupted parent-child relationships, and safety issues.

First, the family often vividly experiences the gambler's degradation. Many respondents spoke of conflict and occasionally of the breakdown of their relationships:

I heard fighting and arguing and stuff like that over gambling—[from] my mom and dad when we were younger, before they got divorced. They were always fighting about my mom gambling.

We separated. I knew it would not be good for my daughter [to stay living with him]. She sometimes asks me, "Where is my dad?" and I simply tell her that he was naughty and did something inappropriate.

Gambling was once the most difficult thing about my family. I now have separated from my husband. I feel relieved.

These interviews confirm the quantitative finding that problem gamblers are more likely to be separated or divorced.

Second, dishonesty and a lack of trust were the main causes cited for the tension and conflict in these relationships. Huge losses created a sense of instability and hopelessness:

I hope I can repay my debts as soon as possible and then rebuild my family. I had properties before. Now I have nothing.

There's a lot of stress in the family—making ends meet, you know, a car's here one day, it's not here the next day.

I've known families that have lost their homes because of their gambling problem. And I also know of a few cases where the couple have separated, have divorced because of a serious gambling problem.

As well, gamblers often sneak around, hide, and have secret lives—all behaviours that can lead to conflict within the family:

It hurts my relationship with my husband. He has been dishonest and has lied to me. We have disputes and quarrels. I am trapped between my husband and my parents, who all gamble.

We used to quarrel a lot when we lived together. He was hiding things from me, lied to me, and I would learn about it anyway ... When you live with a man for many years, you already know by his face if he's lying or telling the truth. Of course, I would learn the truth, and we had awful scandals, terrible rows.

In addition, gambling losses make many families unable to pay off their bills or debts. Asked to name the most difficult things about their family lives, respondents often mentioned unemployment and lack of money. These issues make it hard to fulfill expectations and responsibilities as the head of a family, which ultimately leads to dissatisfaction and conflict. Often, a gambler comes to feel that he has lost his place in the family and in society.

Many of the respondents also viewed problem gambling as an addiction like alcoholism, one that could cause great problems for the family. Often, they associated it with other addictions:

It's a disease. If you get addicted to it ... Some people will gamble everything that they own. I heard about people who commit suicide because they gamble away everything they had. So, it's a sickness or disease, it's addictive like alcohol, and lots of people need help getting away from gambling 'cause it destroys families.

My aunt also has some other problems, she has an alcohol problem as well—she was abused as a child, she had a very violent relationship. So she has a lot of things to deal with. I don't know if they go hand in hand—the alcohol and the gambling—they are all kinds of addictions.

Several respondents also spoke about effects on the parent–child relationship. Often, the gambler focused so much time, money, and emotional energy on gambling that they neglected other people, including their children:

> My father is very preoccupied with money, and everything revolves around gaining or losing money. It has affected our relationship because I find him very self-centred, very consumed with money-making, and [he] doesn't really care about other people's well being aside from making money. Everything is about making money and gaining wealth as quickly as possible.

> My sister was worried about him. Like, she would buy a case of formula for the new baby, and [her husband] would take it back and get the money for gambling.

The children of gamblers sometimes develop feelings of responsibility toward their parents. The gambler's child often has to become the caretaker at an early age, taking up a process that family sociologists have come to call *parentification*:

> My kids recently heard that I had a gambling problem . . . My son, when we are passing the lottery booth, he always tells me that I should buy lottery tickets. My daughter will tell my son, "You shouldn't tell Daddy about gambling because he has a gambling problem . . . And when Daddy has a gambling problem, Daddy won't be here for us as much as he is now."

Family conflicts result from gambling, and they have a negative ripple effect. At their most extreme, these conflicts threaten the physical safety of other family members:

> It's a safety thing too. There were some really serious criminal types that were coming looking for him. And the police warned my sister one time when it got really bad—when they had just found him after he had been kidnapped—not to go near the windows at night. So it was pretty serious. That took a huge toll on her and on his kids!

> It got him into a lot of trouble like with the Mafia, so it was really serious. He was taken to Montreal and held there for a week. He was in some serious, serious, serious trouble.

Qualitative Findings in the 2005 Study

The interviews in the 2005 study suggest common patterns of relationship difficulties after problem gambling develops. The effect on marital relations emerges gradually and in stages. The primary problems of time and money present themselves first. Then, the marital situation gradually worsens, due to deception, emotional withdrawal, negative health effects, and a lack of shared activities. Finally, these problems result in increased conflict or excessive conflict avoidance, and thoughts of divorce. Both problem gamblers and their spouses mention these issues, though partners are more likely to view these as direct effects of the problem gambling.

Money Issues

The gamblers and their spouses both expressed concern about the amount of money lost gambling, for individual losses could add up to seriously substantial amounts:

> Once in a while, she'll go off with friends and I know she'll drop like five hundred or a thousand bucks, and it's kind of a shock.

Some spouses said that all the money spent on gambling could have gone towards other household items or family activities, and it was therefore too much to waste on this habit.

The financial problems that attend problem gambling have a major impact on both the financial and emotional stability of the partnership. Even spouses who have separate accounts or live away from the gambler often become a primary source of loans, which the gamblers do not always pay back. Oftentimes, the gambler accrues even more debt by borrowing from extended family members.

Every member of the family suffers the monetary impact of gambling. The negative financial effects of gambling were felt by this respondent and her daughter:

> Interviewer: How do you think your gambling has affected your daughter?
> M: I know it has affected her a lot. When she was about 13 or 14, she wanted a pair of jeans, and I said, "I don't have the money." "Well mum, if you wouldn't have went to bingo." That would be the first thing at 12 and 13. "If you wouldn't spend three night in bingo, I could have had my money

for my jeans." And it is still that way today, you know, because my daughter has a disability, right. She has a heart condition. So she is not working or anything, and it is still this way today, you know. "Well, why are you taking $40 to go to bingo when I could use that $40 for my jeans?" She's known that money that could have bought her a pair of jeans went to the bingo hall. Say she asked us for $10, and I say, "Well, **** I don't have it." "Well, if you wouldn't have gone to the bingo hall and give it all to the bingo this month, I would have had $10 this night." So she knows.

Conversations between children and parents on these issues gradually increase the stress level in the family, undermining parental authority.

Financial losses may prevent a couple from moving forward in their relationship, as they are unable to take the next big commitment step:

Then we had people phone constantly, You know, "We loaned the money, and we want the money back now, and we'll return your stuff." But he wasn't paying them. He didn't have the money to pay them back . . . You are not there emotionally for each other, because he is too busy thinking about going gambling. Mentally, he is not stable. You know, we can't get ahead, because I am busy covering his tracks. How can one get ahead in life if I am busy doing his part? Kids see that and the arguing—the arguing and the constant bickering for money. The kids see that. It destroys the family.

Spouses often find it difficult to remain committed to a relationship that is going nowhere. Oftentimes, the spouses develop a realistic view of the future:

We haven't bought a house, we don't have enough savings, I don't think we can have kids, which is something that I want. You can't bring up kids with that, you know. You need a new car, there's a lot of new bills.

Unlike their spouses, the gamblers in the study minimized their awareness of the effects of their gambling by focusing on immediate or isolated problems: gambling was *just* time spent away from their spouses or *just* financial trouble that resulted from their gambling. One gambler claimed: "[there are] no major problems, just sometimes money problems . . . bills don't get paid on time, that kind of thing but nothing . . . too major." Another said it was only the time she spent gambling, not the money, that was an issue, believing that her husband "says that I go too much too, you know. It is not the point of spending the money, it is the hours away."

Another major effect of financial problems is the gambler's defection from responsibility. Spouses reported that their gambling partners weren't fulfilling their roles as mates or parents. As a result, budgeting and other financial responsibilities were being added to other responsibilities the spouse was already carrying. This situation often leads to over-burdening, with spouses taking on an almost parent-like role towards the gambler to protect their family lifestyle from the gambler's habits.

For some spouses, taking on the family's financial responsibilities also means trying to moderate the gambler's spending habits. One respondent took on a protective role to try to prevent his wife from spending too much on slot machines:

I don't believe you should get enamoured with a machine. And so I would say, try another, just to break up the monotony. Also, I taught her some of the things that I do know about psychology, which isn't that much; but when you leave a machine, get the hell out of there, 'cause you don't want to have someone sit down at that machine that you just left and win. It is a bad feeling. She would probably feel depressed if that happened. I try to foresee some of that. So, I am the gadfly, the protector saving her from machines. I guess in any area, probably she would feel, with the financial thing, [I'm her] white knight in shining armour on a white horse.

Time Issues

At their most basic, marital problems associated with problem gambling develop out of a shortage of time, as well as out of a shortage of money. As we have seen, one way problem gambling hurts intimate relationships is by reducing the time a couple spends together.

Another adverse effect of problem gambling is a lack of time spent with one's children:

I don't give my kids the time they need, especially on weekends . . . Once a week, on a minimum, I'll go to the casinos.

Many of our respondents admitted that time spent gambling was essentially wasted, which caused many other problems.

Issues Regarding Shared Activities

By spending less time with their family, problem gamblers often miss opportunities to rebuild broken relationships. The most obvious of missed activities is shared leisure time. Many spouses do almost anything to spend time with their gambling partners, so long as it isn't gambling.

However, when spouses propose shared activities other than gambling, gamblers are likely to find ways to avoid taking part in them:

> I've encouraged horseback riding, or bowling, or hiking or that kind of thing. But she says she's been thrown off a horse, she twisted her ankle while hiking, and this kind of thing, so going to a casino, except for the smoking, is pretty safe. (laughing)

Other gamblers even avoid social activities by leaving to gamble:

> My hometown is Orillia, and I like to visit my family and friends there. Every time we go there, she has to go to the casino, and I have a couple of times outright refused to do that. In one instance, for example, we would be visiting people, and she would just tap me on the shoulder and tell me she's going for a drive. She would literally be gone for two or three hours, and I would know that she would drive to the casino.

Gamblers also avoid shared activities by spending all their disposable income on gambling:

> He wants to save his money for other things, and so he uses all of his entertainment money to do gambling and doesn't want to go out to dinner, or go out to a movie, or go out to a show or something . . . It's annoying. It makes me mad. It upsets me sometimes . . . that I want to do other things, go out and see other things and he doesn't want to . . . because he's not interested or because he's got other plans to do a poker night, or he's got no money to do it.

Gamblers frequently respond to suggestions of nongambling activity with flat-out hostility. Even when gamblers come home early or stay home to spend time with their spouses, their emotional state often makes pleasant interaction difficult. As hard as they may try, family members can do little to convince the problem gambler to engage in shared activities that don't involve gambling.

By avoiding shared activities, gamblers miss opportunities to improve their marriage through building emotional and social intimacy with their spouses. One respondent explained how sharing activities with his spouse was rewarding:

Walking, skating, swimming, traveling, taking one or two day trips, vacationing in the Caribbean, watching movies, listening to music, redecorating, sorting through things and throwing things out and taking care of chores—we both feel great about doing these things together, and we both initiate these things together. It's better to do these things together than doing them by yourself. Another person sees the world differently than you do and it becomes a more fulfilling experience.

A lack of shared activities can also deeply affect the development of their children. Children often notice when parents fail to spend time with the family, and they feel an emotional impact:

Oh, he [the son] gets mad. "I get so sick when you are finished in the morning. Been out for two, three days and I'm really sorry for you. I don't know how you can spend the entire weekend going out [gambling], smoking and drinking, and making a lot of (inaudible)." He hates it. "Dad how can you do this to yourself? You are punishing yourself. The whole day and nothing but gambling. What are you gambling for? Going gambling, that's a waste of time! You'll ruin your health, you haven't seen anything, you haven't seen the sunlight, you don't go out. What a waste of time, gambling. What are you going to tell your buddies when you go back to work on Monday morning. 'Oh, I gambled the whole night.' Big deal!" (laughs)

Some gamblers are clear about the ways problem gambling has hurt their relationship:

[Gambling] has actually been instrumental in destroying it. On every level—emotional, I wouldn't say financial but I'd be richer, social—no friends call—so all of a sudden he's alienated himself into a vacuum, and humans are not meant to do that. Including sexual, because you know, when you're angry and upset and depressed, you don't feel like it, you have to be in the mood for it. How often do you win, so you're in the up mood? Most of the time you're losing, that's why the casinos are there.

One spouse confirmed that his spouse's gambling was hurting their marriage:

> It's very bad, extremely bad. If it wasn't for that, we'd have a good relation-
> ship, sex or whatever . . . And she's trying very hard to forget it. But it's very
> hard on her, very hard.

Emotional Issues

Positive descriptions of the effects of gambling were rare in our interviews. Only
two spouses mentioned that the gambling of their spouse was positive, because
they got to share in the winnings. Expressions of concern were far more common.

The gamblers often neglected important aspects of their relationships, which
often resulted in emotional problems for the family. Feelings of stress, guilt,
worry, and neglect weighed heavily on all family members. In this circumstance,
relationships were strained as emotional connections slowly worsened. For
instance, several problem gamblers described how they felt guilty:

> I feel guilty 'cause I spend the money when I shouldn't, when I can use it for
> something else. Then the kids lay the guilt on me and say, "Oh you spent all
> your money on your gambling stuff, you could have bought me this."

One spouse described how her husband's problem gambling led her to worry
for decades:

> I was constantly worrying: he's going there, he'll gamble, he'll lose, he'll
> come back, he'll get angry—you know, it was constant worry—bursts of
> anger, bursts of upsets. Then I had a child staying at home, [and] you didn't
> want it to impact him. He had to do homework, he had to go to hock-
> ey, you don't want to hear your mother and father screaming over there.
> So, you're worrying, [thinking] "I'm not going to scream, I'm not going to
> argue, it'll pass, it'll pass." You're talking to yourself, [while] you worry ex-
> cessively over it.

The spouses' worries were often grounded in real concerns about the financial
implications of gambling:

> I am always worried if we are going to have enough money. When his
> paycheque comes, did he make enough to pay this bill? Or, how much is
> this bill going to want? Or, can I pay half of this bill?

Worrying was even common among respondents who denied that gambling was causing problems for their relationship:

> Maybe, [gambling is] bringing us together—certainly, sharing her joy at doing it and that sort of thing. I enjoy the hell out of people having fun, and if she's having that kind of fun from it, I get a kick out of that too. So, I guess I can't say negative things. I guess it would be a bit of a plus—but there is that niggling concern back there that makes me observant and aware.

Gambling also created personal stress for the respondents. For the gamblers, the stress of lying and maintaining deceptions was causing major emotional strain:

> You lie about cheques that have not being written, people who haven't been paid. My girlfriend asks me if so-and-so's [been] paid, and I am like, "Yeah, of course. It was sent in the mail a couple of days ago," when it wasn't. [Or telling someone] "Here is $200 instead of $500—don't say anything to so-and-so about it, and I'll take care of it next week." And then you forget about that, and it comes up two weeks later. That kind of lying, just to cover my tracks.

Gambling-related stress also affected the spouses:

> I guess sometimes he gets hung up on a loss, and then sometimes that's kind of stressful.

Spouses said they often had to take on emotionally charged responsibilities, that sometimes included keeping their partner's secrets:

> We both agreed I should stop gambling, and she said in return for this, she will co-operate and not tell my family. She also agreed to help in paying my debts.

The responsibility involved in hiding a problem like gambling contributes to the stress the spouses already felt.

In addition, the problem gamblers often gave gambling a higher priority than the relationship, leaving their spouses hurt and rejected by this thoughtlessness.

One spouse described a situation at home when her partner was watching a game he had a bet on:

> If we're in the house and he's watching sports, you cannot talk while the game is on.

A gambler respondent went as far as to claim that his primary emotional loyalty was to gambling:

> I really, really love the cards more than him.

Another described how he focused all his energy on the gambling, whatever the cost:

> Where everyone else grew up and matured and took care of their responsibilities, I just got heavier and heavier into gambling. All my energy was going into that. It was all the energy I was supposed to be putting towards our relationship, putting towards work, my brothers and sisters and the family, [and] other things. There was no balance whatsoever. Everything went into gambling.

Often the gamblers revealed that they felt their relationship problems were, at most, of secondary importance. They usually regarded relationship damage as unimportant.

Even when the gamblers didn't express these views out loud, their spouses could sense that they were lower on the priority list. Many spouses said that this created an overwhelming sense of isolation and secrecy in the relationship and diminished emotional intimacy:

> [The addiction] causes a constant preoccupation with gambling and thinking about gambling. He loses the ability to engage.

Taking second place to gambling left spouses feeling disconnected, neglected, and emotionally abandoned:

> I think he's very sick, you know. It really hurts me. I'm an emotional mess over what's happened between him and I. I'm very, very emotional. It nearly cost me my life at one point.

Moreover, the gamblers showed this disengagement in many ways. They spent less leisure time with their spouses and were emotionally unavailable to them, especially while gambling:

> It's what I call the "gambling zone," where he's constantly preoccupied with it, he's constantly disengaged from his family and the kids, and he's disengaged from positive feelings—having a distinct lack of emotion and [being] hard to get through to and [not responding] to questions.

Spouses who did not gamble found it hard to share the experiences of gamblers and felt emotionally disconnected from them:

> When she loses it creates an unnecessary barrier between us ... Nobody wants to admit when they've lost, so it creates an unnecessary bad feeling because it makes her feel responsible for losing ... I can't share complete joy with her highs because I know it will be followed by another low; and when I suffer through another of her lows, it's another unnecessary low that she is feeling.

Thus, these spouses were struggling, caught between concern for their partner's well-being and resentment for being put into a caretaker position, or for being ignored outright. This emotional disconnect had important and damaging effects on the family:

> Over the years, we drifted apart a little bit. We weren't doing things as a family anymore. Then this last week made me wake up when I realized: This is great, we are cooking together, we are watching a movie for a change. I think it is mostly the time away from my family that has affected [us] the most.

Both spouse and children can feel the emotional absence of a gambling parent. One spouse said that gambling destroyed her marriage and emotionally wounded their son:

> S: There is an emotional impact—latent, but it's there. He keeps saying he doesn't care, but he cares. It's affected him to the degree that now he won't participate in any drinking, gambling, or smoking.

Interviewer: He's totally gone the other way?

S: Yes. A whole 180 degrees.

The emotional barrier caused by gambling can be even more damaging than financial problems, since problem gambling causes all family members to live with constant worry, guilt, and stress, draining away emotional investment from the relationship and towards the gambling. Ultimately, relationships are poorly preserved, and spouses are ignored.

Conclusion

The data from the 2003 and 2005 studies show that problem gambling injects tension and trouble into many relationships. Many couples struggle to overcome these problems through avoidance, discussion, humour, argument, and separate finances. It is surprising just how resilient and determined many of these couples are to solve their problem.

The next chapter examines the spouses' lack of awareness of the extent of the gambling problem and considers the impact of this unawareness on the relationship.

Chapter 8
Lack of Spouse Awareness

Not only are gamblers are walking through life in a dream-state; so are their spouses. Through all the difficulties described in the last chapter, spouses remain largely unaware—or at least uninformed—about the nature of the problem. But how is it possible that in the midst of a gambler's personal crises the spouse remains unaware of the true extent of the gambler's problems? This chapter examines the secret lives of gamblers and their motives for keeping their gambling a secret. It also examines the extent of the spouse awareness of the problem and the spouse's ideas about how to change the gambler's behaviours.

One respondent expressed the problem of awareness succinctly when describing a desire for more emotional and intellectual intimacy with their gambling partner:

> You have a bad day at work and you go into a state, and he'll go gamble instead of letting me know what is going on and maybe trying to give me the opportunity to help. He'll just go on his own tantrum and do what he has to do. You kind of feel shut out of the situation, 'cause if you don't know what is going on, how do you help?

The question, "If you don't know what is going on, how do you help?" resonated throughout the interviews in both the 2003 and 2005 studies. While gamblers often felt misunderstood, their partners often felt powerless to understand what their spouse was going through. Rarely was this gap the result of a spouse's unwillingness to understand. Usually, it was due more to a lack of awareness.

Theoretical Background on Relationships, Groups, and Secrecy

Secrecy and deception are interactive strategies that gamblers use to keep their freedom. By this definition, secrecy and deception are normal parts of everyday life; all social relationships contain some secrecy and deceit, no matter how minor. So, in marriages, secrecy and deception are always present to some degree. But problem gamblers use deceptive strategies more than most people and for the purpose of protecting their gambling habits.

The German sociologist Georg Simmel studied secrecy in the late nineteenth and early twentieth centuries. According to Simmel, secrecy is a condition in which one person intentionally hides something, while another person seeks to discover what is being hidden. Social interaction, then, is a like a game of hide-and-seek. Simmel views secrecy as a characteristic of normal relationships. It is neither a personality trait of individuals nor a sign of psychopathology.

Simmel thought that modern society both permits and requires a high degree of secrecy. As Simmel points out, all relationships rest on the precondition that people know something about each other, and all relationships are located somewhere between complete knowledge and complete ignorance. The possession of full knowledge does away with the need for trust, while ignorance—the absence of knowledge—makes trust impossible. In this sense, relationships differ in their mix of knowledge and ignorance about a person. Marriage, the least secretive of relationships, builds a strong *we-feeling* among those who share the family secrets. The most important duty of each member is to preserve the silence about all things that concern the well-being of the group to which he or she belongs.

Moreover, every relationship causes each person to form a picture in their mind of the other. The detail and truth of that picture depends on information available to each participant. For various reasons, people hide the worse aspects of their personality and actions, often even from intimates. Partly, this is to simplify the interaction between the two; partly, it is to allow each to hold a flattering picture of the other.

Though secrecy erects barriers between people, it also tempts people to break through the barriers with gossip or confession. Information is important to a relationship; for this reason, secrecy always causes tension. In normal relationships, this tension gets released whenever the truth is revealed. Such moments of revelation can be dramatic, because they unveil levels of activity and meaning that had never been guessed at.

In the way families need and use information and secrecy, they resemble intimate cliques. A *clique* is a group of tightly interconnected people, or a circle of people all connected to one another and to the outside world in similar ways. Clique members usually feel strong positive sentiments for each another and contempt for outsiders. In short, cliques are groups characterized by friendship, likeness, interaction, exclusion, and the flow of valuable resources: information, support, and opinions (among others). They receive, censor, and direct information flow. They also produce information, distort it, and send information out as gossip and rumour. Cliques, like families, are stable structures; but they survive largely through what psychologist Irving Janis (1982) called *groupthink*. Leaders within cliques and families use information, secrecy, and abuses of either of these to press members to accept narrow or extreme views.

In their tendency to control information, families are also like secret societies. Simmel defines a *secret society* as a social unit characterized by reciprocal relations that are governed by secrecy. Members of the society are concerned with protecting ideas, sentiments, and information about activities that are important to them. They do this by controlling the flow of information. According to Simmel, everyone is a creator, user, and victim of secrets. Simmel defines the secret as the crowning social technique for regulating the flow and distribution of information. People can and do control social relations by manipulating the ratio of knowledge to ignorance. As a result, people are always struggling to build an understanding of the social environment out of fragmentary and biased information.

In Simmel's view, both secrecy and a lack of secrecy can be harmful. He notes that a lie is especially dangerous in modern societies, because individuals make decisions that rest on assumptions they cannot easily verify. The harmfulness of a lie depends also on the closeness of the relationship. Lies by people who are closest and most important to us also have the most influence and effect on us.

Therefore, intimate relationships normally and necessarily assume a high degree of openness and absence of lying. Yet, Simmel says, some reciprocal concealment is always needed. Sometimes, as with *white lies*, couples can benefit more from concealment than from openness. Every relationship has its own stated and unstated notions about secrecy and discretion.

Paradoxically, Simmel believes that friendship is more likely than marriage to allow complete mutual understanding and confidence. Marriage often draws some of its appeal and romantic power from the "still unrevealed." Since an intimate relationship rests on exchange between the partners, secrecy is a form of commerce in which information is the medium of exchange. So, for Simmel, secrecy through concealment is one of the greatest human accomplishments: it allows people to construct, occupy, and manipulate different social worlds parallel to the commonly shared one. This possibility of multiple worlds (or parallel universes) makes life more interesting and richer with possibilities. It enables delightful, amusing, and creative forms of deception.

However, secrecy also facilitates dangerous deceptions. Simmel states that monetary relationships are too easily undermined by secrecy and deception. Gamblers can easily hide their real activities because money is compact and travels well, can be exchanged for various goods and services, and leaves few tell-tale signs of use (unlike drugs or alcohol). So, gambling is especially well suited to be a hidden problem.

Theories about Lying

Sociologists and social scientists are continuing to research the conditions that lead to lying and the conditions that lead listeners to believe the lies they are told. What follows is a brief overview of more recent research on the topic.

Sometimes people lie to others because they are simultaneously lying to themselves. Self-deception is a trait that simplifies a person's ability to behave in socially censured ways. Yet lies are not always a result of self-deception. Consider high-risk sexual behaviour in the face of HIV/AIDS. Roth *et al.* (2006) note that people can make highly accurate self-assessments of the risks involved; yet they take risky actions anyway, in full awareness of what they are doing. People in our society constantly deceive themselves about the reasons for their everyday conduct.

In addition, lying and self-deception receive support from society as a whole. Conceivably, our need to lie to one another in a complex, individualized way is driven by a need to ignore certain unpalatable truths. Utz (2005) notes people have a wide variety of reasons for lying or hiding the truth. For example, in computer-mediated communication (e.g., the Internet), people often use deception—such as category deception (gender switching), attractiveness deception, or identity concealment—to improve their social standing in some way in the online society. People credit deception to different motivations and evaluate deception according to its assumed motivation. In Utz's (2005) study, people gave negative evaluations only to deceptions with an assumed malicious intent. This suggests that society approves of lying and deception, except where these can cause harm.

Lying as a Cultural, Social, or Organizational Practice

People are likely to lie or hide their behaviour under certain cultural, social, or organizational conditions more than under others. Some organizational and occupational conditions appear to promote lying. Schein (2004) studied various kinds of socialization that people experience in a typical organizational career. He noted that moral dilemmas related to information management occur at different stages in an organizational career. In general, people "climbing the ladder" become moral relativists about the truth. They learn through successive socialization experiences that norms are variable and that "business is business," even when one is personally conflicted.

Many organizations and institutions are based on deceptive practices. Politics is built on deception, or at least on the construction and manipulation of appearances. In addition, some professions struggle with pressures to lie. Lee (2004) tried to answer the following question: Why do journalists use deceptive methods such as impersonations, non-identifications, and untruth in their work? He found that deception is part of a moral-pragmatic framework based on three notions: the harm–benefit balance, the altruism of the act, and instrumental consideration such as convenience, personal safety, and the bottom line. Journalists describe organizational efforts to normalize deceptive behaviour in their profession. In addition, professional demands that insist that all stories have drama, conflict, and strong visual or emotional appeal promote journalistic deception. In similar research on the medical profession, Fainzang (2002) examined the lying of doctors and the lying of patients. He cited examples of medical specialists affirming information to patients, even though they knew of cases that didn't work out that way. Similarly, patients lead their doctors to believe that they have been taking their medication. Fainzang argues that lying is a way of preserving secrecy and therefore expresses and points to a power relationship.

The Effects of Lies

Research on adolescent lying leads to the conclusion that lying, though normal and widespread, reflects troubled circumstances. Warr (2007) finds that lying to parents is a strong and robust correlate of delinquent behaviour. Lying to parents appears to have a progressively negative impact on the parent–child bond. Compared to other youth, lying adolescents hold themselves in lower regard and are more often depressed. Parents are often angered by and distrustful of deceitful children. Their children's lies may say more about the strength of their loyalties to peers than the weakness of their attachment to parents.

Similarly, Engels et al. (2006) report that in a sample of parents and adolescents, lying was moderately associated with other indicators of faulty parent–child communication, a troubled parent–child relationship, and imperfect parenting practices. Baker et al. (2003) studied the agency records of 29 male juvenile sex offenders and 32 comparison youth from three child welfare agencies in New York state. Families of juvenile sex offenders were far more likely to practice family deception. Family deception during childhood and adolescence significantly increased the odds of sexual offending later in life.

Detecting Lies

In general, people are not as good at distinguishing lies from truth as they think they are. Typically, people are more likely to believe information that supports what they already believe. Winneg *et al.* (2005) studied the 2004 American primary election season and focused on three misleading negative claims made by the Republicans and the Democrats. Did these deceptions work? And if so, with whom? The results showed that most citizens believed some of the misleading claims: but Democrats were more likely to believe deceptive negative claims about George W. Bush, whereas Republicans were more likely to believe deceptive negative claims about John Kerry. Recently, Martins (2005) analyzed the opinion dynamics of a neutral observer deciding between two competing scientific theories. The observer had to form his or her opinion solely by reading published articles reporting the experimental results of others. The study found that if the reader sensed even small amounts of deception in the source articles, he or she could never be reasonably sure of which theory was correct, no matter how many articles he or she read. These two studies suggest that deception is very effective at clouding the truth.

By far the most relevant research on this issue comes from Israel, in a study by Elaad (2006). Four distinctive groups of people were asked to assess themselves on their abilities to determine whether other people were telling the truth or telling lies; then they had to persuade other people to believe them when they were telling the truth or telling lies. The results showed that all groups believed that they were better tellers of truth and detectors of truth than they were either detectors of lies or tellers of lies. People also believed they were better at detecting lies than they were at telling lies. People seem to overestimate their ability to detect lies because they dislike the idea that they are easily deceived by others; and they underestimate their ability to tell lies to support their self-perception as honest people.

Case Study of Deception: Zab and Delkash

One couple in the 2005 study—Zab and Delkash[7]—showed the inability of a spouse to detect deception. Zab and Delkash had been married for 11 years,

---

7   See also "Zab and Delkash" in Chapter 3.

and Zab had been gambling as long as they had been together. Delkash linked her effort to curb his gambling to a simple lack of marital understanding. When asked the one thing she would like to change about their relationship, Delkash said she hoped they would learn "to understand each other more. I'm trying to help him get out of this gambling habit."

Throughout their interviews, Zab and Delkash sounded as if they were talking about different marriages. Zab characterized their relationship as conflict-ridden due to the conflict caused by her spending and his gambling. His version of the story made Delkash sound like a shopaholic:

> My wife has a habit of spending lavishly, much more than I will. I will always go for the cheaper option, and she's the opposite. I'll say that we need to save money for the future and we need accidental income saved up in case of an emergency, and that we need to budget for that, and my wife will say, let's spend our savings on vacations and clothing for the kids and herself.

Delkash answered the question differently. She painted a picture of a much more cohesive couple. She said they rarely disagreed about money:

> We very rarely disagree about how money is spent. I prefer to prioritize. I always want to spend more money on clothing and household items and he doesn't want to buy brand names because he thinks it's a waste of time.

This difference in perspective surfaced in discussions of Zab's gambling. Zab claimed that conflicts about his gambling were due to this basic disagreement:

> We discuss strategies, money limits, and I initiate it. We agree on certain money limits, but sometimes I'll get carried away. We disagree on how long to stay at the casinos. I'll talk about strategies and which games to play and the amount of time spent there, and my wife doesn't agree with me. She'll contradict the limits or money spent or length of time spent gambling at the casinos.

By contrast, Delkash said she usually began the discussions:

> We talk about how much he's winning or losing. What games is he playing. Which games have a higher return rate or higher/easier chance of winning.

I usually bring up the topic of gambling. He'll only answer one or two answers. He doesn't go into detail. He says, "Oh, you don't know much about gambling, what's the use in discussing anything with you?"

Sometimes Delkash thought they were having a candid conversation about how much Zab was winning and losing, though they weren't. Delkash knew almost nothing about how much Zab spent when he was gambling, as Zab told us:

I have a secret account that my wife isn't aware of. All my extra income goes into my secret account, which contains money and extra bonuses from work or overtime or double time pay from work goes into the secret account.

No wonder, then, that Delkash took Zab's gambling less seriously than she might if she had known all of the details! As far as she knew, they were dealing with their finances and Zab's gambling in an open and productive way. When asked if she would like him to change his gambling, Delkash reported feeling that *she* has been able to keep it under control, claiming that "till now I've been able to balance it. It hasn't come to the point where I'm fed up."

Zab was much harder on himself than Delkash about the effect of his gambling. And when asked the hardest part of their relationship, Zab said the secrets surrounding his gambling were the hardest part:

Secrets. My wife is aware that I'm going gambling, but she doesn't know how much I've lost.

This couple's experiences reveal several reasons why gamblers' responses don't always match up with what spouses are saying. They likely have different perceptions of the same situation. The lines of communication are often blocked or completely cut, and spouses are left in the dark about the facts of the problem.

Level of Spouse Awareness

Spouses are often unaware of the minute details of their gambling partner's lives, but they may still know a lot about the gambling-related difficulties. It takes some spouses longer than others to learn how to detect these problems. In the end, most of the spouses discover the gamblers' hidden life. Nearly all the spouses in our study said that gambling posed a problem for either themselves or their gambling partner, only one respondent claiming otherwise. Such a uniform answer showed that, regardless of what the gambling respondents claimed to believe, their gambling touched their spouses' lives in negative ways. Yet the spouses often still underestimated the severity of the gambling problem.

Both the gamblers and spouses in the 2005 study were asked to rate the gambling partner using the Canadian Problem Gambling Index (CPGI). The gamblers gave themselves a mean CPGI score of 15.07, whereas the spouses gave their partners a mean CPGI of only 12.23—still in the severe problem range, but much lower. The CPGI responses reveal that many spouses fail to grasp the full extent of their partner's gambling problem. On the item "Needs to gamble with larger amounts of money," 59 percent of the gamblers answered "almost always" or "most of the time," whereas only 43 percent of the spouses answered the same. When asked if "he or she might have a problem with gambling," close to 44 percent of the gamblers expressed a belief that they did have a problem; yet a mere 13 percent of spouses assessed their partners as having a problem.

These discrepancies show that gamblers avoid telling their spouses about their ever-worsening problem. The differences also suggest that spouses lack an understanding of the nature of problem gambling.

Why Do Gamblers Lie?
Gamblers lie for diverse reasons, and often the same gambler has several reasons for hiding his or her activities.

Differing Opinions About Gambling
Though couples need to act together to control a gambling problem, most couples have different opinions about gambling and its impact. Many spouses have extreme objections to gambling, whereas many gamblers don't regard it as harmful. To avoid conflict and argument, gamblers choose to lie about their activities. The degree to which spouses in our study disliked gambling varied. Some spouses expressed strong sentiments against the gambling:

> He hates it. We argue about it. He says (laughs), "You're gonna spend our last cent on gambling."

Most often, spouses said they disagreed over how much money or time should be spent on gambling and the reasons why gambling had taken over their lives. In short, they thought differently about the recreational value of gambling:

He understands why I do it, and he has taken me to casinos. We always rene-
gotiate the limit depending on where we are financially, but he wishes that I
wouldn't feel the need to do it when I get stressed out or use it as a form of
excitement. He looks at it like, "Well if you are going to spend $100, you are
buying $100 worth of entertainment; but when it is done, it is done."

The reasons the spouses disliked gambling vary as much as the extent to which
they condemned the behaviour:

He [says], "Sue, you don't know how to play as much. You don't have as
much experience. This is not a good hand to get into." If I do my own thing,
he'll be like, "See you just lost. Look how much money you just lost. What
a waste of money."

We'll agree [that] if he gambles, then it should just be for fun, that's okay.
If he's going with the intention of having to win money, then I think that's
wrong.

At the other extreme were spouses who held neutral, or even positive, opinions about gambling. These couples experienced less conflict over gambling and
fewer secondary problems:

I don't think [gambling] has affected [our relationship]. It's basically something that we do together every once in a while.

However, few of the couples we interviewed fell into this category.

Trust Issues

The conflict that gamblers avoid with their secrecy is also related to issues of
trust. Once they reveal their deception, it is often hard for the gambler to regain
the spouse's trust, and this deception leads to new conflict. Spouses usually trust
their gambling mate unless they are given a reason to do otherwise. To maintain
this complicity, the gamblers in our study often developed their lies into elaborate deceptions about debt:

The only time they know when I go gambling is weekends, because I go
with this guy. But this guy even goes weekdays, and [my partner] doesn't

know we go weekdays. We don't normally come home before my husband, but I always give the excuse that I have a doctor's appointment. So they think I am at my doctor's appointment, but if they had known [the truth], they would really hit the roof.

Periodically, these liars slipped up and allowed their spouses a glimpse of what they had been hiding:

I started lying about it, and she caught on when they had the traveling casino downtown. Then I lied about it, and she caught on when I lost so much in a month—close to $1,800 in a month. She gave me a choice: her and my son or gambling.

For some, distrust resulted in couples separating their family's financial assets. Some spouses saw this solution as a way to protect the family against huge financial losses. But it did little to rebuild communication and trust. When spouses took over the family's finances and other responsibilities from a gambler, it was because they felt they could not trust the gambler. They no longer felt close enough to feel confident in what the gambler said or did:

We now keep our finances separate. That was something that we decided . . . there was going to be a joint account and there would be separate finance accounts and that kind of stuff. That is how it's being resolved. I really don't know how much debt he's in, but I know it's probably close to tens of thousands of dollars now.

The gamblers admitted that trust was important in a marriage. One respondent described how important trust was in his relationship with his wife:

Trust is a big key; she trusts me, but very slyly. She's very scared to give me a lot of money. I'm going to Europe—to Transylvania—to visit relatives for the last time [and] I guess she's beginning to get edgy. She doesn't want to give me a credit card. She asked me how much cash I want, and I said give me about $4,000 and she says where are you going. And I said there are casinos in Budapest. I want to check them out. And the biggest thing is trust . . . it's always that worry if I am going to go back [to gambling] . . .

Trust is the key and I told her if you want to worry about it for the rest of your life, it's not going to help. If I'm going to do it again, I'm not cured. I'll never be cured. I have to fight against it.

This lack of trust can cause new problems. Some gamblers in the study became afraid to communicate honestly about their actions, thoughts, and feelings related to gambling:

> I have to go see a doctor. Maybe they can't advise me, but at least they are going to listen to my concerns that I don't want to tell my common-law wife the reasons I gamble. Because my concern is perhaps she is going to go.

The trust issue is a cyclical one. Spouses become mistrustful because they suspect deceit from the gambler or have been lied to in the past. Gamblers fear damaging the relationship further by causing conflict, so they continue to hide their activities. Discovery of continued gambling by partners further weakens trust, and the cycle continues.

Increased Conflict
A gambling problem significantly increases conflict, with couples being most likely to argue about the time and money spent on gambling. Gamblers often lie to avoid the heated conflicts that can arise. One respondent said that she and her husband never argued except about her gambling:

> That's about the only thing—the gambling. Like spending on each other, we never have problems like that; or what you spend on the grocery order. It is mostly just gambling.

When the spouse is the gatekeeper to the finances, conflicts arise when a problem gambler asks the spouse for money to gamble:

> We argue until I get my way (laughs). I love bingo and need to play. It isn't free to play, and I love to spend money . . . I need to argue and yell and get mad, and then he gives me money.

Gamblers' mood changes following losses can serve as another source of conflict:

When I'm not gambling, our relationship is pure. We love each other, obey each other, respect each other. But now since I have this problem—most of the time I've lost, you know—I'm mad. Anything, little things—like he say something to me, I disagree. That's the way it happens.

Thus, the gamblers may have felt that arguments over access to money and mood changes were inevitable. Therefore, they lied about anything they could manage to conceal.

The result of gambling-related conflict is usually the same—a strain on the relationship. The conversations our respondents recounted all sounded very similar:

She says you drink too much. I say fine. I tell her she plays bingo too much. She brushes that off. But I only drink when she goes to bingo, I'll go and pick up a little mickey.

I drill into him the responsibility of family. Now that he's married and has kids, he has a responsibility to his family to take care of them.

The undertone of the conflicts is all the same—frustration, anger, and bitterness. In the end, the problem gambler usually got his or her way:

Weekends when I tell him [how I feel,] he is not particularly happy. But then I argue with him, and I say that I am bored . . . "You don't take me anywhere . . . we have not gone anywhere and I am going [to the casino] and I don't care what you say." I get pain . . . it usually happens when I am in a lot of pain, and then I scream like I want to kill somebody, and I say "I am going to go, I don't care what you say." And then he just cools off. I told him it relieves my stress . . . Sometimes, when I am angry I will deliberately go out to the casino. Kind of in a gleeful way or boastful way, I'll say I am going to the casino.

Most of the time, the gamblers and their spouses communicated in ways that hindered the solution of problems. Episodes included explosive arguments that ended without resolution:

We didn't do much talking (laughs). We did a lot of arguing, but our communication wasn't very . . . open . . . and wasn't very calm all the time, so we wouldn't really talk about it. It's just a problem you see is there and you hope that it goes away.

The couples frequently described blowing up at each other and hurting each other's feelings, only to walk away:

[There's] screaming and shouting and she goes away and I go away, and we don't talk together for another three, four days. She goes to her room, I go to my room.

Another ineffective problem-solving technique employed by our respondents was abuse. Several spouses reported suffering abuse at the hands of their gambling partners. Gamblers often resort to abuse when they are overwhelmed by the frequency of conflict or are desperate to make it end:

Because his temper has been rising so much, he's in an anger-management course with the . . . hospital. I had to get the cops involved, [and] I couldn't handle it anymore. It's a very difficult thing to do to call the police. A lot of people say if you're having problems, just pick up the phone and call 911. But, I'd like to see you do that and turn in your spouse of 38 years. Can you sit there and actually do that, watch the police pull up to your house, fill out the form, and watch him being removed?

Spouses may suffer various types of abuse at the hands of their gambling spouses. For example, one respondent felt that his partner's mood swings were a form of verbal and emotional abuse:

[He can be] wonderful to be around. "Let's do things together, let's go to a movie, let's go to a show, spend the money, let's go out for a meal, let's do stuff." [But] when he's not winning he's down, gross, he just wants to sit and watch TV, very easily argumentative . . . and I'll bring this up to him. I'll say, "The mood swings alone are unfair." I'll say, "In the relationship, this gambling has put you into mood swings." I said, "Sure, I love it when you're winning, everyone loves a winner." I said, "When you lose why I should have to pay, why emotionally am I paying for this? If you were by yourself, fine . . . if you want to be in a lousy mood over losing, fine. But I just finished work, I've come home, I want to have a wonderful evening with my partner. I can't because you're in a shitty mood because you just lost at the casino last night, this week, or whatever and you're just thinking how you're going to get that money back. So why am I taking the emotional consequences of your losses?

Some gamblers went so far as to use the marital conflict as an excuse to gamble. In these cases, current issues remained unresolved, and new conflicts were ignited:

We argue quite a bit, and she will say, "I'm going to bingo." "Well go ahead, I'll get a few boys and go play cards." "Oh no, I'm going to come back to another mess . . . " (laughing) It's the name of the game. We argue quite a bit but we get over it. It takes a few days . . . I don't know really how much she spends because . . . if I ask her she starts arguing with me and says "Okay I'm going out for a while." So the best way to deal with that is don't ask her . . . but if I go out and blow a couple hundred dollars on a race, she comes over and looks at me, and we start arguing (laughing).

Almost all the couples in the 2005 study argued over problem gambling, though some respondents downplayed the arguing or rationalized it:

When she's with me, we often disagree on doctrinal issues. It's nothing negative in the sense that we argue a lot, but there are just some disagreements in that area . . . It is somehow pushed that things like gambling are not a good thing to do, and I think she feels uncomfortable when those types of issues are raised. It seems counter to her pleasure centre or doesn't push her buttons the way she would want, and she seeks to avoid talking about those issues as much as possible.

In general, many gamblers choose to use deception to avoid the conflict as much as possible. Through deception, gamblers hope to avoid the conflicts that create opportunities for abuse and aggravation.

Fear and Personal Responsibility

Some gamblers believe that their need to gamble is a personal problem that only they can manage. Respondents in the 2005 study said that they experienced a great deal of fear related to what might happen if they disclosed the truth about their gambling behaviour. Many gamblers told us about the anxiety they felt keeping their gambling secret:

> It's just a matter of time before she finds out. In fact, I kind of wish someone would tell her. I'm starting to feel like I wouldn't care anymore if she found out. I don't want her to call me stupid, though. That would be the worst. I know that her initial reaction will be to call me names. It's so stressful living my life.

For the most part, gamblers wanted to keep others in their life from pressuring them to stop:

> I don't want anybody to know about it. When they start to know, then they start telling me it's a problem, that I'm stupid, that's why my economic situation isn't so great—then it becomes a problem.

Some gamblers felt that their spouses could do little to help them change their gambling. Some appeared to have decided that telling the truth would only anger or hurt their spouses, especially if spouses could do little to help with their gambling problem:

> She has her business and I know that, but I just don't want to talk about it. I know she likes to ask me. But for me it's annoying [so] ... just leave me alone. I never depended on [anyone] for anything.

> They [my family] don't [know about the gambling]. So, I'm just trying to keep it as low-key as I can, to try and figure it out. It's just so hard to get out of that rut ... I'd rather not [talk to my family about it] ... The less people know, the less it haunts me back ... I don't want anybody to know my business, to prevent it [coming] back at me.

Once gambling motivations extended beyond a simple desire to have fun, gamblers often realized that they had "crossed the line" and felt as though they now had something to be ashamed of:

> I tend to gamble for the wrong reasons. I think sometimes that I can just win money to get out of financial problems. I should be responsible and do

the right thing—focus more on work, focus more on my career. [I] try to get out of a financial problem by trying to win money and I know that it is just not going to happen, especially under that kind of stress. It is just not going to happen—it shows on your face, your eyes . . . everything shows.

In this way, realizing that their gambling is no longer of a kind acceptable to society, gamblers often decide to hide their activities from their spouse.

There are strong cultural and social reasons for hiding information about one's condition. For example, a Muslim respondent said that it was against his religion to gamble. Another respondent said her gambling would to bring shame and "loss of face" to the family. These cultural factors can be seen as another source of shame and stigma, which further encourages the gambler to lie.

In addition, a stigma could extend to the gambler's friends and family. Outsiders may see the gambler's associates as blind or insensitive to the problem, or even as its cause. Thus, the gambler's reputation is at stake and so is that of his or her family and friends.

Why are Spouses Unaware?

Spouses lack awareness of the gambling problem for several reasons, the extensive amount of lying being only one of them. Spouses may be unwittingly accommodating the lies:

Conflict Avoidance

Both gamblers and their spouses use *conflict avoidance* as a way to avoid argument. One of the most commonly used techniques of conflict avoidance is *evasive communication*. Many spouses in the study felt they could avoid conflict by avoiding the topic of gambling altogether:

What I try to do now is ignore him. I try to ignore him, because the confrontation is nasty—it's dirty. I just try to pretend he doesn't exist around me sometimes.

Some couples even specifically agreed not to talk about gambling at all:

We don't really talk about it.

In addition, a few respondents described using *nonconfrontational methods of communication* to prevent their spouses from gambling:

I would say to him, "You've got to stop with the Pro-Line stuff, 'cause it is getting way out of hand. Sometimes you spend two dollars, sometimes it's four dollars, sometimes it is six dollars. And I think you are spending way too much money doing it." [He'll say.] "I know, I know, I am sorry, I am sorry." I go, "Yeah, you keep saying you are going to stop, but you never do."

As well, some gamblers used *verbal aggression* to stop a discussion that might have led to conflict:

[My wife] talks about my gambling . . . and I'll tell her to shut up . . . It's none of her business.

At the most extreme end, some gamblers used *threats* to the relationship to stop a discussion. For example, they threatened to leave the relationship if their spouse discussed their gambling:

I'm scared to [try to change his gambling]. I am scared that it is going to get to the point of a really big argument, and then we are going to break up over it, and it is just not worth it. I don't think it is worth losing him over trying to . . . you know.

One gambler and spouse orchestrated a script of threats and counter-threats that became familiar to both:

He'll not want to talk about it and he'll walk away. I get really ticked off about him walking away on me, and I'll be like, "Don't walk away on me," and then I'll start crying and he'll start yelling. He'll start going, "You're trying to be my mother". He'll threaten to leave me and the kids. It is hard. And it all usually has to do with him and his gambling.

Other gamblers took a less confrontational approach, choosing to appease their spouses to avoid disagreement:

I always promise that I will go and see a doctor, that I will improve, that I will stop doing that. But to be honest with you, it doesn't happen. In the moment, I do want to improve and to keep the peace, and I need to take some action. I just don't.

Moreover, some couples thought the problem is not the addiction: it is the frequency of losing. These couples believed they could avoid conflict by solving the money problem through a higher rate of winning. To this end, some couples turned their conflicts into talk about improving the odds of winning:

> We reflect on the past game that we played. Or if it is not that, we are talking about how we shouldn't play as much as we do; or we are talking about strategy.

Faced with the wish to avoid conflict, spouses have a hard time finding ways to help their gambling spouse. Some spouses know that their partner needs help, but they lack the details they need to help them.

Nothing in Common

As we have seen, gambling takes almost everything—time, money, trust, peace of mind—out of a marriage. Couples no longer share common interests, activities, or conversations, and they begin to feel they have nothing in common with the person they had fallen in love with.

The spouses in our study often did not feel that the gamblers understood their concerns or what was expected of them in the relationship. Likewise, the gamblers often said that their spouses did not understand them. One respondent described such a major gap between himself and his wife:

> The only problem [with our relationship] is what we think. We don't think alike. We don't have anything in common; we don't have anything in common.

Another gambler complained about the lost closeness and understanding in her relationship, feeling that she had been a victim of the constant conflict:

> He is not as affectionate as he used to be towards me. He's arguing more with me. Over the years now I can see he is more argumentative. We are still close in our ways, but I can see us drifting. After 21 years of marriage, we don't seem to have nothing in common. He likes one kind of gambling and I like another kind of gambling; but it is mostly the arguing and it upsets my daughter . . . It is mostly because of the gambling.

With both members of the couple feeling misunderstood and neglected, these relationships are hard to rebuild. When a couple feels they have reached an impasse, and they no longer have anything in common, they often decide to part ways.

Ultimatums and Divorce

The gamblers and their partners in the 2005 study often said that one of them was ready to leave the relationship or had left it on occasion. The intent and willingness of spouses to leave the gambler was often preceded by an ultimatum. An ultimatum was their one last try to solve the gambling problem and save the marriage:

> We almost separated a couple of times because of it and we got into a lot of arguments . . . [though] now we're not [arguing as much], 'cause I told her I'm going to slow down on [the gambling] . . . But we used to get into tons of arguments; we were ready to break up a lot. We were supposed to get married and we broke that up.

In general, when gamblers ignore these ultimatums, the partners may decide to leave. But gamblers usually try to prevent the ultimatum by holding back information about their gambling. The feeling that they cannot choose between their relationship and their need to gamble leaves gamblers with few alternatives.

Often, spouses discover that ultimatums don't repair the problems caused by problem gambling. When gamblers refuse to reduce their gambling, their spouses become fed up with the constant worry and frustration. One spouse summed up the feelings of many antigambling spouses:

> I'm going to be on the roller coaster ride with him. I refuse.

Yet while lack of trust, emotional insecurity, resentment, and frustration cause some spouses to leave their relationship, others decide to stay:

> Why didn't I see this sooner? You consider breaking up the relationship, but then I am kind of comfortable. It is easier for the person, despite what is going on, if you just hang around.

Marriages are endlessly varied in the ways they work through problems:

Maybe bringing us together in another element [such as gambling] is a plus—sharing her joy at [gambling]. I enjoy the hell out of people having fun, and if she's having that kind of fun from it, I get a kick out of that too.

Thus, while some respondents were simply willing to remain in conflict-ridden relationships, for others, the conflict, stress, and disconnection that result from avoiding conflict was reason enough to give an ultimatum and get a divorce.

The Concealment and Disclosure of the Gambling Problem

In time, most spouses come to realize the extent of a gambler's problem. When asked how their spouses became aware of the gambling problem, the gambling respondents cited four paths to awareness:

- self-disclosure
- observation
- mistake or outside source
- partner gambles as well and so knows about the problem

Self-disclosure means that the gambler simply confessed to the spouse. One respondent explained that his wife was unaware of his gambling until he self-disclosed:

When I got married she didn't know I was a gambler. I would be away for hours and at odd times and at night. After a period of time she was concerned about where I was. I made excuses and defended myself. Before I told her that I gambled, I made her promise not to tell my parents. It is embarrassing. She was concerned with my being gone every day or several times a week. After a long time of arguments and concerns, I told her.

But gamblers can keep up their lies for a surprisingly long time, stretching even into years, so these self-disclosures can come as a big surprise:

I had to sit down and tell her. I used her bank cards, her cheques, all kinds of stuff and I finally had to tell her. Twenty years and I finally had to sit down and tell her . . . Finally it came out that I had this [gambling problem]. Nobody knew, nobody had a clue. I still lied to her about different things until I finally went, June this year, I went to the gambling seminar in

Windsor and that helped me a lot. I've been seeing [a counsellor] at CAMH [Centre for Addiction and Mental Health] for about a year now. Things are better.

Awareness through observation is slower, while the gambler continues to gamble. One interviewee, who had succeeded in hiding his gambling problem so far, said that his wife suspected there was a problem but didn't know specifically what it was:

> She suspects there's a problem. My wife suspects that I have no money because it's gotta either be gambling or another woman. It's just a matter of time before she finds out.

In addition, positive and negative mood changes alert spouses to the gambling problem:

> You say "bet" and it's like a bomb went off (she laughs). Like a nerve or something . . . like, "Okay, okay, let's go." He is just pumped . . . just hearing about gambling. You think he is going to explode.

> He is much angrier . . . edgier. He snaps. He'll come in and the whole atmosphere is just cold. He is very cold.

One respondent summed up her experience of the behaviour change she witnessed in her husband over a period of 38 years:

> When he's leaving, he's very positive and upbeat. When he comes back, depending on how he fares, if he wins he's still up, if he loses he's down— he's angry, frustrated, you can't say two words to him and everything triggers anger. Everything triggers an argument. He claims nobody understands him, he's alone in this world . . . The first 24 hours is anger, the second 24 hours is depression, and the third 24 hours he's climbing his way out of it, trying to figure out how he's going to get his money back. He's already planning his next trip.

But a few gamblers said their spouses had found out about their gambling by accident or through an outside source:

She never suspected that I go to all these places—[she thought] I was working and whatever . . . [Then] the Visa statement came, and she saw and asked me.

Finally, many gamblers and partners revealed that gambling was always part of their relationship, because the relationship developed around gambling, so there was no need for any kind of disclosure:

When we were dating, I told him that I like to do things like gambling. He knew about the euchre right off the bat. I think he tried to take me out to a movie on Tuesday and that was my euchre night, and I told him that Tuesday was a no-go because I don't do anything on Tuesday with anybody else. I told him about the casinos and he asked me, what kind of self-control do I have and what kind of rules do I give myself. I told him and they seemed fine to him.

Thus, to some extent, most spouses are aware that their partner has a gambling problem. In the 2005 study, all the spouses did eventually become aware of the partner's gambling. However, the severity and details of the problem were harder to uncover.

Spouse Reaction to Disclosure

Some spouses who know gambling is happening don't know the severity or frequency. How one becomes aware of the extent of a partner's problem gambling can have a significant impact on the relationship.

Self-disclosure provides the couple with the most honest and open method for coming to terms with the problem; however, it can be the most shocking and disturbing for the spouse. If the gambler self-discloses at the beginning of the relationship, the disclosure is casual, often just a discussion about recreation activities they enjoy. While most gamblers in the 2005 study admitted their interest in gambling at the beginning of the relationship, it wasn't until later that many spouses realized the severity of the gambling problem:

When we first started dating, she would go to the casinos with her mom. That was just something to do, like a girls-night-out kind of thing. And it wasn't a big deal to me at all. [But] I'm aware of the full extent of her gambling now . . . She would lose everything and then manage to get it back. She has racked up credit card debts quickly, she has borrowed money from her mom, but she pays it back.

M: I met her at a party at my buddy's house. We were playing cards . . . and that's where I met her because she was a friend of my buddy's.
Interviewer: So she became aware of your gambling at that party?
M: Yup. But I guess she didn't think: "There's a gambler, let me hook into him." She didn't know the extent of the addiction, I guess.

Some of the gamblers explained that they kept their gambling hidden until they had to disclose it, either because their spouse was suspicious or because their gambling had gone too far. But by delaying disclosure until the gambling had caused a crisis, these gamblers created a tense, high-conflict situation for the disclosure:

She gave me the money to pay rent, and I said, okay. But I never paid it. Then two weeks later, they were phoning and [asking] "Where's the rent?" and in the meantime I was trying to rustle it up so she wouldn't know about it. Then, yeah, I had to come clean; I said I went and gambled it, and she flipped.

Occasionally, the spouse might learn about the severity of problem gambling by accident or through an outside source. When the spouse learns about the problem in this way, he or she feels betrayed and often expresses bitterness:

Interviewer: When did you first discover that he had a pretty serious problem?
R: I think when people tell he is always at the casino. When he started borrowing money and using my name, I was appalled. Because I was like, we need money for the rent. And people said [my partner] came to borrow money off of me and I was like "I don't have nothing to do with that." And she was like, "Yeah, you borrowed money to pay the rent."

For some respondents, the severity of the problem became apparent only after they moved in together. Eventually, payments were missed or creditors would call. These spouses experienced fear and bewilderment—and a sense of betrayal:

We had just moved in together and there were payments missing on things. I remember sitting in the living room and the phone was ringing with creditors calling.

One spouse recalled that she had an idea that her spouse gambled, though she never thought it was a big issue until it came out in a marital counselling session.

> Interviewer: How did you become aware of your partner's gambling?
> P: Through family counselling and marriage counselling. He disclosed it during counselling. I had an idea that he gambled before but I had no idea that it was an issue. I didn't really think about that up until that point.

Most spouses in the 2005 study were aware that the gambler had a problem, because it was this awareness that motivated them to take part in the study. Therefore, we cannot conclude that most spouses in the general population are as aware of the gambling problems in their relationship as these couples were. But in general, the more honest and forthcoming the gambler is in revealing his or her problem, the better able the couple is to move forward.

Continued Deception

Though spouses often become aware of some details of the gambler's problem, much is still kept hidden. Even after disclosure, many gamblers keep on gambling. To keep the severity of their gambling a secret, they resort to deception:

> If I go weekends, I have to tell because he has to drop me to the place where I have to take the bus that leaves for the casinos. So that is why he came to know weekends; but weekdays he doesn't know. I just take the bus . . . I take the subway all the way to Islington—that he doesn't know. But I have to tell lies.

In addition, some gamblers simply hide the financial details of their activities from their spouses, as one spouse described:

> He would lie on the [loan] application, saying it was his home solely. So that gave him more equity to work with and that gave him a greater credit card balance. It just became crazy and I had no idea. The mail was coming in and he was keeping credit card bills from me, that kind of stuff.

Gamblers also try to put up smokescreens, claiming that they are quitting or cutting back. But in reality, they are still gambling the same amount. Some spouses are not fooled:

> He won't make the attempts to try and stop, and then he lies—he lies about gambling and when he goes—even if he does go to the racetracks. He's been up there, but I don't know how frequent he goes up there. He lies about it.

Thus, even after disclosure, problem gambling continues to be a problem for both the gambler and the spouses. Gamblers lie to continue supporting their habit and focus on creating elaborate charades for their spouses.

How Spouses Feel about Deception

As spouses learn more about the extent of the problem, they are more likely to pressure the gambler to quit or get the gambling under control. But instead of co-operating, gamblers are more likely simply to increase their deception. As a result, spouses often feel frustrated that they can't get their partners to change and that they can't break down the wall of secrecy. They know bits and pieces of information and can't get the whole story. One respondent described his partner's secrecy as a brick wall:

> I don't know why he keeps things from me—whether it's the gambling thing or the feeling of failure—but increasingly so much is kept [secret]. It's almost like he's building this brick wall up so much. If I hadn't accumulated so much [information] at the start, I wouldn't be where I am right now, so far as knowing what I do. It's almost like he's trying to put that wall up so [I won't] get to know too much more. That's getting really scary because I want to know what's behind that wall—"What is so big that you are trying to keep me from knowing?"

Another respondent described herself as being constantly angry with her partner:

> I don't understand this whole "I-have-to-keep-this-a-secret-from-Marjorie" thing. Yes, I'm going to be angry, but don't you think that if I find out from somebody else, I'll be more angry? And I'm like angry 75 percent of the time, so what's another 10? (laughing) Like, we were talking about this, and

I couldn't even discuss spaghetti sauce with him without getting into an argument. We had people over, and he wanted to make spaghetti sauce, and we started yelling about how to make the spaghetti sauce. And his friend was, like, "Is there ever a time when you people can just talk to each other and not yell?" He says I put him down all the time. And I'm, like, "Yes I put you down all the time, but give me something good to say."

Another respondent felt that being kept in the dark made him question the stability of his relationship:

PW: I really don't know how much debt he's in, but I know it's probably close to tens of thousands of dollars now.

Interviewer: So how do you feel about that?

P: Anxious, upset, wondering just how long before the house of cards comes down. Can we get out of this? Are we getting lottery tickets with the idea that a win will take care of everything? I wonder sometimes if the nervous excitement he has is just "I'd be able to erase a lot of debt if I was to win." I know that it has affected my sleep. The climate of secrecy—things aren't as open as they used to be or should be—from his end. I feel a lot of stuff being kept from me and it makes me wonder where I sit.

Most spouses expressed despair both at their lack of details about wins and losses and the frequency of gambling and their inability to successfully intervene:

I don't really know the specifics. I know that this was a problem, really more of a problem, a couple of years ago. Maybe there has been a small change, and maybe that's been enough to satisfy me. Whereas if it had continued the way it had three years ago, then maybe we wouldn't be together right now, because I see that as a big problem.

Conclusion

The deception and secrecy of problem gamblers puts immense stresses on relationships. Partners are torn between their anger and sense of betrayal and their emotional ties with their gambling spouses. Gamblers, in turn, feel guilt and inner turmoil about lying but feel helpless to stop it. How can two people in a relationship live in two such separate worlds? The next chapter explores the impact of couple embeddedness on gambling, secrecy, and spousal control.

Chapter 9
Weak Couple Embeddedness

Spouses are unaware of the dreams and activities and gambling problems of their partner, but this is not because they are asleep and dreaming. It is mainly because they have been excluded from their partner's social world. Spouse lack of awareness of their spouse's gambling contributes to the gradually worsening of marital relations that most of the couples in our study experienced. Because spouses were unaware of the extent of the problem, they were unable to devote the attention, time, and thought needed to help correct it.

Often spouses are unaware of the details of the gamblers' problems because the two partners spend little time together and share few friends, networks, or social activities. In this respect, their lives are not embedded. *Embeddedness* refers to the intertwining of partners' social networks and can be measured through embeddedness scales. Later in this chapter, we discuss the way we measured embeddedness in our own study. According to the measures used here, most of the couples in the study were weakly embedded. Strong embeddedness can help a spouse confront and deal with a gambler's problem; weak embeddedness removes this possibility. Marriage can be useful in helping people cope with their problems, and marriage is more often helpful if the couple is strongly embedded. Embedded partners are more able to supervise each other and apply sanctions for misbehaviour.

A few couples in the study did show *strong couple embeddedness* in their relationship. These couples occupied the same social world, knew each other's families, worked together, spent time with the same group of friends, or belonged to the same organizations. However, most other couples occupied very different social worlds, with neither partner knowing the other's friends or families. These couples displayed *weak couple embeddedness*. If a couple is weakly embedded, neither partner is likely to know much about the other's activities. In turn, this lack of knowledge allows gambling and other problematic behaviours to go unnoticed and uncontrolled.

This chapter explores the tendency of problem gamblers and their partners to occupy different social worlds, and the consequences of this. It begins with a discussion of the ideas of James Coleman and Elizabeth Bott, whose work pioneered our understanding of the role of network embeddedness in shaping the ways couples organize their own relations with one another.

The Embeddedness Research of James Coleman

Let's begin with an interesting observation that made a big splash in the sociological community 20 years ago. Theorist and educational sociologist James Coleman (1988) noted that families and schools in *closed communities*—that is, communities characterized by dense, tightly knit relationships—were better at enforcing family norms than families in more open communities. In this particular case, they were better at keeping teenaged children from dropping out of high school.

Coleman found, in particular, that religious-based schools are more successful at retaining students than non-religious schools. He argues that this is because religious-based schools surround teenagers with a closed community in which parents and teachers are likely to know each other from church as well as from school. As such, the community in which a teenager is embedded can more successfully monitor and guide adolescent behaviour to conform with norms— in this case, to conform with the norm of finishing high school. Coleman explains that closed communities are good at monitoring and sanctioning behaviour because information about malfeasance or misbehaviour in one relationship is easily passed along to other mutual contacts, who then respond negatively. A sequence of negative sanctions instantly goes into play.

This kind of network connectedness, or closure, is related to *social capital*, an important personal and social resource. Writing about social capital, Coleman (1988) claimed that people are better off in densely connected networks characterized by established rules and informal social controls. Collective social capital enforces cooperation and conformity, precisely because it infringes privacy and limits secrecy. Embeddedness in a densely connected network, therefore, reduces the likelihood of extreme or deviant behaviour. This makes dense networks relatively "safe" and makes people more likely to disclose their secrets, even to people who would not otherwise be considered "safe" recipients of information.

Generalizing from a variety of cases that goes well beyond teenagers and religious schools, Coleman writes: "One property of social relations on which effective norms depend is what I will call closure. In general, one can say that a necessary but not sufficient condition for the emergence of effective norms is action that imposes external effects on others . . . Closure of the social structure is important not only for the existence of effective norms but also for another form of social capital: the trustworthiness of social structures that allows the proliferation of obligations and expectations . . . We may say that closure creates trustworthiness in a social structure" (Coleman, 1988: S105–8).

The Embeddedness Research of Elizabeth Bott

Fifty years ago, Elizabeth Bott wrote a book that made much clearer how this process might work in a family setting. Her 1957 book, *Family and Social Network: Roles, Norms, and External Relationships in Ordinary, Urban Families*, was an interdisciplinary study of the relationship between external social networks and internal family organization. The goal of her study was to understand the social and psychological organization of some urban families by analyzing class ideologies and "conjugal norms."

Bott's book focused on marriage and the roles within a marriage, based on a long-term study of "ordinary" families in London in the early 1950s. In her study, Bott distinguishes between two main kinds of spousal relationship—a *complementary conjugal* relationship and a *joint conjugal* relationship—and two kinds of social (including kinship) networks around the spousal unit—a *close-knit network*, with many relationships among its members, versus a *loose-knit network*, with few such relationships. She hypothesizes that, for various reasons, married people in loose-knit social networks will develop and maintain joint conjugal relationships, whereas people in close-knit social networks will develop and maintain complementary conjugal relationships.

In an Appendix B to her study, Bott explains how and why she came to classify conjugal relations as she did. A *complementary conjugal relationship* (occasionally also called *segregated conjugal relationship*) is a relationship in which the husband and wife carry out different, though complementary activities apart from each other (that is, outside each other's company). A *joint conjugal relationship* is a relationship in which the husband and wife typically carry out activities together, whether these activities are shared, parallel, or different; or they carry out similar activities while (occasionally) apart. A *close-knit social network* is a set of people who are connected (or linked together), directly and indirectly, by many connections of various kinds—kinship, friendship, neighbouring, and so on. These networks provide members with a wide range of important resources, including material, emotional, and social support. In contrast, a *loose-knit social network* is a set of people who are connected by few links.

Bott's purpose was to understand the connection between these network structures (especially kinship networks) and the relationships of spouses within a marriage. After empirical study, she concluded that the more separately a husband and wife live (for example, in very gendered roles or in otherwise separate worlds), the more close-knit the social network to which the two spouses belong.

Bott also noted the converse association: that spouses who live a more shared and joint life have somewhat loose-knit networks, especially kin networks. She concluded that in close-knit or high-density kinship networks, all members recognize and internalize the norms of the group. These norms come to dominate family activity. In other words, people in close-knit networks share the same views about marriage and family life and abide by the same rules governing family life. Often, these rules are gendered and encourage married couples to live more separate lives. In contrast, loose-knit or low-density networks have varied social norms; because of this diversity, they can't exert the same dominance over families. This means that families in loose-knit networks are less subject to a "normal" set of views and rules about marriage and family life. They are freer to devise their own rules, which means families in loose-knit networks are more independent and idiosyncratic. Thus, family-specific norms guide married life in loose-knit networks.

As a result, loose-knit and close-knit kin networks create or empower different types of marriage relationships. In close-knit social networks, spouses exchange mutual aid outside the family and spouses have less need for one another's practical aid and companionship. This support from outside the household increases the likelihood of segregated, separate, or gendered marital roles inside the household. It also encourages spouses to socialize outside the household—men with men (fathers, brothers, and male friends) and women with women (mothers, sisters, and female friends).

In contrast, in loose-knit kin networks, domestic (husband-and-wife) roles need to overlap and support one another. Husbands and wives must share the work and co-operate closely in running the household, since they have only each other to rely on. Since kin and social network members are less likely to provide help, spouses have to help each other much more than is usual in "traditional" families in close-knit networks. For example, these couples will often share both domestic tasks and leisure time. As well, they will more often socialize with other couples—husbands forming new friendships with other husbands, and wives forming friendships with their respective wives—rather than with their respective male and female relatives.

We can extrapolate from Bott's work, using Coleman's insights, to make two main arguments. First, spouses in close-knit networks may be able to enlist the help of nearby kin and neighbours to gain the information needed to ensure compliance and generate trust in relations with their spouse. Second, spouses in loose-knit networks can develop joint spousal relationships in which they spend a great deal of time together or with other couples who are friends. These shared relationships offer another way of gaining the information needed to ensure compliance and generate trust in relations with their spouse.

Thus, either the two spouses are embedded closely into each other's lives, or they are embedded closely into their kin and social network. These two types of embeddedness are two alternate strategies for gaining the information on which compliance and trust are built.

However embeddedness arises, it is the key to information flow, norm enforcement, compliance, and marital trust. For this reason, a couple's embeddedness in each other and in their social networks allows a spouse to learn about his or her partner's gambling, and helps to bring it under control.

Quantitative Measures of Couple Embeddedness from the 2005 Study

Measuring couple embeddedness is not easy. The 2005 study measured embeddedness by assessing the shared social networks of each couple, using close-ended questions about the sharing of time, activities, interests, and knowledge about friends, co-workers, and family members. The responses to these items were combined into one measure of partner embeddedness in each couple.

We developed a formal Embeddedness Scale specifically to measure the knowledge spouses have about each other's social networks. A couple's embeddedness helps to explain how (and how well) members of a couple are able to maintain secrecy from each other, whatever their personalities, relationship qualities, or interaction styles. This approach to understanding secrecy and disclosure grows out of social network analysis by researchers like Elizabeth Bott.

Following structural theory, we propose that that a high degree of couple embeddedness makes non-disclosure of gambling (or any other misbehaviour) almost impossible. Disclosure, in these circumstances, is not a rational choice: it is nearly inevitable. Briefly, we expect that people who live in densely connected networks will disclose their secrets more readily than people who live in loosely connected networks. The key concept here is *network connectedness*—the degree to which family, friends, and acquaintances of the problem gambler are linked to one another, directly and indirectly. A high degree of embeddedness ensures a high degree of behavioural visibility. It also increases feelings of trust and safety.

To measure embeddedness in this study, respondents were asked a series of questions that dealt with the nature of their relationship with their spouse in the preceding six months. In total, we developed nine new measures to describe the nature of a couple's relationship, in structural terms. They included the following:

- **Similarity to partner:** Participants were asked how similar they felt they were to their partner, based on the following items and others:
  - sexual orientation,
  - political views,
  - spiritual beliefs,
  - how they like to spend their time, and
  - how they like to spend their money.
- **Time spent with spouse:** Participants were asked how often they spent time with their partner doing a variety of activities that included
  - relaxing at home,
  - doing household chores,
  - going out to restaurants,
  - going out to bars,
  - going out to movies, or
  - entertaining friends at home.
- **Awareness of spouse's hopes and fears:** Participants were asked how much they agreed or disagreed with the following statements:
  - I knew this person's worst fears;
  - This person knew my worst fears;
  - I knew this person's fondest hopes;
  - This person knew my fondest hopes.
- **Common networks:** Participants were asked about the number of people whom they had in common with their partner, within the following three categories:

- close friends,
- acquaintances, and
- co-workers.
- **Knowledge of networks (4 scales):** To determine the inter-connectedness of respondents and their partners, we asked respondents about people they knew by first name. Specifically, they were asked:
  - how many people in their partner's life they knew by first name,
  - how many people in their life their partner knew by first name,
  - how many people in their partner's life knew them by first name, and
  - how many people in their life knew their partner by first name.
- **Embeddedness:** A composite score of couple embeddedness was created by adding the preceding four "knowledge of network" scores.

Subsequent analysis of these data revealed that embeddedness is highly corre-lated with all the other aspects of structural connectedness we measured.

When asked how often they spend time with their partner, most respon-dents replied that they spend *some* time with their partner, such as to relax at home, talk on the phone, or do household chores together. The activities our couples were most likely to share were private activities—just the partners alone together. The gamblers and their spouses claimed to have similar interests in entertainment, sexual orientation, and political views; however, the gamblers were more likely than their spouses to favour spending their time and money gambling.

As well, respondents answered questions about their knowledge of partners' close friends, acquaintances, and co-workers. The results show that our respon-dents shared few close friends, many acquaintances, and few or no co-workers. Generally, partners knew the first names of each others' parents, siblings, and children. They knew only a few of their partners' best friends and co-workers by first name. Similarly, they told us that only a few of their partners' best friends and co-workers would likely know their first name. In short, couples shared the same family and close friend networks to a degree, but their network links ended here.

These measures of network knowledge and embeddedness were based on self-assessment. We have no way of directly measuring how many names of friends, workmates, and family members the partner or spouse *really* knew—only how many names the respondent *believed* his or her partner knows. That said, the data gathered this way likely provides a rough estimate of the couple embeddedness.

Our results compare interestingly with the results from an earlier study of gay couples in Toronto (Tepperman *et al.*, 2002)—the only other study so far that used this measure of network embeddedness. This study found that members of *strongly* embedded couples were significantly more likely than members of *weakly* embedded couples to disclose an important secret—in this case, HIV-positivity—to their partner, and to do so more quickly. By comparing measurements from the two studies, we find that our gambling respondents were more embedded than our gay respondents. This means that in this study, gamblers and their spouses were more embedded than might have been expected, given the frequency and severity of marital problems. We will have to await the use of this measure of embeddedness on a random sample of Canadian couples or high-functioning heterosexual families before we can fully judge how weakly or strongly embedded our couples are in comparative terms.

The embeddedness data from the 2005 study show that the nongambling spouses believed that their parents, siblings, and co-workers do not know the gambler partners very well. On the other hand, the gamblers believed that their spouses were more integrated into the gambler's social networks than the gambler was into the spouse's social networks. If this is true, then the gamblers' invisibility in the partner's social and kin networks may have been a result of the preoccupation with gambling that limited any interest or involvement in the spouse's social lives. If this assumption is correct, then the spouses may be better-known to the gambler's social network than vice versa because the spouses are making conscious efforts to integrate themselves into the gamblers' networks.

Qualitative Data on Embeddedness from the 2005 Study

Qualitative findings from the 2005 study suggest that strongly embedded couples have more emotional and practical "tools" than weakly embedded couples to help correct a partner's gambling problem. Yet these tools are often difficult to use and may not always provide the intended results. Further, it is still difficult for partners to help solve the gambling problem, even if they are strongly embedded. Gambling compounds the relationship problems and the spouse's ability to help the gambler by contributing to a reduction in embeddedness.

Strong Couple Embeddedness

Case Study: Bill

Bill and his partner were both gamblers. Bill's partner was the problem gambler of the two.

Bill described an otherwise healthy relationship with his partner. They share much leisure time together, communicated and resolved conflicts well, and shared family responsibilities equally. Bill admitted having exposed his partner to gambling through his work. He used to get promotional passes for complimentary food and free hotel rooms at nearby casinos. He said that on one of these trips, his partner had a big win and later displayed the common characteristics of a problem gambler—for example, she would go back to recuperate losses and had begun hiding her losses from him.

Bill described spending much time and energy trying to educate his partner about the psychological mechanics of habituation and the wastefulness of gambling, but without any success. Seeing his partner slip into the downward spiral of problem gambling, Bill finally came to the point of trying to regulate her gambling:

> I've been of late a chaperon to her. But the trap that she's caught in now is her trying to win back previous losses and losing more and more.

Trapped in this stressful position, Bill tried multiple strategies. One approach was to use their common friendship network as a source of information and influence. Luckily, Bill knew a lot about his partner's network of friends and fellow gamblers. He revealed his knowledge of the role that friends played in his partner's gambling:

> I think that her friends are also a lot more into gambling and have taught her their ways to have regular gambling as a part of your life.

Recognizing that her friendship network may be teaching her (harmful) norms and behaviours, Bill tried several strategies to manipulate these channels of information, in hopes of diverting or removing the positive messages about gambling. One strategy was to encourage his partner to invite friends to join her in nongambling activities:

I've tried to suggest other activities that she can do with her friends. This whole thing has come up because my hours are not regular, but hers are. So there are lots of times that she has free time when I don't.

Obviously, this strategy was limited, since Bill could not force his partner (or her friends) to engage in these activities. Bill tried to get around this by personally dissuading her friends from gambling:

She would be there . . . talking to her friends, for example . . . asking them what they want to do, and [I'd be] encouraging them that they don't need to go to the casino, that kind of thing . . . We'd go over for dinner two or three times, and we'd begin talking about . . . the joys of going to a casino, and "Oh, do you know what's happening?" and this and that. Then I'd start talking about how I don't think it's a good idea, it's a waste of time, it's a waste of money, hoping that by doing that I would encourage her friends to encourage her not to do it.

Bill hoped his message to stop gambling might reach her through multiple channels this way, and he hoped this increased the message's effectiveness.

The example of Bill shows how a strongly embedded couple might address its problem. With open lines of communication and common friends, there is a solid flow of information, which allows Bill to monitor and sanction his partner's activities. It also allows him to try to manipulate the flow and content of information. However, Bill had only limited success.

Strong Couple Embeddedness and Problem Gambling

Strongly embedded couples share certain features. For one, they enjoy each other's company. As we have seen, respondents cited many joint leisure activities that they participated in, which sometimes involved other people. One respondent even went as far as to say they were so busy they were rarely home:

We go for walks on the beach, walk through the malls, go to the movies, trips, restaurants, um, laundry (laughs). We do all kinds of stuff together. We hardly ever stay home. We are constantly doing something.

Shared leisure time keeps the lines of communication open and helps preserve the quality of the relationship. Also, by engaging in activities with others, couples foster new shared relationships.

In addition, the respondents who had children also described sharing many recreational activities with their children:

> We take the kids to the movies, to Chuck-E Cheese, etc. We like outdoor activities, like bike riding. We have two kids, ages 6 and 9½. I don't think my husband's gambling affects the children because he's always home when they're done school and he only gambles during the night.

In this sense, it appears that having children may help bind a family together. But social activities alone do not prevent the gambler from gambling at other times, although they help by providing distractions and reducing time available for gambling.

A second common characteristic of strongly embedded couples is that they have several common relationships. The most usual shared relationships among strongly embedded partners are those with family members and gambling friends. These are also the shared relationships to which respondents ascribe the most impact.

Yet outside social network relationships come in different types and have different levels of usefulness in combating the problem of gambling. To assess the significance of certain relationships, we must look at the form and influence of relationships on gambling. People have different types of relationships with different types of people, whom they know from different settings. For example, the loving relationship one might have with one's parents is different from the loving relationship one has with one's partner. Each relationship influences people's lives in a different way and to a different degree. The emotional support people get from their family is different from the recreational value they get from their friends. Similarly, some relationships demand more time and involvement than others, since a romantic partner expects much more emotional investment than a co-worker. Each type of relationship offers different ways to influence the gambling.

The single biggest problem spouses face is a lack of reliable information, and their friends and relatives may prove useful, if they are able to provide such information. Beyond this, spouses often need support and encouragement in dealing with the problems caused by problem gambling—for example, indebtedness and financial insecurity. Here too, even friends and acquaintances can serve as normalizing influences on family lives that have been driven by the chaos associated with gambling losses. Reliable friends may also be helpful in dealing with the shame, guilt, and despair a spouse is likely to feel as his or her marital relationship breaks down over gambling.

Often, frustrated spouses try to use and manipulate these relationships in efforts to curb the gambler's habits. But they use different approaches when working with family members and with gambling friends.

Family members are often the most influential social contacts regarding problem gambling. According to interviewees, the most important social ties for gamblers are those with their own family. Therefore, spouses are most successful when they use family members to pressure the gambler to quit. One way a spouse can help influence the gambling is by serving as a *distraction*. Some spouses try to keep the gambler away from gambling by keeping them busy with other activities—for example, by encouraging them to visit their family:

> We clean the house together, go for walks down at the beach once in a while ... We go up north sometimes to my sister's trailer once in a while ... We usually have a good time. And when I do these things with her I am not gambling... things seem to be okay when we go away or do things together.

Spouses can also use the gambler's family as emotional leverage. This is especially true when the gambler's family disapproves of gambling:

> I know her parents wouldn't approve—or her grandfather, who she and I were both close with who just passed away recently in India ... There would be no way that he would understand or approve.

Armed with knowledge the gambler wants to hide from his or her family, a spouse can gain new power over the gambler and can use this to pressure the gambler to change. One respondent admitted to feeling embarrassed about his gambling, saying that his family would kill him if they found out about his habit. After finding out about his gambling, the respondent's wife was able to persuade him to quit by threatening to reveal his secret to his family.

This couple offered an especially interesting example of the moral authority of family. The husband described his marriage as being very shaky since telling his now emotionally-distant wife about his gambling. They had one child, but since the disclosure, they lived in separate homes, and she didn't visit him as often as she used to. When asked how he planned to resolve this problem, he looked to their families. He stated that if he and his wife could not find a way to solve their problems on their own, the parents could force them to resolve things:

> I will try to figure out our differences with her and have family meetings. We will discuss one-on-one, and if that doesn't work we could see coun-sellors. Or we could also discuss things with our elders. We could get our elders involved ... her parents and my parents. So if we don't agree with each other, we will get the elders involved instead of just ignoring each other like we do now.

Another couple we interviewed provides another example of a gambler's family taking initiative. Whenever the couple began to fight, the wife's mother inter-vened or refereed:

> He'll get me crying and, oh man, I do, I cry. I am a very sensitive person, and he'll get me crying, and then my mom will get involved. So we'll get my mom to stand in between, and she'll go, "Both of you stop it, or I will knock you both out." She raised five of us kids, so she knows what to do. We end up working it out a lot better.

Thus, spouses of gamblers can find allies in both the gambler's family and the spouse's family.

Friends are also useful in helping deal with the gambling problem, though friendships have their limitations. First, friends have less emotional leverage than families and so are not as powerful an influence. Second, they often already know about the gambling problem and may have accepted it. Third, the gambler's only friends may be fellow gamblers. However, despite these draw-backs, spouses can still use gambling and nongambling friendships as distrac-tions, keeping gamblers busy with activities other than gambling.

One gambler admitted noticing that his wife employed this strategy by inviting people over to the house to socialize:

> C: We always have people over, always. I mean we drink. Can I say we smoke drugs, or are we going to get arrested?—so that's what we do. That's what she tries to do most of the time.

Interviewer: So, she tries to get you guys to hang out and drink instead of gambling?

C: My wife doesn't do any drugs, but we'll go out on the balcony and talk about it.

Friends can also be sources of information. Spouses can find clever ways to gain access to information through friendship networks. Gamblers' deceit about their problem can be a large obstacle for spouses. So rather than live in constant confusion and suspicion, spouses mine friendships for information. The most useful informants are the gambler's friends, especially if they gamble together.

One respondent described how his partner's friends gave him information that helped him understand his partner's attraction to gambling:

She's a math teacher—she likes things like probability, she likes the thrill of thinking how to beat something—that seems to me anyway to be the case. When we first started this, we didn't really seem to know what we were doing, but now she knows technical things, and she's been talking about buying books to learn how to do things better. Like, she would like to buy a book on how to play blackjack, and her friends tell me she's extremely good at bridge, which she apparently played quite a bit when she was younger. Whether or not if she bets while she plays bridge, I'm not sure.

This spouse's situation is unusual, for his wife's gambling friends often encouraged her to spend time doing other things. As a result, the gambler's friends applied the same kind of pressure as family:

We've only been married for three years. Actually, I knew her four years before we got married, and gambling or going to casinos never was raised; it wasn't until we actually got married that she seemed to reveal to me that she actually liked it. I don't know if she potentially wanted to hide it or what, but then, with speaking with her friends, they really try to encourage her to do other activities as well.

But friendship networks rarely offer this degree of concerted help. Usually, spouses have trouble finding friends to take part in an intervention or confirming suspicions of problematic gambling behaviour.

Spouses can also use the gambler's gambling friends to block gambling opportunities. For example, some spouses find they can position themselves to block the flow of information between the gambler and their gambling networks. One respondent admitted she doesn't always tell her husband when his gambling friends have called, thereby sabotaging his ability to plan gambling excursions:

> He mostly plays with friends, so I always try to have a legitimate excuse ready for why he can't gamble with his friends that night. I also won't give my husband any phone messages from his gambling friends.

To summarize, strongly embedded spouses often try to use the gambler's family and friends to help solve the gambling problem. Families can be used for distraction and emotional leverage because of their moral authority over the gambler. Friends can be useful as distractions, as sources of information, and as a means of blocking information. Friendship networks are also useful for gathering important information that can be used to develop further strategies. For example, friends may be able to supply detailed information about gambling activity or indebtedness that will strengthen a spouse's resolve to take action. Yet, though strongly embedded couples are offered plenty of opportunities to influence the gambling problem, they may fail to use them well.

The Disadvantages of Strong Couple Embeddedness

While strong couple embeddedness is generally healthy and provides good tools to help a problem gambler stop gambling, it is not always successful at solving the problem. Sometimes shared networks cannot be used successfully to deal with a gambling problem. Moreover, a poor relationship between the gambler and spouse may limit the use of personal networks. In addition, counter-productive behaviour by members of the social network (especially of gambling friends) may limit the use of these networks. For whatever reason, spouses often face barriers in accessing and using their partner's social networks.

One factor that can limit the usefulness of friendship and family networks is the conflict over opinions about gambling. Friends and family can only be useful in controlling problem gambling if they disapprove of gambling. Moreover, a network that is being used only as a source of information cannot also be used as a source of influence. Conversely, friends who disapprove of gambling are likely to reveal all they know about the gambler's activities to the partner, in order to help the gambler with their problem.

In addition, if a social or family network is far removed from gambling, its members likely do not have much influence on the gambler. A couple may be involved in many community activities, where none of their friends and acquaintances knows one another, and—outside the gambling network itself—none has any knowledge of the gambling problem. As a result, these friendships are useless for either information-seeking or emotional leverage. In fact, the external focus of shared activities sometimes makes it difficult for shared relationships to help the couples solve their private problems:

> We tend to be involved in activities that are directed to the community rather than personal, between us, so that we do volunteer activities—outside of us and deflecting outward. We have more of those activities together than things we enjoy together, because even some of the normal socializing things that some people would find gratifying, I find it more of a chore.

Social networks can also contribute to the gambling problem if its members are enablers. Families who tolerate gambling are, of course, useless for emotional leverage. In addition, families who support gambling may actually disapprove of a spouse's efforts to intervene, sometimes even becoming hostile towards the spouse:

> When we started dating, I told him to slow down, but it upset me that his mom and dad knew and just didn't do anything about it—didn't ask how much he was spending, didn't ask what kind of financial trouble he was in. [It's] not that he's not able to cope, but that's not the point—the point is you don't have what you should have at that age.

Such a reaction from the family can ostracize the spouse from the gambler's kin network. The family's positive attitude toward gambling and negative attitude toward the spouse make it difficult to reach a family consensus on how to approach the gambler's problem:

> His family again . . . they're big on it. Like his aunt . . . she had to ban herself, she had to go into security and say, "Don't let me in, I have a problem," so, it's in his family, and they all talk about it, they think it's great. They go to the casino, [but] I refuse, when I'm there. I just tell them if everyone

wants to talk about it, that's fine, I don't agree with it, and I'm not going to pretend to agree with it, so I'm not going to talk about it. I guess they don't really like hearing what I have to say, and it looks like I'm this big bitch, because I'm just saying how I feel, that I'm against it.

As this quote shows, a spouse is almost powerless against a family that is set on enabling a gambler.

Another barrier to the use of a social network is the spouse's insufficient knowledge of the network. This knowledge gap may limit the strategies a spouse can realistically use:

I could . . . get together with friends and spouses and talk about it as a group; but I don't know specifically what relationships they have with their spouses, so it might mean me meddling into other people's lives. That definitely is the weak spot in the strategy. But as long as it is for her a social activity, it is beyond her and my control.

The spouse's relationship with members of the gambler's network may also be a barrier. If the spouse gets along poorly with the gambler's friends or family, then the spouse will likely be unable to convince them to take part in strategies aimed at controlling the gambling. One respondent found himself unable to use the blackmail technique with his spouse's family:

She's pretty mainstream, and she comes from a fairly religious, strict religious background where her gambling isn't something her parents know about—they do know she plays lottery, but that's it. I've threatened once to tell members of her family but that immediately blew over. We went into [a] remedy phase and it was again when I was freaked out—multi-thousand dollars missing from our joint account—[I threatened to tell] her mom and her sister, one of her sisters that we are close with . . . It was kind of a dare because I'm close to her sister but not really with her mom and her mom doesn't speak English very well. And her dad—I'm not really close to at all. So I think she knew I wasn't going to do that . . . sort of an empty threat (laughs).

For such strategies to be fruitful, the spouse must have a close and positive relationship with the members of the gambler's networks.

Finally, strong couple embeddedness can also backfire on attempts to reform a gambler. One respondent revealed how her gambling spouse started using her friends and family to justify trips to Niagara Falls:

> Do you know how they have bus trips to go to Niagara Falls? It started like "Let's do that because it's an easy way to get to Niagara Falls instead of driving ourselves." He would spend more time in the casino ... And when I got friends there, it was "Let's go visit them. Oh, well, we happen to be here, so let's go to the casino ... " So it's really more done gradually. He doesn't think it's a problem. He'll sort of put it back on me, like "When I go out to the casino, you can go see your family and your friends." If I participate, [he'll say] "You like it too," and I'm just "Well, I'd like to do something else."

Thus, strongly embedded couples are sometimes no better off than weakly embedded couples. Social networks that overlook gambling, enable the addiction, or are external to gambling are not useful tools for the partner. As well, a spouse with too little knowledge of the network or poor relations with its members has trouble devising suitable strategies.

Weak Couple Embeddedness

The 2005 study found three types of weakly embedded couples: couples who share few social relationships but spend much personal time together; couples who share a few social relationships and little personal time together; and couples who share a few common relationships, but those relationships all centre on gambling. None offers the possibility of using strategies—through influence, communication, and knowledge—that are available to strongly embedded couples. But even for weakly embedded couples, there are advantages to knowing some of each other's friends and families. Spouses who lack any common social contacts are likely to have little influence over the progression of a gambling problem.

Type 1: A Few Social Relationships and Much Personal Time

Some couples in our study shared few social contacts but spent large amounts of shared time alone together. When asked about their shared activities, respondents in this category described typical date activities, such as going to restaurants, watching movies, and so on:

Usually we just stay home and watch TV or rent a movie. Sometimes we go out to a restaurant or a movie. We really like going to restaurants.

These couples shared personal time alone together but remained separate when they were with other people:

We spend a lot of time with each other alone, opposed to there is always people and parties, you know. We just spend a lot of time doing nothing alone. Walks and so forth, where it doesn't take money . . . Obviously, we are on a very tight budget. A lot of personal stuff . . . Outdoors. Exercising is part of my physical activity, and hers is almost identical. That is how we met actually.

Responses like these show that these couples enjoyed very high relationship quality in isolation from other people. Some respondents overtly acknowledged the high quality of their relationship:

We really click, we really love spending time with each other and, well, you can't beat that, can you? I think that's it. We're both pretty active, we like to rollerblade, play volleyball. I play beach volleyball in the summertime a lot, so we go down there a lot; biking, and a lot of outdoor activities.

Many of these couples felt closely tied to each other, but this closeness was insufficient in itself to combat the gambling problem. Often, external information and authority are needed to push gamblers to seek treatment, be truthful, or lessen the frequency of their gambling. These external benefits were unavailable to this first sort of weakly embedded couple, despite their high-level of intimacy.

Type 2: Some Social Activities and Little Personal Time

The second type of weakly embedded couple has no shared social contact or personal activities. Respondents in this type of couple described having mutually isolated relationships. For example, one respondent described her activities with her partner in bleak terms. Besides grocery shopping together once a week, they kept their distance, despite living in the same apartment:

There are two rooms and two TVs . . . He didn't like my shows, so now he watches his and I watch mine. I like my shows.

Often, respondents described their minimal shared time together as a conflicted experience, in which one partner attempted to make contact while the other quietly played along:

> Once in a while ... like when I am watching TV, he'll come and sit and watch. I'll tell him there is a nice program, and he'll sit and watch. [Besides that,] nothing. We don't really do anything.

This respondent went on to explain that her husband often sabotaged her efforts at creating shared time by using her illness to avoid going out to spend time together:

> For instance, for Christmas I said, "You know what, we have to go for Christmas. The last two years we didn't go, because last year I had bunion surgery [and] before that I had bad flu. This year we'll go." "No, no, no, we're not going," he said. I said, "Okay, we'll invite people for Christmas." He said, "No, no, no, you're too sick." And he gets on my nerves, because I want to entertain and he doesn't want to entertain. He says, "You're sick. How can you entertain"? And I said, "Even though I am sick, I like people coming over." And I do most of the work, but he doesn't like. He says, "No."

Couples in this type of a relationship are almost helpless against the gambling problem. They often have no outside support network on which to rely and no personal connection that may help, even though they occasionally engage in social activities together which temporarily distract the gambler from their problem.

Type 3: A Few Common Social Activities, All Related to Gambling

The third type of couple is weakly embedded even though the partners share network contacts. These couples' weak embeddedness is attributable to the fact that the few relationships they do share are exclusively related to the gambling. These social networks, then, are minimally useful to the partner.

In a desperate desire to spend time with their partner, spouses said they often resigned themselves to tagging along at gambling events:

> It almost always has to involve gambling. We can't just go see a movie and come home or rent a movie and stuff like that. More often than not, I would

go [to his friends' homes] because there'd be other people there, and at least I could socialize with the other people—they will do a guys night and the girls will do something else. Like go see a movie together or something like that. [The guys] will stay downstairs in the basement to play poker or whatever, and we'll be upstairs watching a movie or just talking, girl stuff, stuff like that. More often than not, if I didn't go he go anyway, probably . . . and then I would be stuck doing nothing.

Often, spouses used such opportunities to oversee the gambler's activities. Such "shared" time spent gambling rarely involved thoughtful exchanges with the gambler or the gambler's friends. No information could be obtained from friends about the gambler's behaviour. Nor could these friends be used for distraction, as they were only interested in gambling.

Couples who share gambling contacts are only slightly better off than couples with no common social contacts. Moreover, gambling friends may even enable or promote the gambling problem. Spouses may, in fact, end up enabling their partners by accompanying them to gambling.

Couples who share relationships with gambling friends may appear on the surface to be embedded, but it is obvious they are weakly embedded. Gambling friends offer no distraction and rarely offer up useful information about the gambler. Also, shared relationships exclusively with gambling friends finally fail to improve marital relationships and open lines of communication.

The Link between Gambling and Weak Couple Embeddedness

This book argues that marital relationships worsen with the onset of a gambling problem. If embeddedness is used as an indicator of marital quality, it is fair to say that gambling problems weaken embeddedness. Likely, the longer a gambling problem endures, the more weakly a couple is embedded in a shared social world.

According to the interviews, problem gambling undermines and weakens embeddedness for several reasons: suspicion, guilt, resentment, anger, neglect, time spent away from home, lack of money, and social isolation. For many of our couples, anger and resentment that stemmed from the gambling problem permeated all of their interactions. Anger often spilled over into potentially enjoyable social activities. As a result, many couples had trouble enjoying each other's company.

Equally bad, it was often difficult for these couples to spend time with other people. The couple could not get along, and they also risked embarrassing themselves and others by taking part in social activities. Because of their inability to interact privately or socially, these couples often stopped engaging in social activities altogether for fear of embarrassment.

Another reason for refraining from shared social time is that the gamblers felt they could not spare the time from gambling to engage in shared activities. Gamblers often felt compelled to spend their time gambling over socializing with friends and family. One respondent was forced to schedule her shared time with her husband around his gambling:

> It would be like [planning to go] out to dinner with someone else, playing a sport like bowling or skating, or if I wanted to see a play—something like that. I would ask him ahead of time and if it fell on a weekend, he would have to check to make sure that there was no guys' poker weekend. He gets kind of upset if a concert comes by and it's on a particular day . . . then all of a sudden, there's a guys' weekend or a guys' poker night, and he can't miss it because we got tickets four months ago . . . he gets kind of sulky. So, he'll like most of what I'll choose . . . but he prefers to gamble.

Another practical reason for the significantly reduced amount of shared time was lack of money. Often, the gamblers claimed that they had no money to avoid spending time with their spouse:

> It upsets me sometimes . . . that I want to do other things, go out and see other things, and he doesn't want to . . . because he's not interested, or because he's got other plans to do a poker night, or he's got no money to do it. He wants to save his money for other things, and so he uses all of his entertainment money to do gambling and doesn't have or doesn't want to go out to dinner, or go out to a movie, or go out to a show or something.

One final reason for the decreased embeddedness is that gambling is a socially isolating activity. The act of gambling itself isolates gamblers from those around them, even at the casino and bingo hall. One respondent described feeling isolated from her partner, even though they both gamble:

> The only person I gamble with is my partner, but I've noticed the pattern. When we were . . . first going to the casino together, we used to actually

gamble together. And we used to enjoy it together. Like, if I was playing this game, then she would be playing this game next to me. Now, I'm playing over here, and she's playing way over there on this side, [and] it's kind of like we're together, but we're not.

This quote highlights the inherently solo nature of playing a game at a casino. In her interview, this respondent's partner admitted that on occasion they sat in separate seats on the bus ride home to avoid breaking into arguments.

Several respondents mentioned experiencing the isolating nature of gambling. Gamblers and spouses alike admitted that gambling was less social than it appeared on the surface:

It's like being in your own environment and carrying your environment with you; and maybe also because when you go to a casino, it's not meant to be a social activity. You know, people are all . . . focusing on their own gambling, so you are among people but you don't have to interact.

Gamblers also admitted to feeling a disconnection from their family and gambling friends. They often felt embarrassed about their action and misunderstood by their loved ones. One respondent admitted that his lack of money led him to avoid making meaningful connections with people:

I gamble alone. When I go to gambling to the races, I just go by myself without letting anyone know that I do or that I don't . . . I basically isolated myself over the last couple of years. I really don't have any friends, just acquaintances at a bar and that sort of thing . . . Probably the lack of finances or status or whatever you want to call it. I just decided to stick to myself and do my own things, so to speak.

While gambling can be an isolating activity, avoiding gambling can also be isolating for some. Certain gamblers in our study, mainly those with extensive gambling networks, claimed to isolate themselves in hopes of avoiding gambling. Rather than engage in other networks to keep themselves busy and away from gambling, they tried to avoid gambling by sitting at home and doing nothing. One respondent said he used this as a strategy, but that it was ineffective:

Interviewer: What efforts have you made to change your gambling behaviour? I know you mentioned maybe going to Gamblers Anonymous. Has there been anything you've done to try to do to change it?

M: Just staying in the house and isolating. It is not good. You get cooped up after three weeks and you go nuts. [So] you get out and you . . . isolate.

Regardless of the effectiveness of the technique, isolation is never conducive to strong couple embeddedness.

To summarize, gambling is a socially isolating activity in many respects. Anger and tension between the partners often make social outings uncomfortable and embarrassing. Lack of time and money often prevent or excuse gamblers from sharing time with their partners. Gambling itself takes the individual away from reality and loved ones. As a result, couples spend less and less time together, both privately and socially. What was once a strongly embedded couple becomes weakly embedded.

Conclusion

This chapter illustrates how couples who face a gambling problem tend to be or become a weakly embedded couple. They end up sharing few social activities, and the spouses are therefore unable to convince their gambling partners to seek treatment.

As well, this chapter has showed how social networks can be importantly related to problem gambling. We made the general point that all people are embedded in social networks, to a greater or lesser degree. The density—close- or loose-knitness—of the network will largely influence the conjugal arrangements a couple works out. It will also influence the likelihood that a gambler's activities are clearly or frequently visible—to the spouse and/or to other friends and kin of the couple. This, in turn, will influence the ability of the spouse to control the problem gambling. We will discuss this point at much greater length in the final chapter of this book.

In the 2005 study, a few of the couples were strongly embedded. Often, the spouses in these couples used the gambler's family as a source of emotional leverage and distraction. They also used the gambler's friends as a source of information and a means to block information going to the gambler. But strongly embedded couples face several barriers in using shared social networks to their advantage. Social networks are useful only if their members disapprove of excessive gambling. Further, to use such networks to their advantage, partners must have intimate knowledge of and be on good terms with network members.

Research is needed to explore the different uses of various social networks, as well as the practical value of certain social networks over others. Further, the level of intimacy required for the shared social network to be useful should be assessed. The next chapter explores further why most partners are unable to get their gambling spouse to seek treatment.

Chapter 10
Inability to Promote Treatment and Change

As we have seen, couples in weakly embedded relationships are often unaware of the severity of their spouse's gambling problem. As a result, spouses find it difficult to help their partners in changing their behaviour. In our study, couples in this condition generally agreed that spouses were unable to promote treatment for their gambling partner. Here are some vignettes from our study that illustrate this problem.

Case Study: Sonia and Paul[8]
Of all our respondents, one spouse most clearly shows the spouse's inability to promote change. Sonia has been married to Paul for 38 years and has used a wide array of strategies to persuade her husband to quit gambling. All her efforts have met with failure:

> I've gone with him to GA [Gamblers Anonymous], couples therapy, left him twice, each time for a period of a week, then left him a third time for a period of three months; went legal and made a domestic contract that gives me the authority to kick him out of the apartment at any time.

Sonia told us that when support strategies failed, she tried a *tough love* approach by distancing herself from her husband through, for example, multiple separations. She also says they have divided their household expenses so she is no longer economically affected by his gambling:

> The apartment is now in my name, he pays me rent. What I did is I came up with the various expenses for the month, split it down the centre, and anything extra, he pays for—his gambling, his drinking—he pays for that. His smokes, I do not buy that.

Sonia also described the self-doubt and guilt spouses often suffer, carrying a mistaken sense of responsibility for the gambler's actions:

---

8   See also "Sonia and Paul" in Chapter 3.

Could I have done something? When you run out of everything else, you come back to yourself, so now you're doing more damage to yourself. It's time to get out of the relationship when you're questioning yourself, when you know . . . there was nothing else you could have done. The therapist is telling you this, the doctors are telling you, his friends are telling you, your relations are telling you, your family, perfect strangers are telling you this! Why are you doing this to yourself still? It's because you're looking for answers, you're still looking for answers, and you're still looking for a way out.

She admitted that staying enables Paul's actions at her expense, as she assumes all the household responsibilities, thus changing her relationship with her husband to that of a mother and child. In questioning why she remains with her husband, Sonia typifies the emotional turmoil partners experience in their decision to stay or leave their spouse:

Why am I here? It's kind of like a bad itch that you can't get rid of, that you just stay with. You keep putting on various creams, but it just never goes away, it's there, but you don't cut off your leg either. Not a good state to be in.

She expressed a wish to leave, claiming she doesn't have "anything invested to stay in this marriage," but she said she wanted to wait until she is sure her husband is able to take care of himself:

I probably will [divorce him], it's not a question of *if*, it's a question of *when*. It is coming; it's just a question of when it gets done. And I keep hoping every time I go for anything like this that I'll get this magic solution so that when I do cut the cord, hopefully, he will be off and running and be better than he was when he was in the marriage.

While an extreme case, Sonia is not alone in her frustration and feelings of hopelessness in the face of her partner's gambling.

Quantitative Findings from the Current Study

We asked the gamblers in the 2005 study several questions about their problem: specifically, how they felt about it, and how they reacted to it. The responses were mixed.

Half of the gamblers doubted that they had a gambling problem. Further, 34 percent agreed or strongly agreed with the statement that they "have worries but so does the next guy." Given that *all* the gamblers in this study were classified as problem gamblers using the CPGI, many were underestimating their problem. Since they deny the extent of their problem, these gamblers are unlikely to seek the treatment or help they need.

Of those gamblers who admitted to having a problem, roughly three of every four gamblers admitted that they needed treatment. For example, the statements, "I have a problem and I really think I should work at it" and "It might be worthwhile to work on my problem," had agreement values of 70 percent and 78 percent, respectively. Yet, three-quarters (74 percent) agreed with the statement "I wish I had more ideas on how to solve the problem." This shows that most respondents were either unaware of possible treatments or were frustrated with the efficacy of currently available solutions.

Most gamblers in the sample said they were currently dealing with their problem. Nearly two-thirds (62 percent) agree with the statement "Anyone can talk about changing; I'm actually doing something about it." For the item "I haven't started working on my problems but I would like help," over half (57 percent) of the gamblers agreed. These responses show that most gamblers either believed they were trying to or wanted to alter their gambling behaviour.

Finally, the gamblers were asked questions to assess their concerns about slipping back into their downward spiral. Sixty-five percent noted that they have tried to resolve their problem but face a continuing struggle. This response suggests that gamblers, like other recovering addicts, continue to struggle with their problem, even after successful treatment.

The study data show that most of the gamblers felt that they had someone they could count on for help or advice, though we are uncertain if this support was coming mainly from their spouses. Further, it is unclear if their help was useful. Regardless, the presence of social support seemed to help the gamblers in their struggle with problems.

What the Spouses Said

The fact that most spouses in the study were still in relationships with the problem gamblers suggests that they think behavioural change is possible. When asked what they would like their partners to do about their problem, they responded that they wanted the partners to stop gambling, alter their attitude towards gambling, and reduce the time engaged in the activity and the money spent on it.

The findings reveal that the first choice of almost all the spouses was to see the gambling behaviour stop:

> I'd like to have him abstain totally because that's the only way. You can't be a little bit pregnant, you know? And replace it [gambling] with some healthy things.

Some spouses insisted instead that a change in attitude and degree of gambling was acceptable. If their spouse were unable to stop, they said they would settle for a significant decline in gambling:

> I would like it to stop completely, [or] maybe the occasional card game with friends. The occasional visit to the casino, maybe two or three times a year for recreation. Nothing to cause tension or loss of money.

Some spouses believed that complete abstinence from gambling was both unrealistic and unnecessary. Instead, they wanted the gamblers to become more aware and in control of their behaviour:

> I wish he'd cut it out [gambling] ... like, cut out some of it, if not stop completely, because I don't think ... I don't think he can, and I don't think he wants to at least cut it down so we can do other things.

Some distinguished between playing the lottery and going to the casino, and felt that if their partner could stop gambling at casinos, playing the lottery would be acceptable.

> CAMH [Centre for Addiction and Mental Health] will tell you when you're a gambler you can't even play lottery tickets and that. No, I think [he] can play lottery tickets. I've seen him when he plays lottery tickets, and I've seen him when he gambles, and there are two different persons there ... I want him to stop going to the casino.

As well, one respondent wanted her problem-gambling husband to alter his actions when gambling, specifically in relation to superstitious beliefs about luck:

[I want him to be] calmer. Don't say, don't think, everyday, "I got it, I got it." [referring to his belief that he will win the jackpot]. Sometimes just relax. A better approach [is that] if he had the urge . . . ignore it. Ignore your urge sometimes.

In addition, many spouses expressed wishes that the gamblers would recognize their personal limits and set boundaries:

I just want them to realize, you know, that you work so hard for your money, and you don't want to be throwing it away. You want to gamble, but you must know your limit. There's a limit to everything.

Spouses also wanted the gamblers to spend more time with them and less money on gambling:

[I want him to say no to] any type of gambling where it's a lot of money . . . so going over to a friend's house and gambling for poker or something or black jack or going to the casino maybe once every couple of months [is okay]. [That way] we can save and do something else.

Nearly nine out of ten (87 percent) spouses said they had taken actions to help their gambler make these desired changes, though for most, their efforts were unsuccessful. The spouses used different strategies in these attempts—for example, planning alternative activities to distract their partners from gambling:

I have tried to put him in other activities. I put him in a hockey league in the winter and got him to play baseball with the guys in the summer.

Others emphasized the foolishness of continuing to gamble:

I want her to know the odds and that it's just entertainment, but costly entertainment. I've talked about the odds of winning to her.

Some spouses had grown tired of the failure and had chosen to give up:

Give up. There's no point in it. He's either going to go, he's going to come to a string, a row of bad luck, as they say, and the thing is is that I'm covered.

He can't take me down if he goes down, and he knows already that I'm not giving him a penny of my money (laughs), so don't ask me.

Others said they had been partially successful, but the problem persisted:

I've been successful in changing the pattern but not changing the overall goal: to [pay back] the losses back incurred to date which is so far, a few thousand . . . I'm trying to discourage her from thinking that gambling is a social thing and trying to discourage her from believing what any casino is trying to promote.

Other spouses admitted that they were afraid to do anything about the problem:

Maybe I am not the person that is going to be able to help him. Maybe he needs somebody else that is on the outside looking in. Somebody that can professionally help him.

Some spouses said they felt unsuccessful in their efforts, but they remained hopeful that something they were doing may help. Most acknowledged the difficulties in trying to change a gambling spouse.

Ineffective Strategies

Family and Friends

Even though most spouses said they were aware of Ontario's toll-free gambling help line, as well as gambling counselling services available in their community, most turned to a friend or family member for help. This strategy can take several forms, but it can fail in several ways, as one respondent illustrated:

I've tried to find out about his past, to try and find out any information on the parents or family. But, it was very sketchy. I tried to phone the brother once and talk to him about his brother's actions; he told me, if you need to call the authorities, call them.

When spouses turned to the gambler's family to help, they often found the family enabling the problem instead. Thus, their attempts to change their spouse's behaviour became increasingly difficult:

I've had a little heart-to-heart with his father and stepmother one time [when he was at the casino] and said, "You know what, I'm going to put my cards out on the table, and this is how it really is." I had to take his father and mother aside and tell them to stop encouraging him, because they only knew about the winning.

Some parents continued to enable the gambling by bailing the gambler out of difficult financial situations. Doing so put them in opposition to the spouse's goals:

They were aware that he gambled, but they weren't concerned—not to the extent that they wanted to get into an argument with him and dissolve or lose the opportunity of being close with him. So, they gave [the money] to us, but it is one of those situations when you can't hold your head up. You feel a little bit disappointed and upset, it is embarrassing. You are working. You are an adult. You are supposed to be responsible. And here you are almost every month asking someone else for money, or you are pinching pennies.

Some spouses asked the family to appeal to the gambler—to convince him or her to spend time at home rather than going out to gamble. Often, other families resisted requests for help, and gamblers were relieved they did.

Spouses also used the children to try to influence the gamblers' activities. In effect, they tried to make the gambler aware that their actions had consequences for the entire family. One gambling mother of two stated that when her spouse asked her to stay at home with the kids instead of going out to bingo, she told him: "That's what I'm trying to go to bingo for—to get away from you all!"

Some partners went beyond networks of family to seek advice from a religious leader. The gambler usually resisted these efforts too:

I spoke with our minister to see if he could talk some sense into him, and that didn't do much. It just got him upset, 'cause he was like, "You're broadcasting our business. Nobody needs to know what's going on in our house." Blah, blah, blah.

Counselling

Some partners tried couple's therapy to fix the damage caused to their relationship by gambling or to help resolve the gambling problem:

[My partner] suggested marriage counselling because our relationship was ending. Then the marriage counselling suggested we seek further help and recommended that he go for addiction counselling.

As this quote shows, even though the marital difficulties stem from the problem gambling, it may be easier to convince the gambler to attend counselling for marriage rather than for addiction.

Sonia, from this chapter's case study, noted that counselling can fail to improve marital relations. Counselling is only as helpful as the gambler allows it to be:

[Paul] does this with all the psychiatrists. When we were in couple's therapy, it was always if he had to go to therapy, I had to go also. And I always tried to keep quiet in therapy because once you open the floodgates, it's too late. One day the therapist tells me that I can't keep quiet and asks what I think. It was a direct question and I couldn't help it and everything came out. And everything that Paul said, I argued against, because everything Paul told the doctor was incorrect. I mean, come on take some responsibility for your actions. So, by the time we left Paul was very upset, he was banging the steering wheel as we drove home. He tells me I can convince any doctor of anything.

In looking for alternatives, some spouses recommended Gamblers Anonymous meetings to their gambling partners. Others suggested participating in our study:

Interviewer: Did she encourage you to go see Gamblers Anonymous?
P: Oh yeah. [And she gave me] magazines . . . read this, read this.
Interviewer: Did she encourage you to come to this [the interview]?
P: Oh yeah, she make me go [to hear that] gambling is bad and to put some sense into my head.

While counselling is generally a good strategy for achieving change, it is hard to get unwilling gamblers to take part in any form of therapy.

Shared Activities
Several spouses tried planning activities as a distraction and from gambling:

I pushed for the counselling, and I tried to keep as busy for the church or classes and just try to do stuff in the church and join the community centre. Go for walks and you know. When stuff's happening, we'll go to a concert or something. In the summer, we try to keep busy. I figure if I keep him busy with me, there is less chance of him being busy doing that. So I'll try things. If I keep it consistent and I keep pushing and pushing, I hope it will help.

One respondent enrolled her partner in various activities to get him involved in nongambling hobbies:

I'm going to have to put him [her partner] in a hockey league in the winter, summer's over (laughs), get out the old skates, get them sharpened. They have these old leagues, and the only time they can get rink space is 2:00 or 3:00 in the morning, so that cuts into a lot of time. He can't be zipping around and make it back to play; and once he makes a decision on something like that, he will never miss a game, and he will never be late. He's just that kind of person. Like he'll go out the door with his hands up "It's calling to me, it's calling to me!"

But social activities initiated by the spouse, rather than the gambler, can fail. The respondent above stated that she also enrolled her partner in baseball in the summer. Ironically, this backfired as well. Her partner ended up organizing occasional gambling nights with his baseball teammates. When gamblers refuse to take part in activities, partners understandably become frustrated:

I have racked my brain trying to figure out what's in it for him. I've tried to get him away from it, try to get him to think about other things, tried to get him interested in something other than that. I even suggested we play board games. "No."

Nagging
Roughly a quarter of the spouses have tried to "talk to" the gamblers about their problem. Often, the gamblers view this as nagging. The spouses used these discussions to lecture about the randomness of gambling outcomes, in hopes of changing the gamblers' belief in their skill:

I've actually watched one of those poker challenges with her, and I explained to her it's just luck, there's no skill involved, it's just basic luck. I don't care how anyone plays it and says they're skilled, it's just luck, and some people have the luck and some people don't.

Other times, spouses lectured the gambler on interfering with a stable family life, especially stable household finances:

I often explain the bad side of gambling. I talk to him about how much money we could save by him not gambling. I also talk to him about how much money we're losing when he gambles.

But nagging appears to do little to improve the problem and much to worsen it. Several spouses admitted that by discussing the problem, they felt they aggravated it by increasing the gambler's anxiety, reinforcing their behaviour, and causing later conflict:

Sometimes when you press her too much, I think it makes her go out and do more.

Moreover, none of the gamblers recommended nagging as an effective strategy for changing their gambling:

When she just stands behind my shoulder and says how much time I spend gambling, I just ignore her. So the more she nags, the more I'm going to ignore her.

When she says it is bad, I am aware it is bad. This isn't helpful to me, and it becomes a boring matter to hear this.

Similar to nagging, yelling was unproductive because the gamblers ignored it as noise, and it sometimes provoked them to leave to go gamble:

Interviewer: So the swearing is not helping then?
M: No, because then I get angry and I say "fuck it" and I go do what I want.
Interviewer: So what would you do then?
M: Go gamble.

Enabling

Enabling behaviours—usually assigned to the spouse of the substance abuser and usually the female partner—"can best be characterized as learned behavioural responses that may influence drinking or drug using behaviours through either positive or negative reinforcement processes, thus increasing the likelihood of such behaviours in the future" (Rotunda *et al.*, 2004: 272). Sharing gambling activities enables gamblers' behaviour. For example, one respondent did not gamble but she accompanied her partner to the casino or left him there to gamble while she visited friends:

> Interviewer: You will accompany him or . . .
> A: Sometimes yeah.
> Interviewer: And do you play as well . . . do you go gambling?
> A: Not usually, no.
> Interviewer: So when you go, what do you usually do?
> A: I have family around the area so I just visit . . . with family and friends.
> Interviewer: And how long does he stay when he goes?
> A: If I let him, three to five hours . . . or depending if he loses all his money early.
> Interviewer: And if he loses it early, what does he do?
> A: He'll call me and we'll go home.

While some partners who came along felt they were supervising the gambler by merely watching, problem gamblers viewed the same behaviour as sympathetic, caring, or thoughtful. Thus, they concluded that the partner was supportive of their gambling habit:

> A lot of times he'll line up with me in the Wheel of Fortune slot machine [at the casino] and see who'll get the first machine—him or me. And then he'll give me the machine he had if he gets there first. It is almost like lining up twice; or he'll go on the other side of the bank of machines and call me if one becomes available. He'll tell me to sit there and start while he scouts out the whole casino and tells me exactly where all the Wheel of Fortune slot machines are in my price range.

It is possible that in trying to reduce stress on the relationship, these spouses found it easier to engage in activities that enable, rather than inhibit, unwanted behaviour. However, this pattern is disruptive in the long term, hindering progress towards recovery and improved relationships. Rotunda *et al.* (2004) notes that "these behaviours possess adaptive consequences in particular contexts. For example, enabling may (1) reflect the partner's desire to avoid hassles and conflicts with the drinker [or in our case gambler]; (2) be indicative of hopelessness ("I give up, she will never change"); (3) be an effective way to protect the family and substance user [or gambler] from negative economic and social consequences; or (4) be indicative of an intermittent reinforcement process whereby the partner experiences positive periods in the relationship or romanticizes the image of idealized love, and subsequently justifies their own ... behaviours while hoping for future change" (270).

Our study revealed several examples of enabling. For example, one respondent said that when her partner would lose, she would console him and try to raise his spirits. By taking his mind off how bad he felt, she made it easier for him to accept a loss that is damaging to the family:

> J: After a loss, you'll hear me say "Whatever, it happens, we don't have to worry about it. And he'll go like, "I know, and the next time I should do this, or not play those hands".
> Interviewer: So he'll talk about strategy and you'll try to sort of console him.
> J: Yeah, and then try to change the topic (laughing)—"What do you want for dinner?"

Enabling can take other forms. Another respondent said she would fight with her partner when he refused to give her money to gamble, until he gave in to her demands. Instead of holding his ground, this spouse enabled her behaviour by giving her the money. When he refused to give her the money, she threatened to go anyway, which usually caused him to surrender:

> M: He'll say he wants one session of bingo. I want three, right (laughs).
> Interviewer: So [the problem] is the amount of time you are spending there?
> M: Yeah, and money too. But the biggest thing, if I win, I'll say, "I am staying." "No come home. Go back tomorrow." "No. I am staying." That is why I don't call him.

Another respondent described how her spouse gave in and let her spend grocery money on bingo. But she added that he would have been more helpful to her if he hadn't given into her requests:

> He always gives in and gives me the money . . . Don't listen. Don't give me the money when I ask for it.

She said that her spouse enabled her destructive behaviour and only occasionally found ways to keep her from gambling.

Sonia, from this chapter's case study, used her own spending as revenge, which ended up legitimizing her husband's gambling expenditures. Occasionally living apart from Paul, Sonia overspent in an almost wild manner:

> I take the car and I go shopping, go with friends. The free spending—I think that was the way I was equalizing it. [If] I was going out, I never bought one jacket—it was a standing joke at the bank. If I went to any of the petite stores, and they'd say, "This cashmere jacket is $300," I'd buy it in black, navy blue, red, and white . . . If I was going to a wedding, I wouldn't buy one outfit; I'd buy three of them and only use one. When the next wedding came, I'd buy another three outfits—I'd just spend. And of course, the car and the fur jacket—I bought both in one month, and I just blew my budget right out of the water. Free spending. I'd buy furniture, and if I didn't like it, I'd just overhaul everything . . . Free spending. I'd just give away the stuff, I wouldn't keep it. My sister-in-law would say, "What are you doing with the table?" and I'd say, "I'm buying a new one, you want it?" It wasn't a question of what are you going to get for it. It was just "Take it, back your car up and just take it."

This pattern hints at mutual enabling: Paul justified his gambling by pointing to Sonia's overspending, and vice versa:

> One thing I will say is, Paul never stopped me. He never once stopped me. I don't know if he was using that as an excuse, or he thought "Well, I'm gambling and she should be allowed to do this." He [may have] talked himself into this, because he was gambling into the thousands and thousands. I don't know if this was his way of coping, I'm guessing. I don't know; we've never discussed it.

Similarly, another respondent's ex-partner used to encourage her to gamble so he had time to maintain an affair:

> K: He'd tell me to go to bingo, that the jackpot numbers were high or . . . sometimes, the numbers will be high and I think that they are going to win a ton of money and the bingo hall will be crowded . . . every fourth day.
> Interviewer: So he would tell you to go, or encourage you?
> K: Yeah, or else he was wanting to get rid of me so he could go out, telling me "There's $30 or $40, why don't you go to bingo?"
> Interviewer: Why did he want you to get out?
> K: He already had a girlfriend.

Causing the gambler stress is another form of enabling. When relationship stresses increase, the likelihood of gambling increases too. One respondent cited the stress of household responsibilities as a reason why she gambles, explaining that her family was unsympathetic about an illness she had:

> Everybody is stressing me out to the limit. I wish [my husband] would be more understanding. I wish he would do more work in the house. [So] I go to gambling. There's a guy who organizes trips and he calls me and actually I am going tomorrow. I am going to the casino. That is the only thing that gives me joy. Otherwise, I am whole day depressed. The whole day I want to die. I just get so . . . because I have fibromyalgia, I have pain all over and I am constantly taking painkillers. [Gambling] is the only thing that relieves the stress, and life at home is not all that particularly good. So, everybody blames me for everything.

Another respondent also admitted to this kind of behaviour, using gambling to avoid household conflict, since she and her spouse lacked effective or calm strategies for resolving conflict:

> My thinking is, if I stay in this environment, things are going to escalate, she is going to push me, I'm going to say forget it, or even if she doesn't touch me, lay a finger on me, she's gonna start yelling and then we're both going to have hurt feelings, so forget this. I'm going to get out of here. So that's when I will go, and I will take a long ride to the casino.

Loneliness is another reason why partners enable gambling. One respondent said she had few recreational interests in common with her husband, so she used gambling as a substitute for the enjoyment she was missing in her marriage:

> The gambling is an entertainment and a substitute for other things. If there didn't need to be a substitute, that would be helpful—if we had other activities that we could share that were enjoyable and [would] fill the time together, as opposed to me getting satisfaction with gambling and going to casinos . . . If we were more on the same wavelength about other things that would be helpful. And in that sense, gambling is a substitute—I guess that's the way with most other addictions . . . whether you are drinking or something else, it is a substitute for something else. So in that sense, it is a problem because it is a substitute. Instead of dealing with the issues, you side-step them.

She echoed a similar sentiment expressed by gamblers—that their spouses did not understand them:

> Our ideas of entertainment are also different. He likes the stimulation of having three TV's on at the same time, all on different stations. He likes to flip through—he [needs] this constant stimulation and he thrives in it. I'm the opposite person. I want to come home and turn everything off and just have some quiet time. That balance is becoming unbalanced . . . It is becoming more extreme between us, because I don't have a place in my own home where I can maintain my own environment. So I guess that is part of the other attraction of going out, it's the substitution thing.

Relationships that lack both understanding and emotional and intellectual intimacy can promote or enable gambling. Spouses may misdiagnose a problem or overlook it completely as the gambler spirals further into their gambling habit. Many respondents cited inattention or inaction from their partner as a reason their behaviour continues.

Some gamblers claimed that their spouses facilitated their gambling in various ways, such as by providing tips, money, leaving them alone when they were gambling online, and watching and being excited about sporting events on which they had placed Pro-Line bets. Gamblers described other actions as enabling as well. For example, two gamblers noted that their partners kept their problem a secret from friends and family. Keeping the problem a secret places a great deal of stress on a relationship. It also may prevent the spouse or gambler from seeking advice and help from a therapist or counsellor.

The gambling respondents said they were grateful to their spouses, whose actions may have reduced feelings of stress, anxiety, or depression. Because they felt that their spouses supported them, the gamblers would be more likely to rely on their spouses for additional help later. On the other hand, going to the casino with their spouse, avoiding discussions of the problem, and providing the gambler with money served to enable the problem behaviour.

Separate or Joint Bank Accounts

Some spouses decide to separate financial accounts to protect their assets. Yet as a result, they then remain unaware of the extent of the gambler's losses and financial troubles. In contrast, joint accounts—often used by partners to monitor the gambler's spending—may not help unless the gambler is forced to account for their finances or their behaviour:

> We have a joint account. And you'll notice money disappearing and a few things. The bills are not paid and the groceries are not bought and you wonder "Where is the money going"? I am not stupid.

The Emotional Impact of Failed Attempts

Spouses feel hurt when they cannot help bring about change in their spouse. With every failed attempt, their hope for change wanes. Yet, many spouses are reluctant to give up hope entirely because they feel responsible for their loved ones.

Often, because of these feelings, spouses are less likely to discuss their own emotional instability in the face of this growing problem. Many respondents hinted at the emotional toll as they expressed fear and anger related to their partner's gambling:

> I'm not superstitious, but knock on wood, I think it's mostly better . . . I wish I could feel confident that she's not going to fall off the wagon again . . . and I feel that way sometimes. I guess coming to this [interview] and reading some of the questions and thinking about it . . . it's sort of a feeling that I haven't really articulated to myself yet . . . but mostly [I wish] that she would limit herself to one type of gambling.

In the same manner, another respondent talked about gambling as selfish behaviour that made him feel alienated in the relationship:

> Once [my partner starts] gambling, I don't feel a part of this relationship anymore. I find it's very selfish behaviour. Then I try to analyze it and then I [wonder], is it an addiction.

Some spouses in the study had already visited professional counsellors. These spouses were most likely to discuss how they had been affected by the gambling problem. They may have been more forthright with their feelings because a therapist had validated their experiences. It is also possible these respondents had lost their tolerance for the situation. For example, Sonia, from the chapter case study, expressed her declining tolerance for her husband's behaviour and her frustration that she could not change an "addict":

> Interviewer: So, what do you want him to do to change his behaviour?
> S: Quit! There's no other way. Or, I've got to leave, there's no other way. It's a tough decision, but it's come to a point where self-preservation has set in. I'm getting older, and I can't handle it anymore. I am drowning. It's my health; it's my age, my realization that I can't do this anymore. Maybe I'm a slow learner; people told me this 35 years ago that you can't change a gambler. I'm sitting here telling you no matter how many of these [studies] you do, addictions you cannot change. Don't tell them quit, they never quit, they cope, so give them coping mechanisms.

Lack of success leads to an overwhelming sense of helplessness, where many spouses feel there is little they can do. In many respects, they are right. Until the gambler realizes he or she needs to stop, nothing will change:

> I really don't think that I can stop this man from doing this, because it just doesn't fizz on him. But at one point, I got so angry about his going up there that I wanted to phone up the casino and say "Hey, please do not offer him anything, get him off the mailing list, have no contact with him". But they have to ban *themselves*, you can't ban somebody. They would have to ban themselves right, but they're not going to take him off the mailing list because they know he's making them money up there.

To change, you have to be willing to get help. You have to want to help your-self and you want to change yourself and that won't happen until you, yourself want to change. People can do tons of stuff to help you, whatever, but until inside you feel it, you'll change. Until then, you will always be the same.

This sense of helplessness was evident in many of the interviews. Some respondents felt the only way gamblers could change was if they lost everything:

Homeless, on the streets somewhere with nothing in his pocket ... It's terribly stressing. He needs to get professional help. I know there is a number to call but he refuses ever to acknowledge.

Because spouses are intertwined in the lives of the gamblers and are themselves affected by the gambling problem, treatment programs need to stress strategies that include both the spouse and the gambler. Yet spouses often know little about treatment options. For instance, when asked if they have sought information about any treatment, one spouse responded: "I wouldn't know where to start." We asked if there is anything that spouses could do to change a gambler's behaviour:

Not at this stage. I've just run out of options. I have nothing more to offer. If you can give me some, I'd be more than happy to listen.

When Nothing Works: Withdrawing from their Gambling Partners

Some spouses said they had reached a point where they felt there was nothing they could do to help. Because of failed attempts to help and an increasing awareness that change cannot happen if someone refuses help, these spouses often distanced themselves from the relationship. Several respondents spoke candidly about their awareness of not being able to help their partners:

He's got to take the first step himself and try to get away from it and stay away from it.

Leave him [all that she can do to help him with his problem] ... I've told him he needs Gamblers Anonymous or if he stops he certainly has to fill the void with something else because so much time is spent gambling.

One respondent said she continuously fell into the trap of thinking her partner would change, only to be disappointed:

> We were split for two months and we weren't seeing each other. [Now] when we see each other, he's on his perfect behaviour, and I just can't take that risk that he's going to stay on that perfect behaviour. He's slowly getting into the old patterns, I can't handle that anymore, I have to realize that this is the way he is and this is what is always going to happen. But, I can't see him stopping.

Many spouses described how they disengaged from the relationship after similar failures and emotionally charged confrontations. In addition, some respondents said they no longer took part in activities with their partner because of their partner's mood swings and lack of interest in nongambling activities:

> He is always snapping . . . He goes, "I am coming" [to join them in activities together as a family] and then after, he will come with us. After, we will have problem—we are eating and something erupts, and then we start arguing. Just to be on the safe side to have a nice quiet evening, we don't include him.

Many spouses said they ceased trying to alter their partners' behaviour. Reasons for this included feelings of frustration over failed attempts to help, anger over deceitful behaviour, and financial strain. As well, they wanted to protect their own and their children's well-being. They realized that they could only help once their spouse admitted to having a problem and sought treatment for the problem. If they felt the gambler would not change, they often pulled back emotionally from the relationship.

Why do Strategies Fail?

The Role of the Gambling Industry
Several spouses said they were aware of tactics used by the gaming industry to encourage gambling. Others said they believed that the gaming industry should alter their policies to protect people with gambling problems.

First of all, several spouses noted the persuasive recruitment techniques used by the gambling industry. These techniques cause the gambler to overlook the problems in their behaviour and focus on the perks they might receive:

I told him that gambling is for rich people. Rich people have lots of money, and he doesn't have it. It went in one ear and out the other. He didn't absorb it at all. He talks a lot about the buffet there, and he thinks it's wonderful that he gets this big free meal there.

One respondent commented on the VIP passes that casinos mail to frequent visitors, giving special privileges (for example, free meals or upgraded hotel suites). These casinos target people with records of high losses. They make people with low self-esteem feel like a "big shot" by glamourizing their lifestyle:

He goes to Casino Rama so many times, he is the VIP. He has the VIP pass. So they always have him . . . we get the letters all the time. When they have something big happening you will be the first to know . . . you are a VIP member, so you are always there. They always invite you to their weekend while you gamble, because they have those VIP privileges.

The spouses in the study were aware of these tactics and tried to make their gambling partners aware of them:

I fear that she is being sucked into the marketing of it and the pseudo-sanctioning of it because it is run by the government and "It's not all that bad." So we have discussions as to why the government is involved and that it is really an additional tax that we don't have to pay if we don't want to. She is sucked into the market machinery of gambling, and this can work on otherwise intelligent people. It's easy if you don't have your guard up to think that it's another social activity but it's a costly social activity.

Another respondent explained that the best strategy to help problem gamblers may lie in the hands of the gambling industry:

Maybe if the advertising was maybe a little more explicit, like maybe if they threw in the real odds of winning. I've seen on the back of the ticket they have a help line, but maybe they should have more information on the front . . . [about] this whole process of buying a ticket and going through. It just happens so quickly and the outcome doesn't matter once you've won once, it just happens so fast, you buy a ticket and you win money, it's like "Oh, my God!" This happened so quickly . . . So I think that's how the problem needs to be addressed. Like with these tickets . . . it has to be made more in touch with reality, because you can get caught up. So they need to make it more certain, by including odds on the front maybe not making them so flashy, or more straightforward—like giving more expression to the amount of winnings.

Other respondents felt the government should engage in the prevention of gambling:

The government should be doing more . . . in terms of prevention . . . instead of encouraging [gambling]. But they seem to encourage it more than discouraging it. I think it's a problem for people. I don't see it as a major, major problem for my wife at this time, but I am concerned that it may be, because I'm not finding things that interest her as much, and now they are coming up with these [gambling] incentives and such.

Sonia, from this chapter's case study, talked about her frustrations with the gambling industry in their failure to protect gamblers and their families:

If such a strong person as myself has so much suffering, what is happening to the weaker personalities? How much are they drowning? And if they're drowning, they can't help themselves. How the hell do you think they are going to help their partners that are gambling? They can't. So, is the province going to step in? Is the country going to step in? Are these various establishments—these health organizations—are they going to step in, like they have with smoking and drinking? Or are they going to keep sprouting up these casinos everywhere, which in turn you're paying right back into mental health, and family break-ups, into social problems? Are we any better off than we were five years ago? No. If anything, we're worse.

Gambling is an activity that is actively encouraged in our society, without regard for its harmful effects. Some gamblers have difficulty resisting the perks and extensive advertisements by the gambling industry. The constant temptation is hard for gamblers and partners to fight against.

Poor Treatment Experiences
Several spouses expressed difficulty in promoting treatment for their partner because they had previously received poor counselling. Most gambling respon-

dents told us they were not currently seeking treatment nor had they ever sought help:

> Interviewer: Have you ever sought treatment for your gambling?
> S: No.
> Interviewer: have you ever thought about seeking treatment?
> S: Yeah, yeah.
> Interviewer: How often do you think about it?
> S: Every time I go to the casino.

Other problem gamblers in the study said that they had thought about and had made small efforts to seek help:

> M: I phoned Gamblers Anonymous [GA] once, but no, I've never been to a GA meeting. No I've never gotten to one. Well, I knew I had a problem. It was just that ... It was family members that said "I think you should phone GA."
> Interviewer: And what made you decide not to go?
> M: I don't know. I guess, maybe it is you are vulnerable, I, I, I can't ... I don't know.

The gamblers hated feeling vulnerable to their problem. This feeling of weakness, paradoxically, caused them to leave or avoid treatment.

Some problem gamblers sought some form of professional treatment, such as Gamblers Anonymous or counselling at the Centre for Addiction and Mental Health (CAMH) in Toronto. But few found the programs helpful:

> [I went] twice. But even the second time I was there [Gamblers Anonymous], I left. I didn't fit there because I know that I'm going to play again.

> I saw [a therapist] a long time ago ... I think five years ago. But they just asked me how many weeks I gambled ... it doesn't help me. I don't know why. If there was an injection or patch, maybe I'd patch me here, like a cure, you know. But no, they asked me [questions] for four weeks, and after that I stopped ... Since then, I never [went]. I think it's five or seven years ago.

Feeling the help was ineffective, these gamblers were unlikely to stay or return to treatment.

Some gamblers had attended 12-step meetings or couple's therapy, even those who had refused to admit they had a problem. But they also refused to attend most of the meetings, resulting in ineffective treatment:

> The first time he flipped—"You are all sick, you [the 12-step group] are all a bunch of losers. I'm not like you."

A common barrier to seeking help among the problem gamblers was insufficient awareness and understanding of available options. One respondent discussed the 1-800 gambling line, stating she had "no idea how it works or what the process is." Others were unaware the 1-800 line existed.

Lack of Interest in Radical Behaviour Change and Denial of Problems

Some gamblers in the study denied having a gambling problem, so they believed there was no need for change. Others were inclined to decrease the frequency of gambling, decrease the money spent gambling, or decrease the time spent on gambling. Some wanted to quit gambling while others simply wanted to win more.

Most of the gamblers answered "no" when asked if they had sought or thought about getting treatment. For various reasons, the few gamblers who had sought treatment in the past failed to follow their programs all the way through:

> Just only once, I went into that group [Gamblers Anonymous], and I was considering [going] to see a doctor and I made the appointment, but then I cancelled it. But I'm still considering to see a doctor and to shake it out.

Many gamblers were interested in making small changes that did not involve directly addressing their problem. When asked to elaborate, several said they would just like to win more. Thus, it is effectiveness of their gambling behaviour that they would like to change, not the behaviour itself:

> I'm trying to get better at thinking at betting wise, so planning, stuff like that, so I know how to take less risks, ah, not playing certain cards, ah, things like that, just concerning the game, that's it.

> I would like to know better the odds of winning and play only those games that have better odds.

Some respondents said they did want to curb their gambling behaviour but only in certain respects, such as spending less time or money gambling. Several gamblers would just like to "cut down" on their gambling. For example, some said that they would like to go less often, buy fewer tickets, or play less. One respondent said that she wanted to decrease the time she spent gambling because of the monotonous nature— particularly when she is losing:

> It takes like three or four hours to get to any casino outside of the city and you'll go there and after six, or seven, or eight hours. I'll think "What are we doing here—why are we here? This is so boring." I've actually had episodes where I've gotten up and walked away from a game, and my partner has gotten up and said "This is dull," and "Let's go get a burger or something"— it becomes unbelievably dull.

Roughly one-third of respondents said that they wanted to limit the amount of money they spent gambling:

> Maybe gamble less money . . . I tried and I set an amount—you know, I am only going to play with this much—but it never works, because when you lose, you have to take more money so you can get it back. That is how I get in trouble you know.

While several gamblers merely wanted to make superficial changes, some gamblers truly wanted to fix their problem. Yet there is a big difference between expressing the wish to change and actively working towards that goal. As noted above, many expressed a desire to change their behaviour but had taken no sincere steps to do so:

> I went to a 12-step program for a short period of time. It didn't really help me. I did one-on-one counselling and that helped a bit. I guess through the one-on-one counselling, I see what my past experiences were and what it got me and what happened to my money and where it went and comparing how many times did I actually win to comparing how much money I've thrown. And I've seen the scales are one side over here and one over here.

> [I want to] stop it. My biggest loss was $500 in a day. Are you giving away any gambling coupons for the casino at the end of this interview?

Most gamblers believed there was little their spouses could do to help because the gambling problem was solely *their* problem. Several respondents claimed that there was nothing helpful their partner could do or say. Despite their partners' actions, they felt alone in their struggle, which isolated them from spouses who continued their attempts to find a solution:

> I am learning through my therapist to just depend on myself.

> He can't tell me not to go there at all—because whenever someone tells me not to do something, that is when I want to do it. So that wouldn't work either.

> If I could change, she would be a better person. She is already a better person, okay, don't get me wrong. But my habit, I've got to change that myself.

One respondent was forthright in explaining how ineffective any effort to change his gambling would be:

> Nah, she knows me. I ain't changing. If I don't feel like changing, then I ain't going to change, I ain't no fucking mule, no. You know, you're wasting your time with that shit.

Another respondent did not want people to know about his problem, and that was why he did not seek help:

> I try to reduce . . . And the gambling itself, I did try to stop cold turkey; I did go on the Internet to try and find some advice, like a step program—by myself. I prefer to keep this low-key. Not many people know this is that serious for me.

Most respondents doubted that their spouses could help. They felt that change was a personal responsibility. Other respondents held conflicting views: they wanted their spouses to help them change (for example, by not enabling, by doing more activities together, or by including them in household chores), but they could not imagine leading a life without gambling:

> [We're] not that quite involved into each other, as well. Aside from the ultimatum thing, that's it. Mostly involving all strictly myself . . . her

involvement is very little here. Maybe it would be nice to have a person here to pull me away from that, but again, I don't want her to have that kind of pressure for herself, so I haven't really put that strain on her.

Another respondent believed that gambling was ultimately his problem and that the spouse's assistance could go only so far:

> I guess she's helping me quit in the sense that I know that she doesn't like it, and I don't want it to be an issue in our relationship. In that sense, she is helping me quit. But I think it is more my decision anyways to do it.

Above all, a gambler's willingness to change is essential if a spouse's input is to be effective. While this may seem obvious, it explains why some couples struggle unsuccessfully to stop or reduce gambling while others succeed. One spouse described the difficulty in trying to promote change:

> You have to want to help yourself and want to change yourself. [Change] won't happen until you, yourself, want to change. I mean, people can do tons of stuff to change, help you, whatever—but until inside you feel it, you won't get changed. Until then, you will always be the same.

Few gamblers in the study were completely committed or willing to change their behaviour, which is why the spouse's strategies were often ineffective. Problem gamblers who deny the existence of a problem are the hardest to help. They are reluctant to define the gambling as problematic yet need a solution that reduces the gambling.

Conclusion

Most spouses in the study wanted their gambling partner to change in some respect. Almost all of the spouses we interviewed had used several strategies to get the gambler to change or seek treatment. Usually, their efforts were unsuccessful.

The most frequent and ineffective approaches include nagging and enabling. Spouses become very frustrated with continued failure when fighting this uphill battle. The gaming industry, negative treatment experiences, and resistance on the part of the gambler all hinder a spouse's attempt to help the gambler.

The next chapter examines strategies that have proven successful for some couples in helping gamblers tackle their gambling problem.

Chapter 11
Ability to Promote Treatment and Change

Not all dreams of easy wealth wreck the families of gamblers. The previous chapter discussed ineffective strategies aimed at encouraging gamblers to seek treatment. This chapter focuses on effective strategies, as reported by gamblers and their partners. It addresses two questions:

- What are effective strategies for promoting change?
- What factors make these strategies effective?

The second question becomes especially significant when we look at strategies that fail for some people but succeed for others.

Interestingly, many strategies described as unsuccessful in the previous chapter resurface here, but with the missing details that can make them successful. We discuss what can make the same strategy effective for some people and not for others. We begin by noting that the same general principles about successful marriage apply to problem gamblers and their spouses, just as they apply to non-gamblers and their spouses. In general, for both, marital relationships can be healthy and helpful.

Literature on the Rules of Emotional Engagement

Research shows that close relations—despite the effort they take and the conflict they often breed—*are* good for people. Committed relationships can do people much mental and physical good, though bad ones can do them much harm. Best of all, people can *choose* to form close relationships, and they can act to improve their relationships. So, in the end, the benefits of a close relationship are available to everyone.

Research also shows that the closer the relationship, the better: so, for example, marriage is better than a dating relationship, and dating is better than nothing. Other things being equal, married people are healthier and happier than unmarried people. Compared with married people, separated, divorced, and unattached people are, on average, less happy, less healthy, and more disturbed, and they run a higher risk of early death. Cohabiting people are typically less stable and satisfied than married people. Yet, other things being equal, people in long-term committed cohabiting relationships are happier and better-off than unattached people.

Among attached people, happiness and health depends a lot on the quality of a relationship—on how the couple gets along. In some relationships, the two partners are just incompatible. In other relationships, the partners are compatible but do not know how to solve their problems. This chapter discusses the ways that couples improve troubled relationships—especially, relationships harmed by problem gambling.

Relationship problems can infect every part of a person's life. Often, relationship dissatisfaction and unhappiness take physical forms. Symptoms of stress from relationship dissatisfaction occur in an ever-widening range of illnesses. For example, people with cancer vary in their adjustment to the illness. Cancer patients in bad relationships report more depression and anxiety, less commitment to good health, and more illness-related family problems than patients in good relationships (Rodrigues and Park, 1996). Marital functioning can thus indirectly influence health by moderating daily life habits and mood swings.

Marital stressors are related to various health problems, both mental and physiological (Kiecolt-Glaser and Newton, 2001) The cause-and-effect relationship goes both ways. For example, psychiatric symptoms can lead to marital difficulties, or marital difficulties can aggravate psychiatric symptoms. People in unhappy relationships often show more signs of psychological difficulty— a weaker will to live, less life satisfaction, and reported poorer health—than people in happy relationships (Shek, 1995a). A bad relationship may even lead to work loss, especially for men in the first decade of an unhappy relationship (Forthofer et al., 1996).

Note that men and women sometimes view and experience marriage differently. For example, relationship quality affects the mental health of wives more than husbands (Horowitz et al., 1998). Women tend to respond in a more directly emotional manner to adverse experiences. Under conditions of stress, men tend to act out—for example, to drink or act violently. Under the same conditions, women are more likely to experience depression.

Why does a good relationship increase life satisfaction, health, and longevity to such a degree? The likeliest explanation is that a good relationship provides practical and emotional support. Emotional stability in turn strengthens the immune system, making partners more able to avoid or recover from illness. It also increases the will to live and promotes prudence and self-care. Other things being equal, people who want to live longer and healthier lives usually end up doing so.

Defining a "good" relationship is easier than it might seem. People in good relationships manage to achieve a good fit between the partners' own needs, wishes, and expectations, a fit that they regard as unique and irreplaceable (Wallerstein, 1996). Yet, as we have seen, reported well-being varies from one relationship to another—for example, from marriage to cohabitation to dating. Likely, people in different kinds of relationships evaluate their relationships and their lives together using different standards.

People in different kinds of relationships may also draw satisfaction from different activities and attributes in the relationship. Cohabiting couples place more emphasis on spending time together and enjoying physical intimacy, while married couples place more emphasis on emotional stability (Cannon, 1999); for the longer-lived marital relationships, physical intimacy tends to become less significant. As well, cohabiters report less commitment than married people, as well as a greater conflict frequency (Stafford et al., 2004): it seems marriage brings stability to a relationship. Less instability and more happiness are found in cohabiters who get married than in those who remain cohabiting (Brown, 2003). Brown also notes that cohabiters expressing plans to marry enjoy levels of relationship quality similar to those who did marry.

Most people would agree that feelings of intimacy are also important for making people satisfied with their relationship. *Intimacy* comes from the Latin word meaning *inward* or *inmost*. To become intimate with someone else means admitting them to our largely private, unique world and trusting them with our most valued possessions. Building this intimacy with a partner is the key to a mature, surviving relationship.

Literature on Intimacy and Communication

Intimacy in couples is not mainly about sex. Many couples who are sexually active are not emotionally intimate with each other, and many who are emotionally intimate rarely (if ever) have sexual relations. Consider the odd status of friendship—especially, same-sex friendship—in our culture: often, friendships are far more intimate (in the original sense of the word) than sexual relationships.

Typically, men consider cheating by their partner to mean sexual interaction with another man. In contrast, some women consider emotional intimacy with another woman to be cheating, whether sexual relations occurred or not. Good relationships have intimacy of both kinds, sexual and emotional. Satisfied partners are more sexually intimate with each other, as measured by how often they display affection physically, touch each other, kiss each other, cuddle, and have sex. These loving behaviours are two-sided. Shows of affection by one partner in a good relationship usually prompt loving behaviour by the other partner. Intimacy grows naturally in a sympathetic social relationship.

None of this is automatic and should not be taken for granted. For example, a loving, committed couple can have problems with emotional intimacy if one or both partners has never learned how to express feelings or respond to others' expressions. Couples can also have problems with sexual intimacy when they have different levels of desire. For example, men and women experience sexual intimacy differently and may want, need, and expect different things. Opposites may attract, but all the problems of difference need to be dealt with. Women need to talk about their feelings, and they want their men to do the same. Some men act as if communication is a big waste of time. It is no wonder that opposite-sex relationships have problems to solve.

This gender difference can affect every aspect of a couple's relationship, including sex. Many wives typically report less sexual satisfaction than husbands. As well, the predictors of sexual satisfaction differ for husbands and wives (Song, Bergen, and Schumm, 1995). For women, sex occurs within a gendered or gender-unequal society. Many women have to find sexual pleasure within a relationship that also provokes feelings of powerlessness, anxieties about contraception, and exhaustion from child care and outside employment.

For many reasons, including these power issues between men and women, sexual incidence and frequency decline with time. Age, length of relationship, and the presence of children all affect the frequency of sex. Yet despite all these variables, happily married people still have sex more often than less happily married people. The cause-and-effect relationship remains unclear. Is it that people who are happy together are more inclined to make love, that making love often helps a couple stay happy, or that other factors affect both happiness and sexual frequency? Likely, the answer is all of the above.

Literature on Coping and Conflict Management

How well a couple manages the conflicts that arise in their relationship controls their relationship satisfaction, and these conflicts and stresses come in many forms.

Less satisfied couples are more likely to avoid discussing important aspects of their relationship as a means of coping and avoiding conflict. For example, they tend to avoid talking about financial situations and problems with their children, and they are more likely to just make small talk (Nielsen, 2002). When talking about important issues, they also talk more negatively than couples with high marital satisfaction (Nielsen, 2002).

Major problems are difficult for many couples to cope with. For example, financial difficulties increase the likelihood of depression in both partners. Depression then leads partners to withdraw their social support and undermine each other. These behaviours, in turn, reduce relationship satisfaction and intensify the depression (Vinokur, Price, and Caplan, 1996). Similarly, health-induced strains also reduce the couple's ability to cope. Taking care of a severely ill partner puts an enormous strain on a relationship. This leads to dissatisfaction, especially for the caregiving partner. Dissatisfaction is especially likely if a caregiver feels the ill partner brought on his or her own health problems, or if the caregiver has other reasons for feeling cheated in the relationship (Thompson, Medvene, and Freedman, 1995).

Similarly, work and roles can strain a couple's ability to cope. For example, the birth of children often lessens relationship satisfaction by increasing conflict and parenting stress (Lavee, Sharlin, and Katz, 1996). The stresses of work can also reduce relationship satisfaction. Conflicts resulting from a partner's employment can cause distress and, in turn, produce hostility and reduce warmth and encouragement between the partners (Matthews, Conger, and Wickrama, 1996). Unemployment because of job loss also causes relationship conflict, either because of the loss of ordinary ways of family living or because of an unwanted role reversal (especially for males). Material privation and relationship conflict over financial issues also play a part (Lobo and Watkins, 1995).

As a major role change, retirement from work can either increase or decrease relationship satisfaction. On the one hand, leaving a high-stress job normally increases satisfaction. On the other hand, poor health and other changes that often cause or go with retirement reduce satisfaction (Myers and Booth, 1996). Retirement, like unemployment, may also reverse gender roles or reduce social support. In general, people need to prepare for retirement and adjust their close relationships to handle their new situation.

Married people can rarely avoid conflicts, whatever the cause. Trying to avoid disagreements altogether is usually unwise. Research has shown that relationship adjustment is affected less by the presence or absence of hardship than by relationship skills and beliefs. With the passage of time, many couples figure out how to defuse and even laugh at their disagreements. In older couples, conflict resolution is usually less hostile and more loving than in middle-aged couples. Styles of conflict resolution vary by gender, and often it is this difference that causes more conflicts. Wives tend to be more emotional than husbands, and husbands are more defensive and less expressive (Carstensen, Gottman, and Levenson, 1995).

Which is better—making a noise or refusing to say anything at all? Actually, something in between is best. Many new parents cope effectively with the increased stress of parenthood by adopting a strategy of *quiescence* (Crohan, 1996)—calm, even silent reserve, followed by addressing the troubles in a careful and measured way. Yet sometimes this is only a short-term strategy while the couple decides how to address their problem in a more useful way. Research shows that a quiet, careful approach keeps the peace and preserves relationship happiness, so long as there is no attempt to avoid discussing problems in the long run.

On the other hand, hostile argument is definitely unhelpful. It neither makes the disagreement disappear nor improves the relationship. Partners who lack the skill to argue constructively may fall into a pattern in which both partners assert but neither accepts the other's effort at control (Sabourin, 1995). Each responds to the other's comments with one-up-manship, and the argument intensifies, sometimes even resulting in violence.

In short, some mixture of emotional expression and emotional restraint is usually called for under conditions of stress. In the end, everything has to be discussed in a calm, friendly, but honest and firm way. Most important, the partners should understand that each has his or her own way of dealing with the stress. They need to show patience and sympathy for each other.

Effective Strategies for Problem Gambling

Strategies from Family and Religion

Spouses in the 2005 study often stressed the importance of family when encouraging the gambler to seek treatment. Targeting the importance and value of children and the gambler's responsibility to his or her family is a common strategy. One problem gambler—a father of two—said his wife gave him a picture of his family to keep in his wallet:

This helps me to remember to put family first. The photo is supposed to make me think of the family and to help me not to gamble until I have debts. It also reminds me to have more control.

Another problem gambler and a mother of one child said her husband highlighted the importance of staying home and spending time with the family, rather than gambling:

> He says: "You realize how much better it is to sit with us instead of being in the bingo hall? Now don't you feel better? You had a night with us instead of a night in a bingo hall with strangers. You are here with your family." And then I look at him and say "Maybe you're right."

Family responsibilities for household management also help to reduce the time spent gambling. As previously noted, problem gamblers often leave most household responsibilities to their partners. Those gamblers who assumed a significant household responsibility claimed it helped them cut down on gambling. For example, one respondent said that his wife's disability required him to spend more time at home taking care of her and helping her with household chores:

> It seems to be helping [me] because I have less time to gamble now . . . My wife is basically partially blind now . . . so I have to do more for her, to help her.

While extra responsibilities may cause some gamblers added stress, which makes them head out gambling, it may give others a reason to spend time at home.

Several problem gamblers explained that their spouse's emphasis on the harmful effects of their gambling helped them to see the need for change. Often, these lessons emphasized the negative impact that gambling was having on the family, both for individual family members and the family as a whole. They explained how gambling put a stress on the family finances and strains marital relations:

> [She says to] put the family first . . . She talks about the family and tells me to be a family man. She says that I should think about my family first. I do that now.

She tries to convince me that it is a bad habit. She reminds me of what it could do to my family.

I am trying to focus on getting out of this gambling, because I know how much more money we would have in the family household to spend.

One problem gambler said that his wife's dislike of gambling was a major factor in his effort to change his gambling Another gambler said his wife tried to convince him his behaviour was destructive by "by showing me [the] worst consequences that could happen. Her worst fear is losing me." To influence her spouse's actions, another partner drew on the wider family and on social networks in which the couple was embedded:

She also gives me cultural, religious, proofs and experience from faraway. She talks about relatives and how their lives were affected and how their situations became worse.

Religion is another option to use to explain the bad effects of gambling. The wife of the respondent quoted above was urging him to assess the morality of his behaviour. Other gamblers highlighted the importance of religion in combatting their problem:

The best thing for me is having spirituality in my life. Without spirituality I don't know where I would be. I now have a new way of thinking about gambling. There are losses and wins when you gamble and I realize the losses outweigh the wins. It was important for me to realize that.

These examples show the effectiveness of drawing on social institutions—both the family and religious affiliations—to frame the impact of gambling's destructive effects on a gambler's personal life.

Shared Activities

In the previous chapter, partners engaged gamblers in alternative activities to distract them from their gambling. Gamblers who are open to discussing their problem with their partner are more willing to engage in these activities. But whereas the couples in the last chapter were unsuccessful with these strategies, other couples were able to move ahead with them. The difference seems to rest on the cohesiveness and adaptability of the spousal relationship, and the couple's greater commitment to making the relationship survive and prosper. Often, it came down to something simple—for example, the partners really liked each other and enjoyed each other's company.

Many gamblers in the study expressed openness to this approach:

She's trying to lead me away from [gambling] by doing other activities together . . . Like going out and watch races . . . Car races, horse races. Stuff like that . . . for about a year now. It's starting to work . . . I don't go as much and I don't feel like I have to gamble as much.

M: He does try to encourage me from not going to bingo. He'll say "Just stay home and maybe we'll make something together . . . or watch a movie together that you want to see". You know, to try to get me to stay home.
Interviewer: So what types of things do you make together?
M: Oh he and I cook together. The last week now—I haven't been out to bingo, which I am real proud of myself, right?—I had to make some desserts for the Salvation Army for Wednesday, so he helped me make a peach upside down cake and then I made cinnamon loaf and I wasn't sure how to put the cinnamon into the bread, so he showed me how to do it . . . So we are doing things together you know, finally again. We are getting back to each other again.

In both cases, the gambler was being engaged in other activities that he or she enjoyed. This appeared to decrease the need to gamble.

Even gamblers whose spouses had not yet used this strategy thought it might help. They felt that if there were other activities they could do with their partner, it might reduce the time spent gambling:

The gambling is an entertainment and a substitute for other things. If it didn't need to be a substitute that would be helpful . . . if we had other activities that we could share that were enjoyable and [would] fill the time together, as opposed to me getting satisfaction with gambling and going to casinos.

Another respondent said that she and her spouse—both gamblers—decided that they should take part in other recreational activities as a change from gambling.

They saw their decision as an investment in themselves. Because they made the decision together, based on shared interests, the strategy had some chance of success:

> Once every couple of months, we go [gambling] together . . . But neither one of us does it like we [used to] because I guess we are getting older and finally realized what is happening . . . if we had that money we could take a nice cruise or if we had put that money in a piggybank we could have gone here on a trip or gone there . . . A hundred bucks can be gone in an hour, then it's finished . . . I think between the two of us we started thinking the same: we're getting older now and [gambling's] not giving us anything except for the enjoyment so let's find something else like Harbourfront and walking around—we both like the Beaches and walking around, we like the Zoo, so we have our Zoo pass—so yeah, find other things to do.

Enriching their own couple relationships can significantly help in the battle to help one partner quit or at least reduce gambling. The couple above have a rich intimacy and understanding when it comes to their gambling—something that is often lacking in couples with only one gambler. Since both are gamblers, they can better understand the thoughts and feelings that inspire gambling. Also, they can engage in alternative activities together in the same way that they engage in gambling as a couple. By making this shift away from gambling, they lose none of the time they enjoy spending together. Compared to nongamblers and anti-gamblers, who must first work to understand the problem behaviour, mutual gamblers can use their common interest to take the first steps away from the problem.

This understanding is essential for moving forward in the relationship and combating the problem as a couple. Generally, many gamblers said they would like to improve the sense of togetherness or understanding they had with their partners. Shared activities are a great and often successful way to do this.

Requests to Avoid Gambling
When spouses think like their gambling partners, they can more effectively use the right words to dissuade gamblers from their activity. In relationships with open lines of communication, gamblers respect and value their partner's input. But the gambler must be ready to accept these requests for them to have any impact; otherwise, they will come across as nagging. One respondent explained

to his gambling partner that she had a gambling problem and insisted that she avoid it. This seems to have helped:

> L: He would try to explain to me and say, you know, "You have to avoid gambling, because you like it too much and you might like it even more if you keep going." So, we've had a couple of conversations like that.
> Interviewer: Did you find the conversations helpful?
> L: [Yes,] because it is basically something that I agree with too. I know I have to avoid those places. I can still play the lottery, because it is not a lot of money and it is just once a week that you play. But, casinos, slots, and things like that—I know I have to avoid them as much as possible (laughs).

Another gambler showed that he was responsive to his spouse's requests because he was aware that he needed to quit:

> On particular occasions, she's said, generally, you should stop—like, I don't even think she sees it as a problem, only if it affects my schoolwork—[and] when she says it's time to stop, in the back of my mind, I know I should stop, but when someone else tells you to stop then it just reinforces it, and I'll do it. So, I think that's helpful in that way.

This gambler had already admitted to himself that there was a problem; for this reason, his partner's pressures were not offensive. Thus, a spouse can use words and reminders to reinforce the gambler's own beliefs. In this way, the spouse supports the gambler without demanding a change in behaviour.

Many problem gamblers said that their spouses helped just by asking them to avoid or reduce their gambling and to avoid the friends in their gambling networks. But one gambler thought it was helpful for her spouse and friends to avoid the topic of gambling altogether. She explained that talking about bingo (in this case) increased her need to play:

> M: I am starting to feel better about myself already in these last ... even that one week away from being away from bingo. Do I need to be there? But right now, I am almost dying to be there ... talking about it.
> Interviewer: Oh, now that you are talking about it?
> M: Right, because that is the one thing that [my friends] won't do. If I am not in bingo, they won't mention the word *bingo* ... They know if they say the word *bingo*, I'll be thinking about it and I'll want to go.

For this gambler, avoiding all talk about the subject reduces her feelings of temptation. Thus, her spouse would be most supportive through silence and distraction than through direct requests.

Support

Some gamblers in the study felt that the most effective way to help is by supporting the gambler's decision to take part in—or avoid taking part in—gambling. What mattered was to make the gambler feel supported, accepted, and loved. A few gamblers said that their spouse helped by providing continued support and encouragement to seek counselling for their gambling problem. One gambler said that "just listening to me and being encouraging of my recovery" was meaningful. A spouse's willingness to discuss—but not control—the gambler's behaviour appeared to be a useful strategy for several couples:

> We just try to work on it together with our thoughts and feelings about it. He doesn't say to me "Don't go" because I'm bull-headed, and if you tell me not to do it, I'm going to do it.

Sometimes, avoiding an argument with the gambler is helpful in reducing the strain and stress that gamblers feel. One respondent wanted to protect her relationship, so she limited her discussions about gambling and the way she responded to her partner's behaviour. The result was sometimes confusion and ambivalence:

> I am not being strict enough with him ... I want to help him, but I don't want to treat him like a child either. I don't want him to feel like I am being like his mother either. I don't want him to cause a big fight and have him be like, "Oh, you're just trying to be my mother." I don't want him to feel like that.

Supporting the gambling habit may allow the spouse to reduce the stress the gambler feels and avoid relationship conflicts. And when gamblers seek help with their problem, support for change is extremely important. Realizing he had a problem, one respondent sought help and started trying to change. He credited the support from his partner as a source of strength and encouragement:

> She is very supportive when I go out to meetings ... In everything she is very supportive.

Supporting the gambler's behaviour is a useful way for spouses to help gamblers at any point in their gambling career. Offering support is different from nagging, because it focuses on the positive and relies on the couple's concern for each other.

Counselling

According to Rotunda *et al.* (1994), working to change problem behaviours through couples therapy may "(1) help those that engage in enabling to decrease or eliminate these behaviours; (2) teach and foster the use of positive coping responses in what are usually very difficult situations; (3) help family members provide a socially supportive environment for recovery without becoming overly responsible for the impaired person; and (4) help mitigate psychological and physical strain that may result from frustration and long-term interaction with those struggling with alcohol or drug dependence" (274). Thus, productive counselling depends on positive attitudes and an openness to change.

A few respondents mentioned seeking counselling for themselves and also for their children, so that the entire family could learn how to help themselves and the gambler:

> He [her partner] says, "Why are you guys going—you don't need it." I said, "Yeah we need it." Now we are better people. Now we [she and their children] understand more about gambling. You learn something. You sometimes overlook it. [And] until he is ready, you just don't support him as much. You have to back off with the support. When he is ready, then you know. You know he has the support, but he doesn't help himself.

One respondent sought advice from a counsellor on how to deal effectively with his partner. When the counsellor proposed that he stop enabling the gambling and end the relationship, this insight was a turning point:

> I've had to say, "This is the last line in the sand, I have the agreement of a counsellor on this . . . A professional told me this. I talked with someone who deals with people who have gambling problems like you and they said if you cross this line, we've got to go our separate ways." . . . Yeah, I've been accused of being an enabler. [The counsellor] said basically, "You got to start using the word *I* more often."

This respondent also hoped his partner would follow his example and seek help for himself, once he acknowledged the problem to himself:

> In the rare occasions I'm able to tell him about what I'm getting out of this counselling, I can see it in his face ... like someone who gets an idea that "Maybe they can help me." I'm trying to encourage him to think there might be something they could say to help him. "Now if you get past the problem, the part where you deny you have the problem ... then you might just find someone has a few answers for you."

Counselling can be an effective way to help partners and children understand the gambler's problem—when both parties are open and ready to accept the uncomfortable truths they might have to face. This knowledge can help the family deal with the gambler, which may benefit the entire group.

Offering Treatment Information

Awareness of options is important, since many gamblers and spouses don't know what is available. Offering information about services is very different from counselling, since it simply makes the information accessible, rather than pushing the gambler into using it.

Some spouses tried to help by providing their partners with information about available resources or by talking to them about their need for help:

> Show some kind of support, I guess ... you know, talk more. Keep on giving him the pamphlets. Keep on assuring that there is help out there and it is free of charge. Just keep on showing him. Give assistance.

> I've mostly talked to him. I haven't shown him materials about it; I've got materials about it for him to see, but he's never asked me about gambling—he's never asked me how he could stop.

A few spouses tried to tell their partners about available types of help in more subtle and creative ways:

> I've brought home a few sheets from that Pro-Line—you know, how it has that gambling hotline number? Well, I put it down, and a few times, I've put it as a screen saver (laughs).

Some spouses were able to get the gamblers to seek therapy using these methods, though they usually meet resistance at first:

> He was a little bit difficult at first, but he came around. And he is [in] counselling now. He is getting some help ... It is going slow, but anything you want really bad takes time. So we are going through that, but he didn't take it very well at first. He was like, "How could you be judging me and telling me who I am?"

While admitting there is a problem is the first step in changing behaviour, many gamblers also said that they were unaware of resources that could help them. Here, information provided by spouses about counselling, gambling hotlines, and other means of help are a significant source of support for gamblers who want to deal with their problem.

Bank Accounts

Several respondents—both spouses and gamblers—said that greater *financial intimacy*—where partners share resources or are aware of the other's financial position—may help moderate a gambler's behaviour. Because their spending can be traced, gamblers who share a joint account with their spouse are more likely to be truthful about the amounts of money they spend. Some even admit to moderating their own behaviour, saying the joint bank account helps control their spending:

> I usually tell her [how much is spent on gambling]. I usually tell her, because I feel guilty if I don't tell her. She is going to find out anyways because she works in a bank, so she is going to know. So I usually tell her, because she is going to find out anyways, but I thought about it—I thought about taking a little bit extra money out.

This respondent knew he could not lie to his wife, since she had access to bank account information. That he still thought about keeping withdrawals secret from his wife showed the strength of his habituation. That he felt guilty about thinking of deceiving her showed that his emotional concern for her played an important role too. The strength of their emotional connection to each other was in effect helping him struggle against the pull of gambling. He understood the risk he was running with their relationship.

Joint accounts can also be useful when the partner controls access to the money and forces the gambler to practise restraint:

> It's going good because she controls the money, and I can't touch it. I got a bank card but I let her hold onto the bank cards 'cause I won't have the itchy finger to grab money out and spend it if I don't. If I want it, I'll ask. I like it like that. If I want to borrow money, I'll say "Can I take some money out of the bank?" Okay, I'll take the bank card and take, like, 20 bucks out.

Even when joint accounts do not have this direct effect on the gamblers' choices, they pressure gamblers to think about being honest about their activities. One respondent admitted that she would have told her husband white lies about how much she was spending; but because they had a joint account, she would have to tell him the truth if he asked:

> S: I always tell him that I am going to gamble and I tell him that I don't spend a lot, which is a lie of course. I tell him that I have my limits. When I lose, I just go out and I sit. And he doesn't actually ask me a lot of questions, because he doesn't really care about gambling. All he says is "Don't go." He never once asked me if I went to the bank or withdrew money.
> Interviewer: If he did ask you, what would you say?
> S: I would say "Yes," because it comes out of the bankbook. I would say it, but he never asked me.

Sometimes spouses make other arrangements to achieve the financial intimacy of a joint bank account. For example, one respondent asked her partner to save his winnings and bring them home for her to check:

> I take half his money when he comes home when he's won, and that offsets the days [he loses] ... so I keep that money, so next time he goes and he loses, I still have the money there ... In his mind, he hasn't really lost, you see? Because he knows that I have kept the winnings. So he takes another bit of money and goes out and plays with that, and if he loses with that he says "Oh well, it was a bad day."

This strategy is effective because of her partner's willingness to let her manage his playing money.

Many of the problem gamblers stated that their spouse's emphasis on money was useful for persuading them to cut back on the gambling. This emphasis ranged from underscoring the amount of money lost and its effects on family finances, to encouraging gamblers to budget, and even to taking total control of the gambler's finances. One gambler said that his spouse stressed the importance of saving money while noting that he could play bingo another day:

[My partner] says to save the money when I have it and to relax—that there's another day to spend money and to go to bingo . . . He says that if I save money then the next day I will know I have money. I have a bad thing of going and buying lottery tickets when I have money and losing it all—25 dollars' worth.

Similarly, another respondent said that her partner has encouraged her to make positive financial decisions:

S: Controlling the money and trying to put the decision in my hands. That's been helpful because I really have been trying to say "No, we can't do this, no." Interviewer: And how successful do you think you are in making that decision not to go? S: Pretty good. This is the first weekend, I guess, coming here and going "Oh no, I am not going gambling this Saturday. Oh, I must have this problem." I'm just realizing that.

By being honest and open about the financial aspects of gambling, couples can limit gambling and increase trust in the process. Also, as we saw in the previous example, forcing gamblers to become aware of and responsible for their financial spending may lead to the revelation they have a problem.

Ultimatums

For many couples, the strategies described so far don't end up working. For some problem gamblers, only the most severe ultimatum—where the spouse threatens to leave the relationship—causes the gambler to take action. Spouses often resort to this strategy when they have exhausted all others.

Of the two respondents who were in therapy when interviewed, both had begun counselling because their spouse had given them an ultimatum. How effective ultimatums are in the long term remains unclear. Also, how personally invested these gamblers are in their counselling is also uncertain. Therefore, the effectiveness of this strategy is hard to assess. Interestingly, some of the gamblers who had not received an ultimatum thought that counselling might be something that could encourage them to change. Yet none had so far started any counselling. This suggests that the ultimatum is necessary to push some gamblers to start changing.

Some gamblers also said that the threat of their spouse leaving made them consider quitting gambling. This contrasted with other gamblers who negotiated the terms of their relationship in a way that allowed them to gamble. Fearing instability, these latter gamblers felt endangered by the possible loss of their spouse:

> This is a problem, because at the time, I have a relationship, and I don't want to be alone. So I have to put it in balance—my girlfriend and my gambling. I hope my relationship will be there in the future, because I'm growing old, and I want to have a person next to me, to be with me.

If the gambler wants the stability and companionship of a relationship, the spouse can manipulate these vulnerabilities and pressure the gambler to seek help for their problem. One respondent described his need for his spouse:

> The problem is, I don't want to be alone, so I have to explain things to her.

Another respondent connected the fear of losing his spouse with thoughts about quitting gambling.

Threats and ultimatums only work if they are consistent and can be backed up. The partner must be willing to put something at risk to affect great change. Unfortunately, this *something* is usually the relationship. If a relationship is good and the gambler values it, the threat may have an effect. The more important the relationship is to the gambler, the more likely the gambler will react when it is put at risk. Therefore, fostering and preserving a strong relationship is one of the best things a partner can do to promote change in the gambler's behaviour.

What Helps the Relationship?

The relationship between a gambler and spouse needs to be strong in order to face the challenges of defeating a strong habit. Couples need to find ways to strengthen their relationship and cope with the stresses of financial problems, workload, and fears.

Open Communication

The problems of persuasion and conflict resolution faced by respondents in the study are by no means unique to gamblers and their spouses. All close relationships experience conflict and need to find ways to reduce conflict. Increased conflict makes solving any problem slower, more difficult, and more painful. As well, certain styles of communication inflame conflict.

One communication style that increases relationship conflict is the *demand/ withdrawal pattern*. In this pattern, one party—the demander—tries to engage in communication by nagging, bullying, or criticizing the other partner. Partners with more power in the relationship are more likely to be the demander. The withdrawer, on the other hand, tries to avoid such discussions through silence, defensiveness, or withdrawal (Walczynski, 1998).

Like any behaviour that can reduce relationship satisfaction, the demand/ withdraw pattern of communication has health outcomes. Research has found that among married couples, withdrawers—the nagged spouses—have higher blood pressure and heart rate reactivity than the other groups. Husbands of withdrawer wives have even higher blood pressure than the husbands of demander wives. Demander (that is, nagging) husbands with withdrawer wives experience the highest blood pressure of all the groups (Denton *et al.*, 2001).

Neither nagging nor being nagged is a recipe for good communication. For the couples in the study, nagging and intensified conflict tended to propel the gambler out the door, back to the casino. These gamblers tended to use nagging as an excuse and gambling as a means of reducing stress. But in general, nagging alienates the partner and drives him or her away. So, demanding and withdrawing is a poor communication pattern, as is mutual nagging or mutual withdrawing.

Partner communication patterns must be effective and similar enough to uphold relationship health and couple happiness. As well, when partners discuss their problems of communication and express what they both want, their commitment to their relationship often increases.

Talking openly is easier when partners are already satisfied with their relationship; yet good communication is hardly ever the automatic result of a good relationship. Couples who love each other intensely and are committed to each other may still have trouble learning to talk effectively. Like all other social skills, communication is something people learn, and continue to learn, throughout their lives.

What counts as good, effective communication varies over time and across cultures, to some degree. In Western society, most people agree that certain forms of communication harm the relationship because they undermine the listener's self-esteem. For example, personal insults, ridicule, questioning of a person's authority or competence, or dismissing or belittling of a partner's achievements are negative, hurtful, even emotionally abusive, forms of communication. Giving a partner the cold shoulder can sometimes hurt even more than a personal insult.

Some rules of successful communication emerge from sociological research on families. One purpose of communication is to send information, either of a factual or an emotional nature. So, the first rule is that communication must be clear if it is to be effective. Both partners should say what they mean and mean what they say. Many people have learned at an early age that communication is a powerful tool for hurting and controlling people. They need to remember that communication is also a tool for making our thoughts and feelings known.

A second rule of communication is: Be willing to hear and to respond to your partner's comments, complaints, and criticisms. A key to beginning and continuing good communication in a relationship is recognizing our own defects and trying sincerely to work on correcting them. Communication is important at all stages of a close relationship—especially in the beginning. This is because during the so-called honeymoon period, partners have a heightened sensitivity when communicating with each other, and a strong wish to please and understand the other person. It is during this period that couples set up the basic interactional patterns of the relationship. For people who have long been in a relationship with faulty communication, they need to expend some effort to relearn how to listen and how to talk to one another in open and non-injurious ways.

A third rule of good communication is: Let your behaviour speak for you (and be sure to "listen to" your partner's behaviour too). Often, people have trouble putting their thoughts and feelings into words. That's why actions can be meaningful in communicating feelings and desires. Establishing family rituals can help a couple build and express stability. Among couples with small children, relationship satisfaction is highest for people who have created family rituals and believe that these rituals are important. Even small things—quiet time spent together in trivial activities—can count for a lot if they convey the feeling that people care for each other and enjoy each other's company.

Some couples we studied have managed to achieve successful communication and conflict resolution strategies. They have found these strategies useful for avoiding disputes and also for neutralizing the negative effects of gambling on the relationship. Our results show that couples who have found neutral—that is, unemotional—ways to discuss gambling have fared better than couples who get into heated battles about the topic. Calm discussions of their problem help to foster emotional and intellectual intimacy and increase the partner's ability to help the gambler with his problem. Each successful couple found its own specific tools to open conversations comfortably. In general, careful, quiet, and purposeful discussions are better rather than random nagging sessions:

> Talking it out is part of constructive arguing; it helps to listen to each other.

One respondent elaborated on how using objective language helped her and her partner avoid needlessly hurting each other emotionally:

> We are not really big on arguing, and when we do argue, we don't insult each other or say false things or exaggerate. We are pretty much to the point. It is more like a debate rather than an argument. I think that actually helps, you know, because you can filter out all the crap . . ." You always do this and you never do this and you're so stupid." You filter all that stuff and go right to the actual part of the problem. I think that helps us solve it.

The recurring element here is *talk*—talking about the gambling, talking through the problem, and turning bitterness into a productive and practical discussion:

> We talk about it, we follow up on our talk and comfort each other and . . . help each other. [If] there is an issue we immediately start talking about it. We are very open with each other. One person usually notices a change of behaviour before someone else and someone says "What's wrong?" and someone opens up.

> We usually talk about it. We will sit down together and try to talk things through. Sometimes we do argue . . . Talking things over with my friend and then coming back to talk to him is helpful. I also like communicating with him—talking things through.

> Yeah, we talk about it, sometimes argue about it, and we just come up with a plan to deal with it. We find ways around it.

This may sound very simple—almost naive. Yet, the ability to do this—to confront problems openly and honestly and talk them through—is, sad to say, missing from many relationships in our society. The reason is that it forces the partners to admit their faults and mistakes, their fears and misgivings. It forces them to be emotionally intimate with each other in ways that many couples never risk and many other couples may have lost. Honesty can be painful. It calls for a lot of trust and confidence in the relationship. This is true whether the problem at hand is gambling, drinking, or infidelity, or much more common problems, such as the way that work is shared at home or how the children are being disciplined. The problems we face with problem gambling, then, are merely specific versions of generic marital issues.

How to Discuss Gambling

As previously noted, gamblers often have a hard time opening up or being honest about their gambling. They may find it especially difficult to discuss these matters with their partners, who have been affected—often repeatedly—by the sometimes upsetting results.

Couples in the study had to develop their own methods for discussing gambling without causing conflict. One respondent explained she and her partner have developed a routine way of approaching the subject of gambling, in a neutral, nonconfrontational manner:

> It's more of an issue for him in terms of how much money we spend—he has more anxiety about it—and so recently, I have been using this technique where, if he is spending money on gambling, he has to give me that money in cash . . . So, for $50 he spends on gambling, he has to pay me $50 for whatever I want. That has also helped bring the behaviour to the forefront, and that has been in conjunction with the counselling . . . I think that it has helped us to have a neutral way of discussing it; because for him, it is a way to admit what he has done in a very neutral way . . . Instead of having to say "I gambled today," which is kind of a heavy statement, he can say "I owe you $20." And then we can initiate the discussion.

Another respondent and his partner referred to shared financial goals as way to discuss potentially problematic gambling:

> I feel that we've been pretty successful just talking it though. We have some fairly clear goals on saving. If we fail to meet those goals then, [we] talk about that and show these concrete objectives haven't been met and so, we're in trouble, kind of thing.

Some respondents avoided openly criticizing their partner's gambling while discussing their partner's behaviour. One respondent referred to a technique she learned in counselling:

> I use . . . a way of outing the behaviour, which is not to let him get away with saying he was doing something else when he was actually doing the gambling. So something that I have done is to make sure that it is clarified that that's what's happening and that I'm aware of what's happening.

Such methods of discussion are important for problem gamblers who try to hide their problem, rather than discuss it. Spouses who fail to develop these techniques often feel shut out and helpless in facing this situation.

Important Factors for Promoting Change

Relationships with problem gamblers can include financial insecurity, emotional neglect, and gambling-induced mood swings. The couples in our study have confronted these problems with various types of intimacy—emotional, intellectual, and financial—each with varying levels of success. But several factors influence whether change is even possible for a couple.

Severity of the Problem

The severity of a gambling problem is an important influence on whether the gambler seeks and accepts help. Tragically, the more severe a gambler's problem, the less likely efforts to change their behaviour will succeed. A heavily habituated gambler is usually less willing to admit having a problem, to think about getting treatment, to seek information about treatments, to enter treatment, to comply with the rules of treatment, or to stay in treatment. A heavily habituated gambler is also less likely to follow through on personal commitments like financial and household responsibilities. Many of our respondents also reported thinking about gambling as an addiction and they described what this addiction meant for their families:

> Well I was naïve when I was younger . . . I didn't understand the game or the addiction. To me it was just "Oh, they're gambling" or "Oh, they're at the track." But now that I've been through it—like been through the wringer— I can understand what they were going through . . . And I understand how

hard it is to quit. Or, I understand the addiction, and the need to be there. And everything else that goes with it.

Gamblers who are less heavily invested in their problem respond more favourably to a spouse's efforts to replace gambling with alternative activities and added responsibilities. It helps if the gambler feels he or she has personal efficacy or a locus of control over the gambling problem.

Quality of the Relationship

The interviews showed that assertive spousal intervention is the best way of encouraging gamblers to consider treatment. Yet there is no easy path to improving injured marital relations and promoting treatment. Even when marital relations are good, a gambler may still decline the spouse's support or requests to seek treatment. Doing so may also lead to a worsening of marital relations and a downward spiral in the gambler's behaviour.

Regardless, the data from our study suggest that strong marriages benefit gamblers. This is especially true for those who practise honest communication in their relationship. These gamblers are typically more receptive to help from their spouses. One condition for success is the gambler's willingness to place a higher value on their personal relationship than on their gambling. Gamblers in more stable, happy marriages, and who value their spouse over their gambling are usually more receptive to proposals that they change their behaviour. The conscientious, committed partner will help to find alternative activities and remember his or her family responsibilities:

> Interviewer: What would you like to see your partner do to help with this problem?
> C: I want him to understand what he is losing by having this problem. I want him to start helping out. I don't want to have to worry that he is going to go out with his friends and gamble away the money. I can't even go shopping for clothes, because I have to save money in case he gets into one of his moods and spends all the extra money. I want him to get involved with things and not focus on gambling . . . I want him to join a baseball team or do things to keep himself occupied so that I don't always have to think of things to keep him occupied. I plan activities for us to do, because I worry that he will gamble.

Interviewer: What efforts have you made to get your husband to make these changes?

G: I often explain the bad side of gambling, I talk to him about how much money we could save by him not gambling. I also talk to him about how much money we're losing when he gambles. I drill into him the responsibility of family. Now that he's married and has kids, he has a responsibility to his family to take care of them.

Shift of Gambling Lens

Both the way gamblers view their behaviour and the way they understand the role of gambling in their lives affect the gambler's likelihood of accepting help. A few respondents spoke to us about the need to shift their gambling outlook. Instead of viewing gambling with the dream of a big win, they described shifting their perspective to view gambling as a simple distraction or entertainment:

It's better not to hope from gambling, I believe. To cut the hope from gambling, that would be the best way.

I just want to make sure it doesn't become an entity on its own . . . it doesn't take on a life of its own. That it stays just entertainment or whatever, a distraction. It doesn't become a substitute for something else.

I wish I didn't have that feeling . . . when I just feel really ugly when I lose. It is just this bad feeling and it is that feeling that fuels me to play more. I wish I didn't have that.

A few respondents said that they regretted the time away from their partner and family. They viewed this as a good reason to change their behaviour. One gambler explained that more important than the lost money was the lost time:

Just the amount of time that I waste gambling. It's not the money . . . I don't play for a lot but the time I could be spending on something else . . . it's a waste of my time when I could be making money or spending time with my partner.

Another problem gambler explained that she wanted to reduce her gambling because she was spending too little time with her husband and daughter:

I am not thinking about being at home with them [my husband and daughter] . . . but I would like to change that pattern . . . start thinking more of them as they are getting older. My husband is sixteen years older than I am, you know. I should be spending more time here than I am there. So that is the one thing that I would consider about my gambling ways.

Because some respondents regarded gambling as a way of getting away from the family, addressing unresolved family issues may help stop this cycle. These gamblers need to understand why they feel the need to escape their home life and must work out with their spouse how that home life can be made more enjoyable and attractive than gambling. By changing the way they view their problem—from a gambling problem to a family life problem—gamblers become more open to the possibility of quitting or cutting down. However, if a gambler's perspective is unalterable, it is difficult for spouses to have any success in promoting change or treatment.

Conclusion

The downward spiral in gambling is often interconnected with a downward spiral in the marital relationship. In effect, for married gamblers, we cannot talk about the gambling separate from the relationship. The lack of embeddedness causes both the partner's lack of awareness about the gambling problem and the gambler's ability to make gambling a higher priority than spouse and family. Combined with the gambler's usual unwillingness to enter treatment, a weak relationship makes it nearly impossible for the spouse to force change in the gambling pattern.

This is the majority experience in our sample. Yet, there were exceptions to this rule. Some spouses were able to surmount these difficulties. Some were able to promote change or treatment for their gambling spouse. Often the successful strategies were minor or sentimental actions, such as giving the gambler a family picture for their wallet, to remind them of what they miss when they gamble. More significant acts include issuing an ultimatum: change or I will leave you.

Speaking broadly, successful strategies have several features. First and most important, they increase visibility and surveillance. Successful spouses take active steps to see more and know more about their partner's gambling. They monitor his or her activities more closely. In addition, these strategies control the flow of household money and make a point of discussing gambling and spending. Finally, successful strategies work to strengthen the relationship, by providing new activities to share, creating time for each other, or developing distractions to gambling. This last point is critical: the spouses who were effective in influencing their partners exercised their influence in a steady, consistent, warm, and usually even-tempered way.

Successful spouses also realized that they were not responsible for their partner's gambling and could not take responsibility for controlling it or ending it. They could only support actions by the gambler that would control or end the gambling. The spouses, then, had to remain encouraging. They had to show faith in their own efforts and in those of their partners to quit or control the gambling. The gamblers needed to know they could rely on their spouse for support, but that their spouse unyieldingly and unambiguously opposed their current practices of gambling. In general, partners of gamblers had to avoid providing the gambler with excuses or provocations to gamble, had to recognize the gambler's weak self-control, and had to supply stability and encouragement.

The next chapter summarizes the overall findings of this research. It then considers the implications of these findings for future research and treatment. Finally, it proposes and examines a theory about the therapeutic role of partners that grows out of the findings of this study.

III.

FUTURE DIRECTIONS

Chapter 12
What Have We Learned?

This study explored in what ways, and with what success, spouses try to regulate their partner's gambling. It examined this regulation within committed relationships that include both common-law and married couples. It provided useful information about the extent and character of problem gambling in relationships, the degree of network embeddedness in gambling-affected couples, and gamblers' openness for change or treatment.

Because our research was an exploratory study, it mainly identifies patterns in the comments of our respondents, within the context of very basic quantitative information measured on widely trusted scales. While we cannot be sure that these findings are statistically significant or generalizeable, the patterns warrant further investigation.

The foundation questions of this study asked: Do spouses play a role in regulating or controlling problem gambling? If so, what role do they play, and what role could they play? Moreover, what prevents them from playing a larger role? According to the data we gathered, spouses do play a role in regulating gambling, but they are often unsuccessful in their attempts.

Summary of the Results

Let us summarize the main findings of this study. Some of the findings relate to the gambler and his or her situation:

- Problem gambling is associated with a *downward spiral*.
- Contrary to what some literature says, the downward spiral is a continuum, not a clear set of stages. Each gambler experiences a unique downward spiral, though there are common elements, such as disastrous financial loss.
- Each person experiences these elements differently. What this means is that therapists must attend to the unique features of each gambler's own downward spiral, as well as the unique factors that led the person to gamble excessively.

- One such element in the downward spiral is *comorbidity*. A cross-addiction of another kind—for example, to drugs or alcohol—is common among problem gamblers. Often, gambling treatments fail to help gamblers with their comorbidities, and in ignoring them, may encourage or promote them.

Some of the findings relate to the partner and his or her response to the gambling problem:

- The spouses of gamblers often lack a full awareness of what is going on: for example, the full extent of gambling losses. They may catch glimpses of the gambling, but because their partner keeps them in the dark with continuing lies, they know little.
- Spouses often participate in gambling. When they do so, they legitimate and enable the gambler's problem behaviour. If partners are to help solve the problem, they must avoid such enabling actions.
- Gamblers generally ignore gentle or subtle efforts from spouses to regulate gambling behaviour. To increase a gambler's willingness to enter treatment, remain in treatment, and comply with treatment, a spouse often has to use significant threats and pressure.
- Spouses sometimes use the gambler's family and friends to help solve the gambling problem. Co-operation from friends and family members may help the partner push the gambler to quit. Yet friends and family may take the gambler's side and counter efforts to get the gambler to reduce his or her gambling.
- Some spouses are frankly hostile to gambling in general, while others are indifferent or even sympathetic. Different opinions about gambling are often at the root of conflicts between partners about gambling.
- Almost all the spouses we interviewed report they have tried to change their spouse's gambling behaviour. Most spouses and gamblers alike admit that these efforts have been largely unsuccessful.

Many of the findings relate to the couple's relationship:

General Observations
- Problem gambling weakens family cohesiveness. We found little evidence that weak family cohesiveness causes problem gambling.

- Because of their preoccupation, problem gamblers often respond neutrally or casually when we probe their opinions about the quality of their spousal relationship.
- Debt resulting from gambling forces the couple to sacrifice goals and opportunities that were integral to their vision of the relationship. Spouses resent this limiting of their horizons and, often, strike back in concealed as well as open ways.

Lack of Embeddedness
- A significant reason for the spouses' lack of awareness is a lack of network embeddedness. Gamblers and their spouses often live in different social worlds. This isolation results from the gamblers' secrecy and lies and often culminates in creating alternative lives organized around gambling.
- Many spouses of problem gamblers are far from happy about their marriages.
- Neither gamblers nor their spouses express a consistently high degree of unhappiness. This may reflect a long-term progressive deadening of their hopes and expectations—an adjustment to the gambling problem.
- Some couples we studied were more cohesive than others. They were more embedded in the same social world and as a result, they were more likely to know their partner's innermost hopes and fears, and have a good relationship with their partner. These couples were in a better position to address the gambling problem.

Communication Problems
- Resentment is often hard to detect, since many spouses avoid discussing gambling in a frank open way. Gamblers, for their part, try to stifle discussion about the effects of gambling on their family's problems.
- Many spouses also have trouble thinking about these problems or putting their thoughts into words, leaving them feeling frustrated and angry.
- Both gamblers and spouses may feel misunderstood and feel they have little in common. This can lead to ultimatums and divorce.
- Many gamblers and spouses avoid direct conflict, instead using evasive communication, nonconfrontational methods, and dishonesty in dealing with their problem.

Our data hint that the quality of a marital relationship predicts a willing-ness to undertake change. Gamblers in good, strong relationships are more likely than gamblers in weak or conflictual relationships to report a willingness to cut back on their gambling or seek treatment. This supports the underlying premise of our study, that intimate family relationships can influence, promote, and leverage the personal change of problem gamblers. But keep in mind that the statistical relationships here are weak. This may speak to peculiarities of this sample or to the multiplicity of factors—marital and otherwise—that influence a gambling problem.

The Gambler's Path

Regardless of the efforts of partners, problem gamblers tend to follow a similar path. As time progresses and losses mount, gamblers go further into debt. Many believe the solution is to gamble more until the big win comes along. Then, all problems will be solved, and they will again ride the wave of prosperity. They believe it's just a matter of time until their luck turns. They fight panic by invoking patience.

At some point, gamblers face a financial crisis and have to consider alterna-tives. While paying their debts, they consider cutting back to affordable levels or quitting altogether. This transition is significant, for it involves abandoning (or at least challenging) their own closely held beliefs, values, magical thinking, and self-image, while resisting overwhelming urges and temptations to continue gambling.

At this point, many problem gamblers spend considerable time back-tracking—that is, looking again for less drastic and painful solutions. Some try to devise better odds of winning, some search for new sources of cash, and some reduce the time they spend playing. Even as they take action—to either cut back or quit—they must still withstand the environmental pressures (such as the widespread advertising of gambling) and dependence-oriented psycho-logical states that argue for a return to former patterns of play. Many relapse, only to re-encounter their problems and return to thinking about alternatives. As new disasters accumulate, they reluctantly prepare for and take new steps, only to face the same pressures to resume gambling. In short, problem gamblers increasingly face conflicting demands and increasingly more urgent solutions.

What results are debt loads that are difficult or impossible to manage. Imagine earning $26 an hour at a factory and owing $100,000 in gambling debts! For these people, treatment demands that they quit the very activity that they need to engage in to have any chance at all of recouping their losses. From their perspective, treatment is counterproductive in relation to solving the debt problem that dominates the problem gambler's concerns. This significant phenomenon is absent from the other major dependencies—for example, in problem drinking and smoking. Only in problem gambling does the dependent person perceive that the habit can help pay off debts. We have yet to quantify or fully understand the power this idea exerts on the person trying to change his or her behaviour.

The Gambler's Isolation

The study results show that the financial costs of gambling are troubling for most people with low incomes. Even when the absolute amounts that are lost daily are small, they are pressing if the gambler's income is small and fixed, and the losses mount up. Money management and banking strategies would be useful in these situations. Some couples opt for separate accounts as a way of managing household funds and protecting them from the gambler's urge to wager them. Yet, the same money and banking arrangements may promote deception by allowing gamblers to hide how much they spend on gambling.

Meanwhile, gamblers systematically keep their spouses in the dark. This deception is a source of tension in these couples' relationships. Gamblers often prevent their spouse from learning how much money they spend on gambling or how often they go gambling. To hide their gambling, they regularly lie to their spouse and family about their whereabouts. Some spouses (rightly) suspect their partner of gambling and lying about it. This doubt causes added stress in their already strained relationship.

Gamblers and their spouses lead largely separate, isolated lives. They scarcely occupy each other's worlds. It is no wonder then that spouses know little about the problem gambling that is affecting their relationship and the thoughts that preoccupy the gambler. While problem gamblers are likely to understate the problem because they want to deny it, spouses are likely to understate the problem because they have limited information about it. Both partners understate the extent or impact of gambling, but most relationships in this study showed strain because of gambling. Even relationships in which the spouses tried to ignore or deny gambling-related problems suffered these problems. A failure to recognize and deal with them may worsen these problems.

While spouses may think they have many friends and acquaintances in common, gamblers are more likely to report they have few. Spouses may think that they know all or many friends of their gambling partner, but gamblers say that their spouse only knows some of their friends. Gamblers are in the best position to make these judgments, since in many cases they have created alternative social worlds from which they have excluded their partner.

By creating double lives and separate worlds, the gambler can more easily keep his or her spouse in the dark about the extent of gambling. This strategy also gives the gambler new sources of social support and sociability that reduce reliance on the spouse. This, in turn, gives the spouse less control over the gambler's behaviour.

Talking to the Gambler

Yet when the gambler is at home, there are opportunities for discussion and influence. As long as the gambler wants to preserve the relationship, he or she needs to pay at least some attention to what his or her spouse has to say. But what is said, and how it is said, can be part of the problem too.

The interviews showed that when spouses talked about problem gambling, the talk ranged from whispering and conflict avoidance at one end of the spectrum to open confrontation and drawn battle lines at the other. The spouses in our study often described how they had a great deal of difficulty influencing their gambling spouse. Typically, they were unable to prevent them from gambling or even consider treatment. Thus, the spouses of problem gamblers need support and encouragement themselves.

Conflict and tension was evident in many relationships we studied. Almost all the spouses disapproved of gambling, and most considered themselves unable to change their partner's gambling or lead their partner towards treatment. Their conversations about treatment usually ended in heated arguments, leading to a future avoidance of the topic altogether. As a result, many of these couples were unable to talk about gambling, even to vent their frustrations or offer support. Problem gambling became the elephant in the room: imposing, unavoidable, yet something that (seemingly) cannot be discussed or corrected.

Most of the respondents believed there was little a spouse could do to change or moderate their partner's problem gambling. Almost all the respondents—gamblers and spouses alike—said that responsibility for changing the pattern rested in the hands of the problem gambler alone.

Yet some spouses had adopted strategies that were moderately successful. These strategies stressed prudence with money; highlighted the importance of family relations; emphasized the harm done by problem gambling; encouraged the gambler to avoid gambling and gambling acquaintances; and urged the gambler to seek counselling. The gamblers commonly cited these actions as helpful strategies their partners use to help control their gambling.

The Big Issue of Comorbidities

Like earlier studies, this study has found that problem gamblers often suffer from addiction to cigarettes, alcohol, or recreational drugs. This is an important finding, for several reasons. First, it further validates the study by showing that the problem gamblers we studied are like the problem gamblers others have studied. As well, it reminds us that dealing effectively with problem gambling may mean dealing with other addictions as well. Finally, it helps us understand why problem gambling is so hard to control. Often, co-occurring addictions (or comorbidities) complicate the relationship problems of problem gamblers and their partners.

If problem gambling is caused by or co-occurs with addictions like alcoholism and drug abuse, treating the comorbid disorders may help prevent or relieve the symptoms of problem gambling (Scherrer et al., 2007). Comorbidity may also influence both access to and willingness to remain in treatment. As noted in the literature, problem gamblers often encounter barriers to treatment (Winters and Kushner, 2003). They may not view their behaviour as problematic and thus not seek treatment. Equally important, the confusion about whether problem gambling is a behavioural or psychiatric disorder may make treatment less certain. Also, financial limits may hinder access to treatment. Treatment programs for alcohol and drug addiction are far more common and better funded than treatment programs for problem gambling.

Ironically, problem gamblers with other disorders may suffer fewer barriers to treatment access (Winters and Kushner, 2003). For example, the presence of an identifiable comorbid psychiatric disorder may make it easier for the gambler to get treatment for the problem gambling. No evidence is available yet to support this speculation.

Among the few problem gamblers who do seek treatment, only a few go on to complete the treatment. No research currently examines whether problem gamblers with comorbid disorders leave treatment earlier than problem gamblers without comorbid disorders. Other addiction research shows that people with more than one disorder are more likely to drop out of treatment. For example, one study finds that substance abusers with an antisocial personality disorder are more likely to leave treatment early than those without an antisocial personality disorder (Winters and Kushner, 2003).

The current literature on treatment outcomes is limited. Evaluating the effectiveness of treatment choices is complicated and expensive. Even the research literature on treatment outcomes for problem gamblers without comorbidities is sparse (Shaffer and Korn, 2004). As a result, it is uncertain how effective current treatment choices are and whether certain treatments are preferable for treating specific subtypes of problem gamblers. Further, many of the published outcome studies lack a rigorous experimental design and display poor treatment descriptions. Winters and Kushner (2003) credit these failures to low sampling size, low base rates, and lack of resources.

The literature is also inconclusive about pharmacological treatments. Dell'Osso *et al.* (2005) show in a review of the literature that various pharmacological treatments are effective in treating problem gamblers with comorbidities. Like previous reviews of the literature, this study finds large inconsistencies in treatment outcome between the different studies reviewed. From this, Dell'Osso *et al.* infer that there are various subtypes of problem gamblers, and their treatment outcome varies with their comorbidities and treatment. Some studies find positive results; but more research is needed to accurately assess the various treatments. None of these studies discusses the impact different comorbidities have on the treatment outcome. Interestingly, Stinchfield *et al.* (2005) find that a history of substance abuse predicts more severe symptoms of problem gambling, though it has no apparent effect on treatment outcomes.

Should therapists treat the problem gambling and other disorders simultaneously or sequentially? If they treat the disorders sequentially, which disorder should they treat first and on what basis? Questions like these are unanswered and make treating problem gambling and its comorbidities so difficult.

Implications of this Research for Sociology of the Family

The research from the 2005 study has implications for people who are trying to understand problem gambling, for personal or professional reasons. Some may be people who themselves have a gambling problem, have a friend or family member with a gambling problem, or employ someone with a gambling problem. The remainder may be people who do research on problem gambling or provide treatment for problem gamblers and their loved ones.

The findings in this book should contribute to the theoretical understanding of the ways families work—that is, to the sociological study of family life. The study connects the theoretical (sociological) literature on families to families of problem gamblers. What we have found out about families in this study mainly confirms sociological knowledge on the topic.

1. Families are social systems seeking balance.

First, this study has reminded us that families are social systems. Each member of the family is affected by and responds to the other members' behaviours. All family members influence one another. The way some members play their family roles influences the way other family members play their roles—whether as husbands, wives, sons, daughters, fathers, mothers, and so on. As groups, families develop shared understandings of their lives and shared ways of dealing with their problems.

Most important, these shared ways of dealing with family life often resist change. Often, families respond to gambling crises with enabling behaviour, in order to preserve the existing family equilibrium. In so doing, they turn the gambling problem into a family disorder. The extent of the family disorder becomes obvious when family members become obsessed with trying to control the gambler's gambling.

Some spouses seemingly take on a full-time job of trying to regulate their partners' gambling:

> She tries to hide my money. Right, she hides my bankcards. She tries to make me take different directions to avoid the stores, and if we go on the bus, she makes sure the sports page is out of the paper, so I won't look at it and see the horse racing and not watch it on TV.

Other spouses take responsibility for gamblers' mistakes, by covering bills and lending them money. This is especially hard for spouses who live with their gambling partners, and the gamblers' losses create consequences for the both of them. To preserve their normal lives, they start changing their own behaviour to allow the gambling. For example, one respondent told us she saved her money for about a year so that she would have enough to pay her boyfriend's share of the bills:

> It was going on for almost a year. I felt like I was scrimping my money just to make sure that we had ends to meet. [Then] I just blew up on him. It was

like, "This is ridiculous. This can't happen." He didn't take it very well, but [I said] "You know what, if you want to be in a relationship and you want me to be part of the relationship then you have to meet me halfway."

Similarly, when another respondent arrived home at midnight after eight hours at the bingo hall, she was surprised that her husband and teenage daughter grilled her about the reasons she did not at least call. They didn't know if she had stayed late, or if something happened to her on her way home. They were spending large parts of their lives worrying about her gambling-related behaviour.

Seeing the family as a system helps us understand the role of collective habits in family life. Though some interactions or exchanges are one-time-only—*spot transactions*—much of what people do in families are habitual patterns. Partners usually respond the way they have in the past when they try to stop the behaviour that is disrupting their usual family life. Thus, arguments erupt as gamblers and their spouses struggle to develop a new pattern of interactions that can include the problem gambling.

Often the biggest arguments erupt when the gambler announces that he or she is leaving to gamble and the spouse challenges this. Such conflict leads many gamblers to lie about their plans and whereabouts:

> Usually there's an argument when I tell her that I'm going to the casino. [So] I'm basically not telling her anymore when I'm going to the casino ... [for] about a year now [I'm] just trying to avoid confrontation ... I just say I'm going out to have a couple of beers with friends or that I'm just going out to do something ... She says "That's fine. I just hope that you aren't going to no casinos.

Under these circumstances, secretive and obsessive patterns develop around the gambling. Fictionalizing the problem infantilizes the gambler and forces both the gambler and spouse to live out a fantasy.

In the interviews, we heard that a desire for peace, balance, and equilibrium can often be important enough to motivate gamblers to quit gambling. If the gambling was leading to big enough financial losses, or risky enough behaviours, the spouses said they might threaten to leave, or they actually did so. The gamblers committed to preserving the relationship would then promise to quit and might quit or slow down substantially for a time to reduce conflict in the relationship. But once peace and balance were restored, many of these gamblers slowly began to gamble again as they increasingly felt it was safe to do so.

But if peace and balance are so important to couples, why do gamblers continue to jeopardize them by gambling? And if efforts to restore peace and balance rarely work, why do spouses continue making these efforts? As we found, most things that spouses do to reduce gambling do not work. Most partners do not know what else to do. For many, this attempt to control gambling gives them a (possibly false) sense of security. They try to re-assert control, to secure old or idealized family patterns. In family systems, habits and illusions of control are seemingly better than a frank admission that control is lost, that the family is effectively out of control.

This systems approach takes account of the ways family members react to the gambler, and also the ways the gambler reacts to their reactions. Usually, gamblers are happy to take advantage of the spouse's enabling behaviour—even if this means they have to make elusive promises to stop gambling.

Occasionally, extended family and friends, as part of the wider social system around a family, can act in ways that pressure the gambler to lessen or stop gambling. One respondent told us how she and the wives of her husband's poker friends slowly stopped enabling card games at home. As the games became harder to plan and carry out, the men eventually stopped playing:

> The first thing was preventing the gambling parties from coming in to the house. I refused to cook, but I would clean. The second stage was I didn't cook or clean for these parties. When I stopped doing that, other wives started refusing to cook and clean for these parties, and the men started having to do it. Then the men started bickering with each other, fighting, yelling, booze would be brought out in the morning and never put away, now the men were too drunk to drive home, so they called the wives to pick them up. So we'd go and pick them up and bring them back home, and eventually we stopped doing that too. They had to start taking cabs, we told them. It didn't work out, they started getting angry with each other, and now they've broke up and haven't played cards together in the last three years. No more house games.

This example shows a sequence of moves and counter-moves by the spouses (in this case, the wives) and gamblers (in this case, their husbands). As the wives stopped supporting the poker activities, the husbands had to make and carry out their own plans. This did not immediately and directly stop the gambling behaviour. By staying out of the way and making it harder to continue the gambling, these spouses forced the gamblers to take more responsibility for their own behaviour. Sometimes, this can force them to slow down or stop. In this way, a change in family patterns and habits can bring about a change in unwanted behaviour and restore peace and balance to the family.

While this systems approach explains why families are often so slow to change, it fails to explain how and why many families do manage to change. How can cohesion improve in a family broken apart by gambling? The systems framework offers us no easy answers to this question.

2. Even disruptive behaviour can be fulfilling for families.

Why do many spouses enable the gambling behaviour of their gambling partners? It is difficult to think of disruptive behaviour like problem gambling as being useful or fulfilling for families—and yet it may be. Otherwise, it is difficult to understand why gambling behaviour persists and why many families are complicit in its persistence. This persistence hints at a payoff or reward—to the gambler, the spouse, or the family system as a whole—and we must acknowledge this payoff if we are to deal effectively with gamblers and their families.

Sometimes, people's seemingly irrational behaviours may be rational, in the sense that they bring sometimes non-obvious rewards. This *rational choice framework* may provide useful perspectives on both gamblers' behaviours and spouses' responses. For example, it can lead us to consider how seemingly irrational actions can be seen as instrumentally profitable or as part of a continuing emotional exchange that is more symbolic than instrumental in its nature.

For the gambler, the payoff is obvious—a chance at the big win. Gambling is inherently tempting for the potential long-term rewards it offers. Even though it usually results in loss, gamblers have no way of knowing beforehand if they will lose or win. It is the uncertainty—the unlikelihood and yet the possibility of gaining a large profit—that drives their behaviour. It is always this chance of winning that encourages them to go, even if common sense sometimes tells them otherwise.

For example, one respondent admitted he knew his gambling was getting him and his spouse into a lot of financial trouble. But he ignored this and focused on the possibility of winning this time. That chance was always there:

[He says,] "You might lose again, you better not go." Sometimes I respect what he said, and I don't go, and sometimes [I say] "No, no, no. Maybe I win this time" ... So he let me. I said "Oh, don't worry, I'm going to win." But I don't win, and that's it.

Since the outcome is always unpredictable, both playing and not playing can be seen as rational or irrational decisions.

Since the costs of gambling usually affect the family as a whole, families think they are behaving rationally when they respond to the crises by pooling their resources and trying to protect the family from the results. When asked who is responsible for paying bills, for example, one respondent told us that she had to take over this responsibility once creditors started cutting off household services. She did this mainly to protect their children:

He was in charge of paying the bills. But since the gambling became [a problem] ... Banging on the door, you know ... "Rent is still not paid." "What do you mean rent is still not paid?" "You pay the money ... No, you didn't pay the money." So when you see things not happening ... like, cable getting cut off or water getting cut off, bills that should be paid are not being paid—then you know there is a problem ... At first, he was defensive, but then I go, "I refuse to live on the street. When I am working, I shouldn't live on the street. If you want to live on the street then that is your problem, but I refuse to put the kids through this stress."

When partners share their resources, both partners find themselves in over their heads if one goes under financially. Interviewees often spoke about "our" money, either because they had formally pooled their resources in joint accounts, or because they considered each other's money their money, despite separate accounts. These couples often responded to financial crises by taking out joint loans. Doing so converted what was initially the gambler's mistake into the couple's shared dilemma. In the long term, this behaviour enables—that is, promotes—gambling by protecting gamblers from the results of their own behaviour. It would be more rational for spouses to protect themselves and their children by refusing to do this.

As the severity of gambling increases, gamblers increasingly divert resources and emotional attention away from the family, often leaving the partner to pick up the slack. This places unequal and unfair financial responsibilities on the spouse, and it also infects the family's emotional exchanges. Increasingly, all family life becomes focused on gambling activity and the gambling problem, since gambling has come to preoccupy all thoughts and consume all resources.

Thus, the gambler's isolation and the spouse's loneliness create further reasons for irrational behaviour. One respondent said that her husband spent time with her only if she went to the casino with him. Once they got there, he tried to minimize their contact as much as possible because he was busy with his gambling:

> It's not like it's a family outing . . . [I say] "Let's meet at 12:00 or 1:00 p.m. and have lunch together and then we can carry on." [He says] "Why break for lunch?] He just wants to have ice cream. I say "Sure," because I'm willing to meet him more than 90 percent of the way as long as there is somewhere that I can meet him. But if he's going a full 360 degrees, then there's no place for me to meet him.

The more this spouse tried to adapt to her husband's needs—first by going to the casino with him, then by accepting that they would not even have lunch together—the more he and the gambling shaped the marital interaction at her expense. Her language described the unequal contribution they are each making to their marriage: she was willing to do 90 percent of the relationship work, if he would only just meet her the last 10 percent. Thus, her husband's gambling habit was forcing her to take on an irrational burden of the relationship work, including showing fake approval for his habit.

In addition, the irrationally self-centred priorities of gamblers often put their families at risk. Some spouses in the study sensed a lack of concern from their partners, in more subtle ways. For example, one gambler habitually faced his spouse's lack of concern for his health:

> On Sundays, driving home from London, she'll want to stop off at the casino. And when there's traffic, and it'll already take us a while to get home, that's a problem, because I'm a diabetic, and it then becomes a health risk.

Naturally, spousal frustration from this constant lack of equity mounts. Given the mood changes that gamblers often experience around gambling, the relationships become hotbeds for conflict. Gamblers often become short-tempered and moody, either when they want to gamble, just after gambling, or both. Frustrations about gambling can erupt into disagreements about unrelated matters, much like one respondent's report of an argument over spaghetti sauce:

> I couldn't even discuss spaghetti sauce with him without getting into an argument. We had people over, and he wanted to make spaghetti sauce and we started yelling about how to make the spaghetti sauce. And his friend was like, "Is there ever a time when you people can just talk to each other and not yell?" He says I put him down all the time. And I'm like "Yes, I put you down all the time, but give me something good to say."

Under these conditions, couples can find themselves locked into recurring patterns of negative exchange:

> [I'll say to him] "We'll do whatever you want to do, we just won't go to the bar." Or, "I will leave you if you go to the bar." Or, "I'm not coming there with you, if you go to the bar. Not going to happen." Or, "I will call you all sorts of awful names if you go." Like, "'I will sit and talk to your mother, the whole time you are there and we will talk shit about you if you go." He gets really mad about that.

Thus, thinking of families as exchanges with both rational and non-rational (i.e., symbolic or sentimental) content provides a useful perspective on gamblers' behaviours and spouses' responses. Actions that seem irrational may really be attempts to regain order in the family and fulfill unmet personal needs.

3. Family members are all engaged in interpreting their situation.

As discussed in Chapter 2, human behaviour is based on interpretations of reality, not on reality itself. People spend much of their everyday life developing and applying interpretations to everyday experience. In gambling families, members spend much time trying to understand and interpret gambling behaviour. For many, this means coming to terms with the reality that they have an unmanageable gambling problem.

The symbolic interactionist framework asserts that what humans define as real has real effects. Furthermore, families are a place where a great deal of manufacturing of meanings takes place. So, actions (like gambling), perceived problems (like debt), and perceived solutions (like quitting the gambling rather than trying to win the money back by gambling more) are all debated and reasoned in the family setting. In this framework, families can exert considerable influence on the gambler to get him or her to admit that gambling is causing problems and that the solution is to stop gambling.

Thus, to create change, spouses have to influence the way their gambling partner defines reality, without getting into repeated, explosive arguments. The spouses in the study tried many different strategies, such as speaking calmly, setting objective goals, and finding neutral language. One respondent explained how after years of joking with her husband that he was addicted to gambling, one day, he finally agreed with her:

> The first big step that he took was admitting that he had a problem with it. Because I was always joking around with him ... "Boy, you're addicted to Pro-Line, man!" That was always a joke between us. He goes, "You know what, I think I *am* addicted to Pro-Line. You're right." Just out of the blue one day he came out and said it.

Sometimes gamblers admit they have a gambling problem but do not accept that quitting is the solution. For example, one respondent in the study discussed the many problems his gambling has caused his marriage. He even said that gambling was the worst thing about his marriage and admitted to having thought about quitting. Yet when asked what strategies could help him quit, he responded that he still liked gambling too much to quit, despite the adverse outcomes:

> C: I'm just not ready to quit. I don't know how to answer that.
> Interviewer: Okay, why do you think you are not ready to quit?
> C: I don't know. I just like to gamble.

The interviews revealed another pattern that gamblers use to define their situation. When asked about the scope of their gambling problem, they often described it in language that diminished or downplayed the problem. For example, they ignored the consequences, such as the emotional distance it created, the artificial bad moods, and so on, and asserted that "only" the time or money spent was a problem. Many gamblers said that they only needed to cut back on the time or money spent gambling. For example, one respondent described his gambling only in terms of the time he spent doing it. He denied that he needed treatment:

> I don't think I have a problem. I just do it for fun, for entertainment. The only thing is, rather than working sometimes, because I work from home, I'll play on-line instead. So it's only the time issue that is a problem ... When my partner asks me to get off the computer and to spend time with her, sometimes I will. I haven't tried to do anything about my gambling because it's not a problem.

Thus, the way a gambler defines the situation shapes the way he or she will define appropriate solutions to the problem.

Having come to view themselves as "gamblers," gamblers often experience a strain between their role in the family (as parent, spouse, or son or daughter) and their role as gambler. As they get further into the downward spiral, the gambling role comes to dominate all other roles and identities. Gamblers then increasingly neglect their duties as a partner and parent. One respondent, who had progressed far into the downward spiral, said that he habitually chose gambling with his friends over spending time at home with his family.

When the "gambler" role blinds gamblers to all their other roles, their perceptions of their financial responsibilities change too. For example, much to his spouse's chagrin, one respondent habitually spent family rent and food money on gambling. His spouse reacted by refusing to give him any money. He felt (correctly) that this showed she did not trust him to play his role as a contributing partner in the relationship. Evidently, trust has been lost in this relationship:

> It's got to stop ... Yeah, even money she gives me to get things for the house ... It's money that we haven't got. I'm spending money [intended for] rent and food and it's not fair to her. And she, she won't give me money no more. She doesn't give me nothing (laughs).

Spouses participate in the shifting definitions too. When gamblers fail to perform their roles in the relationship, spouses have to invent new roles for themselves and change their own behaviour. Sometimes these changes amount to freeing and enabling the gambler to do more harm. Yet role-changing can be part of the partner's attempts to find a solution. One respondent (Sonia from the case study in Chapter 10) tried many things to get her husband to change. Each time she tried creating a new role for herself: being sympathetic and encouraging, then dishing out tough love:

> I've gone with him to GA; left him twice, each time for a period of a week, then left him a third time for a period of three months; went legal, and made a domestic contract that gives me the authority to kick him out of the apartment at any time.

Finally, spouses have to contend with the reality that they are no longer central to the gambler's world. Repeatedly, spouses in the study said they felt demeaned when treated as a lower priority than gambling—for example, when the gamblers spent all their time or money on gambling. But the low status takes other forms as well. For example, one respondent described how her spouse ignored her the first time she went to the casino with him, when they had just started dating. Later, he ignored her wish to leave the casino, because he was so engrossed in his gambling:

> At first it was okay. I thought one or two hours and then we are gone, right. We were there all night. And I was just getting so tired. I'd be saying, "I am tired, I'm tired, I'm tired." And he was like, "One more hand, one more hand, one more hand."

This respondent had failed to understand that early situation: that her boyfriend considered gambling a higher priority than his relationship with her.

4. All families change over time.

Though families hold onto old patterns for a long time and may even go to great lengths (for example, through enabling and interpretation) to keep things as they have always been, they also change naturally over time. This evolution occurs in part because family members grow up, get older, confront new opportunities and challenges, and gradually detach from unrewarding patterns of action. Typically, family life develops in stages—periods of time when distinct patterns of interaction take place and major events mark transitions through stages. The stages of family life are useful in understanding the personal histories of gamblers and how personal history shapes family reactions to the gambler.

The interviews yielded strong evidence that key events shape a gambler's career. For example, gamblers often described a noticeably large win early in their gambling career, which sparked enthusiasm about winning:

> The first time that I played Pro-Line, I didn't know what I was doing at the time. I just selected the teams that they had selected to win, and it was hockey, and I didn't really know a thing about hockey, and I ended up winning like 600 bucks off of it.

Other events, such as having a child, can change gambling behaviour for the better. One respondent described how she became more responsible with the money she spent to gamble once her daughter was born:

> Since the daughter's been born, we have to have a roof over our heads. So after she was born I never touched it again ... My lifestyle changed a lot when she came along, you know. I have to bring this kid up, you know. I can't let her suffer and be out on the streets like we were when we were down in Nova Scotia.

The family developmental stage model is important because it recognizes that change is built into all human life—indeed, life of all kinds. The trouble with a gambling problem is not that it never lessens or goes away, but that it may not change at the rate that a partner or family needs it to change. Future research can focus on finding and devising interventions that speed up natural processes of change that can work for different kinds of families.

This stage model is also useful because it considers gamblers' personal histories, and it can help explain why certain behaviours become dangerous for the family. For example, one respondent explained how she would start to panic whenever she heard her boyfriend say he was going out with the boys, because she knew a big loss usually followed. Thus, a few words out of a partner's mouth can trigger a panic response in the other spouse. The stage model also includes the impact of trust. Since spouses watch as the gamblers go through cycles of extreme gambling, then promise and try to stop, and then slip back into the gambling, they get to know their partners' habits. Thus, they learn to feel insecure and lose trust in their partners, specifically when they are alone. Many spouses learn to worry about future events that may never come to pass. For example, they live in fear that their partner will lose a huge sum of money. They know from experience that it can happen at any time, in any way.

> I wish I could just sort of feel confident that she's not going to fall off the wagon again ... [or even] that she would limit herself to one type of gambling.

5. Families of addicts are locked in conflict.

Finally, and most obviously, gambling problems are a source of great conflict to families and their members. Problem gambling strains the family's financial resources, especially its ability to plan, save, and spend as a group. Conflict over saving and spending reveals the structure of power (mainly financial) between gamblers and their spouses. Many spouses in the study sample were stay-at-home parents, financially dependent on their partners to take care of the family. In single-income families, a gambling loss is much more stressful than in a dual-income family, and it reveals an imbalance in power, status, and security. Spouses who lack an independent income may have extraordinary difficulty influencing their partner's spending habits.

For example, one respondent explained how after her husband suffered a huge loss, she put her foot down and demanded he stop gambling. He reminded her then that it is "his" money and he could do what he'd like with it:

> I just told him, you know what? It is not just your money that you are gambling away, it is mine too. And he got really mad about it. "Oh, it's my name on that cheque. That cheque belongs to me, and I can do what I want with it."

Thus, addiction skews gamblers' perception of family income and encourages them to assert a new role of power and unequal resources. But some family members lose more than others. Typically, they are the ones who are more dependent financially and have far more at risk. Children and spouses without an independent income particularly find themselves in this condition.

Models of family relationships can help us understand why problem gambling has such a deeply disturbing effect on family life, and why families have such a hard time changing their patterns. Families of problem gamblers may be appropriate areas for further research to study the way groups adapt to persisting misfortune.

Conclusions

This study has shown the benefit of using a sociological model to examine gamblers within their social networks. Gamblers, like all people, are social beings, influenced by those around them.

By taking this perspective, this study has been able to reveal that problem gambling has a dramatic effect on the financial, social, and psychological lives of the gamblers and their partners. The impacts include emotional costs to problem gamblers and partners such as stress, worries, and guilt. Intimate relationships are systematically eroded by deception and loss of trust, increased conflict, and a decrease in the time spouses spend together. Parent–child relations also suffer. Children in these families are often aware of problem gambling and its effects, and are often caught in the middle of their parents' conflicts. As well, children often suffer from the parent's gambling losses and absences from the family home. Finally, problem gambling often damages the family's or couple's social circle, which becomes constrained by the presence of a secret, stigmatized problem.

As social beings, people do not invent their lives. They rarely create their problems alone or solve them alone. The purpose of this study has been to explore the intimate social worlds within which gamblers experience their problems. It is obvious from this exploratory study that problem gamblers affect the lives of their loved ones. To only a small degree, the reverse is true. This has clear implications for treatment and social policy.

Chapter 13

Recommendations for Treatment, Policy, and Research

This study finds that many gamblers have never sought treatment, nor are they currently considering treatment. Many feel there is nothing their spouse has done, can do, or will do that could change their gambling. This chapter draws conclusions from the findings that imply practical applications in treatment, policy, and research.

The chapter starts with a sociological analysis of *role exits*—the way people change their roles and identities—and relates role exits to problems that occur when counsellors and therapists try to hasten behaviour change in problem gamblers. The gambler's partner needs to play a role in this change process. The process varies from one couple to another, and from one gambler to another, which is why programs must be tailored to the individual and family. This chapter also offers a short discussion of treatment programs that provide *caring significant others* (CSOs), including spouses, with better strategies to deal with family members who are problem gamblers. Finally, it briefly explores how we can improve gambling policy to help problem gamblers and their families.

A Sociological Approach to Behaviour Change

Sociologists view behaviour as mainly a result of past learning and current situational requirements. They think of people *dramaturgically*—that is, as role-players on a social stage, where they find rewards for playing their roles properly and a withdrawal of rewards for failing to do so.

The socially structured roles people play generally have two types of long-term consequences. First, people tend to internalize the roles they play as *identities*. That is, they come to see themselves in terms of their roles. This identification is reinforced by the responses of others, who likewise come to see them in terms of their roles and come to expect and even reward a continued performance of these roles.

Second, roles are often structured into *careers*, in the sense that they lead logically and organizationally into other roles. Playing one particular role can increase the access to another role or reduce the access to a different role. For example, high rates of recidivism among ex-convicts may be a result of learning better criminal skills in prison, thereby increasing the likelihood of moving from amateur to professional crime. It may also be a result of narrowed opportunities for other educational and occupational opportunities, thereby reducing access to non-criminal activities. So, for sociologists, problematic behaviour may simply reveal the hidden social structuring of deviant roles and deviant careers.

Career is a broad term that includes both accepted and unwelcome life progressions. While most people have educational careers and occupational careers, some people also have deviant careers as problem gamblers, alcoholics, or drug abusers. Changing a person's long-time behaviour—for example, ending a career as a gambler—involves changing that person's motivations (including beliefs and cognitions). It also involves changing social expectations in the family and community, and changing the constraints and opportunities that promote gambling.

Often, people live out their particular careers in particular communities or social worlds, such as a gambler living out the gambler role in a gambler's world. These communities promote shared sentiments and identities through common activities and mutually affirmed values. Changing behaviour—for example, ending a person's career as a gambler —usually means dislodging the gambler from the gambling community and embedding that gambler in a nongambling community with different common activities and shared values.

Leaving careers behind is not easy. Counsellors and therapists need to be aware that behaviours they do not understand and views they do not hold are not always the result of error, pathology, or irrationality, as many psychological observers of problem gambling seem to think. Therapists must learn see the world as the gambler sees it and help the gambler understand why it is to his or her advantage to act differently. For example, they can help problem gamblers understand why and how to leave behind their role as gamblers—that is, accepting the emotional challenges of abandoning a long-standing career, community, subculture, and identity.

Thus, in asking a problem gambler to give up or significantly reduce the time spent gambling, therapists are asking the problem gambler to leave a role that has been important and turn his or her back on an identity—"gambler"—forged over many years.

Role Exits

Zena Smith Blau wrote the classic theoretical work on *role exit* in 1972. She noted that role exit occurs whenever any stable pattern of interaction and shared activities between two or more people ends (Blau, 1972). During the exit from a social role, people often experience feelings of loss and anxiety about separation. Yet role exits occur repeatedly in social life, and some bring less of a sense of loss, sadness, depression, and doubt than others. Role exits are particularly difficult when they are unplanned, unwanted, unexpected, and premature. People have particular difficulty with role exits they did not choose freely.

Within this framework, the transition from gambler to ex-gambler is like any other major life transition: difficult, puzzling, and stressful. Signs of weariness, wariness, confusion, and stress are normal in such difficult transitions. We should not rush to pathologize these signs; these are all normal parts of any major life transition. Both therapist and spouses of problem gamblers must be made aware of the personal challenges involved in such a major transition.

Role exits also have important observable effects of varying intensity and duration. The sense of loss (for example, the loss of social contacts and excitement) is one example. Reintegrating the person's identity in one or more new roles helps compensate for the losses suffered in role exit. People must compensate socially after a role exit, to end the bereavement and reintegrate their identity around new activities. One way of compensating for losses in a role exit is a standard *role succession*—a socially accepted process for transitioning from the exited role into a new role. However, for many key role exits, such as widowhood, divorce, and retirement, there are no standard role successions to follow the emotionally and socially draining end of the previous role. The same absence of a standard role succession also affects exits from problem gambling. This is an area where further work can be done so that exiting gamblers can anticipate their next role and feel safe with the changes.

In the absence of a standard role succession, therapists can instead promote *role replacement*—replacing the lost role with an alternative activity. Alternative activities can include new sports, new hobbies, and new social interests. A third alternative is *involvement reallocation*—making more thorough use of the remaining roles in the person's repertoire. For example, exiting gamblers who no longer spend time at the casino may spend more time fulfilling family roles and sharing activities with their spouse and children.

The availability of these alternatives depends on the gambler's stage of life when the role exit occurs and the extent of a person's role resources. Gamblers who were previously socially isolated and who used gambling to provide social contacts may find role exiting particularly difficult, since it makes them uniquely dependent on their spouse for social contact and support.

Social attitudes toward the role exit also affect the ease of transition. Generally, the transition is easiest when the exit is a considered a normal and acceptable occurrence among the person's peers and contemporaries. For example, even though widows and divorcees share common problems (loss of companionship, love, and security, and economic problems), women experience these two role exits very differently. Dickerson and Thompson (1977) found that divorcees suffer much more from role exit than do widows: they receive less support from traditional institutions and often shoulder blame for dissolving the marriage. In a similar way, gamblers often receive little assistance from traditional institutions and are frequently blamed for their poor choices and inability to quit. Thus, the gambler's exit often occurs under a blanket of disapproval, which makes it all the more difficult.

In 1981, Blau wrote a paper comparing widowhood and retirement as two role exits typically associated with aging (Blau, 1981). She found that certain factors influence the ease of role exit and resocialization in both cases: the quality of the relationship with adult children, the availability of friends, health, and preparedness for new social roles in later life. Similar conditions are likely to apply in the case of an exit from gambling: the extent and quality of supports outside the family are likely to play a large part in easing the transition from gambler to ex-gambler (or even, moderate gambler).

Blau never tested her seminal theory of role exit on empirical data. This task was left to Helen Ebaugh (1988), who used data from interviews to study 185 people who had exited various roles they had considered central to their self-identity. Ebaugh focused on significant role exits and the establishment of new identities in new roles, specifying sequences of events and variables that show that role exit is a social process. Typically, role exit progresses through four basic stages:

(1) First doubts,
(2) Seeking alternatives,

(3) Turning point, and

(4) Creating the ex-role.

Certainly, the gamblers we studied showed evidence of passing through these stages, with much backsliding. But problem gamblers are different from the people Ebaugh studied in one significant respect: Ebaugh's widows and retirees essentially had no choice in their role exit. In contrast, problem gamblers have more freedom in their choice to quit or continue gambling. Only a few of the people in Ebaugh's study (for example, divorcees and nuns leaving the convent) had any real range of choice. In those instances, delay, mind-changing, and back-sliding were as common as among the problem gamblers in our study.

In a similar study, McClure (2003) studied how people manage the role transition from student to worker. He noted that all successful life transitions, whether important or trivial, include role exit and role entry and depend on social support and access to financial and personal resources. Even graduates need help moving from the relative freedom and irresponsibility of student-hood to the constraints and opportunities of paid employment. Like McClure's students, problem gamblers also need social support and access to financial and personal resources to be successful in their transition to ex-gamblers. Therapists can foster social support and access to personal resources by including partners in treatment approaches.

Another challenge of role exits for problem gamblers is the duration of the gambling role. Roles and identities that have been held publicly for a long time are harder to change than those that are more recent. Certainly, people who are famous in association with a particular role are likely to find role exit more difficult than people whose role is more anonymous. For example, first-ranking Tiger Woods can be expected to have harder time leaving the role of pro golfer than a 200th-ranked and largely unknown competitor. Stier's study of profes-sional tennis players (2007) reveals that professional athletes frequently experi-ence this problem related to career retirement, role exit, and related identity issues. In professional sports, role-changers faced a problem that Stier called *role-identity fusion*—that is, a difficulty in separating the person's identity from the role the person played.

The same happens to a lesser degree to people whose role and identity have been fused over a long period. For example, Milne (2007) studied the role exits of soccer referees. Using a sample of 940 current and former soccer referees, the author found that several role-set background factors and social characteristics affect role exit. For example, social characteristics (such as social connections (social capital) or educational credentials (human capital)) can make leaving a role easier. Yet social characteristics do not influence behaviour automatically: they are mediated by people's conceptions of themselves. Social characteristics influence how strongly a person has come to identify with—or been identified with—the role. They also affect if and how people can imagine themselves changing their lives in important ways. Generally, people with more social, economic, and psychological resources are more flexible in their views—including views about their own future. For this reason, people with many competing roles (including interests, resources, and social contacts) find it easier to disengage from one valued role and identity because of the availability of others.

Under some circumstances, successful role exit requires a plan, including a rationale and rhetoric of their motives. So, for example, it is usually easier for gamblers to gain support for and save face over a role exit if they cite health issues or relationship issues as the driving force behind the change. Changing a role on a whim (e.g., suddenly refusing to socialize with gambling friends) is likely to lead to a loss of friends and public sympathy. Thus, therapists need to put effort into helping their clients work out their public explanations for the role exit. This rhetoric would allow the role changer to exit the old role and enter a new one with dignity. Addressing the issue of humiliation is likely to help problem gamblers, who frequently avoid admitting they have a problem for fear of being embarrassed. Furthermore, no one wants to admit to themselves or others that they wrecked their health, wasted their wages, risked their job, ruined their marriage, and jeopardized their children's future all on a whim. For this reason, some gamblers like to use the rhetoric of *addiction*—a health explanation—to keep them blameless for their problem gambling and to explain why they are seeking a change. The question is, what other rhetoric—if any—would help the problem gambler publicly rationalize his gambling and intention to quit.

The research literature reports that processes of role exit from so-called *deviant roles* are similar to the processes of role exit from normal, conforming, or typical roles. For example, Anderson and Lynn (1996, 1998) found that Ebaugh's theory applies well to the role exits of recovering drug addicts. Drug addicts who go into recovery—that is, exit the drug abuse role and enter the recovery role—follow Ebaugh's four stages (first doubts, seeking alternatives, turning points, and creating the ex-role) in sequence. Still, our own research reveals that one size does not fit all. Contrary to earlier research, our research indicated that it is not always possible to identify turning points or critical moments among addicts who were exiting roles. Moreover, there are other variations, based on race and gender differences, which can also affect the process. So design of treatment programs must take into consideration individual differences while following the four-stage model.

Along similar lines, Boeri (2002) studied the role exits of cult members. The central issues that emerged were alienation, depression, spiritual confusion, changing gender roles, limited friendships, sexual abuse, lack of education and work history, and health concerns. Likely, the minority status and social marginality of cult members—like that of drug addicts, celebrities, and others mentioned above—increases their engagement with their deviant role (and deviant identity). This makes role exit and identity change more difficult than it might be for ordinary people leaving a job or a marriage.

Moreover, Sanders' (2007) study of the role exits of sex workers found that economic, political, cultural, and legal factors as well as ways of thinking and levels of self-confidence are key factors that trap women in the industry. In a similar way, problems gamblers are trapped by the gambling industry—through inducements (free meals, transport, or accommodation), misinformation (a lack of information about the true odds of winning), and an absence of needed barriers (ineffective exclusionary practices for self-proclaimed problem gamblers). It's true that no one forces the gambler to gamble; but social influences (a manufactured desire for excitement and glamour through gambling) can often be just as influential as force.

Other research shows that the issues that affect leaving a life of crime apply to exits from other deviant roles, such as homelessness, substance abuse, welfare reliance, and problem gambling. Put another way, it is always difficult to leave a role: but it is particularly difficult to leave a deviant role, especially if person has paid a high cost to occupy that role. Yet people do leave deviant and criminal roles: witness the large number of juvenile delinquents who become law-abiding adults, and the large number of street people who leave the streets when they get a paying job.

As we have said, there is a tendency in the research literature to psychologize problem gambling, stressing the abnormality of problem gamblers and their difficulties in changing. In contrast, the sociological literature shows that major life changes are normally difficult, that difficulties are often normal, and that normal people have seemingly abnormal difficulties when making important changes.

In making important changes, people form new identities or self-schemas around new roles and subsequently develop new role-appropriate thoughts and behaviours (Lee, 2002). Once the change has started, then everyday social experiences (for example, people's expectations that you act like the person you say you are) set up conditions that help the person change his or her identity along with the changing role.

The assumption underlying sociological approaches to problem gambling is that if you change a person's social context, you change his or her identity. If role change brings about identity change, and because of this, stable new behaviour, then you have solved the problem Homans posed of how to lead someone to conform to group rules freely (see Chapter 2). Though oversimplified, this approach is an essentially correct representation of the principles involved.

However, no one can deny the role of psychological factors, such as motivation and mental health, when trying to lead someone into a new role and new identity. On this issue, Wray (2000) has shown that mental health affects transitions out of paid work through retirement. Typically, "mentally healthy" people are much more able to make choices and carry through on choices and are permitted much more latitude in these choices than are psychological unstable or unwell people. Likewise, psychological issues would be expected to affect a gambler's ability to make choices about quitting the habit.

The Need for Tailored Programs

Little research has explored the effectiveness of treatment programs for problem gamblers. The development of treatments for problem gambling lags behind the development of treatments for other addictions and mental disorders (Potenza, 2002). Partly, this is because our society still denies or doubts that problem gambling is a serious problem with serious consequences (Blaszczynski, 2006; Erickson and Wilcox, 2006). The persistence of this debate has kept policy-makers from paying the necessary attention to problem gambling, compared with other problem behaviours that are better understood (Petry *et al.*, 2006:157). As well, as the owners of many casinos and lotteries, governments have a significant vested interest in promoting gambling as a recreational activity, rather than in expressing concerns about problem gambling or funding research in this area.

Moreover, some treatment programs currently available to problem gamblers seem designed to help an imaginary, homogeneous group of gamblers. Treatments need to match variations in the gambling population, such as problem severity and types of game played (Toneatto and Ladouceur, 2003). Our findings point to a need for treatment that is sensitive to differences in the problem behaviour. For example, different ethnocultural groups hold strikingly different views about gambling and gamble for different reasons. Our findings show that problem gamblers from particular religious or cultural backgrounds feel less need than others to seek counselling, given their culture's willingness to accept or encourage gambling. Conversely, some religious or cultural groups view gambling as a counterculture. This causes some group members to be ashamed of their problem and encourages them to keep their gambling secret. In both cases, treatment must be sensitive to ethnocultural differences in the gambling population, to effectively target or treat those in need of therapy.

Gender is another variable that needs to be incorporated into treatment programs. Our study, unlike Wiebe's (2005), found no strong association between gender and gambling; but many women we studied said they gamble because of boredom, loneliness, or the need to relieve anxiety or depression. The men said they gamble for some of the same reasons, but more than then women, they said they enjoyed the risk, excitement, and danger tied to these activities. Treatment programs need to consider these and other gender differences in problem gamblers.

Also, poorer (lower socioeconomic status) people run a higher risk of developing a gambling problem and the harmful secondary effects of habituation. Nearly eight in ten problem gamblers in our sample have a household income of $50,000 or less. Some low-income people gamble in hopes of escaping poverty. Likewise, some gamblers gamble more often and chase losses, in hopes of solving their financial problems, which makes them even more poor. Therapists need to pay more attention to socioeconomic status in treatment, since poor clients likely gamble for poverty-related reasons. Additionally, treatment programs need to include units that teach clients to manage their debts related to gambling.

Furthermore, like other published studies, our study points to a need to develop treatment interventions that target the flawed beliefs of gamblers. Many gamblers in our study believed that they could control gambling outcomes with play strategies and techniques; they seemed to lack awareness of the true odds of winning. For people with these distorted beliefs, cognitive-behavioural approaches have the best treatment outcomes (Toneatto and Ladouceur, 2003). Moreover, treatment approaches with a cognitive focus, which treat illusions of control and other mistaken beliefs, are the best treatments for all problem gamblers. These treatments also train gamblers to manage money more effectively, to avoid gambling, and to resist the urge to gamble when near a gambling venue (Toneatto and Ladouceur, 2003).

In addition, psychological counselling may be appropriate for many problem gamblers if they suffer from mental health problems that cause or result from their gambling. In fact, McCormick *et al.* (1984) reported that three-quarters of their sample of problem gamblers had a major depressive disorder, 38 percent had hypomanic disorder, and 26 percent had both disorders. Our study yielded no comparable statistics on the incidence of mental disorders. However, one-third of our sample reported having felt seriously depressed at some point in their lives. Despite some debate on this issue (Becona, 1993), researchers often report that problem gambling is associated with substance abuse (Ramirez *et al.*, 1983; Lesieur *et al.*, 1986). In our study, gamblers reported that if something painful were to happen in their lives, over 50 percent would feel an urge to drink, and 37 percent would feel an urge to use drugs or medication. Our study also found that alcohol was the drug most widely used by the problem gamblers.

Overall, gamblers vary in their severity of problems, game played, gambling behaviour, ethnicity, religious affiliation, gender, socioeconomic status, cognitive issues, mental health problems, and substance abuse problems. All of these factors must be incorporated into programming to ensure that gamblers successfully exit their role.

Reasons to Involve Spouses

By definition, problem gamblers are people with a problem. They need to decide whether the personal costs of gambling outweigh the personal benefits. Studies show that most problem gamblers feel ambivalent about entering treatment. Typically, they refuse to seek treatment or drop out of treatment programs before completing them (Toneatto, 2005). In our study, many gamblers were also ambivalent about change and continued to gamble despite the negative effects on themselves and their families. Regardless of their original motivations to gamble—irrational beliefs, chasing losses, the thrill involved, avoidance of personal problems—their attachment to gambling was often stronger than the wish to stop gambling.

When designing treatment programs, therapists need to remember that problem gamblers may feel ambivalent about stopping their gambling. Most gamblers in our study felt that they could not give up gambling. Their sense of efficacy and motivation to change were both low. The best programs for treating such people, then, may be those that take a *harm reduction approach*, instead of an *abstention approach*. Also, in line with Anderson and Lynn's findings (1996, 1998), gamblers who are ambivalent about change may become convinced to make a role exit if they participate in a new role that initiates doubts about their old role. More treatment programs with this leaning need to be developed and made available to people with gambling problems.

It is within this context that family members—especially spouses—can help the treatment process. At present, many spouses try to change the behaviour of problem gamblers, but they often irritate the problem by using ineffective strategies. In fact, some theories of addiction (for example, codependency theory and family systems theory) view spouses as contributors to the addict's problem. Many of these theories identify family members as enablers who can hinder behaviour change and reduce treatment success (Orford, 1992). This perspective likely deters many therapists from incorporating spouses into the treatment programs. As well, problem gamblers and their spouses often interact in ways that feed marital conflict. But according to our research and other litera-ture, spouses are likely to benefit from treatment that helps them detach from unhealthy relational patterns and learn new ways of dealing with the gambler. Because they do not know how to go about this, they need help learning ways to motivate and instruct problem gamblers.

Another problem that some therapists observe is that the spouses may be too soft on the gamblers to be useful participants in treatment. According to Lorenz (1989), problem gamblers tend to choose mates with warm and loving qualities, who are likely to tolerate and, in that way, enable their problem behaviour. Child-hood experiences aside, there are reasons why people knowingly and willingly marry people with problems. For example, living with a problem gambler gives the spouse effective control over the family and makes him or her feel needed. Other spouses may respond to their feelings of helplessness with resentment. For these reasons, therapists might decide that the spouses will be in the way.

So the question remains, what can spouses who choose to stay married to a problem gambler do to promote change? And how can therapists help spouses to change their own behaviour?

Several current approaches incorporate spouses in the program, all of which are discussed in detail later in this chapter. One approach, Gamblers Anonymous, focuses on improving the well-being of the partner while downplaying his or her role in promoting behaviour change. A second approach, the Johnson Intervention, uses family intervention to force the gambler into treatment: the gambler who refuses family help is threatened with a list of the ways his or her close relationships will likely change. Community Reinforcement and Family Training (CRAFT) is a third approach, which teaches spouses various skills (for example, ways to interest their partner in competing activities or raise the topic of treatment) to promote change in themselves and their partners. As supporters of the CRAFT program point out, there are excellent reasons for working with spouses. Engaging them makes it easier to access problem gamblers who are resisting treatment. As well, spouses often need help themselves. In addition, many former problem gamblers report that family influence (by spouses and others) has helped them quit gambling.

Empirical research shows that the CRAFT method in particular achieves its stated goal and is seemingly more effective in bringing about change in gamblers than 12-step programs (like Gamblers Anonymous) and the Johnson Intervention (Miller *et al.*, 2000). Typically, programs aimed at empowering family members to promote change teach spouses to "listen nonjudgmentally, provide useful information, counsel nondirectively about ways of coping, and help strengthen social support and joint problem-solving in the family" (Orford, 1994:425). Overall, these treatment approaches try to increase the amount of social support available to the gambler. Such social support plays a key role in the success of role exits.

The therapeutic literature also shows that problem gambling is rarely the only problem in a marriage marked by problem gambling. In a survey of the spouses of problem gamblers, Lorenz and Shuttlesworth (1983) reported that gambling typically become a problem only after the marriage, with many spouses saying that problem gambling played a large part in worsening the marriage. Other studies have shown that marital problems can begin before the problem gambling and may contribute to the development of the problem (Petry, 2002). As noted earlier, some research shows that many problem gamblers and their spouses have grown up in environments that have left them emotionally scarred and without effective coping strategies (Heineman, 1987). Thus, both spouses may need therapy that helps them cope as individuals and as couples.

Whatever their background, both spouses stand to gain from therapy that helps them resolve past issues and begin to work on interactional patterns the spouses want to change. Therapy that includes both partners and heals a damaged relationship is especially valuable. In a report on marital therapy groups, Boyd and Bolen (1979) state: "Marital couple group therapy was selected because of the chronic and severe marital difficulties, the relationship of specific marital stress to the onset of problem gambling, and the anticipated poor prognosis in individual therapy" (78).

One effective method of starting to treat the gambling problem is by directly addressing the couple's chaotic, troubled, and dysfunctional marriage. Typically, when a problem gambler first enters treatment, his or her marriage is chaotic. Spouses of a problem gambler who is reluctant to change are often the first point of contact for therapists. Despite the difficulties involved, a spouse's engagement in therapy is often critical to promoting behaviour change in the gambler (Makarchuk et al., 2002). In addition to spouses, other members of the family and members of the larger community can help problem gamblers. So, therapists need to consider the role that spouses and other family members can play in controlling or regulating problem gambling.

Steinberg (1993) gives five reasons to include spouses in treating problem gamblers:

- Including them acquaints spouses with the treatment plan and prepares them for further involvement.
- Through their involvement, spouses are likely to gain a more accurate picture of the gambler's problem.
- By viewing spousal interaction, the therapist is able to understand the interpersonal strengths and weaknesses of the couple.
- The therapist is more likely to receive early and honest warnings of failure or relapse.
- Involvement at an early stage increases the chance a spouse receives needed treatment even if the gambler drops out. (Steinberg, 1993)

In short, including the spouse helps to develop a strong therapeutic relationship. The primary "patient" is the gambler, but the spouse is also a patient, often suffering significant difficulties because of their partner's gambling.

As well, spouses should be included in the treatment programs to help them complete their own role exit. While the problem gambler is the one primarily changing roles, the spouse is experiencing a secondary role exit—from spouse of a problem gambler to spouse of an ex-gambler. Both role exits are important because the shared pattern of interaction between the two partners is changing dramatically. Coordinating these changes likely helps the partner abandon their enabling behaviours.

Including a spouse in the treatment also allows the gambler's partner to gain awareness of his or her own problems and admit his or her own role in the troubles. Gamblers Anonymous (GA) can also play an important role here by giving the gambler an opportunity to connect emotionally with other problem gamblers and develop empathy with them (Steinberg, 1993). In this way, spouses help the treatment process run smoothly. Two ways spouses can help secure the success of a GA program treatment are by increasing compliance and supporting abstinence.

Increasing Compliance

In many treatment programs, partners can be useful by helping a gambler remain in treatment and comply with the demands of that treatment. On this topic of treatment compliance, there is a substantial literature both inside and outside the field of gambling research.

The term *compliance* refers to a patient's adherence to a recommended course of treatment. In the gambling field, as elsewhere, treatment compliance is a matter of therapeutic concern, since dropouts are more likely to lapse back into gambling than gamblers who complete their course of treatment. In fact, most problem gamblers who complete their treatment show improved symptoms when interviewed in follow-up sessions (Pallesen *et al.*, 2005; Grant *et al.*, 2004). Thus, completion of a full course of treatment helps gamblers quit, so it is important to keep gamblers from dropping out. Several studies have found the strongest protective factor against treatment dropout is social support (Grant *et al.*, 2004; Brown, 1986; Stewart and Brown, 1988; Sayreet *et al.*, 2002). The main predictor of treatment completion is whether a patient has someone who they feel supports their treatment and cessation efforts (Grant *et al.*, 2004). Therefore, spouses can play an important role in encouraging compliance.

Spouses can play another important role by getting their gambling partner to attend treatment sessions regularly. When spouses drop out of the treatment process, for whatever reason, gamblers are also likely to drop out as well. Brown (1986) found that gamblers who drop out of Gamblers Anonymous are less likely than average to have a spouse who had ever attended GA meetings. This shows that spousal support is crucial in helping the gambler adapt to the new friends and activities that come with their new nongambling role.

In contrast, individual-level, or psychological, variables are surprisingly weak in predicting a gambler's ability to remain in treatment. For example, researchers have been unable to find a consistent link between a gambler's motivation to quit gambling and his or her remaining in treatment (Joe, Simpson, and Broome, 1998; Leblond *et al.*, 2003). Nor do other gambling-related variables, such as the size of a gambling debt (Echeburua *et al.*, 1996; Brown, 1986) and the measured severity of the gambler's problem (Echeburua *et al.*, 1996; Leblond *et al.*, 2003; Sylvain *et al.*, 1997), have a consistent link with staying in treatment. Social variables, such as the strength and consistency of a partner's support, appear to play a much more important role in maintaining compliance.

There are good reasons to expect that strong social support makes treatment dropout less likely. First, social support reduces a gambler's stress level. Stressful life situations increase the risk of non-compliance with treatment. For example, major life changes—such as the loss of a job or the arrival of a new baby—are highly correlated with dropping out of Gamblers Anonymous treatment programs (Brown, 1986). Social support may help gamblers to cope with these stressful situations, thereby preventing dropout. Also, spouses who can share financial debts and care for the gambler and their family may also help and encourage the gambler to continue treatment. A financial cushion is useful when the gambler is transitioning into a new role.

Second, spousal support reduces impulsive decisions. Impulsive gamblers are more likely to drop out after making a hasty decision to terminate treatment without consulting others (Grant *et al.*, 2004; Leblond *et al.*, 2003; Melville *et al.*, 2007). Having a sympathetic social network, especially a sympathetic spouse, may reduce the gambler's impulsiveness, in this way reducing the chance of dropout.

Third, social support may also reduce the likelihood of dropout among gamblers who face the greatest challenges in quitting. Gamblers with an earlier onset and/or longer period of gambling behaviour are more likely to drop out of treatment than shorter-term gamblers (Sylvain *et al.*, 1997; Milton *et al.*, 2002). They may experience more frustration with the treatment and need more help from support networks to stay in treatment.

Fourth, social support can help gamblers deal with the fear of stigma, shame, or embarrassment that often leads to treatment dropout, such as when gamblers have to confront their own gambling problems during treatment sessions. Social supports—especially through spouses—may be able to convince gamblers that continuing treatment is good for their relationship. Ending treatment would only allow the gambler's problems to go on unabated and endanger the marriage.

Aiding Abstinence

Spouses can also play an important role in promoting abstinence. First, the spouse is someone the ex-gambler can talk to about his or her difficulties with abstinence. Gamblers need to spend time with people who reward them for not gambling, and supportive spouses can do that. Second, ex-gamblers need stimulus control. They have to avoid people and places that would pull them back into gambling. Spouses can help by creating diversions and arranging new social activities. Third, ex-gamblers need counter-conditioning. That is, they need to learn to distract themselves by keeping busy with other activities. Spouses can help ensure that the gambler's time is occupied. Fourth, gamblers need reinforcement management. For example, they need to spend time with people who reward them for not gambling (cited in Petry, 2005:159). Spouses have a vested interest in the success of treatment and are more likely to provide these rewards.

Family relationships can encourage people to distance themselves from their previous deviant behaviours. They can also help ex-gamblers successfully reintegrate into society or into a new community and role. In this respect, families provide resources, motivation, and social capital. However, at times, family support has its limitations. Families with badly deteriorated relationships may not provide much support to the gambler. However, helping these families to work at preventing relapses may heal the family after profoundly negative experiences.

Treatment Interventions that Incorporate Spouses

Like other extreme and unusual activities, problem gambling has a trickle-down effect that ends up harming anyone who is closely involved with the gambler. In fact, Lobsinger and Beckett (1996) estimate that a person's gambling problem harms as many as 8–10 other people—often those who are most intimately involved with the gambler. Since spouses, children, and extended family are all affected by the gambler's behaviour, any therapy that makes use of spouses and family members is likely to be more effective than a method that excludes them (Copello et al., 2006). All types of therapy benefit the entire family.

Moreover, if treatment does not include the spouse, marital conflict is likely to continue, undermining the effectiveness of therapy for the individual gambler(Boyd and Bolen, 1979; Taber, 1985). Under some circumstances, the family may even sabotage the gambler's efforts at recovery (Lorenz, 1989). To avoid these problems, many treatment approaches for alcohol and drug abusers, and problem gamblers stress family and marital therapy (Harrison and Donnelly, 1987; Lorenz, 1989; Ciarrochi and Hohmann, 1989; Wildman, 1989).

As previously mentioned, the inclusion of spouses in the treatment process is also crucial because spouses are also involved in a role transition. Involving the spouse and even other family members also makes it easier to change their enabling behaviours. When everyone closely associated with the gambler are involved in the treatment, more people are reorienting their lives in ways that promote change.

Few, if any, of the families we studied knew about couple counselling programs related to problem gambling. Few of the gamblers we studied had ever been in couples therapy. In part, this is because most gamblers and their partners feel the problem is mainly the gambler's problem to solve: only gamblers can initiate change. With spouse involvement, partners and other family members are given license (and skills) to engage gamblers who are resisting change. Generally, programs that most involve spouses and other family members are most successful at bringing about change in problem gamblers.

Gamblers Anonymous

In our study, few problem gamblers admitted to seeking treatment or thinking that treatment could help them. Many had never sought treatment. Others had dropped out of treatment before completing a program.

This may explain the ineffectiveness of programs like Gamblers Anonymous (GA), one of the few programs widely available to problem gamblers. GA makes little use of spouses and other family members. One study found that only 8 percent of problem gamblers were still going to GA after one year. Most gamblers left after only a few sessions (Stewart and Brown, 1988). Another study (Brown, 1987; cited in Petry, 2005) shows that GA may be more effective for gamblers with severe gambling problems than for those with milder problems.

Some gamblers say they feel uncomfortable with GA's public meetings. Perhaps this is because problem gamblers tend to be loners. In our study, 61 percent of problem gamblers report gambling alone. On the other hand, many may feel they can recover without treatment, and many are able to do so. As

Slutske (2006) notes: "Many individuals with a history of problem gambling eventually recover, most without formal treatment" (297).

Even within the context of GA, spouses could probably play a useful role by helping gamblers move towards abstinence or even self-control. Yet spouses often distance themselves from their partner to avoid conflict and disappointment. Most spouses need help re-engaging with their partner and creating a new social world with them. By failing to engage and train spouses sufficiently, Gamblers Anonymous achieves only a low level of treatment recruitment, retention, or completion.

The Johnson Intervention

At the other extreme, the Johnson Intervention makes explicit, forceful use of spouses and other family members. This intervention is based on the belief that regardless of the stage of the problem, pressure and support from family and friends can convince a problem gambler to enter treatment and ultimately overcome their problem (Fernandez *et al.*, 2006). Ways of applying pressure include threatening divorce or loss of employment unless treatment is sought.

A study by Logan (1983) found that 90 percent of families who participated were successful in engaging their loved ones in treatment. Further, 75 percent completed the treatment program. But according to a random assignment study conducted by Miller *et al.* (1999), only 30 percent of families approached were willing to participate in the intervention. Also, only 23 percent were successful in convincing their loved ones to seek treatment. It appears the Johnson Intervention may be too confrontational for some families. So, this is a method that may work well for families with a high level of motivation and a high degree of tolerance for threats and conflict. It may frighten off many other gamblers and their families.

Community Reinforcement and Family Training (CRAFT)

Makarchuk *et al.* (2002) adapted the CRAFT approach—developed originally for the spouses of alcoholics (Meyers and Smith, 1997)—for use with the spouses of problem gamblers. Practitioners of CRAFT have found that involving spouses in therapy usually helps promote behaviour change. As noted in Chapter 2, CRAFT is a cognitive-behavioural approach that teaches spouses to use behavioural strategies to reduce the gambling and encourage the gambler to change.

In addition, CRAFT teaches family members how to manage and cope with problem gamblers and the effects of their gambling. In treating spouses of alcoholics, CRAFT has shown to be more effective than Alcoholics Anonymous and individual interventions (Miller *et al.*, 1999). Recent research by Hodgins and his colleagues (2007a, b) has shown this method works very well with problem gamblers too. In short, the CRAFT program seems to strike a very healthy balance between too much and too little engagement of both gamblers and their partners. It provides both with a deeper understanding of the problem to be solved and with coping strategies that are useful.

Couples and Family Therapy

Couples therapy is a broadly generic treatment option that involves partners in encouraging gamblers to change their behaviour. Couples therapy engages both the problem gambling and the spouse's role in promoting change. One subtype, Behavioural-Couples Therapy (BCT), is a well-researched, effective mode of treatment for resolving relationship problems (Hahlweg and Markman, 1988). It has been widely used to treat mental health, substance abuse, and drug abuse problems in couples (O'Leary and Beach, 1990; Fals-Stewart *et al.*, 1996; Winters *et al.*, 2002).

Couples therapy encourages the expression of positive sentiments in shared activities and social interactions between the spouses. In this way, it helps the couple to begin rebuilding their relationship, which has been so harmed by the problem gambling.

Social Behaviour and Network Therapy (SBNT)

Another therapy that incorporates spouses is Social Behaviour and Network Therapy (SBNT). In SBNT, the client starts with individual therapy (Galvani, 2007) to work on building a positive social network that will support recovery and role exit. The unique aspect of this therapy is its focus on the client's social network. But once the gambler completes the individual program, the supportive network of family and friends takes part in six or seven group additional therapy sessions. The therapist teaches and encourages positive forms of coping—coping skills other than avoidance or escapism—and helps build networks that encourage problem behaviour cessation (Galvani, 2007).

Issues to be Addressed in Counselling

With the exception of Gamblers Anonymous, these therapy or counselling programs are similar in important ways, with only slight differences in emphasis.

They all combine cognitive and behavioural counselling. They all help the gambler and spouse understand each other and improve their communication. And, to a greater or lesser degree, they all stimulate the building of new social networks, social supports, social worlds.

Few spouses in our study knew about any programs that could help them with their partner. Many knew about programs designed for gamblers only—counselling programs such as those provided by the Centre for Addiction and Mental Health (in Toronto), Gamblers Anonymous, or gambling hotline counselling. A few spouses had tried individual counselling, relationship counselling, and family counselling (without the gambling partner present) to learn how to help their partner. But these programs usually focused on improving the spouse's well-being. Some spouses who had started out seeking help for their partners stayed in therapy to help themselves, after concluding that they could not control the gambler. None of the spouses in our study sought help from Gam-Anon, which is specifically designed to help the families of problem gamblers.

Our research shows that many spouses need to be educated about the impact of problem gambling on their personal well-being. They need to learn which strategies fail. They need expert advice on how to bring about change. Therapists and spouses cannot change people who firmly resist change. Yet sometimes something a spouse does cuts through the resistance and pushes the gambler toward change. In our data, gamblers reacted positively to "tough love" and threats. For example, faced with losing his or her spouse, a problem gambler is more likely to agree to treatment. Such threats also make gamblers more willing to have their spouse take over the family's finances and oversee their spending. This is just the beginning, but it is at least a beginning.

Our study also found that spouses who calmly express their emotions and concerns about the gambling problem and act on their threats or ultimatums are more successful in helping their partners to change than those who are antagonistic or who fail to make firm decisions. Fixated on the gambling behaviour and the problems it has produced, spouses often cannot see the harmful behaviour patterns they have themselves brought into the relationship or developed in response to the gambling problem.

For many spouses, gambling becomes an obsession, just as it is for the gambler. Preoccupied with gambling in this way, both partners develop an unhealthy relationship with gambling and with one another. In addition to educating spouses and gamblers about the issues mentioned above, treatment should also focus on repairing particular aspects of the marital relationship.

Emotional Intimacy

Our study showed that problem gamblers often have unstable or distant relationships with their spouses. Many couples in our sample are weakly embedded, with few or no shared activities, or a pattern in which gambling is the only shared activity.

How bad is the problem of intimacy? In our study, couples tended to disagree about this. For example, the gamblers were more likely to say that they spend quality time with their spouse, whereas the spouses were more likely to report that shared time, especially quality time, is sorely lacking. They said they wanted to reduce their partner's gambling in order to strengthen their relationship. Yet many spouses reported that they have been unsuccessful at promoting change and this has left them feeling helpless. Some couples reported marital problems that were rooted in even earlier social and emotional experiences that predated the gambling problem.

The road to recovery begins with couples learning to feel comfortable with each other. During the gambler's most severe gambling phase, the couple spends little time together. To help them develop a more fulfilling relationship, the therapist may get the couple involved in role-playing and problem solving. Once they engage in new activities as part of their transition into the ex-gambler role, gamblers are better able to rebuild the emotional intimacy. Some of the time that was previously spent on gambling is then available to spend as a spouse, parent, friend, or child. They share more activities with their children, spouses, and parents. This increase in shared activities helps increase the emotional intimacy, as the two members of the couple begin to share the same social world.

Sexual Intimacy

The emotional and interactional problems these couples suffer often translate into sexual problems. Some gamblers have even said that gambling can be more stimulating than sex (Steinberg, 1993). Other research has found an association between problem gambling and sex addiction.

In addition, often the spouses of gamblers lose interest in sex as well, for various reasons. When gamblers are in their gambling phase, they may be sexually self-centred. The spouse may feel sexually rejected, given the gambler's preoccupation with his own needs during sexual intercourse. Or, during the intense gambling period, the gambler may express no sexual interest towards his or her spouse. In some cases, owing to the secrecy associated with problem gambling, the spouse may even suspect that the gambler is having an affair. Once the gambling ceases or at least slows down, the problem gambler may be able to redirect attention to the couple's previously neglected sexual relationship.

The therapist must teach couples to be more expressive and assertive with each other. The gambler must learn to be more open in expressing his or her emotions during sexual interactions. Likewise, the spouse must learn to voice his or her feelings and concerns during intercourse to re-establish a flow of intimate communication.

An Important Note about Protecting Spouses

There are dangers associated with staying closely tied to someone who is self-destructing. If involvement with the problem gambler risks a spouse's safety, the therapist should be able to identify other social network members who can get involved in the addict's recovery efforts. Spouses should never compromise their own safety for that of someone who is abusive and resistant to change. Also, it is important that spouses avoid a cycle of enabling behaviour that sabotages their own well-being and that of the problem gambler.

Improving Gambling Policy

What can the larger community do to help gamblers transition roles more effectively? Several spouses in our study spoke about the aggressive recruitment techniques used by the gambling industry. These include VIP passes, upgraded hotel suites, and free buffet meals at the casino. Communities and governments may need to reevaluate these strategies and control such recruitment techniques.

The gambling industry also needs to present clear and unequivocal information about gambling odds. People with low incomes are especially vulnerable to prospects of "hitting the jackpot." Many fail to consider the high risk of losing, and many don't understand the odds of winning or losing. To reduce the prevalence of irrational and mistaken views about the chances of winning, all casinos and all lottery tickets should be required to display the odds of winning a particular game.

Further, shuttle buses that ferry gamblers to and from casinos increase the accessibility, and therefore the probability, of gambling among the poor. All such buses should display and provide information about problem gambling and the treatment services available for problem gamblers. A more thorough approach would eliminate free transport services entirely—if you can't afford to get there yourself, then you can't afford to gamble.

Communities may want to make gambling more difficult to access. The easier it is to gamble, the more people do it. As more people do it, more people develop gambling problems. A National Gambling Impact Study Commission (United States) report states that having a casino nearby doubles the prevalence rates of problem gambling within a 50-mile radius (cited in Shaffer and Korn, 2002:177). Certainly, some people with problem-gambling tendencies will move to Nevada so they can gamble more readily; but most rely on local opportunities to gamble. Thus, the more casinos and lotteries there are, the more our society stimulates problem gambling.

What is Needed for Successful Treatment

1. Involve Both Partners

Families can play a critical role in recruitment, treatment retention, and treatment outcomes for problem gamblers, as they do for alcoholics and drug addicts (McCrady, Epstein, and Hirsch, 1999). Family and spouse involvement in treatment can be expected to increase the likelihood that a client completes and complies with the treatment. Treatment programs involving spouses vary but they have similar goals and methods.

Most important, research shows that couple-based therapy works better than individual-centred therapy. Combining the two seems to work best of all. McCrady and colleagues (1999) compared Alcohol Behavioural Couples Therapy (ABCT) alone with Alcohol Behavioural Couples Therapy, coupled with either Alcoholics Anonymous (ABCT-AA) or with relapse prevention sessions (ABCT-RP). Along several dimensions of comparison, ABCT and ABCT-RP proved superior to ABCT-AA.

Research on problem gamblers is still limited. It would be of interest to find out whether relapse prevention sessions can be applied to problem gamblers as well, to prevent relapses.

2. Promote Full Awareness of the Problem

Gamblers see their problem as a personal problem. They are not necessarily aware of the impact their habit has on others, nor of the potential for spouses to help them. Moreover, many spouses are not fully aware of the extent of the gambling problem either.

Doctors should be sure to encourage both gamblers and their loved ones to seek treatment together so that everyone is aware what is going on. When gamblers seek treatment, therapists should encourage them to be honest about their problems, talk to their spouses about their progress, reaffirm their commitment to treatment, and express any concerns about it.

Gamblers may feel hesitant about admitting the full extent of their past activities to their spouses. The couple and their therapist need to look upon this as a "truth and reconciliation" undertaking, with amnesty granted for past misdeeds if (and only if) there is a full exposure of the problem to be solved.

3. Help the Couple Rebuild Tarnished Relationships

Because the spouses likely feels a sense of betrayal, their needs must be prioritized at the beginning of therapy, when they are being inundated with new awareness about the problem behaviour.

Therapists need to keep in mind that solid, supportive relationships promote progress toward change. They need to know and emphasize that backsliding is a normal part of role transition. Shame often causes partners to resist seeking help or support from friends and family, so the therapist has to help them build a supportive network. Spouses need a network of support too if they are to stay with someone who has refused to change or who appears unable to change even when they are engaged in the treatment.

Some therapists ask the gambler to write the spouse a letter formally disclosing his or her activities and feelings, with the goal of making amends. This activity helps the spouse gain clarity about his or her underlying emotions. If the spouse needs added sessions to discuss the betrayal, those should be made available. Once the spouse accepts the gambler's efforts to repair the relationship and make amends, then the real work of re-building the relationship can begin. This includes work on communication, intimacy, trust, emotional openness, and shared activities.

4. Discuss Attachment Styles

Helping a troubled relationship involves understanding the attachment styles involved. The therapist must figure out the attachment pattern between a gambler and his or her spouse, and the roots of these patterns in family backgrounds. The goal of therapy is to stabilize a relationship that has been strained by problem gambling. To do so, spouses first have to let the gambler know they need boundaries in the relationship to ensure "safety and stability" (Corley and Kort, 2006:182).

Often, re-establishing a damaged relationship means revisiting the reasons why a couple got together in the first place: what they shared then, what they liked about each other, what they aspired to as a couple, and so on. The deep study of these original motives may unearth feelings or perceptions that were misguided at the time, or grew misguided with the passage of time.

5. Provide Social Support

Therapists use various techniques to strengthen their patients' commitment to therapy. For example, a therapist can pretend to be a member of the patient's social support network. The therapist then helps the client develop a sense of personal efficacy and commitment to the treatment (Milton *et al.*, 2002; Miller and Rollnick, 1991).

So far, only two studies have studied the impact of therapist compliance-enhancing interventions on dropout. They report 25 percent and 30 percent cuts, respectively, in dropout rates (Wulfert *et al.*, 2006; Milton *et al.*, 2002). These therapist-based interventions are also reported to hasten the rate of improvement in problem gamblers' symptoms (Melville *et al.*, 2007). It is unclear under what circumstances the therapist, the spouse, or other friends and family are best equipped to promote treatment compliance and retention. Likely, widely diffused social support works more reliably and durably than if all support is vested only in the therapist.

6. Increase Embeddedness

Two tactics used in Behavioural Couples Therapy—building positive attitudes towards shared activities and improving communications skills (Walitzer and Dermen, 2004)—help couples contend with a partner's problem behaviour by increasing the positive interaction and strengthening couple embeddedness.

Our study suggests that more embeddedness leads to more fulfilling relationships and closer supervision of the gambler's activities. Gamblers in our study rarely shared the full extent of their problem with spouses and led a double life shrouded in secrecy. CRAFT and BCT may both promote couple embeddedness and treat the problem behaviour. More research is needed to improve therapeutic interventions with this focus.

Currently, according to various studies, the most effective therapeutic approaches incorporate both BCT and addiction-focused spousal involvement to improve both behavioural outcomes and marital functioning (O'Farrell and Fals-Stewart, 2000, 2003). Most BCT programs incorporate addiction-focused spousal involvement when necessary. BCT could be an effective therapeutic intervention for couples dealing with partner problem gambling. So far, no one has yet systematically evaluated the application of these therapies to problem gamblers.

7. General Recommendations for Therapeutic Practice

Therapists can consider some topic areas that merit further discussion because of the findings of our study:

(1) Both our study and the review of the literature show that therapeutic interventions should recognize that problem gamblers are a diverse population. They differ in the severity of their problem, game type, gender, and sociocultural factors. Moreover, some problem gamblers need therapy that helps them contend with their gambling problem and with concomitant affective and psychiatric disorders and multiple addictions. One size of therapy does not fit all.

(2) Our study shows that gamblers tend to gamble alone. Treatment programs should be sensitive to this fact and treat gamblers individually or in couples therapy or family therapy, rather than in large-group programs such as GA, which run the risk of anonymizing the participants. Most of the gamblers in our study found GA ineffective or unappealing.

(3) In general, gamblers are unwilling to change or to admit that their problem and its cure lie in their own hands. They are often unaware of the full impact their gambling has on spouses and other family members and doubt that spouses can help promote change. This means that a key aspect of therapy is to clarify the effects of problem gambling on the gambler's intimate relationship. Therapy uses the threatened loss of this relationship to induce gamblers to enter and comply with treatment.

(4) Spouses can be helpful in promoting change in problem gamblers. Enlisting spouses in the treatment should be made a primary focus when developing and implementing treatment programs for problem

gamblers. The role of the spouse continues to be important in helping the gambler successfully resist returning to gambling.

(5) Finance is a critical issue in couples' therapy for gamblers, as money (and the lack of it) is usually a main focus of the spouse's struggle for control in the relationship. Financial security is also helpful in successful role transitioning. Therapists need to help the gamblers and their spouses think about money issues and the reasons why money is important to them.

(6) There are fewer studies of problem gambling than of addictions, such as alcoholism or drug abuse. There also seems to be a lack of resources available for gambling research. Yet we need to identify and improve treatments that are both effective and cost-effective. It should be noted that with every $100 spent on treatment, BCT produced greater improvements than IBT, as showed in several treatment outcome variables (for example, more days of abstinence, fewer legal problems, and improved marital and social functioning). (Fals-Stewart *et al.*, 1997)

Last Words

We started the book by noting that gambling has social antecedents and several social outcomes for families and communities. Our study has showed that gamblers suffer disastrous financial losses because of their gambling. Moreover, spouses and children of these gamblers are affected too. The data indicate that problem gambling can destroy families, careers, relationships, and future prospects. The social problems caused by problem gambling are important and growing.

At present, we cannot rely on government and the gambling industry to protect people with current or potential gambling problems. For this reason, families—which often play such an important role in teaching and rewarding gambling—may also have to play an important part in regulating gambling.

Our study purposely focused on the role of spouses: how they are affected by problem gambling and what they can do to deal with it. Its final goal—to develop a sociological approach to problem gambling that truly helps people—is now a few steps closer to realization. Researchers, therapists, and other people who want to help the families of problem gamblers have a lot more work to do.

The next chapter presents a sociological theory that builds on the data collected in this exploratory study.

Chapter 14

Regulation Theory: A Statement and Proposed Tests

Exploratory studies usually examine the literature and data on a topic and end with a theory, and this monograph ends in just that way. The theory proposed here, the result of our exploration, has implications for research and for therapy. This chapter asks how we may now apply theory to improve our therapies and organize therapy to test our theories.

This book has focused on the ways spouses can help gamblers control their gambling problem. We have seen that spouses face great difficulties in doing so. Many feel angry, frustrated, or guilty that they are unable to do more or do better. Most are unaware of the extent and the details of their partner's gambling problem. Gamblers want to resist treatment and keep their spouses in the dark about the problem. Figuratively speaking, they have locked themselves in the closet with a loaded gun and refuse to come out.

Why then focus on spouses and the limited role they currently play? The answer is, there is no one else to call on. Spouses are closer to the problem and more motivated to help than anyone else. Governments and the gaming industry take only the narrowest view of their responsibility for this gambling problem. No significant increases in help are evidently coming from those quarters.

Some readers may demand that the government tighten its regulations of the industry and provides problem gamblers with more treatment. They stress that government and the gaming industry—not problem gamblers and their families—are most to blame for problem gambling. Even if government and industry eventually admit some responsibility and act on it, these solutions may take a long time to reach the people who need help today. In short, spouses may be unaware and largely unqualified to help, but they are the single strongest ally these gamblers have, and they are on-site right now.

Embeddedness and Regulation Theory

This study has shown that spouses face two main problems in trying to control or regulate their gambling spouses, or help their gambling spouses control and regulate themselves. These are problems of unawareness and enabling. We have also said that spouses and gamblers occupy different social worlds.

But this separation of social worlds is not in itself necessarily a problem. Chapter 9 examined the embeddedness of gamblers and their spouses through Bott's research on family roles and kinship networks. Typically, couples with close roles usually have loose-knit family networks; couples with segregated roles usually have close-knit family networks. In short, spouses tend to be more active in their partner's life in societies where other relatives have decreased importance in the couple's life—and vice versa. However, in close-knit family networks, the gambler is often visible to many relatives and life-long friends.

What this means is that as long as the couple has some kind of social embeddedness (either with each other or with the wider family network), they are visible *either* to the spouses or to other relatives and friends. We call these typical conditions *spouse regulation* and *kin regulation* respectively.

But if both kinds of embeddedness are absent, then it's possible that nobody is watching. For example, a partner could be visible to neither to his or her spouse nor to relatives. This condition might arise if a couple from a traditional ethnocultural community with segregated gender roles had recently migrated to a new community where they had no friends or relatives and had yet failed to adopt shared spousal roles. As a result, the couple might go through a period of mutual estrangement and hostility. On the other hand, one or both spouses might have been drawn into work-specific activities that excluded the other. In such a case, a person would find him- or herself almost never visible to either spouse or relatives and friends. This condition is called *underregulation*. As the name implies, people need a minimum amount of surveillance by family and close friends to have healthy relationships.

In the opposite theoretical possibility, the couple lives a life that is visible to both the spouse and to their relatives. This might occur if a couple were to adopt shared roles within the household, form joint friendships with other couples, and preserve a close-knit network of relatives and friends. As a result, the person would find him- or herself continuously visible to spouse, relatives, and friends. We call this condition *overregulation*—a name that implies people do not always benefit from being constantly on view.

To show this diagrammatically, the four types are presented in Table 3.

Table 3: Regulation Theory

| | | Shared Activities with Spouse | |
		Yes	No
Shared Activities	Yes	Overregulation	Kin regulation
with Relatives	No	Spouse regulation	Underregulation

The theory proposed here, provisionally named *Regulation Theory* and obviously derived from Durkheim's theory of suicide, asserts the following:

(1) People typically need and benefit from social regulation.

(2) Without the right amount and kind of regulation, people are likely to behave erratically, in ways that injure themselves and/or others.

    a. Too much regulation—usually, a result of constant surveillance by intimates—is likely to produce rebellious or escapist behaviour that may be injurious.

    b. Too little regulation—sometimes a result of little or no surveillance by intimates—is likely to produce *anomie* (i.e., normlessness) and reckless behaviour that may be injurious.

(3) People who receive the right *amount* of regulation may not receive the right *type* of regulation. For example, they might receive tolerant or enabling responses for a deviant behaviour.

(4) Regulation that tolerates or encourages reckless behaviour through enabling will not prevent injurious behaviour.

Regulation Theory proposes, then, that therapists providing treatment for problem gamblers must pay primary attention to four variables:

(1) the gambler's connection with his or her spouse;

(2) the gambler's connection with his or her relatives;

(3) the amount of regulation provided by spouse and relatives; and

(4) the type(s) of regulation provided by spouse and relatives.

Therapy must be tailored separately to each of the four conditions we mentioned above.

Spouse Regulation

Therapy for gamblers who are spouse-regulated—visible mainly or only to the spouse—may suffer from either too little regulation or the wrong type of regulation. The therapist should work with the spouse on the kinds of shared activities mentioned above. The therapist should also help the spouse recognize signs of a gambling problem. Finally, the therapist should help the spouse strengthen resolve against enabling behaviour.

In addition, the therapist should help the gambler and spouse identify a goal—whether total abstinence or reduced gambling—and then develop agreed-on strategies for enforcing that goal, through regulating time and dollars spent on gambling. A written contract may be useful here. There should be no discussion of gambling except what is needed to enforce the stated agreement. The spouse should avoid taking part in gambling, as this encourages the behaviour.

Kin Regulation

Therapy for gamblers who are kin-regulated—visible to relatives more than to spouse—may also suffer from either too little regulation or the wrong type of regulation. The therapist may need to work with the relatives on the kinds of shared activities mentioned above. The therapist should help them recognize signs of a gambling problem and strengthen their resolve against enabling behaviour.

As above, the therapist should help the gambler and relatives identify a goal—whether total abstinence or reduced gambling—and then develop agreed-on strategies for enforcing that goal, by regulating the time and dollars spent on gambling. A written contract may be useful here too. There should be no discussion of gambling outside enforcing the stated agreement. The relatives should avoid taking part in gambling, as this encourages the behaviour.

Conceivably, for both spouse-regulated and kin-regulated types, it would be worthwhile including both spouse and other relatives in therapy. So for example, if relatives are not already involved, the therapist may want to encourage their inclusion, providing this does not lead to conflict between relatives and the gambler's spouse.

Occasionally, it may prove feasible to shift from kin-regulation to spouse-regulation, or at least to increase the spousal role in regulation—especially if relatives are less willing or able than the spouse to carry out the stated therapeutic practices. Such a shift, if needed, would best accompany the development of shared spousal rituals and activities discussed in the paragraph on corrections for underregulation.

Underregulation

Therapy for gamblers who are underregulated—visible to neither relatives nor spouse—may suffer from a problem of *anomie* and social isolation. The therapist should work with the spouse (and perhaps, the gambler's family) to build shared activities that increase surveillance. This includes, for example, developing group rituals such as nightly dinners together and weekend or holiday special events (e.g., family outings, Sunday dinners with the family, Saturday night dates, and vacations together). It also includes developing group relationships: for example, joint friendships with other couples and joint involvement in neighbourhood or community groups (e.g., school parent committees, bowling leagues, charities, or public service groups).

Overregulation

Therapy for gamblers who are overregulated—visible to both relatives and spouse—may suffer from two main types of problem that need attention. First, these gamblers may be motivated to engage in risky behaviour just to individuate themselves and escape from feeling drowned by other people's (possibly too rigid) expectations. If so, the therapist should work with the spouse and family on issues around freedom and inadequate flexibility.

Second, these gamblers may be receiving stated or implied encouragement for their gambling, either from their spouse or from relatives. If so, the therapist should work with the spouse and family on issues around enabling, tolerance, and tacit encouragement for reckless and risky behaviour.

Further Research

The therapeutic recommendations stated above flow directly from the data we have examined in this study, and from the literature on therapeutic interventions. In this sense, it is a piece of *grounded theory* with some practical applications. Of course, in science, a theory must be testable with new empirical data. This means several things in the current context.

More studies of gamblers and their spouses are needed to further examine issues of spousal control. We need to find out whether these studies also reveal that problems of spousal visibility and enablement are key to understanding regulation, and whether they identify informal regulation as a key factor in controlling reckless and harmful behaviour.

Ideally, such studies would be informed by our own explorations and would improve on the current study in several ways. First, the ideal study would select a larger sample of both gamblers and spouses for study over a longer period. This study would use a sampling screen that included questions on visibility and enabling, so that equal numbers of the four gambling types (that is, under-regulated, over-regulated, spouse-regulated, and kin-regulated) could be studied. The study would be longitudinal, covering several years. More pointed and thorough questions would be asked about behavioural visibility. These would include better questions about embeddedness and shared activities. One or more kin members would also be interviewed, to gain a better understanding of the role of non-household kin members in the gambling problem. The purpose of such extra research would be both to confirm the results of this current study, and to table more variables for consideration.

Second, new research findings would help in the development of more effective treatment strategies. Certainly, our study generated the treatment strategies listed in this chapter, based on Regulation Theory. What logically comes next is an empirical test of these strategies.

If these strategies fail to help the gambler achieve the treatment goals set by the gambler, spouse, and therapist, then one of only four explanations is possible:

- the therapist applied the theory incompetently;
- the gambler and spouse failed to co-operate with the therapist or falsified information they provided to the therapist;
- the therapy was incorrectly deduced from Regulation Theory; or
- Regulation Theory is invalid and should be rejected.

What science calls for is a series of demonstration projects that directly test the therapeutic value of Regulation Theory. The results of these demonstrations, after publication and debate in both the therapeutic and research communities, would allow us to draw conclusions about the validity of the theory and the usefulness of the therapy.

However, there are some practical difficulties in applying this treatment and testing this theory. Gaining compliance from the gamblers may be extremely difficult; that is the nature of a compulsive gambling habit. Currently, few spouses and families willingly allow gambling family members to be completely unregulated by their expectations and ties. Our study showed that despite spouse efforts to regulate behaviour, gamblers find ways to evade these attempts.

The task we now face is to determine how to get gamblers involved in family and spousal relationships. Setting mandatory shared activities does not ensure the gambler engages emotionally or intellectually in these activities. Moreover, families and spouses cannot regulate gamblers 24 hours a day.

If gamblers do not see their gambling as problematic, the more their family tries to regulate them, the more conflict erupts, and the more secretive they become about their gambling. Even if gamblers want to stop, it is still an internal battle to overcome their impulses. So, even if domestic regulation succeeds in slowing down or diverting the gambling career, in the short term, it will also strain relationships.

Clearly, some families are good at adjusting to new activities promoted by therapy and find it easier to be understanding, yet assertive. But families who already experience a lot of conflict probably face a much harder struggle with this proposed solution. Given the existing levels of conflict in many of the families we studied, this model requires family or couples therapy to work on relationships while also treating gambling. For gamblers in relationships, treatment should not ignore the couple relationship while addressing purely individual (psychological or psychiatric) concerns.

Final Words

By proposing a treatment based on Regulation Theory, this book does not recommend leaving the entire burden of problem gambling on the shoulders of the gambler and his or her spouse. Nor does it say that this is sum total of the sociological imagination. Other sociological research should study schools, workplaces, cyberspace, advertising, mass consumerism, and ethnocultural traditions for other sources of motivation and opportunity for gambling.

Moreover, there is plenty of work needed in other areas. First, we need to learn more about public opinion and public knowledge about gambling and its associated problems. Research is also needed on the legal (that is, formal) regulation of gambling: how legal regulations restrict or enable people's gambling, and how the gambling industry influences policy-making that affects gambling. In addition, as noted several times in the book, we have yet to understand gambling careers: how people progress from gambling to problem gambling, and then how they find their way back again (if they do).

Most of all, we need better to understand a society that leads large numbers of adults to believe they have their best chance for happiness and a good life sitting at a slot machine or bingo table. Something is deeply wrong with the way such a society is organized and how it affects ordinary human beings. We may have created an "iron cage" for ourselves, as sociologist Max Weber feared. For the time being, we cannot rely on government and the gambling industry to prevent gambling problems or significantly help problem gamblers.

This book offers a set of theoretical and practical observations with full awareness that problem gamblers typically resist change. As well, it recognizes how hard it is for spouses to build a social world together with a gambling spouse. Increasingly, married people are leading independent, isolated, and even solitary lives, because of the demands of their work. We live in an increasingly individualized world. As Putnam illustrates in *Bowling Alone*, there are ever fewer cohesive collectivities for people to join.

This book argues in favour of a new, sociological way of understanding problem gambling that adds new variables and insights. This sociological approach, in turn, may improve both the theories and treatments currently in use.

The current evidence shows there is room for improvement.

Works Cited

Abbott, D. A., S.L. Cramer, and S.D. Sherrets. 1995. "Pathological gambling and the family: Practice implications." *Families in Society: The Journal of Contemporary Human Services* 76:4.

Ahlberg, B.M., E. Jylkäs, and I. Krantz. 2001. "Gendered construction of sexual risks: Implications for safer sex among young people in Kenya and Sweden." *Reproductive Health Matters* 9(17):26–36.

Ainsworth, M., M. Blehar, E. Waters, and S. Wall. (1978) *Patterns of Attachment*. New Jersey: Erlbaum.

Alexander, J.C. 2002. "On the social construction of moral universals: The 'Holocaust' from mass murder to trauma drama." *European Journal of Social Theory*, 5 (1): 5-86.

American Psychiatric Association. 2000. *Diagnostic and Statistical Manual of Mental Disorders* (4th ed., text revision). Washington, DC: APA.

Anderson, S.C. 1994. "A critical analysis of the concept of codependency." *Social Work*. 39:6:677–685.

Anderson, T. L., and L. Bondi. 1998 (Summer). "Exiting the drug-addict role: Variations by race and gender." *Symbolic Interaction* 21(2): 155–174.

Anglin, M.D., M.W. Booth, C. Kao, L.L. Harlow. 1987. "Similarity of behavior within addict couples: II. Addiction-related variable." *International Journal of Addiction*. 22(7):583–607.

Baker, A.J. L., R. Tabacoff, G. Tornusciolo, and M. Eisenstadt. 2003 (Spring). "Family secrecy: A comparative study of juvenile sex offenders and youth with conduct disorders." *Family Process* 42(1):105–116.

Barber, J.G. 2002. *Social work with addictions*. (2nd ed.). New York: New York University Press.

Bartholomew, K., and L. Horowitz. 1991. "Attachment styles among young adults." *Journal of Personality and Social Psychology* 61:226–244.

Baucom, D.H., V. Shoham, K.T. Mueser, A.D. Daiuto, and T.R. Stickle. 1998. "Empirically supported couple and family interventions for marital distress and adult mental health problems." *Journal of Consulting and Clinical Psychology* 66:53–88.

Bauer, R.H., and J.H. Turner. 1974. "Betting behavior in sexually homogeneous and heterogeneous groups." *Psychological Reports* 34(1):251–258.

Baumer, E.P., R. Wright, K. Kristinsdottir, and H. Gunnlaugsson. 2002. "Crime, shame, and recidivism: The case of Iceland." *British Journal of Criminology* 1 (Winter):40–59.

Beach, S. R., F.D. Fincham, and J. Katz. 1998. "Marital therapy in the treatment of depression: Toward a third generation of therapy and research." *Clinical Psychology Review* 18:635–661.

Becker, H. 1963. *Outsiders: Studies in the Sociology of Deviance*. Glencoe: Free Press.

Becona, E. 1993. "The prevalence of pathological gambling in Galicia." *Journal of Gambling Studies* 9: 353–369.

Benhsain, K., A. Taillefer, and R. Ladouceur. 2004. "Awareness of independence of events and erroneous perceptions while gambling." *Addictive Behaviours* 29:399–404.

Bergner, R.M., and A.J. Bridges. 2002. "The significance of heavy pornography involvement for romantic partners: Research and clinical implications." *Journal of Sex and Marital Therapy*, 28:193–206.

Blaszczynski, A. 2006. "To formulate gambling policies on the premise that problem gambling is an addiction may be premature." *Addiction* 100:1230–1231.

——— 2002. "Pathways to pathological gambling: Identifying typologies." *eGambling: The Electronic Journal of Gambling Issues* 1:1–14.

——— 1999. "Pathways to Gambling Addiction." Paper presented at the 1999 conference of the Canadian Foundation on Compulsive Gambling. Ottawa.

Blau, Z.S. 1972. "Role Exit: A Theoretical Essay." Paper presented to a Conference of the American Sociological Association.

Blumer, H. 1971. "Social problems as collective behavior." *Social Problems* 18(3): 298–306.

Boeri, M.W. 2002 (June). "Women after the utopia: The gendered lives of former cult members." *Journal of Contemporary Ethnography* 31(3): 323–360.

Bookwala, J. 2005. "The role of marital quality in physical health during the mature years." *Journal of Aging and Health* 17(1):85–104.

Bott, E. 1957. *Family and Social Network*. London: Tavistock.

Bowlby, J. 1973. *Separation: Anxiety and Anger. Attachment and Loss* (Vol. 2). New York: Basic Books.

Boyd, H.W., and D.W. Bolen. 1979. "The compulsive gambler and spouse in group psychotherapy." *International Journal of Group Psychotherapy* 20:77–90.

Brown, R. 1985. "The effectiveness of Gamblers Anonymous." In: W. R. Eadington (Ed.), *The Gambling Studies: Proceedings of the 6th National Conference on Gambling and Risk-Taking*. Reno, NV: University of Nevada.

Brown, R.I.F. 1986. "Dropouts and continuers in Gamblers Anonymous: Life-context and other factors." *Journal of Gambling Behavior* 2:130–140.

Brown, S., and L. Coventry. 1997. *Queen of Hearts: The Needs of Women with Gambling Problems*. Melbourne, Australia: Financial and Consumer Rights Council.

Brown, S.L. 2003 (July). "Relationship Quality Dynamics of Cohabitating Unions." *Journal of Family Issues* 24(5):583–601.

Browne, B.A., and D.J. Brown. 1994. "Predictors of lottery gambling among American college students." *Journal of Social Psychology* 134:339–347.

Burman, B., and G. Margolin. 1992. "Analysis of the association between marital relationships and health problems: An interactional perspective." *Psychological Bulletin* 112:39–63.

Caetano, R., and S. Ramisetty-Mikler. 2005. "Alcohol use and intimate partner violence as predictors of separation among U.S. couples: A longitudinal model." *Journal of Studies on Alcohol*, 66(2):205–212.

Calzavara, L., L. Tepperman, W. Medved, N. Ramuscak, A. Burchell, and the Polaris HIV Seroconversion Study Team. 2003. "To tell or not to tell: An exploratory study of social networks and HIV disclosure." Presented at the 12th Annual Canadian Conference on HIV/AIDS Research, April 10–13, Halifax, Nova Scotia.

Canadian Partnership for Responsible Gambling. 2007. *Canadian Gambling Digest, 2006-2007.*

Cannon, B. 1999 (December). "Marriage and cohabitation: A comparison of adult attachment style and quality between the two types of relationships." Dissertation *Abstracts International: Section B: The Sciences & Engineering.* 60(5–B): 2332.

Carnes, P. 1985. *Out of the Shadows: Understanding Sexual Addiction* (2nd ed.). Minnesota: CompCare Publications:

Carr, P.J. 1998. *Keeping Up Appearances: Informal Social Control in a White Working Class Neighborhood in Chicago (Illinois).* Chicago: University of Chicago Press.

Carruthers, C. 1999. "Pathological gambling: Implications for therapeutic recreation practice." *Therapeutic Recreation Journal* 33(4):287.

Carstensen, L.L., J.M. Gottman, and R.W. Levenson. 1995 (March). "Emotional behavior in long-term marriage." *Psychology and Aging* 10:140–149.

Carter, C.A., and W.M. Kahnweiler. 2000. "The efficacy of the social norms approach to substance abuse prevention applied to fraternity men." *Journal of American College Health* 49(2):66–71.

Ciarrocchi, J., and A.A. Hohmann. 1989. "The family environment and married male pathological gamblers, alcoholics and dually addicted gamblers." *Journal of Gambling Behavior* 5:283–291.

Ciarrocchi, J.W., and D. F. Reinert. 1993. "Family environment and length of recovery for married male members of Gamblers Anonymous and female members of GamAnon." *Journal of Gambling Studies* 9(4):341–352.

CNN. 2007 (April 4). "Living paycheck to paycheck." Available at http://www.cnn.com/2007/US/Careers/04/04/cb.paycheck/index.html.

Coleman, J.S. 1988. "Social capital in the creation of human capital." *American Journal of Sociology* 94: Supplement S95–S120.

Collins, R.L., K.E. Leonard, and J.S. Searles. 1990. *Alcohol and the Family: Research and Clinical Perspectives.* New York: Guilford Press.

Conference of the Canadian Foundation on Compulsive Gambling.1999. *Commission Final Report.* Retrieved November 1, 2003, from http://govinfo.library.unt.edu/ngisc/reports/fullrpt.html .

Conger, R.D., X.Ge, and G.H. Elder, Jr. 1994 (April). "Economic stress, coercive family process, and developmental problems of adolescents." *Child Development* 65: 541–561.

Cooley, C. 1902 (1922). *Human Nature and the Social Order.* New York: Charles Scribner.

Copello A., R. Velleman, and L. Templeton. 2005. "Family interventions in the treatment of alcohol and drug problems." *Drug Alcohol Rev* 24:369–385.

Copello, A.G., L. Templeton, and R. Velleman. 2006. "Family interventions for drug and alcohol misuse: Is there a best practice?" *Current Opinion in Psychiatry* 19, 271–276.

Corley, D.M., and J. Kort. 2006. "The sex-addicted mixed-orientation marriage: Examining attachment styles, internalized homophobia and viability of marriage after disclosure." *Sexual Addiction and Compulsivity* 13:167–193.

Costantini, M.F., L. Wermuth, J.L. Sorensen, and J.S. Lyons. 1992. "Family functioning as a predictor of progress in substance abuse treatment." *J. Subst. Abuse Treat* 9: 331–335.

Cotler, S.B. 1971. "The use of different behavioral techniques in treating a case of compulsive gambling." *Behavior Therapy* 2:579–584.

Cowan, A.E., and P.A. Cowan. 2005. "Couple attachment and the quality of marital relationships: Method and concept of the validation of the new couple and attachment coding system." *Attachment and Human Development* 7(2): 123–152.

Crisp, B. R., S.A. Thomas, A.C. Jackson, N. Thomson, S. Smith, J. Borrell, W. Ho, and T.A. Holt. 2000. "Sex differences in the treatment needs and outcomes of problem gamblers." *Research on Social Work Practice* 10(2):229–242.

Crittenden, P. M., and M. Ainsworth. 1989. "Child maltreatment and attachment theory." In: D. Cicchetti and V. Carlson (Eds.), *Child Maltreatment: Theory and Research on the Causes and Consequences of Child Abuse and Neglect* (pp. 432–463). Cambridge: Cambridge University Press.

Crohan, S.E. 1996 (November). "Marital quality and conflict across the transition to parenthood in African American and white couples." *Journal of Marriage and the Family* 58:933–944.

Currie, S.R., D.C. Hodgins, J. Wang, N. el-Guebaly, H. Wynne, and S. Chen. 2006. "Risk of harm among gamblers in the general population as a function of level of participation in gambling activities." *Addiction*, 101(4):570–580.

Darbyshire, P., C. Oster, and H. Carrig. 2001. "The experience of pervasive loss: Children and young people living in a family where parental gambling is a problem." *Journal of Gambling Studies* 17(1):23–45.

Darvas, S.F. 1981. *The Spouse in Treatment: Or There Is a Woman (or Women) . . . A Survey of Gambling Attitudes and Behavior.* Ann Arbor, MI: Institute for Social Research.

Davis, D. 2002. "The queen of diamonds: Women and compulsive gambling." In: S. Straussner and S. Brown (eds.), *The Handbook of Addiction Treatment for Women* (pp. 99–126). San Francisco: Jossey-Bass.

Dawson, P., and C.J. Rosenthal. 1996. "Wives of institutionalized elderly men: The first stage of the transition to quasi-widowhood." *Journal of Aging and Health* 3(3):315–334.

Deal, J.E., K.S. Wampler, and C.F. Halverson, Jr. 1992 (December). "The importance of similarity in the marital relationship." *Family Process* 31(4): 369–382.

Delfabbro, P. 2004. "The stubborn logic of regular gamblers: Obstacles and dilemmas in cognitive gambling research." *Journal of Gambling Studies* 20(1):1–21.

Delfabbro, P., and L. Thrupp. 2003. "The social determinants of youth gambling in South Australian adolescents." *Journal of Adolescence* 26(3):313–330.

Dell'Osso, B., A. Allen, and E. Hollander. 2005. "Comorbidity issues in pharmological treatment of pathological gambling: A critical review." *Clinical Practice and Epidemiology in Mental Health* 1: 1-9.

Dickerson, B.E., and L.M. Thompson. 1977. "The Widow and the Divorcee: A Comparative Study of Role Exit." Paper presented to a conference of the Southwestern Sociological Association.

Dickerson, M. 1995. "Problem gambling in Australia." In: *Proceedings of the Inquiry into the Social Impact of the Extension of EGMs beyond Casinos in Tasmania.* Tasmanian Council of Social Services, November 15–17.

DiClemente, C. 2003. *Addiction and Change: How Addictions Develop and Addicted People Recover.* New York: The Guilford Press.

DiClemente, C., M. Story, and K. Murray. 2000. "On a roll: The process of initiation and cessation of problem gambling among adolescents." *Journal of Gambling Studies* 16(2–3):289–313.

DiClemente, C.C., and J.O. Prochaska. 1985. "Processes and stages of self-change: Coping and competence in smoking behavior change." In: S. Shiffman and T A. Wills (eds.), *Coping Behavior and Drug Use* (pp. 319-343). San Diego, CA: Academic.

———— 1982. "Self-change and therapy change of smoking behaviour: A comparison of process of change in cessation and maintenance." *Addictive Behaviours* 7:133–142.

Dinkmeyer, D., and R. Sherman. 1989 (March-June). "Brief Adlerian family therapy: Individual psychology." *Journal of Adlerian Theory, Research and Practice* (Special Issue: Varieties of Brief Therapy) 45(1–2): 148–158.

Downs, W.R. 1982 (January). "Alcoholism as a developing family crisis." *Family Relations* 31(1): 5–12.

Earle, R.H., and M.R. Earle. 1995. *Sex Addiction: Case Studies and Management.* New York: Brunner/Mazel.

Ebaugh, H.R.F. 1988. *Becoming an EX: The Process of Role Exit.* Chicago: University of Chicago Press.

Echeburua, E., C. Baez, and J. Fernandez-Montalvo. 1996. "Comparative effectiveness of three therapeutic modalities in the psychological treatment of pathological enhancement." *Behavior Modification* 30:315–340.

Elaad, E. 2006 (Summer). "How ideological crisis and prolonged external threat affect self-assessed abilities to tell and detect lies and truths." *Social Issues in Israel* 1(2):160–173.

Engels, R.C.M.E., C. Finkenauer, and D.C. van Kooten. 2006 (December). "Lying behavior, family functioning and adjustment in early adolescence." *Journal of Youth and Adolescence* 35(6):949–58.

Erickson, C., and R. Wilcox. 2006. "Please, not 'addiction' in DSM-V." *American Journal of Psychiatry* 163(11):2015–2016.

Evans, L., and P.H. Delfabbro. 2005. "Motivators for change and barriers to help-seeking in Australian problem gamblers." *Journal of Gambling Studies* 21(2):133–155.

Faber, R.J., T.C. O'Guinn, and R. Krych. 1987. "Compulsive consumption." *Advances in Consumer Research* 14:132–135.

Fainzang, S. 2002 (August). "Lying, secrecy and power within the doctor–patient relationship." *Anthropology and Medicine* 9(2): 85–95.

Fals-Stewart, W., G.R. Birchler, and T.J. O'Farrell. 1996. "Behavioral couples therapy for male substance-abusing patients: Effects on relationship adjustment and drug-using behavior." *J Consul Clin Psychol* 64(5):959–972.

Fals-Stewart, W., T.J. O'Farrell, and G.R. Birchler. 1997. "Behavioral couples therapy for male-substances abusing patients: A cost outcome analysis." *Journal of Consulting and Clinical Psychology* 65:789–802.

Favorini, A. 1995. "Concept of codependency: Blaming the victim or pathway to recovery?" *Social Work* 40(6):827–830.

Fernandez, A.C., E.A. Begley, and G.A. Marlatt. 2006. "Family and peer interventions for adults: Past approaches and future directions," Psychology of Addictive Behaviors 20(2):207–213.

Ferrari, J.R., J. Harriott, and M. Zimmerman. 1999. "The social support networks of procrastinators: Friends or family in times of trouble?" *Personality and Individual Differences* 26:321–334.

Ferrari, J.R., L.A. Jason, R. Nelson, M. Curtin-Davis, P. Marsh, and B. Smith. 1999. "An exploratory analysis of women and men within a self-help, communal-living recovery setting: A new beginning in a new house." *The American Journal of Drug and Alcohol Abuse* 25(2):305–317.

Ferris, J., and H. Wynne. 2001. *The Canadian Problem Gambling Index: Final Report.* Submitted to the Canadian Centre on Substance Abuse.

Fincham, F. D., and Beach, S. R. 1999. "Conflict in marriage: Implications for working with couples." *Annual Review of Psychology* 50:47–77.

Finzi-Dottan, R., O. Cohen, D. Iwaniec, Y. Sapir, and A. Weizman. 2003. "The drug-user husband and his wife: Attachment styles, family cohesion, and adaptability." *Substance Use and Misuse* 38(2):271–292.

Forthofer, M.S., H.J. Markman, M. Cox. 1996 (August). "Associations between marital distress and work loss in a national sample." *Journal of Marriage and the Family* 58:597–605.

Franklin, J., and D.R. Thomas. 1989. "Clinical observations of family members of compulsive gamblers." In: H.J. Shaffer, S.A. Stein, B. Gambino, T.N. Cummings (eds.),*Compulsive Gambling: Theory, Research, and Practice* (pp. 135-146). Lexington, MA: Lexington Books.

Fredriksen, K. 1996. "Gender differences in employment and the informal care of adults." *Journal of Women and Aging* 8(2):35–53.

Freidenberg, J., and M. Hammer. 1998 (Spring). "Social networks and health care: The case of elderly Latinos in East Harlem." *Urban Anthropology* 27(1): 49–85.

Gaboury, A., R. Ladouceur, G. Beauvais, L. Marchand, and Y. Martineau. 1988. "Cognitive and behavioural dimensions in regular players and occasional blackjack players." *International Journal of Psychology* 23:283–291.

Galski, T. (ed.). 1987. *The Handbook of Pathological Gambling.* Springfield: Charles C. Thomas.

Galvani, S.A. 2007. "Safety in numbers? Tackling domestic abuse in couples and network therapies." *Alcohol Review* 26(2):175–181.

Gamblers Anonymous. 2007. "Twenty questions." *Gamblers Anonymous Online.* Retrieved August 16, 2007 from http://www.gamblersanonymous.org/20questions.html.

Ganster, D.C., and B. Victor. 1988 (March). "The impact of social support on mental and physical health." *The British Journal of Medical Psychology* 61(1): 17–36.

Getty, H., J. Watson, and G.R. Frisch. 2000. "A comparison of depression and styles of coping in male and female GA members and controls." *Journal of Gambling Studies* 16(4):377–391.

Gittelsohn, J., K.M. Roche, C.S. Alexander, and P. Tassler. 2001. "The social context of smoking among African-American and white adolescents in Baltimore City." *Ethnicity and Health* 6(3–4):211–225.

Goffman, E. 1963. *Behavior in public places: Notes on the social organization of gatherings.* Glencoe: Free Press.

Goldstein, M.Z. 1990. "The role of mutual support groups and family therapy for caregivers of demented elderly." *Journal of Geriatric Psychiatry* 23(2): 117–128.

Gottlieb, B.H. 1985 (July–August). "Assessing and strengthening the impact of social support on mental health." *Social Work* 30(4): 293–300.

Government of Nova Scotia: Health Promotion and Protection. 2004. "What is problem gambling?" Retrieved from http://www.gov.ns.ca/hpp/gambling/whatIsGambling/5-problem.html.

Grant J.E., S.W. Kim, and M. Kuskowski. 2004. "Retrospective review of treatment retention in pathological gambling." *Compr Psychiatry* 45:83–87.

Grant, J.E., and M.A. Steinberg. 2005. "Compulsive sexual behaviour and pathological gambling." *Sexual Addiction and Compulsivity* 12:235–244.

Grasmick, H.G., and R.J. Bursik. 1990. "Conscience, spouses, and rational choice: Extending the deterrence model." *Law and Society Review* 24(3):837–861.

Grella, C., and V. Joshi. 1999. "Gender differences in drug treatment careers among clients in the national drug abuse treatment outcomes study." *American Journal of Drug and Alcohol Abuse* 25(3):385–406.

Griffiths, M.D. 1989. "Gambling in children and adolescents." *Journal of Gambling Behaviour* 5:66–83.

Gruber, K.J., and T.W. Fleetwood. 2004. "In-home continuing care services for substance use affected families." *Substance Use and Misuse* 39(9):1379–1403.

Guebaly, N., S.B. Patten, S. Currie, J.V.A. Williams, C.A. Beck, C.J. Maxwell, and J.L. Wang. 2006. "Epidemiological associations between gambling, substance use and mood and anxiety disorders." *Journal of Gambling Studies* 22: 275–287.

Gupta, R., and J.L. Derevensky. 1997. "Familial and social influences on juvenile gambling." *Journal of Gambling Studies* 13:179-192.

Hahlweg, K., and H.J. Markman. 1988. "The effectiveness of behavioral marital therapy: Empirical status of behavioral techniques in preventing and alleviating marital distress." *Journal of Consulting and Clinical Psychology* 56:440–447.

Hardoon, K.K., R. Gupta, and J.L. Derevensky. 2004. "Psychosocial variables associated with harm among gamblers in the general population as a function of level of participation in gambling." *Society for the Study of Addiction* 101:507–580.

Harrison, C., and D. Donnelly. 1987. "A couples group for alcoholics, gamblers and their spouses in recovery: A pilot study." *Sexual and Marital Therapy* 2:139–143.

Hawkins, D., and A. Booth. 2005. "Unhappily ever after: Effects of long-term, low-quality marriages on well-being." *Social Forces* 84(1):451–471.

Hazan, C., and Shaver, P. 1987. "Romantic love conceptualized as an attachment process." *Journal of Personality and Social Psychology* 52:511–524.

Heineman, M. 1987. "A comparison: The treatment of wives of alcoholics with the treatment of wives of pathological gamblers." *Journal of Gambling Behavior* 3(1):27–40.

Hendrix, H. 2001. *Getting the Love You Want: A Guide for Couples.* New York: Owl Books.

Higgins, S.T., A.J. Budney, W.K. Bickel, and G.J. Badger. 1994. "Participation of spouses in outpatient behavioral treatment predicts greater cocaine abstinence." *Am. J. Drug Alcohol Ab* 20(1):47–56.

Hodgins, D.C., and N. El Guebaly. 2000. "Natural and treatment-assisted recovery from gambling problems: A comparison of resolved and active gamblers." *Addiction,* 95(5):777–789.

Hodgins, D.C., K. Makarchuk, N. El Guebaly, and N. Penden. 2000. "Why problem gamblers quit gambling: A comparison of methods and samples." *Addiction Research and Theory* 10:203–218.

Hodgins, D.C., N. Peden, and E. Cassidy, E. 2005. "The association between comorbidity and outcome in pathological gambling: A prospective follow-up of recent quitters." *Journal of Gambling Studies* 21: 255–271.

Hodgins, D.C., W. Shead, and K. Makarchuk. 2007a (January). "Relationship satisfaction and psychological distress among concerned significant others of pathological gamblers," *Journal of Nervous and Mental Disease* 195(1): 65–71.

Hodgins, D.C., T. Toneatto, K. Makarchuk, W. Skinner, and S. Vincent. 2007b. "Minimal treatment approaches for concerned significant others of problem gamblers: A randomized controlled trial." *Journal of Gambling Studies* 23:215–230.

Hodgins, D.C., H. Wynne, and K. Makarchuk. 1999 (Summer). "Pathways to recovery from gambling problems: Follow-up from a general population survey." *Journal of Gambling Studies* 15(2):93–104.

Homans, G. 1950. *The Human Group.* New York: Harcourt Brace.

Horowitz, A.V., J. McLaughlin, and H. Raskin White. 1997. "How the negative and positive aspects of partner relationships affect the mental health of young married people." *Journal of Health and Social Behavior* 39:124–136.

House, J.S., K.R. Landis, and D. Umberson. 1988. "Social relationships and health." *Science* 241:540–545.

Huang, I-C. 1991. "Family stress and coping." In: S.R. Bahr (ed.), *Family Research: A Sixty-Year Review, 1930–1990,* Volume 1 (pp. 289–334). New York: Lexington Books, Maxwell Macmillan International.

Hurcom, C., A. Copello, and J. Orford. 2000. "The family and alcohol: Effects of excessive drinking and conceptualizations of spouses over recent decades." *Substance Use and Misuse* 35(4):473–502.

Jacob, T. 1992 (May–June). "Family studies of alcoholism." *Journal of Family Psychology* (Special Issue: *Diversity in Contemporary Family Psychology*) 5(3–4): 319–359.

Jacobs, D. 1986. "A general theory of addictions: A new theoretical model." *Journal of Gambling Behavior* 2:15–31.

Jacobs, D., A. Marston, R. Singer, K. Widaman, T. Little, and I. Veizades. 1989. "Children of problem gamblers." *Journal of Gambling Behavior* 5:261–267.

Jacobs, D.F. 1987. "A general theory of addictions." In T. Galski (ed.), *The Handbook of Pathological Gambling* (pp. 169-194). Springfield, IL: Charles C. Thomas.

Joe, G.W., D.D. Simpson, and K.M. Broome. 1998. "Effects of readiness for drug abuse," *Journal of Gambling Studies* 18:207–229.

Judge, S.L. 1998 (July). "Parental coping strategies and strengths in families of young children with disabilities." *Family Relations: Interdisciplinary Journal of Applied Family Studies* 47(3): 263–268.

Kausch, O. 2003. "Patterns of substance abuse among treatment-seeking pathological gamblers." *Journal of Substance Abuse Treatment* 25:263–270.

Keating, N., J. Fast, J. Frederick, K. Cranswick, and C. Perrier. 1999. "Eldercare in Canada: Context, content and consequences." Ottawa: Statistics Canada, Housing, Family and Social Statistics Division.

Kelly, A.B. W.K. Halford, and R.M. Young. 2002 (September). "Couple communication and female problem drinking: A behavioral observation study." *Psychology of Addictive Behaviors* 16(3):269–271.

Kennedy, B.P., N.E. Isaac, T.F. Nelson, and J.D. Graham. 1997. "Young male drinkers and impaired driving intervention: Results of a U.S. telephone survey." *Accident Analysis and Prevention* 29(6):707–713.

Kiecolt-Glaser, J.K., and T.L. Newton. 2001. "Marriage and health: His and hers." *Psychological Bulletin* 127(4):472–503.

Kliska, B., and C.E. Aronoff. 1997. "Facing up to a loved one's addiction." *Nation's Business* 85(9):70–72.

Korn, D., and Shaffer, H. 1999. "Gambling and the health of the public: Adopting a public health perspective." *Journal of Gambling Studies* 15:289–365.

Kumar, R., P.M. O'Malley, L.D. Johnston, J.E. Schulenberg, and J.G. Bachman. 2002. "Effects of school-level norms on student substance use." *Prevention Science* 3(2):105–124.

Ladouceur, R. 1996. "The prevalence of problem gambling in Canada." *Journal of Gambling Studies,* 12:129–142.

Ladouceur, R., J.M. Boisvert, M. Pépin, M. Loranger, and C. Sylvain. 1994 (December). "Social cost of pathological gambling." *Journal of Gambling Studies* 10(4):339–409.

Lamberton, A., and T.P.S. Oei. 1997. "Problem gambling in adults: An overview." *Clinical Psychology and Psychotherapy* 4(2):84–104.

Laudet, A., S. Magura, R.T. Furst, and N. Kumar. 1999. "Male partners of substance-abusing women in treatment: An exploratory study." *The American Journal of Drug and Alcohol Abuse* 25(4):607–627.

Lavee, Y., and D. Altus.2001. "Family relationships as a predictor of post-treatment drug abuse." *Contemporary family therapy* 23(4):513–530.

Lavee, Y., S. Sharlin, and R. Katz. 1996. "The effect of parenting stress on marital quality: An integrated mother-father model." *Journal of Family Issues* 17:114–135.

Leblond J., R. Ladouceur, and A. Blaszczynski. 2003 (June). "Which pathological gamblers will complete treatment?" *British Journal of Clinical Psychology* 42(1): 205–209.

Lee, B.K., and M. Rovers. 2008. "'Bringing torn lives together again': Effects of the first Congruence Couple Therapy training application to clients in pathological gambling." *International Gambling Studies* 8(1):113-129.

Lee, B.K., M. Rovers, and L. Maclean. 2008. "Training problem gambling counselors in Congruence Couple Therapy: Evaluation of training outcomes," *International Gambling Studies* 8(1):95–111.

Lee, J.D. 2002. "How Did I End Up Like This? An Identity Theory Explanation of Gradual Self-Change." Paper presented to a Conference of the Southern Sociological Society.

Lee, S.T. 2004 (March). "Lying to tell the truth: Journalists and the social context of deception." *Mass Communication and Society* 7(1):97–120.

Lemert, E.M. 1951. *Social Pathology: A Systemic Approach to the Theory of Sociopathic Behavior*. New York: McGraw-Hill.

Le Poire, B.E. 2004. "The influence of drugs and alcohol on family communication: The effects that substance abuse has on family communication and the effects that family members have on substance abuse." In: A.L. Vangelisti (Ed). *Handbook of family communication* (pp. 609–629). Mahwah, NJ: Lawrence Erlbaum Associates.

Lesieur, H.R., and S.B. Blume. 1987. "The South Oaks Gambling Screen: A new instrument for the identification of pathological gamblers." *American Psychiatry Journal* 144:1184–1188.

Lesieur, H.R., S.B. Blume, and R.M. Zoppa. 1986. "Alcoholism, drug abuse, and gambling." *Alcoholism: Clinical and Experimental Research* 10:33–38.

Lesieur, H.R., J. Cross, J. Frank, *et al.* 1991. "Gambling and pathological gambling among university students." *Addictive Behaviours* 16:517–527.

Lesieur, H.R., and J. Rothschild. 1989. "Children of Gamblers Anonymous members." *Journal of. Gambling Behavior* 5:269–282.

Littell, J. H., and H. Girvin. 2002. "Stages of change: A critique." *Behavior Modification* 26(2):223–73.

Lloyd, J.J., E.P. Ricketts, and S.A. Strathdee. 2005. "Social contextual factors associated with entry into opiate agonist." *The American Journal of Drug and Alcohol Aabuse* 31(4):555–570.

Lobo, F., and G. Watkins. 1995. "Late career unemployment in the 1990s: Its impact on the family." *Journal of Family Studies* 1(2):103–113.

Lobsinger, C., and L. Beckett. 1996. *Odds on the Break Even: A Practical Approach to Gambling Awareness*. Canberra: Relationships Australia, Inc.

Logan, D.G. 1983. "Getting alcoholics to treatment by social network intervention." *Hosp Commun Psychiatry* 34(4):360–361.

Lorenz, V. 1989. "Some treatment approaches for family members who jeopardize the compulsive gambler's recovery." *Journal of Gambling Behavior* 5(4): 303–312.

Lorenz, V., and R.A. Yaffee. 1988. "Pathological gambling: Psychosomatic, emotional, and marital difficulties as reported by the spouse." *Journal of Gambling Behavior* 4(1):13–26.

———— 1989. "Pathological gamblers and their spouses: Problems in interaction." *Journal of Gambling Behavior* 5(2):113–126.

Lorenz, V.C., and D. Shuttlesworth. 1983. "The impact of pathological gambling on the spouse of the gambler." *Journal of Community Psychology* 11:67–76.

Makarchuk, K., D.C. Hodgins, and N. Peden. 2002. "Development of a brief intervention for concerned significant others of problem gamblers." *Addictive Disorders and Their Treatment* 1:126–134.

Marshall, K., and H. Wynne. 2003. "Fighting the odds." *Perspectives 5 Statistics Canada.* December: 5-13.

Martins, A.C.R. 2005 (March). Deception and convergence of opinions." *Journal of Artificial Societies and Social Simulation* 8(2). Available at http://jass.soc.surrey. ac.uk/8/2/3.html.

Matthews, L.S., R.D.Conger, and K.A.S. Wickrama. 1996. "Work-family conflict and marital quality: Mediating processes." *Social Psychology Quarterly* 59(1): 62–79.

McClure, S.M. 2003. "Navigating the Post-College Transition: Emotional Complexity, Normative Alternatives, and Neolocality for the 21st Century Female College Graduate." Paper presented to the Southern Sociological Society.

McCollum, E.E., T.S. Nelson, and R.A. Lewis. 2005. "Partner relationship quality and drug use as predictors of women's substance abuse treatment outcome." *The American Journal of Drug and Alcohol Abuse* 31(1):111–127.

McCormick, R.A., and J.I. Taber. 1987. "The pathological gambler: Salient personality variables." In: T. Galski (ed.), *The Handbook of Pathological Gambling* (pp. 137-168). Springfield: Charles C. Thomas.

McCown W.G., and W.H. Howatt. 2007. *Treating gambling problems.* New Jersey: John Wiley and Sons, Inc.

McCrady, B.S., and E.E. Epstein. 1996. "Theoretical bases of family approaches to substance abuse treatment." In: F. Rotger, D.S. Kekker, and J. Morganstern (eds.), *Treating Substance Abuse: Theory and Technique* (pp. 117–142). New York: Guilford Press.

McCrady, B.S., E.E. Epstein, and L.S. Hirsch. 1999. "Maintaining change after conjoint behavioral alcohol treatment for men: Outcomes at six months." *Addiction* 94: 1381–1396.

McCrady, B.S., N.E. Noel, D.B. Abrams, and R.L. Stout *et al.* 1986 (November). "Comparative effectiveness of three types of spouse involvement in outpatient behavioral alcoholism treatment." *Journal of Studies on Alcohol* 47(6): 459–467.

McCrady, B.S., R. Stout, N. Noel, D. Abrams, H.F. Nelson. 1991. "Effectiveness of three types of spouse-involved behavioral alcoholism treatment." *British Journal of Addictions* 86:1415–1424.

McGue, M., R.W. Pickens, and D.S. Svikis. 1992. "Sex and age effects of the inheritance of alcohol problems: A twin study." *Journal of Abnormal Psychology* 101:3–17.

McIntyre, R.S., S.L. McElroy, J.Z. Konarski, J.K. Soczynska, K. Wilkins, and S.H. Kennedy. 2007. "Problem gambling in bipolar disorder: Results from the Canadian Health Survey." *Journal of Affective Disorders* 102:27–34.

Mead, G.H. 1934. *Mind, Self, and Society.* Ed. by Charles W. Morris. Chicago: University of Chicago Press.

Meichenbaum, D., and D.C. Turk. 1987. *Facilitating Treatment Adherence: A Practitioner's Guidebook.* New York: Plenum Press.

Mellan, O. 1995. *Overcoming Overspending: A Winning Plan for Spenders and their Partners.* New York: Walker and Company.

Melville K.M., L.M. Casey, and D.J. Kavanagh. 2007 (December). "Psychological treatment dropout among pathological gamblers." *Clin Psychol Rev* 27(8):944–958.

Meyers, R.J., W.R. Miller, J.E. Smith, and J.S. Tonigan. 2002. "A randomized trial of two methods of engaging treatment-refusing drug users through concerned significant others." *Journal of Consulting and Clinical Psychology* 70:1182–1185.

Meyers, R.J., and J.E. Smith. 1997. "Getting off the fence: Procedures to engage treatment-resistant drinkers." *Journal of Substance Abuse Treatment* 14:467–472.

Miller, W., R. Meyers, and S. Tonigan. 1999. "Engaging the unmotivated in treatment for alcohol problems: A comparison of three strategies for intervention through family members." *Journal of Consulting and Clinical Psychology* 67(5):688–697.

Miller, W.R., and S. Rollnick, eds. 1991. *Motivational Interviewing: Preparing People To Change Addictive Behavior*. New York: Guilford Press.

Milne, J.S. 2007 (April). "An identity theory of role exit among soccer referees." *Dissertation Abstracts International, A: The Humanities and Social Sciences* 67(10):3999.

Milton, S., R. Crino, C. Hunt, and E. Prosser. 2002. "The effect of compliance-improving interventions on the cognitive-behavioural treatment of pathological gambling." *Journal of Gambling Studies* 18(2):207–229.

Molassiotis, A., O.B.A. Van Den Akker, and B.J. Broughton. 1997 (February). "Perceived social support, family environment and psychosocial recovery in bone marrow transplant long-term survivors." *Social Science and Medicine* 44(3): 317–325.

Moore, S.M., and K. Ohtsuka. 1999. "Beliefs about control over gambling among young people." In: National Research Council (ed.), *Pathological Gambling* (pp.339–347). Washington, DC: National Academy Press.

Moos, R.H., *et al.* 1990. *Alcoholism Treatment: Context, Process and Outcome*. Oxford University Press.

Myers, S.M., and A. Booth. 1996. "Men's retirement and marital quality." *Journal of Family Issues* 17(3):336–357.

National Council of Welfare. 1996. *Gambling in Canada*. Report No. 94.

National Gambling Impact Study Commission. 1999. *National Gambling Impact Study Commission final report*. Retrieved November 1, 2003, from http://govinfo.library. unt.edu/ngisc/reports/fullrpt.html.

National Research Council. 1999. *Pathological Gambling*. Washington, DC: National Academy Press.

Nielsen, M. 2002. "Are all marriages the same? Marital satisfaction of middle-class couples." *Dissertation Abstracts International, A: The Humanities and Social Sciences* 64(11), 4108A–4109A.

Oei, T.P.S., and N. Raylu. 2004. "Familial influence on offspring gambling: A cognitive mechanism for transmission of gambling behavior in families," *Psychological Medicine* 34(7):1279–1288.

O'Farrell, T.J. 1996. "Marital and family therapy in the treatment of alcoholism." In: *The Hatherleigh Guide to Treating Substance Abuse*, Part 1 (pp. 101–127). The Hatherleigh Guides Series 7. New York: Hatherleigh Press.

——— 1995. "Marital and family therapy." In: R.K. Hester and W.R. Miller (eds.), *Handbook of Alcoholism Treatment Approaches: Effective Alternatives* (pp. 195-220). Boston: Simon and Schuster.

O'Farrell, T.J., and W. Fals-Stewart. 2003a (January). "Alcohol abuse." *Journal of Marital and Family Therapy* 29(1):121–146.

—— 2003b. "Marital and family therapy." In: R.K. Hester and W.R. Miller (eds.), *Handbook of Alcoholism Treatment Approaches: Effective Alternatives,* 3rd ed (pp. 188–212). Boston: Allyn and Bacon.

—— 2000. "Behavioral couples therapy for alcoholism and drug abuse." *Journal of Substance Abuse Treatment* 18:51–54.

O'Farrell, T.J., K.A. Choquette, and H.S.G. Cutter. 1998. "Couples relapse prevention sessions after behavioral marital therapy for male alcoholics: Outcomes during the three years after starting treatment." *Journal of Studies on Alcohol* 59:357–370.

O'Farrell, T.J., and J. Hooley. 1998. "Expressed emotion and relapse in alcoholic patients." *Journal of Consulting and Clinical Psychology* 66(5):744–752.

O'Leary, K.D., and Beach, S.R.H. 1990. "Marital therapy: A viable treatment for depression and marital discord." *American Journal of Psychiatry* 147:183–186.

Olsen, M. 1978. *The Process of Social Organization.* New York: Holt, Rinehart, Winston.

Orford, J. 1992. "Control, confront or collude: How family and society respond to excessive drinking." *British Journal of Addiction* 87:1513–1525.

Pallesen, S., M. Mitsem , G. Kvale, *et al.* 2005. "Outcome of psychological treatments of pathological gambling: A review and meta-analysis." *Addiction* 100:1412–22.

Paolino, T.J., B. S. McCrady, and K.B. Kogan. 1978 (February). "Alcoholic marriages: A longitudinal empirical assessment of alternative theories." *Addiction* 73(2): 129–138.

Park, R.E. 1928 (May). "Human migration and the marginal man." *American Journal of Sociology* 33: 881–893.

Peele, S. 2002. "Is gambling and addiction like drug and alcohol addiction? Developing realistic and useful conceptions of compulsive gambling." *The Electronic Journal of Gambling Issues* 3. Retrieved July 4, 2002 from http://www.camh.net/egambling/issue3/index.html.

Pescosolido, B.A., E. Wright, and W.P. Sullivan. 1995. "Communities of care: A theoretical perspective on case management models in mental health." *Advances in Medical Sociology* 6:37–79.

Petry, N.M. 2006. "Should the scope of addictive behaviors be broadened to include pathological gambling?" *Addiction* 101(1):152–160.

—— 2005. *Pathological gambling: Etiology, comorbidity, and treatment.* Washington, DC: American Psychological Association.

—— 2004 (November). *Behavioral Treatments for Problem and Pathological Gambling.* American Public Health Association Conference, Washington, DC.

Petry, N.M., Y. Ammerman, J. Bohl, A. Doersch, H. Gay, R. Kadden, C. Molina, and K. Steinberg. 2006. "Cognitive-behavioral therapy for pathological gamblers: A controlled study," *Journal of Consulting and Clinical Psychology* 74(3):555–567.

Phillipson. C. 1997. "Social relationships in later life: A review of the research literature." *International Journal of Geriatric Psychiatry* 12:505–512.

Pietrzak, R.H., B.J. Morasco, C. Blanco, B.F. Grant, and N.M. Petry. 2007. "Gambling levels and psychiatric and medical disorders in older adults: Results from the national epidemiology survey on alcohol and related conditions." *American Journal of Geriatric Psychiatry* 15:301–313.

Platt, F.W., and K.N. Keating. 2007. "Differences in physician and patient perceptions of uncomplicated UTI symptom severity: Understanding the communication gap." *International Journal of Clinical Practice* 61(2):303–308.

Pokorny, M.R. 1972. "Compulsive gambling and the family." *British Journal of Medical Psychology* 45(4):355–364.

Potenza, M. 2002. "A perspective on future directions in the prevention, treatment, and research of pathological gambling." *Psychiatric Annals* 32(3):203–207.

Poulin, C. 2000. "Problem gambling among adolescent students in the Atlantic Provinces of Canada." *Journal of Gambling Studies* 16(1): 53–78.

Powers, K.I., 1993. "Cumulative versus stabilizing effects of methadone maintenance." *Evaluation Review* 17(3):243–270.

Powers, K.I., and M.D. Anglin. 1996. "Couples' reciprocal patterns in narcotics addiction: A recommendation." *Psychology and Marketing* 13(8):769–784.

Prochaska, J.O. 2004. "Population treatment for addictions." *Current Directions in Psychological Science* 13(6):242–246.

Prochaska, J.O., and C.C. DiClemente. 1986a. "Toward a comprehensive model of change." In: W.R. Miller and N. Heather (eds.), *Treating Addictive Behaviors* (pp. 3–27). New York: Plenum.

——— 1986b. "The transtheoretical approach: Towards a systematic eclectic framework." In: J.C. Norcross (ed.), *Handbook of Eclectic Psychotherapy* (pp. 163–200). New York: Brunner/Mazel.

Prochaska, J., J.C. Norcross, and C.C. DiClemente. 1994. *Changing for good: A revolutionary six-stage program for overcoming bad habits and moving your life positively forward.* New York: Avon Books.

Putnam, Robert D. (2000). *Bowling Alone: The Collapse and Revival of American Community.* New York: Simon & Schuster.

Ramirez, L.F., R.A. McCormick, A.M. Russo, and J.I. Taber. 1983. "Patterns of substance abuse in pathological gamblers undergoing treatment." *Addictive Behaviours* 8: 425–428.

Riehman, K.S., Y.I. Hser, and M. Zeller. 2000. "Gender differences in how intimate partners influence drug treatment motivation." *Journal of Drug Issues* 30(4):823–838.

Riehman, K.S., M.Y. Iguchi, M. Zeller, and A.R. Morral. 2003. "The influence of partner drug use and relationship power on treatment engagement." *Drug and Alcohol Dependence* 70:1–10.

Rodrigues, J.R., and T.L. Park. 1996. "General and illness-specific adjustment to cancer: Relationship to marital status and marital quality." *Journal of Psychosomatic Research* 40(1):29–36.

Room, R., S. Bondy, and J. Ferris. 1996. "Determinants of suggestions for alcohol treatment." *Addiction* 91(5):643–655.

Ross. C.E., Mirowsky, J., and Goldsteen, K. 1990. "The impact of the family on health: The decade in review." *Journal of Marriage and the Family* 52:1059–1078.

Rotunda, R., and K. Doman. 2001. "Partner enabling of substance use disorders: critical review and future directions." *The American Journal of Family Therapy* 29:257–270.

Rotunda, R.J., D.G. Scherer, and P.S.Imm. 1995. "Family systems and alcohol misuse: Research on the effects of alcoholism on family functioning and effective family interventions." *Professional Psychology: Research and Practice* 26(1):95–104.

Rotunda, R.J., L. West, and T.J. O'Farrell. 2004. "Enabling behavior in a clinical sample of alcohol-dependent clients and their partners." *Journal of Substance Abuse Treatment* 26:269–276.

Rowe, C.L., and H.A. Liddle. 2003. "Substance abuse." *Journal of Marital and Family Therapy* 29(1):97–120.

Rush, B., S. Veldhuizen, and E. Adlaf. 2007. "Mapping the prevalence of problem gambling and its association with treatment accessibility and proximity to gambling venues." *Journal of Gambling Issues* 20:193–214.

Sabourin, T.C. 1995. "The role of negative reciprocity in spouse abuse: A relational control analysis." *Journal of Applied Communication Research* 23(4):271–283.

Sanders, T.L.M. 2007 (January). "Becoming an ex-sex worker: Making transitions out of a deviant career." *Feminist Criminology* 2(1):74–95.

Sayre, S.L., J.M. Schmitz, A.L. Stotts, P.M. Averill, H.M.Rhoades, and J.J. Grabowski. 2002. "Determining predictors of attrition in an outpatient substance abuse program." *The American Journal of Drug and Alcohol Abuse* 28(1):55–72.

Schein, E.H. 2004. *Organizational Culture and Leadership*. San Francisco: Jossey-Bass.

Scherrer, J.F., W.S. Slutske, H. Xian, B. Waterman, K.R. Shah, R. Volberg, and S.A. Eisen. 2007. "Factors associated with pathological gambling at 10-year follow-up in national sample of middle-aged men." *Addiction* 102:970–979.

Schneider, J.P. 1989. "Rebuilding the marriage during recovery from compulsive sexual behaviour." *Family Relations* 38:288–294.

——— 2003. "The impact of compulsive cybersex behaviours on the family." *Sexual and Relationship Therapy* 18(3):329–354.

Shaffer, H.J., M.N. Hall, and J. Vander Bilt. 1999. "Estimating the prevalence of disorder skills and thinking dispositions of problem gamblers: A dual processing taxonomy." *Journal of Behavioral Decision Making* 20:103–124.

Shaffer, H. J., and D.A. Korn. 2002. "Gambling and related mental disorders: A public health analysis." *Annual Review of Public Health* 23:171–212.

Shek, D.T.L. 1995. "Marital quality and psychological well-being of married adults in a Chinese context." *Journal of Genetic Psychology* 156(1):74–95.

Simmel, G. 1906 (1950). *The Sociology of Georg Simmel*. Compiled and translated by Kurt Wolff. Glencoe, IL: Free Press.

Simpson, J.A., W.S. Rholes, and J.S. Nelligan, J. S. 1992. "Support seeking and support giving within couples in an anxiety-provoking situation: The role of attachment styles." *Journal of Personality and Social Psychology* 62(3):434–446.

Skinner, H.A. 1999 (December). "Gambling: Achieving the right balance." *Journal of Gambling Studies* 15(4):285–287.

Slutske, W.S. 2006. "Natural recovery and treatment-seeking in pathological gambling: Results of two U.S. national surveys." *The American Journal of Psychiatry* 163:297–302.

Sobell, L.C., J.A. Cunningham, and M.A. Sobell. 1996. "Recovery from alcohol problems with and without treatment: Prevalence in two population surveys." *American Journal of Public Health* 86:966–972.

Sobell, M.B. *et al.* 2000. "Does enhanced social support improve outcomes for problem drinkers in self-change treatment?" *Journal of Behavior Therapy and Experimental Psychiatry* 31:41–54.

Song, J.A., B.M. Bergen, and W. Schumm. 1995. "Sexual satisfaction among Korean-American couples in the Midwestern United States." *Journal of Sex and Marital Therapy* 21(3):147–158.

Spanier, G.B. 1976. "Measuring dyadic adjustment: A new scale for assessing the quality of marriage and similar dyads." *Journal of Marriage and the Family* 38:15–28.

Spotts, E.L., N.L. Pedersen, J.M. Neiderhiser, D. Reiss, P. Lichtenstein, K. Hansson, and M. Cederblad. 2005. "Genetic effects on women's positive mental health: Do marital relationships and social support matter?" *Journal of Family Psychology* 19(3):339–349.

Stafford, L., S.L., Kline, and C.T. Rankin. 2004 (April). "Married individuals, cohabiters, and cohabiters who marry: A longitudinal study of relational and individual well-being." *Journal of Social and Personal Relationships* 21(2):231–248.

Stanton, D.M. 2004. "Getting reluctant substance abusers to engage in treatment." *Journal of Marital and Family Therapy* 30(2):165.

Steinberg, M.A. 1993. "Couples treatment issues for recovering male compulsive gamblers and their partners." *Journal of Gambling Studies* 9(2):153–167.

Stewart, R., and Brown, R. 1988. "An outcome study of gamblers anonymous." *British Journal of Psychiatry* 152: 284–288.

Stier, J. 2007 (March). "Game, name and fame: Afterwards, will I still be the same? A social psychological study of career, role exit and identity." *International Review For The Sociology Of Sport* 42(1):99–111.

Stinchfield, R., R. Govoni, and G.R. Frisch. 2001 (November). "An evaluation of diagnostic criteria for pathological gambling: Final report." Windsor, ON: University of Windsor.

Stinchfield, R., M.G. Kushner, and K.C. Winters. 2005. "Alcohol use and prior substance abuse treatment in relation to problem gambling severity and gambling treatment outcome." *Journal of Gambling Studies* 21: 273–297.

Stonequist, E.V. 1930. *The Marginal Man*. New York: Charles Scribner.

Sutherland, E.H. 1924. *Principles of Criminology*. Chicago: University of Chicago Press.

Sutherland, E.H. 1949. *White Collar Crime*. New York: Holt Rinehart and Winston.

Sutherland, E.H. (Chic Conwell, pseudonym) (ed). 1937. *The Professional Thief: By a Professional Thief*. Annotated and Interpreted by Edwin H. Sutherland. Chicago: University of Chicago Press.

Svendson, R., and T. Griffin. 1998. *Gambling: Choices and Guidelines*. Minnesota: Minnesota Institute of Public Health.

Sylvain, C., R. Ladouceur, and J.M. Boisvert. 1997. "Cognitive and behavioral treatment of pathological gambling: A controlled study." *J Consult Clin Psychol* 65(5):727–732.

Taber, J.I. 1985. "Pathological gambling: The initial screening interview." *Journal of Gambling Behaviour* 1:23–34.

Tavares, H., S.S. Martins, D.S.S. Lobo, C.M. Silveira, V. Gentil, and D.C. Hodgins. 2003. "Factors at play in faster progression for female pathological gamblers: An exploratory analysis." *The Journal of Clinical Psychiatry* 64(4):433–438.

Tavares, H., M.L. Zilberman, F.J. Beites, and V. Gentil. 2001. "Gender differences in gambling progression." *Journal of Gambling Studies* 17(2):151–159.

Tennstedt, S.L., and J.B. McKinlay. 1987. *Predictors of Informal Care: The Role of Social Network Characteristics.* American Sociological Association (ASA).

Tepperman, J.H. 1985. "The effectiveness of short-term group therapy upon the pathological gambler and wife." *Journal of Gambling Behavior* 1:119–130.

Tepperman, L., L. Calzavara, W. Medved, N. Ramuscak, A. Burchell, and the Polaris HIV Seroconversion Study Team. 2002 (July). "To Tell or Not to Tell: An exploratory study of structural embeddedness and HIV disclosure by men who have sex with men." Presented at the World Congress of the International Sociological Association, Brisbane, Australia.

Tepperman, L., D. Korn, and M. Lynn. 2003 (June). *At Home With Gambling.* Guelph: ON: Problem Gambling Research Centre.

Thompson, S.C., L.J. Medvene, and D. Freedman. 1995. "Caregiving in the close relationship of cardiac patients: exchange, power and attribution perspectives on caregiver resentment." *Personal Relationships* 2(2):125–142.

Toneatto, T. 2005. "A perspective on problem gambling treatment: Issues and challenges." *Journal of Gambling Studies* 21(1): 75–80.

Toneatto, T., and J. Brennan, J. 2002. "Pathological gambling in treatment-seeking substance abusers." *Addictive behaviors* 27(3):465–469

Toneatto, T., and R. Ladouceur. 2003. Treatment of pathological gambling: A critical review of the literature." *Psychology of Addictive Behaviors* 17(4): 284–292.

Toplak, M.E., E. Liu, R. Macpherson, T. Toneatto, and K.E. Stanovich. 2006 (September). "The reasoning skills and thinking dispositions of problem gamblers: A dual-process taxonomy." *Journal of Behavioral Decision Making* 20(2):103–124. Published on-line.

Tracy, S.W., J.F. Kelly, and R.H. Moos. 2005. "The influence of partner status, relationship quality and relationship." *Journal of Studies on Alcohol* 66(4):497–505.

Trevorrow, K., and S. Moore. 1998. "The association between loneliness, social isolation and women's electronic gaming machine gambling." *Journal of Gambling Studies* 14: 263–284.

Turner, N., N. Littman-Sharp, M. Zangeneh, and W. Spence. 2002. "Winners: Why do some develop gambling problems, while others do not?" Retrieved from http://www.problemgambling.ca/Research/Research_Reports/reportpage21482.hml.

Ulmer, J.T., and J.W. Spencer. 1999. "The contributions of an interactionist approach to research and theory on criminal careers." *Theoretical Criminology* 3(1):95–124.

Umberson, D. 1992. "Gender, marital status and the social control of health behavior." *Social Science and Medicine* 24:907–917.

Umberson, D., K. Williams, D.A. Powers, H. Liu, and B. Needham. 2006. "You make me sick: Marital quality and health over the life course." *Journal of Health and Social Behavior* 47:1–16.

Utz, S. 2005. "Types of deception and underlying. motivation: What people think." *Social Science Computer Review* 23:49–56.

Velasquez, M.M., G.G. Maurer, C. Crouch, and C.C. DiClemente. 2001. *Group Treatment for Substance Abuse: A Stages-of-Change Therapy Manual.* New York: The Guilford Press.

Velicer, W.F., C.C. DiClemente, J.O. Prochaska, N. Brandenburg. 1985. "Decisional balance measure for assessing and predicting smoking status." *Journal of Personality and Social Psychology* 48(5):1279–1289.

Velleman, R., G. Bennett, T. Miller, J. Orford, and A. Tod. 1993. "The families of problem drug users: A study of 50 close relatives." *Addiction* 88 (9): 1281–1289.

Vinokur, A.D., R.H. Price, and R.D. Caplan. 1996. "Hard times and hurtful partners: How financial strain affects depression and relationship satisfaction of unemployed persons and their spouses." *Journal of Personality and Social Psychology* 71:166–179.

Wadsworth, A.P., W. Wilson, and H.R. Barker. 1975. "Determinants of marital happiness and unhappiness rated by alcoholics and their wives." *Journal of Studies on Alcohol* 36(5):634–644.

Waite, L., and M. Gallagher. 2000. *The Case for Marriage: Why Married People Are Happier, Healthier, and Better Off Financially*. New York: Doubleday.

Walczynski, P.T. 1998 (April). "Power, personality, and conflictual interaction: An exploration of demand/withdraw interaction in same-sex and cross-sex couples." *Dissertation Abstracts International: Section B: The Sciences and Engineering* 58(10–B): 5660.

Walitzer, K.S., and K.H. Dermen. 2004. "Alcohol-focused spouse involvement and behavioral couples therapy: Evaluation of enhancements to drinking reduction treatment for male problem drinkers." *Journal of Consulting and Clinical Psychology* 72(6):944–955.

Walker, M.B. 1992. *The Psychology of Gambling*. New York: Pergamon Press.

Wallerstein, J.S. 1996 (April). "The psychological tasks of marriage: Part 2." *American Journal of Orthopsychiatry* 66:217–227.

Ward, R.M., W.F. Velicer, J.S. Rossi, J.L. Fava, and J.O. Prochaska. 2004. "Factorial invariance and internal consistency for the Decisional Balance Inventory—Short Form." *Addictive Behaviours* 29(5):953–958.

Warr, M. 2007 (July). "The tangled web: Delinquency, deception, and parental attachment. *Journal of Youth and Adolescence* 36(5):607–622.

West, M.O., and R.J. Prinz. 1987 (September). "Parental alcoholism and childhood psychopathology." *Psychological Bulletin* 102(2):204–218.

Westphal, J.R., and L.J. Johnson. 2007. "Multiple co-occurring behaviours among gamblers in treatment: Implications and assessment." *International Gambling Studies* 7: 73–99.

Wetchler, J.L., and D.L. DelVecchio. 1995. "Couples therapy for a female heroin addict." *Journal of Family Psychotherapy* 6(4):1–13.

Wiebe, J., E. Single, and A. Falkowski-Ham. 2001 (November 30). *Measuring Gambling and Problem Gambling in Ontario*. Canadian Centre on Substance Abuse/Responsible Gambling Council (Ontario).

Wiebe, J., P. Mun, and N. Kauffman. 2006. *Gambling and Problem Gambling in Ontario 2005*. Guelph, ON: Ontario Problem Gambling Research Centre.

Wildman, R.W. 1989. "Pathological gambling: Marital-familial factors, implications and treatment." *Journal of Gambling Behaviour* 3:37–40.

Williams, K. 2003. "Has the future of marriage arrived? A contemporary examination of gender, marriage, and psychological well-being." *Journal of Health and Social Behavior* 44:470–487.

Winn, M.E. 1995. "Drawing upon the strengths of couples in the treatment of chronic drug addiction." *Journal of Family Psychotherapy* 6(3):33–54.

Winneg, K., K. Kenski, K.H. Jamieson. 2005 (September). "Detecting the effects of deceptive presidential advertisements in the spring of 2004." *American Behavioral Scientist* 49(1):114–129.

Winters, J., W. Fals-Stewart, T.J. O'Farrell, G.R. Birchler, and M.L. Kelley. 2002. "Behavioral couples therapy for female substance-abusing patients: Effects on substance use and relationship adjustment." *Journal of Consulting and Clinical Psychology* 70:344–355.

Winters, K.C., and M.G. Kushner. 2003. "Treatment issues pertaining to pathological gamblers with a comorbid disorder." *Journal of Gambling Studies* 19:261–77.

Winters, K.C., and T. Rich. 1998. "A twin study of adult gambling." *Journal of Gambling Studies* 14:213–225.

Wray, L.A. 2000. *Does Mental Health Affect Transitions out of the Labor Force in Older Workers?* Paper presented to a Conference of American Sociological Association.

Wright, E.R. 1994 (August). "Caring for those who "can't": Gender, network structure, and the burden of caring for people with mental illness." *Dissertation Abstracts International, A: The Humanities and Social Sciences* 55(2):380–A.

Wulfert, E., E.B. Blanchard, B.M. Freidenberg, and R.S. Martell. 2006. "Retaining pathological gamblers in cognitive behavior therapy through motivational enhancement." *Behavior Modification* 30(3):315–340.

Wynne, H.J. 2003. *Introducing the Canadian Problem Gambling Index.* Edmonton, AB: Wynne Resources.

Wynne, H.J., and G. Smith. 2002 (February). *Measuring Gambling and Problem Gambling in Alberta. Final Report: Using the Canadian Problem Gambling Index, CPGI.* Prepared for the Alberta Research Gambling Institute.

York, G.Y. 1987(Summer). "Religious-based denial in the NICU: Implications for social work." *Social Work in Health Care* 12(4): 31–45.

Zion, M.M., E. Tracy, and N. Abell. 1991. "Examining the relationship between spousal involvement in Gam-Anon and relapse behaviors in pathological gamblers." *Journal of Gambling Studies* 7(2): 117–131.

Zubin, J., and Spring, B. 1977. "Vulnerability: A new view of schizophrenia." *Journal of Abnormal Psychology* 86:103–126.

Index

CPSIA information can be obtained at www.ICGtesting.com
Printed in the USA
LVOW070824250212

270324LV00003B/2/P